Japanese

3rd Edition

by Hiroko Chiba and Eriko Sato, PhD

Japanese For Dummies®, 3rd Edition

Published by: **John Wiley & Sons, Inc.,** 111 River Street, Hoboken, NJ 07030-5774, www.wiley.com

Copyright © 2019 by John Wiley & Sons, Inc., Hoboken, New Jersey

Published simultaneously in Canada

For general information on our other products and services, please contact our Customer Care Department within the U.S. at 877-762-2974, outside the U.S. at 317-572-3993, or fax 317-572-4002. For technical support, please visit https://hub.wiley.com/community/support/dummies.

Wiley publishes in a variety of print and electronic formats and by print-on-demand. Some material included with standard print versions of this book may not be included in e-books or in print-on-demand. If this book refers to media such as a CD or DVD that is not included in the version you purchased, you may download this material at http://booksupport.wiley.com. For more information about Wiley products, visit www.wiley.com.

Library of Congress Control Number: 2018963461

ISBN 978-1-119-47540-8 (pbk); ISBN 978-1-119-47542-2 (ebk); ISBN 978-1-119-47541-5 (ebk)

Manufactured in the United States of America

SKY10030809_102521

Contents at a Glance

Table of Contents

PART 3: JAPANESE ON THE GO

Introduction

We live in a wonderfully global and amazingly diverse society. Exchanging ideas, products, foods, and friendship across national and cultural boundaries is the key to making our lives richer and more meaningful and peaceful. Besides, traveling abroad is a lot of fun and an eye-opening experience. Grabbing your passport and setting off on an adventure is always exciting, but it's even more special when you can communicate with people in a different country in their own language.

If Japanese is the language you want to learn, for whatever reason, *Japanese For Dummies,* 3rd Edition, can help. It provides substantial learning materials and some of the cultural background behind the language. Now, I'm not saying that you'll be fluent overnight, but you will gain confidence, have fun, and continue to pick up more and more Japanese so that you can carry on a conversation with your Japanese-speaking co-worker, family member, friend, or neighbor.

About This Book

Japanese For Dummies, 3rd Edition, can help you whether you want to get familiar with Japanese because you're planning a trip to this island nation, because you deal with Japanese companies at work, because you want to understand Anime/Manga in Japanese, or because your new neighbor is Japanese and you want to be able to say *good morning* to him or her. (Try **ohayō gozaimasu** [oh-hah-yohh goh-zah-ee-mah-soo].) This book provides you with helpful and commonly used Japanese words and phrases on subjects as diverse as shopping, money, food, and sports in self-contained chapters and sections.

Simply turn to the topics that interest you the most, play the online audio examples, and start speaking! That's right, you don't have to go through this book in order. If I think you may want to know information that's contained in a different chapter than the one you're currently reading, I include a handy cross-reference so you can find the additional information when you're ready for it.

I also use a few conventions in this book to help your reading go smoothly:

» In many places throughout this book, Japanese terms appear in two forms: Japanese scripts (like what you would read if you were in Japan) and the Romanized forms of words (which appear in **boldface** so you can easily find them in the text). The official term for Romanized Japanese is **rōmaji** (rohh-mah-jee).

» Pronunciations in parentheses and meanings or English equivalents in another pair of parentheses follow the Japanese terms. Note that meanings and English equivalents appear in *italics.*

» Verb conjugations (lists that show you the basic forms of a verb) are given in tables in this order: the dictionary form, the negative **(nai-)** form, the stem form (or the form before the polite suffix **-masu**), and the **te-**form. You find Japanese scripts in the first column, **rōmaji** in the second column, and pronunciations in the third column. Here's a sample conjugation of the verb **taberu** (tah-beh-roo) (*to eat*):

Japanese Script	Rōmaji	Pronunciation
食べる	taberu	tah-beh-roo
食べない	tabenai	tah-beh-nah-ee
食べ(ます)	tabe (masu)	tah-beh (-mah-soo)
食べて	tabete	tah-beh-teh

» Keep in mind that Japanese verbs don't conjugate like English verbs. You can't find exact counterparts for English verb forms such as infinitives, gerunds, and participles. In addition, you don't conjugate Japanese verbs in terms of the person and number, so **taberu** can mean *I eat, you eat, he eats, she eats,* and *they eat.* This difference may take a little getting used to, but it should make your verb-learning life a little easier.

To help you remember the most important new words and see the language in context, this book includes some special elements to reinforce the Japanese terms you're studying:

» **Talkin' the Talk dialogues:** Hearing actual Japanese conversations is the best way to learn Japanese, which is why I include many dialogues under the "Talkin' the Talk" heading in this book. These exchanges show you the Japanese words in **rōmaji,** their pronunciations, and the English translations so that you can see how the language is actually used. All Talkin' the Talk dialogues are accompanied by audio recordings so that you can hear and pick up the natural intonation and rhythm that are essential in conversational interactions.

>> **Words to Know blackboards:** Here's where you find key words and phrases from the Talkin' the Talk dialogues.

>> **Fun & Games activities:** Located at the end of chapters, these amusing activities help reinforce the vocabulary you practice in each chapter. You can find the solutions to these activities in Appendix C.

This book also features compact yet convenient mini-dictionaries — both Japanese-English and English-Japanese — in Appendix A. They include only very basic vocabulary words, mainly content words such as nouns, adjectives, adverbs, and verbs. For your convenience, I mark the conjugation class of the verbs: **u** for u-verbs, **ru** for **ru**-verbs, and **irr** for **irregular** verbs. Slightly irregular u-verbs are specified as **u (irr)**. In the English-Japanese mini-dictionary, I also designate verbs with (v.) because some English verbs also function as nouns. Last but certainly not least, I mark the type of adjectives: **i** for **i**-type adjectives and **na** for **na**-type adjectives. A few **i**-type adjectives with minor irregularities are specified as **i (irr)**.

Speaking of language quirks, you should know that English and Japanese sometimes express the same concept in very different ways. And Japanese has many words and phrases that you can't translate into English at all. In this book, I want you to focus on what is actually said (the content and intended meaning) rather than how it's said. So instead of giving you a literal translation, I give you a nonliteral, natural English translation. For example, the phrase **yoroshiku** (yoh-roh-shee-koo) can be literally translated as *appropriately,* but the phrase really means *pleased to meet you* if you say it when meeting someone new. This book gives the nonliteral, pleased-to-meet-you type translations (sometimes with the more literal translation for reference).

Your exploration of Japanese will also show you different ways of looking at the world of language because Japanese doesn't contain the same type of grammar items as European languages do. For example, Japanese doesn't have equivalents of English articles like *a* and *the.* Some verbs in English correspond to adjectives in Japanese. Here's another example: The verb *to want* is best represented by the Japanese adjective **hoshii**, so be ready to see some mismatch in the part-of-speech categories. And Japanese doesn't have a singular/plural distinction, such as *dog* and *dogs,* either. The information about specificity and numbers is expressed in very different ways. Also, Japanese sometimes has linguistic systems that European languages don't have. For example, Japanese speech styles clearly indicate degrees of respect or familiarity within conversational contexts.

Foolish Assumptions

To write this book, I had to work off of some assumptions about you. I'm thinking that

>> You don't know much Japanese, except maybe for a few words like **karate** and **sushi.**

>> You're not planning on taking a language-proficiency test for Japanese next month, and you're not planning on becoming a professional Japanese translator in the near future. You just want to be able to communicate basic information in Japanese and get to know the Japanese language.

>> You don't have time to spend hours and hours memorizing vocabulary and grammar rules.

>> You want to have fun in addition to learning Japanese.

Icons Used in This Book

To help you find certain types of information quickly, I've placed some icons throughout the book. Here are the six icons to keep an eye out for:

CULTURAL WISDOM

If you're interested in information and advice about culture and travel, look for these icons. They draw your attention to interesting tidbits about Japan and Japanese culture.

GRAMMAR CHAT

If you understand grammar, you can create an infinite number of sentences, so I use this icon to point out discussions of grammar facts.

REMEMBER

To ensure that you don't forget information important to the language, this icon serves as a reminder, just like a string tied around your finger.

TIP

This icon highlights suggestions that can make learning Japanese easier.

WARNING

This icon can keep you from making embarrassing or really foolish mistakes.

Beyond the Book

This book is full of useful information, but you can find even more online! Check out this book's Cheat Sheet, which contains useful questions, common expressions and phrases, Japanese numbers, and more all in a handy portable format. Just go to www.dummies.com and search for "Japanese For Dummies Cheat Sheet."

You can also hear all the Talkin' the Talk dialogues provided in the book to get a better handle on correct pronunciation. Just go to www.dummies.com/go/japanesefd.

Where to Go from Here

You can read as much or as little as you want of this book and the chapters in it. Decide what topic you're interested in, consult the index or table of contents to find the proper section, and quickly discover what you need to know to speak about that topic in Japanese. Of course, if you're looking to get a foundation in the basics, I recommend turning to Chapters 2 and 3 first. These chapters introduce the fundamentals of Japanese pronunciation, writing systems, and grammar. Read them now and then refer to them later if you get hung up on how to read Japanese scripts or build sentences.

Well, are you ready? Head for the chapter that interests you or listen to the online audio examples. And make sure to use your favorite Japanese phrases when you hang out with your friends or family. If you think your family probably won't understand what you say, you can teach them Japanese. With a little dedication, you'll be able to confidently answer **Hai!** (hah-ee!) (*Yes!*) when people ask **Nihongo wa hanasemasu ka.** (nee-hohn-goh wah hah-nah-seh-mah-soo kah.) (*Can you speak Japanese?*)

1
Getting Started with Japanese

Chapter **1**

Japanese in a Nutshell

Welcome to Japanese! Now that you've decided to learn this intriguing language, I'm sure you're eager to find out as much as you can as quickly as you can. After all, you probably have co-workers, friends, neighbors, and others to impress with your newfound language skills. Well, here's your chance to dive into Japanese. This chapter offers you a mini-preview of what you can find throughout *Japanese For Dummies,* 3rd Edition.

Discovering Basic Japanese Sounds and Script

Japanese sounds are pretty easy to pronounce. For one thing, Japanese has only five basic vowels: **a** (ah), **i** (ee), **u** (oo), **e** (eh), and **o** (oh). In addition, you don't see a long string of consonants before or after a vowel, unlike in Russian or Polish. You just have to pay attention to a handful of strange consonants, such the Japanese **r,** which makes a sound somewhere between the English **l** and **r.** You can pronounce basic sounds in Japanese along with the online audio recordings featured in Chapter 2.

Japanese writing, on the other hand, can be confusing because Japanese scripts don't look at all like Western alphabets. The Japanese scripts consist of two sets of **kana** (kah-nah) — phonetic symbols for Japanese syllables — and about 2,000

kanji (kahn-jee) characters, which are Chinese characters adapted for Japanese. If you just want to learn how to speak Japanese, you may want to skip focusing on these Japanese scripts and use **rōmaji** (rohh-mah-jee), the Romanized spellings of Japanese words. However, getting used to the Japanese scripts is a good idea, especially if you plan to use your Japanese skills to travel. If you can recognize some of the Japanese scripts, you can get around in a Japanese town more easily because all street signs are written in only the Japanese scripts.

Another advantage of being able to recognize the Japanese scripts, especially **kana,** is that you can avoid reading Japanese like English. For example, the Japanese word that means *bamboo* is **take.** As an English speaker, you may have an urge to read **take** as teh-ee-koo because you know the English word *to take,* but the Japanese pronunciation of this word is tah-keh. In this case, the **rōmaji** may mislead you, but the **kana,** たけ, wouldn't because your existing knowledge in English can't interfere. Chapter 2 shows all **kana** characters and some representative **kanji** characters for your reference.

Getting a Grip on Basic Grammar

Japanese grammar is quite different from English grammar, particularly when it comes to word order in sentences. Even if grammar was your most hated subject, you can't avoid learning grammar if you want to speak Japanese like a native speaker. Without grammar, you'll sound like a big 2-year-old, saying things like the Japanese counterparts of *Brian car, me kiss Mary,* or *John in office.*

REMEMBER

You generally put the verb at the end of the sentence and add the particle **o** (oh) after the direct object noun. So to mean *to eat sushi,* say **sushi o taberu** (soo-shee oh tah-beh-roo), where **taberu** means *to eat.*

For further insight into Japanese grammar, head to Chapter 3, which tells you all about parts of speech; conjugation patterns; and the structure of words, phrases, and sentences.

Counting on Numbers

Numbers dominate everyday life. What time do you wake up? How many glasses of water do you drink a day? How many guests are you expecting? How much does buying groceries cost? Chapter 4 lets you count both small and large numbers and use them with the right counters.

Counters, you ask? The Japanese use a short, suffix–like element called a *counter* right after the number. The counter you use varies depending on the type of things you're counting or the kind of notions you're specifying. To start with, count the bare simple numbers from one to ten:

>> 一 **ichi** (ee-chee) (*one*)

>> 二 **ni** (nee) (*two*)

>> 三 **san** (sahn) (*three*)

>> 四 **yon** (yohn) *or* **shi** (shee) (*four*)

>> 五 **go** (goh) (*five*)

>> 六 **roku** (roh-koo) (*six*)

>> 七 **nana** (nah-nah) *or* **shichi** (shee-chee) (*seven*)

>> 八 **hachi** (hah-chee) (*eight*)

>> 九 **kyū** (kyooo) *or* **ku** (koo) (*nine*)

>> 十 **jū** (jooo) (*ten*)

TIP

Japanese also frequently uses the Arabic numerals (1, 2, and so on) that you're used to seeing.

You can read more about using numbers, including using them to tell time and specify dates, in Chapter 4.

Speaking Japanese around the House

You spend at least half of your time in your house every day — sleeping, cooking, eating, watching TV, and so on. Here are some terms to help you name the rooms in your house in Japanese:

>> ダイニング **dainingu** (dah-ee-neen-goo) (*dining room*)

>> 風呂場 **furoba** (foo-roh-bah) (*bathing room*)

>> キッチン **kitchin** (keet-cheen) (*kitchen*)

>> リビング **ribingu** (ree-been-goo) (*living room*)

>> 寝室 **shinshitsu** (sheen-shee-tsoo) (*bedroom*)

Chapter 5 introduces the Japanese words you need for naming things in your house and expressing what you do in your house.

Using Japanese in Social Scenarios

I can't stress enough that a language is a wonderful tool for communication. You can put yourself into someone else's shoes by learning a language and step into a new world. You communicate with people not only for socialization and entertainment but also for completing daily tasks successfully with your family, friends, and colleagues. That is, developing good language skills is the key to your success in your life! The following sections introduce you to some of the vocabulary you need in various social situations.

Beginning (and ending) conversations

It's always nice to hear warm greetings. Hello and goodbye are so important in our communication. This section introduces basic greetings and making small talk, as well as how to address people properly.

If you want to say something more than just "hello" when you see someone, make a point of knowing Japanese phrases that can help you initiate small talk. Start with questions like the following:

» どちらまでですか。 **Dochira made desu ka.** (doh-chee-rah mah-deh deh-soo kah.) (*Where are you heading to?*)

» いい天気ですね。 **Ii tenki desu ne.** (eee tehn-kee deh-soo neh.) (*It's nice today, isn't it?*)

» ご兄弟は。 **Go-kyōdai wa** (goh-kyohh-dah-ee wah.) (*Do you have any siblings?*)

» メールアドレスは。 **Mēru adoresu wa.** (mehh-roo ah-doh-reh-soo wah) (*What's your email address?*)

Chapter 6 shows you how to politely start a basic conversation in Japanese.

Getting to know you

When you make new friends, you may chat about your life — your family, your job, your hobbies, and so on. And you may want to know about them as well. If you tell new friends what your hobbies are, maybe they will have the same interests.

» **Oshigoto wa nandesu ka.** (oh-shee-goh-toh wah nahn-deh-soo kah.) (*What is your job?*)

>> **Watashi wa ani ga imasu.** (wah-tah-shee wah ah-nee gah ee-mah-soo.) (*I have a(n older) brother.*)

>> **Jon san wa yoku tenisu o shimasu ka.** (John sahn wah yoh-koo the-nee-soo o shee-mah-soo ka.) (*John, do you often play tennis?*)

Chapter 7 introduces words and expressions you may use to get to know someone.

Asking for directions

REMEMBER

When you need to ask for directions to somewhere, name the place you want to go, add the particle **wa** (wah) after it, and say **doko desu ka** (doh-koh deh-soo kah), as in **Eki wa doko desu ka.** (eh-kee wah doh-koh deh-soo kah.) (*Where is the train station?*)

Chapter 8 shows you how to ask for or give directions in Japanese.

Making sense of money

You need money no matter where you go, and if you're headed to a foreign destination, you need to be prepared **ryōgae suru** (ryohh-gah-eh soo-roo) (*to exchange*) your country's currency for that of your destination country. Be sure to bring enough **genkin** (gehn-keen) (*cash*) to the exchange counter.

TIP

Even at a foreign **ginkō** (geen-kohh) (*bank*), you may be able to use your ATM card to withdraw funds from your **kōza** (kohh-za) (*account*) in the right currency.

For more money-related words, as well as information on the Japanese **en** (ehn) (*yen*), see Chapter 9.

Going shopping

Who doesn't love shopping? If you're looking for something in particular, name it, add **wa** (wah) after it, and say **arimasu ka** (ah-ree-mah-soo kah), as in **Sukāfu wa arimasu ka.** (soo-kahh-foo wah ah-ree-mah-soo kah.) (*Do you have a scarf?*) Definitely check the price, though. You can do so by asking **Ikura desu ka.** (ee-koo-rah deh-soo kah.) (*How much?*)

Turn to Chapter 10 for more words and phrases that can help you have successful shopping experiences in Japanese.

Dining out and exploring entertainment opportunities

Hanging out at home is fun, but if you do that 7 days a week, 365 days a year, it's going to get boring. So why not head out and explore the great restaurants and entertainment opportunities your community has to offer? If you love eating Japanese foods, you need to know how to place an order at a restaurant in Japanese. Your server will ask you, **Go-chūmon wa** (goh-chooo-mohn wah) (*Your order?*). That's your opportunity to say, for example, **Sushi o onegai shimasu.** (soo-shee oh oh-neh-gah-ee shee-mah-soo.) (*Sushi, please.*) Here are some words you may look for:

>> レストラン **resutoran** (reh-soo-toh-rahn) (*restaurants*)

>> ハンバーガー **hanbāgā** (hahn-bahh-gahh) (*hamburger*)

>> 美術館 **bijutsukan** (bee-joo-tsoo-kahn) (*art museums*)

>> 劇場 **gekijō** (geh-kee-johh) (*theaters for performing arts*)

>> 博物館 **hakubutsukan** (hah-koo-boo-tsoo-kahn) (*museums*)

>> カラオケ **karaoke** (kah-rah-oh-keh) (*karaoke*)

>> クラブ **kurabu** (koo-rah-boo) (*nightclub*)

Chapter 11 introduces how to dine out and go to fun places and shows you what you can do there, in Japanese.

Doing business and using technology

Do you want to work in Japan or in a Japanese company in the United States? If the answer to either question is *yes,* you need to have a bunch of business-related vocabulary under your belt. Chapter 12 provides such words, including

>> ヴォイスメール **boisu-mēru** (boh-ee-soo-mehh-roo) (*voice mail*)

>> 配達する **haitatsu suru** (hah-ee-tah-tsoo soo-roo) (*to deliver*)

>> 確認する **kakunin suru** (kah-koo-neen soo-roo) (*to confirm*)

>> コピーする **kopī suru** (koh-peee soo-roo) (*to make copies*)

>> 会議 **kaigi** (kah-ee-gee) (*meeting, conference*)

>> メール **mēru** (mehh-roo) (*email*)

>> パソコン **pasokon** (pah-soh-kohn) (*computer*)

Tackling Travel-Related Topics

After you've been studying Japanese for a while and the travel bug bites, you may feel like making the journey to Japan to really immerse yourself in the language and culture. From packing your bags to choosing accommodations and navigating emergencies, the next sections give you some of the basic vocabulary you need when traveling in Japan.

Preparing for a trip

The first step in preparing for your trip is to decide where to go. Then, depending on your destination, you'll need to get a passport and book a flight. Here are some Japanese terms to consider as you're getting ready to take a trip:

>> チケット **chiketto** (chee-keht-toh) (*ticket*)

>> 飛行機 **hikōki** (hee-kohh-kee) (*airplane*)

>> ホテル **hoteru** (hoh-teh-roo) (*hotel*)

>> パスポート **pasupōto** (pah-soo-pohh-toh) (*passport*)

>> スーツケース **sūtsukēsu** (sooo-tsoo-kehh-soo) (*suitcase*)

Chapter 13 helps you make your travel plan and pack your suitcase.

Getting around with local transportation

Make sure you know the best ways of getting from place to place in a foreign country you're planning on visiting. In large urban areas, people often walk or take the **chikatetsu** (chee–kah–teh–tsoo) (*subway*). Other common methods of transportation may include one (or more!) of the following:

>> 電車 **densha** (dehn-shah) (*train*)

>> フェリー **ferī** (feh-reee) (*ferry*)

>> 自転車 **jitensha** (jee-tehn-shah) (*bicycle*)

>> タクシー **takushī** (tah-koo-sheee) (*taxi*)

I cover transportation information in Chapter 14.

Securing a place to stay

You have several options to choose from when choosing your accommodations in Japan:

>> ビジネスホテル **bijinesu hoteru** (bee-jee-neh-soo hoh-teh-roo) (*business hotel*)

>> 観光ホテル **kankō hoteru** (kahn-kohh hoh-teh-roo) (*tourist's hotel*)

>> カプセルホテル **kapuseru hoteru** (kah-poo-seh-roo hoh-teh-roo) (*capsule hotel*)

>> 旅館 **ryokan** (ryoh-kahn) (*Japanese-style inn*)

>> ユースホステル **yūsu hosuteru** (yooo-soo hoh-soo-teh-roo) (*youth hostel*)

Chapter 15 helps you choose the right accommodation for your needs, make a reservation, check in, and check out at the end of your trip.

Taking action during emergencies

No one likes to think about experiencing an emergency while traveling, but if you're in a foreign country, you're better off knowing what to do if an illness, injury, or emergency pops up. Chapter 16 provides you with the confidence and the Japanese to act wisely when you face an emergency.

REMEMBER

Memorize these phrases now — and hope you don't need them later:

>> だれか! **Dareka!** (dah-reh-kah!) (*Someone help!*)

>> 泥棒! **Dorobō!** (doh-roh-bohh!) (*A thief!*)

>> 火事! **Kaji!** (kah-jee!) (*Fire!*)

>> 助けて! **Tasukete!** (tah-soo-keh-teh!) (*Help me!*)

Chapter 2

Checking Out the Japanese Sounds and Scripts

This chapter lets you open your mouth and sound like a totally different person — a Japanese person! Get ready to find out all about the basic Japanese vowel and consonant sounds. You also discover the core concepts of the Japanese writing systems.

Pronouncing Basic Japanese Sounds

Japanese sounds are very easy to hear and pronounce; each syllable is short and simple. With a little practice, you'll get used to these sounds quickly. The following sections get you off on the right foot (or should I say the right sound) by looking at vowels, consonants, and a couple of combinations of each.

Vowels

The Japanese language has only five basic vowels — **a, e, i, o,** and **u,** all of which sound short and crispy — plus their longer counterparts. Long vowels have the same sound as short vowels; you just draw out the sound for a moment longer. The long vowels are sometimes represented by double letters — **aa, ee, ii, oo,** and **uu** — but the more common presentation uses single letters with a bar (ˉ) over them, as in **ā, ē, ī, ō,** and **ū.** This second method is what I use in this book.

REMEMBER

The difference between a long vowel and a short vowel can make all the difference in the meaning of a Japanese word. For example, **obasan** (oh-bah-sahn) with the short vowel **a** means *aunt,* but **obāsan** (oh-bahh-sahn) with the long vowel **ā** means *grandmother.*

Listen for the difference between short and long vowel sounds online at www. dummies.com/go/japanese while you look at Table 2-1 to get the idea about vowel length.

TABLE 2-1   ## Japanese Vowel Sounds

Letter	Pronunciation	English Word with the Sound	Example
a	ah	ah<u>a</u>	おばさん **obasan** (oh-bah-sahn) (*aunt*)
ā	ahh	no equivalent	おばあさん **obāsan** (oh-bahh-sahn) (*grandmother*)
e	eh	b<u>e</u>d	セル **seru** (seh-roo) (*cell*)
ē	ehh	no equivalent	セール **sēru** (sehh-roo) (*sale*)
i	ee	f<u>ee</u>t	おじさん **ojisan** (oh-jee-sahn) (*uncle*)
ī	eee	no equivalent	おじいさん **ojīsan** (oh-jeee-sahn) (*grandfather*)
o	oh	d<u>o</u>me	とり **tori** (toh-ree) (*bird*)
ō	ohh	no equivalent	とおり **tōri** (tohh-ree) (*street*)
u	oo	f<u>oo</u>t	ゆき **yuki** (yoo-kee) (*snow*)
ū	ooo	no equivalent	ゆうき **yūki** (yooo-kee) (*courage*)

Unlike in English, vowels can appear next to each other without being separated by a consonant in Japanese. You may be inclined to pronounce them as one vowel, but the Japanese actually pronounce each vowel so that the sequence is multiple syllables. Listen online at www.dummies.com/go/japanesefd to hear some examples of these sequential vowels and their pronunciations:

>> あお **ao** (ah-oh) (*blue color*)

>> あおい **aoi** (ah-oh-ee) (*blue*)

>> いえ **ie** (ee-eh) (*house*)

>> いう **iu** (ee-oo) (*to say*)

>> うえ **ue** (oo-eh) (*up, above, on*)

>> おい **oi** (oh-ee) (*nephew*)

TIP

The vowels **i** (ee) and **u** (oo) come out as a downright whisper, in normal or fast speech, when they fall between the consonant sounds ch, h, k, p, s, sh, t, or ts or when a word ends in this consonant–vowel combination.

Consonants

Most Japanese consonants are pronounced like their English counterparts, but check out the descriptions of the sounds you need to pay attention to in Table 2-2 (you can hear them pronounced online at www.dummies.com/go/japanesefd).

TABLE 2-2 **Japanese Consonants Very Different from English**

Consonant	Description of the Sound	Examples
r	Almost like a Spanish **r,** where you tap your tongue on the roof of your mouth just once — almost like an English **d** or **l,** but not quite.	りんご **ringo** (reen-goh) (*apple*)
f	A much softer sound than the English **f** — somewhere between an **f** and an **h** sound. Make it by bringing your lips close to each other and gently blowing air through them.	ふゆ **fuyu** (foo-yoo) (*winter*)
ts	The combination of **t** and **s** is hard to pronounce at the beginning of a word, as in *tsunami,* although it's easy anywhere else. My advice is to say the word *cats* in your head and then say *tsunami.*	つなみ **tsunami** (tsoo-nah-mee) (*tsunami*)
ry	The combination of **r** and **y** is difficult to pronounce when it occurs before the vowel **o.** Try saying **ri** (ree) and then **yo** (yoh). Repeat many times and gradually increase the speed until you can pronounce these two sounds simultaneously. Remember that the **r** sounds almost like a **d** in English.	りょう **ryō** (ryohh) (*dormitory*)

Like most other languages, Japanese has double consonants, which are pronounced as single consonants preceded by a brief pause. Check out the following examples and listen to the pronunciation online.

>> きっぷ **kippu** (keep-poo) (*transportation tickets*)

>> きって **kitte** (keet-teh) (*postage stamp*)

>> けっこん **kekkon** (kehk-kohn) (*marriage*)

>> まっすぐ **massugu** (mahs-soo-goo) (*straight*)

>> バッグ **baggu** (bahg-goo) (*bag*)

>> ベッド **beddo** (behd-doh) (*bed*)

Sounding Fluent

If you want to sound like a native Japanese speaker, you need to imitate the overall stress accent, the pitch and intonation, the rhythm, and the speed of native Japanese. These almost-musical aspects of the language make a big difference, and the following sections show you how to achieve them.

Don't stress

English sentences sound like they're full of punches, one after another, because English words have stressed syllables followed by unstressed syllables. But Japanese sentences sound very flat because Japanese words and phrases don't have any stressed syllables. So unless you're very angry or excited, suppress your desire to stress syllables when you speak Japanese.

Watch out for pitch and intonation

Although Japanese speakers don't stress their syllables (see the preceding section), they may raise or lower their *pitch* on a specific syllable in certain words. A raised pitch may sound like a stress, but it's not quite the same concept; if you think in terms of music, higher-pitched notes aren't necessarily stressed more than low notes. But even though pitch differences don't change the emphasis in a word, these slight shifts can change the word's meaning. That, however, also depends on what part of Japan you're in. For example, in eastern Japan, the word **hashi** (hah-shee) said with high-to-low pitch means *chopsticks*, but with low-to-high pitch, it means *a bridge*. In western Japan, it's exactly the opposite: High-to-low pitch means *a bridge*, and low-to-high pitch means *chopsticks*.

How can you tell what anyone means? For one thing, the eastern dialect is standard because that's where Tokyo, the capital of Japan, is located. In any event, the context usually makes it clear. If you're in a restaurant and you ask for **hashi,** you can safely assume that, no matter how you pitch this word, no one will bring you a bridge. Listen to such pairs online and try to hear what I mean by pitch.

>> 箸 **hashi** (hah-shee) (*chopsticks*) versus 橋 **hashi** (hah-shee) (*bridge*)

>> 雨 **ame** (ah-meh) (*rain*) versus 飴 **ame** (ah-meh) (*candy*)

>> 神 **kami** (kah-mee) (*god*) versus 紙 **kami** (kah-mee) (*paper*)

Similarly, a single phrase can be said or understood in different ways depending on the *intonation,* an overall pitch flow that applies to the entire phrase or sentence. Suppose someone said that math is the easiest subject in the world. You can respond to this statement by saying **Sō desu ka.** (sohh deh-soo kah.) If you say it with a falling intonation, you're acknowledging the statement: *Oh, I see.* If you say it with a falling-rising intonation, you're showing your doubt or slight disagreement: *Really?* Listen to the difference online.

CULTURAL WISDOM

Another interesting fact about pitch: The Japanese raise their overall pitch range when they speak to their superiors. So people speak to a boss, client, customer, or teacher as if they (the speakers) are chirping birds and to their friends, assistants, and family members in a more normal pitch range. This shift is most noticeable among women. Female workers raise their pitch greatly when they deal with business customers. They don't mean to scare their customers; they're just trying to be super polite. Women also raise their pitch when they speak to young children, just to indicate a friendly attitude toward the little ones. A Japanese woman's flattering high pitch in these contexts has a totally different tone of voice from the high pitch that she uses when she raises her pitch out of anger.

Get in rhythm

English sentences sound very smooth and connected, but Japanese sentences sound chopped up because each syllable is pronounced more clearly and separately in Japanese than in English. You can sound like a native speaker by pronouncing each Japanese syllable separately.

TIP

Each syllable is represented by each **kana** character, so seeing Japanese scripts can help you pronounce words and sentences well. For the scoop on the Japanese scripts, including **kana,** see the next section.

BODY LANGUAGE

Gestures are very important for communication. Japanese probably use fewer gestures than Westerners; for example, they don't hug or kiss people in public. But they do have some unique gestures. If you know these gestures' meanings and functions and can use them as you interact with Japanese people, you'll seem like part of the crowd. Try some of the following gestures yourself. And if you see native Japanese people in a Japanese grocery store, at the mall, at a party, or anywhere else, observe them carefully. You'll definitely see some of these gestures.

- **Banzai:** When a bunch of people gather to celebrate something, they often stand up at the same time, raise both arms over their heads simultaneously, and shout "万歳! **Banzai!** (bahn-zah-ee!) (*Hurrah!*)" together three times.

- **Bowing:** For Japanese, bowing is an absolutely important and necessary everyday communication tool. You bow to thank someone, to apologize, to greet, and even to say goodbye. By bowing, you express your politeness and respect for others. But you don't have to bow very deeply. In most cases, you can just tilt your head for a second or two. Save the deep bow, using the upper half of the body, for those times when you make a horrible mistake, receive overwhelming kindness, or associate with extremely formal people.

- **Nodding:** Whenever someone says something to you, nod immediately. Otherwise, the speaker will think you're not paying attention or that you're upset.

- **Waving:** If you want Japanese folks to understand your waves, you must know that Japanese waving is all in the wrist. If you greet your American neighbor by moving your hand up and down from your wrist, like a toddler waving bye-bye, he'll understand that you mean to say *hi*. However, your Japanese neighbor will think you're beckoning her to come to you. The Japanese use a sort of palm-down scooping motion to say *come here* — just a 180-degree turn from the palm-up scooping motion Americans use to say the same thing.

Keep your speed up

The shortcut to sounding like a Japanese native is to pay attention to your speech speed. Try to say the entire phrase or sentence in normal speed. If you speak too slowly, the listener may lose track of what you are trying to say even if your pronunciation is precisely perfect. I'm not asking you to speak fast, but try to speak close to the normal speech speed of native speakers. Chances are that no one will notice your minor pronunciation problems if you speak in normal speed with the right intonation and rhythm.

Introducing the Japanese Scripts

Japanese uses multiple writing systems simultaneously even in the same sentence, combining two sets of phonetic symbols called **kana** (**hiragana** and **katakana**) and Chinese characters called **kanji.** Each **kana** character represents a syllable sound, but each **kanji** character represents a meaning. This book provides **kana** and **kanji** in most sections so you can get used to authentic Japanese texts, but don't worry; I also provide **rōmaji** (rohh-mah-jee) (*Roman letters*) throughout the book so you never get lost or feel intimidated. It's really up to you whether you want to learn Japanese by using **rōmaji,** using **kana** and **kanji,** or using both!

Kana

In modern Japanese, **hiragana** is mainly used for representing grammatical elements and native words not written in **kanji,** while **katakana** is used for representing foreign names and foreign vocabulary. The next sections introduce you to the symbols and the sounds they stand for, as well as some basic writing-related rules.

The characters

Table 2-3 shows basic **hiragana** and **katakana** characters. Try reading them aloud along with the online audio. (*Note:* Some people pronounce the second-to-last entry in the table as **woh,** but only some of the time.)

TABLE 2-3

Basic Hiragana and Katakana

Rōmaji	Pronunciation	Hiragana	Katakana
a	ah	あ	ア
i	ee	い	イ
u	oo	う	ウ
e	eh	え	エ
o	oh	お	オ
ka	kah	か	カ
ki	kee	き	キ
ku	koo	く	ク
ke	keh	け	ケ

(continued)

TABLE 2-3 *(continued)*

Rōmaji	Pronunciation	Hiragana	Katakana
ko	koh	こ	コ
sa	sah	さ	サ
shi	shee	し	シ
su	soo	す	ス
se	seh	せ	セ
so	soh	そ	ソ
ta	tah	た	タ
chi	chee	ち	チ
tsu	tsoo	つ	ツ
te	teh	て	テ
to	toh	と	ト
na	nah	な	ナ
ni	nee	に	ニ
nu	noo	ぬ	ヌ
ne	neh	ね	ネ
no	noh	の	ノ
ha	hah	は	ハ
hi	hee	ひ	ヒ
fu	foo	ふ	フ
he	heh	へ	ヘ
ho	hoh	ほ	ホ
ma	mah	ま	マ
mi	mee	み	ミ
mu	moo	む	ム
me	meh	め	メ
mo	moh	も	モ

Rōmaji	Pronunciation	Hiragana	Katakana
ya	yah	や	ヤ
yu	yoo	ゆ	ユ
yo	yoh	よ	ヨ
ra	rah	ら	ラ
ri	ree	り	リ
ru	roo	る	ル
re	reh	れ	レ
ro	roh	ろ	ロ
wa	wah	わ	ワ
(w)o	oh	を	ヲ
n	n	ん	ン

The basic rules

The character ん **(n)** represents an independent syllable for Japanese even though it may sound like part of an existing syllable to you. を is usually pronounced as **o**, like the character お, but it's exclusively used as a direct object marker (see Chapter 3 to find out about direct objects in Japanese). A few **kana** characters have an exceptional pronunciation: は **(ha)** (hah) is read as **wa** (wah) when used as a topic particle, and へ **(he)** (heh) is read as **e** (eh) when used as a particle that shows directions. (I cover particles in Chapter 3.)

Japanese uses two diacritic marks: two short dashes (˝) and a small circle (°). By adding (˝) at the right upper corner of a **kana** character that starts with the consonant **k, s, t, h,** or **f,** you can make that consonant voiced. For example, か represents **ka** (kah), while が represents **ga** (gah). So you can convert **k** to **g, s** to **z,** and **t** to **d** by using (˝). Strangely, **h** and **f** are converted to **b.** Also remember that じ and ぢ both sound **ji** (jee) and ず and づ both sound **zu** (zoo). (However, **ji** and **zu** are almost always represented by じ and ず, respectively.)

What does *voiced* mean? To understand voiced and unvoiced sounds, say **k** and **g** while lightly touching your throat. You feel a vibration only when you say **g,** even though you're doing largely the same thing with your mouth when you say **k,** right? Linguists call vibrationless sounds such as **k, p, t,** and **s** *voiceless* sounds, and sounds that do vibrate, such as **g, b, d,** and **z,** are *voiced* sounds.

On the other hand, by adding a small circle (°) at the right upper corner of a **kana** character that starts with **h** or **f**, you can convert the consonant to **p**. Check out the following example words that include these diacritic marks:

ぶんぷ **bunpu** (boon-poo) (*distribution*)

ちぢむ **chijimu** (chee-jee-moo) (*to shrink*)

ふぶき **fubuki** (foo-boo-kee) (*snowstorm*)

がか **gaka** (gah-kah) (*painter*)

はば **haba** (hah-bah) (*width*)

かんぱい **Kanpai!** (kahn-pah-ee!) (*Toast!*)

しじ **shiji** (shee-jee) (*instruction*)

すず **suzu** (soo-zoo) (*bell*)

つづき **tsuzuki** (tsoo-zoo-kee) (*continuation*)

You can represent complex syllables with the sound quality of **y** by adding a small-sized や **(ya)** (*yah*), ゆ **(yu)** (*yoo*), or よ **(yo)** (*yoh*) after a syllable with a vowel **i** (*ee*). I'm not talking about lowercase or uppercase. You just need to make the size of the character smaller by 50 to 75 percent. For example, き **(ki)** (*kee*) followed by the small-sized や yields きゃ **(kya)** (*kyah*). The same applies to **katakana**. The size difference is a bit hard to see in print, but I hope you gradually get used to it. Here are examples with such complex syllables:

ひゃく **hyaku** (hyah-koo) (*hundred*)

シャツ **shatsu** (shah-tsoo) (*shirt*)

しゅじゅつ **shujutsu** (shoo-joo-tsoo) (*medical operation*)

The small-sized つ **(tsu)** (*tsoo*) isn't pronounced; rather, it represents a moment of pause found with double consonants. The same applies to **katakana**.

きって **kitte** (keeht-teh) (*postage stamp*)

みっつ **mittsu** (meet-tsoo) (*three pieces*)

ソックス **sokkusu** (sohk-koo-soo) (*socks*)

Long vowels are represented by an additional letter, あ **(a)** (ah), い **(i)** (ee), う **(u)** (oo), え **(e)** (eh), or お **(o)** (oh) in **hiragana**, but by an elongation mark (ー) in **katakana** (check out the earlier section "Vowels" for more on long vowels). For example

おばあさん **obāsan** (oh-bahh-sahn) (*grandmother*)

おじいさん **ojīsan** (oh-jeee-sahn) (*grandfather*)

コーヒー **kōhī** (kohh-heee) (*coffee*)

The pronunciation of some **kana** changes slightly in normal–fast speech in some contexts. For example, the **kana** う **(u)** (oo) that follows another **kana** with the vowel **o** is read as a part of a long vowel **ō,** and the **kana** い **(i)** (ee) that follows another **kana** with the vowel **e** is read as a part of a long vowel **ē.** You can see what I mean in the following examples:

おとうさん **otōsan** (oh-tohh-sahn) (*father*)

せんせい **sensei** (sehn-sehh) (*teacher*)

Kanji

Kanji characters were imported from China. Many of them are made from pictures and signs, and others are combinations of multiple **kanji** characters or components. For example

Kanji made from pictures: 山 (*mountain*), 川 (*river*), 木 (*tree*), 日 (*sun*), 月 (*moon*), and 人 (*person*)

山 (*mountain*)

木 (*tree*)

月 (*moon*)

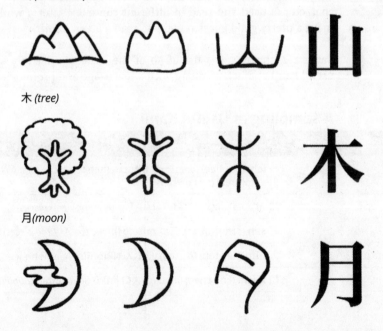

Kanji made from signs: 一 (*one*), 二 (*two*), 三 (*three*), 上 (*top*), 下 (*bottom*), and 中 (*middle*)

Kanji made by combining multiple kanji or kanji components: 明 (*bright*), made of 日 (*sun*) and 月 (*moon*); 森 (*forest*), made of three instances of the **kanji** 木 (*tree*); and 休 (*rest*), made of the **kanji** component 亻 (*person*) and the **kanji** 木 (*tree*)

Most **kanji** characters have multiple pronunciations, including Japanese-based and Chinese-based versions. For example, you pronounce 人 as **hito** (hee-toh) in the Japanese way when it appears by itself, but you most likely read it as **jin** (jeen) or **nin** (neen) when it's a part of a compound noun. For example

人 **hito** (hee-toh) (*person*)

日本人 **Nihonjin** (nee-hohn-jeen) (*Japanese person*)

三人 **sannin** (sahn-neen) (*three people*)

Kanji characters for verbs and adjectives are usually followed by **hiragana**. For example

明るい **akarui** (ah-kah-roo-ee) (*bright*)

食べる **taberu** (tah-beh-roo) (*to eat*)

REMEMBER

Unfortunately, I can't give you an easy tip for knowing how to pronounce the **kanji** characters; you just have to learn them one by one. Look at how each character is used and read in different contexts. After a while, you'll be able to make a pretty good guess on how to read a given **kanji**.

Table 2-4 shows you a list of 50 of the easiest (relatively speaking) and most useful **kanji** characters, along with a few usage and pronunciation examples.

TABLE 2-4 **A Sampling of Useful Kanji**

Kanji	Core Meaning(s)	Examples
一	one	一 **ichi** (ee-chee) (*one*), 一つ **hitotsu** (hee-toh-tsoo) (*one piece*), 一人 **hitori** (hee-toh-ree) (*one person*)
二	two	二 **ni** (nee) (*two*), 二つ **futatsu** (foo-tah-tsoo) (*two pieces*)
三	three	三 **san** (sahn) (*three*), 三つ **mittsu** (meet-tsoo) (*three pieces*)
人	person	人 **hito** (hee-toh) (*person*), 日本人 **Nihonjin** (nee-hohn-jeen) (*Japanese person*)
口	mouth	口 **kuchi** (koo-chee) (*mouth*), 人口 **jinkō** (jeen-kohh) (*population*)

Kanji	Core Meaning(s)	Examples
目	*eye*	目 **me** (meh) (*eye*), 一つ目 **hitotsu-me** (hee-toh-tsoo-meh) (*the first piece*), 目的 **mokuteki** (moh-koo-teh-kee) (*purpose*)
木	*tree*	木 **ki** (kee) (*tree*), 木曜日 **mokuyōbi** (moh-koo-yohh-bee) (*Thursday*)
森	*forest*	森 **mori** (moh-ree) (*forest*), 森林 **shinrin** (sheen-reen) (*woods and forests*)
山	*mountain*	山 **yama** (yah-mah) (*mountain*), 富士山 **Fujisan** (foo-jee-sahn) (*Mt. Fuji*)
川	*river*	川 **kawa** (kah-wah) (*river*), 川口 **Kawaguchi** (kah-wah-goo-chee) (*Kawaguchi, a family name*)
日	*sun*	日 **hi** (hee) (*the sun*), 日曜日 **nichiyōbi** (nee-chee-yohh-bee) (*Sunday*)
月	*moon*	月 **tsuki** (tsoo-kee) (*the moon*), 月曜日 **getsuyōbi** (geh-tsoo-yohh-bee) (*Monday*)
年	*year, age*	年 **toshi** (toh-shee) (*year, age*), 去年 **kyonen** (kyoh-nehn) (*last year*)
本	*book*	本 **hon** (hohn) (*book*), 日本 **Nihon/Nippon** (nee-hohn/neep-pohn) (*Japan*)
明	*bright*	明るい **akarui** (ah-kah-roo-ee) (*bright*), 明日 **asu** (ah-soo) (*tomorrow*)
行	*to go*	行く **iku** (ee-koo) (*to go*), 銀行 **ginkō** (geen-kohh) (*bank*)
来	*to come*	来る **kuru** (koo-roo) (*to come*), 来週 **raishū** (rah-ee-shooo) (*next week*)
私	*I, me, private*	私 **watashi** (wah-tah-shee) (*I, me*), 私立大学 **shiritsu daigaku** (shee-ree-tsoo dah-ee-gah-koo) (*private university*)
男	*male*	男の人 **otoko no hito** (oh-toh-koh noh hee-toh) (*man*), 男性 **dansei** (dahn-sehh) (*man*)
女	*female*	女の人 **onna no hito** (ohn-nah noh hee-toh) (*woman*), 彼女 **kanojo** (kah-noh-joh) (*she, her, girlfriend*)
母	*mother*	母 **haha** (hah-hah) (*one's own mother*), お母さん **okāsan** (oh-kahh-sahn) (*someone else's mother*)
父	*father*	父 **chichi** (chee-chee) (*one's own father*), お父さん **otōsan** (oh-tohh-sahn) (*someone else's father*)
車	*car*	車 **kuruma** (koo-roo-mah) (*car*), 電車 **densha** (dehn-sah) (*train*)
食	*eat*	食べる **taberu** (tah-beh-roo) (*to eat*), 食事 **shokuji** (shoh-koo-jee) (*meal*)
入	*enter*	入る **hairu** (hah-ee-roo) (*to enter*), 入学 **nyūgaku** (nyooo-gah-koo) (*admission to a school*)
出	*come out*	出る **deru** (deh-roo) (*to come out*), 出口 **deguchi** (deh-goo-chee) (*exit*), 出発 **shuppatsu** (shoop-pah-tsoo) (*departure*)
学	*learn*	学ぶ **manabu** (mah-nah-boo) (*to learn*), 学生 **gakusei** (gah-koo-sehh) (*student*), 学校 **gakkō** (gahk-kohh) (*school*)

(continued)

TABLE 2-4 *(continued)*

Kanji	Core Meaning(s)	Examples
先	*ahead, previous*	先に **saki ni** (sah-kee nee) (*on ahead*), 先生 **sensei** (sehn-sehh) (*teacher*), 先月 **sengetsu** (sehn-geh-tsoo) (*last month*)
生	*live, birth*	生きる **ikiru** (ee-kee-roo) (*to live*), 生まれる **umareru** (oo-mah-reh-roo) (*to be born*)
金	*gold, money*	金 **kin** (keen) (*gold*), お金 **o-kane** (oh-kah-neh) (*money*), 金曜日 **kinyōbi** (keen-yohh-bee) (*Friday*)
上	*top, above*	上 **ue** (oo-eh) (*top, above*), 上がる **agaru** (ah-gah-roo) (*to go up*), 上手 **jōzu** (johh-zoo) (*skillful*)
下	*bottom, below*	下 **shita** (shee-tah) (*bottom, below*), 下がる **sagaru** (sah-gah-roo) (*to go down*), 地下 **chika** (chee-kah) (*basement*)
中	*inside, middle*	中 **naka** (nah-kah) (*inside, middle*), 中国 **Chūgoku** (chooo-goh-koo) (*China*)
水	*water*	水 **mizu** (mee-zoo) (*water*), 水曜日 **suiyōbi** (soo-ee-yohh-bee) (*Wednesday*)
土	*soil*	土 **tsuchi** (tsoo-chee) (*soil*), 土地 **tochi** (toh-chee) (*land*), 土曜日 **doyōbi** (doh-yohh-bee) (*Saturday*)
火	*fire*	火 **hi** (hee) (*fire*), 火曜日 **kayōbi** (kah-yohh-bee) (*Tuesday*), 火山 **kazan** (kah-zahn) (*volcano*)
大	*big*	大きい **ōkii** (ohh-keee) (*big*), 大学 **daigaku** (dah-ee-gah-koo) (*university*)
小	*small*	小さい **chīsai** (chee-ee-sah-ee) (*small*), 小学生 **shōgakusei** (shohh-gah-koo-sehh) (*elementary school student*)
犬	*dog*	犬 **inu** (ee-noo) (*dog*), 番犬 **banken** (bahn-kehn) (*watchdog*)
高	*expensive, tall*	高い **takai** (tah-kah-ee) (*expensive*), 高校 **kōkō** (kohh-kohh) (*high school*)
安	*cheap, peaceful*	安い **yasui** (yah-soo-ee) (*cheap*), 安心 **anshin** (ahn-sheen) (*peace of mind*)
右	*right*	右 **migi** (mee-gee) (*right*), 右折する **usetsu suru** (oo-seh-tsoo soo-roo) (*to turn right*)
左	*left*	左 **hidari** (hee-dah-ree) (*left*), 左右 **sayū** (sah-yooo) (*left and right*)
円	*circle, yen*	円 **en** (ehn) (*circle, yen*), 円周 **enshū** (ehn-shooo) (*circumference*)
長	*long, chief*	長い **nagai** (nah-gah-ee) (*long*), 校長 **kōchō** (kohh-chohh) (*principal*)
朝	*morning*	朝 **asa** (ah-sah) (*morning*), 朝食 **chōshoku** (chohh-shoh-koo) (*breakfast*)
昼	*noon, daytime*	昼 **hiru** (hee-roo) (*noon, daytime*), 昼食 **chūshoku** (chooo-shoh-koo) (*lunch*)
晩	*evening*	晩 **ban** (bahn) (*evening*), 今晩 **konban** (kohn-bahn) (*tonight*)
時	*hour*	時 **toki** (toh-kee) (*time*), 時間 **jikan** (jee-kahn) (*time*)
分	*minute*	分かる **wakaru** (wah-kah-roo) (*to understand*), 5分 **go-fun** (goh-foon) (*five minutes*)

FUN & GAMES

For each English word, circle the correct Japanese word in the parentheses. The solution is in Appendix C.

1. grandmother (おばさん **obasan**, おばあさん **obāsan**)

2. grandfather (おじさん **ojisan**, おじいさん **ojīsan**)

3. postage stamp (きって **kitte**, きて **kite**)

4. Toast! (かんぱい **kanpai**, かんばい **kanbai**)

5. Japanese person (日本人 **Nihonhito**, 日本人 **Nihonjin**)

Chapter **3**

Warming Up with Japanese Grammar Basics

I f grammar rules are the branches of a tree, words are the tree's beautiful leaves. Checking the branches before enjoying those leaves is the shortcut to your success in understanding the entire tree. This chapter shows you what the branches of the Japanese language tree look like. You discover the importance of speech styles in speaking Japanese like a native, as well as how to form sentences and ask basic questions. You also find out the basics of parts of speech such as pronouns, verbs, adjectives, and adverbs. All that and more await you in this overview of Japanese grammar basics.

You can listen to all the Talkin' the Talk dialogues featured in this chapter. Go to www.dummies.com/go/japanesefd and click on the dialogue you want to hear.

REMEMBER

Using Appropriate Speech Styles

Japanese use different speech styles depending on whom they're talking to. For example, you ask a simple question like *Did you see it?* differently to different people. When speaking to your boss, use the formal style of speech and say **Goran**

ni narimashita ka. (goh-rahn nee nah-ree-mah-shee-tah kah.) When speaking to your colleague, use the polite/neutral style and say **Mimashita ka.** (mee-mah-shee-tah kah.) And with your kids, use the plain/informal style and say **Mita no.** (mee-tah noh.) Notice that the phrase becomes shorter and shorter as you go down in the relative hierarchy from your boss to your kids.

If you use the plain/informal style of speech with your boss, he will probably start looking for some official reason to kick you out of his group. If you use a formal style with your own daughter, you'll sound like a commoner whose daughter got married to a royal prince. The tricky part of choosing the correct speech style is that the choice depends on both social hierarchy (in terms of position and age) and social grouping (such as insiders and outsiders). Depending on the audience, the informal forms can sound rude or very friendly; the formal forms can sound very polite or awfully cold. In some cases, which style you should use can be very unclear. What if your assistant is older than you are? What if your son is your boss? These scenarios are where your personality can influence your speech style; different people treat them in different ways, even in Japan. If you don't want to offend anyone, your best bet is to use the polite version, at least at the beginning. Table 3-1 gives you some general guidelines on when to use which speech style.

TABLE 3-1

Speech Styles

Style	Whom to Use It With
Formal	Your business customer, a person who is much older than you, your boss, your teacher
Polite/neutral	Your classmate, your colleague, your neighbor, your acquaintance, your friend's parent
Plain/informal	Your parent, your child, your spouse, your student, your assistant, your close friend

REMEMBER

In this book, I use the speech style appropriate to the context, but don't worry — you can tell the difference after you learn the basic verb forms.

TIP

As you're beginning your Japanese study, my advice is to start from the polite/neutral style and gradually play with formal and plain/informal styles.

Forming Sentences

It took me about 20 months to start forming a Japanese sentence after I was born. Twenty months! I was very cute at that age, or so my mom says. Today, you can start forming a Japanese sentence in just five minutes — I promise. You're saving a lot of time! The following sections cover the important points for creating Japanese sentences.

Ordering the words correctly

REMEMBER

The basic word order in English is subject-verb-object, but the order in Japanese is subject-object-verb. Instead of saying *I watched TV*, you say *I TV watched*. Instead of saying *I ate sushi*, you say *I sushi ate*. Now you know the pattern. So repeat after me: Put the *verb at the end! Verb end! Verb end!* Go ahead and try it! *I sake drank*, *I karaoke did*, and *I money lost!* Good, you the basic word order in Japanese have.

Marking nouns with particles

Subject-object-verb is the basic word order in Japanese, but object-subject-verb is also okay. As long as the verb is at the end of the sentence, Japanese grammar teachers are happy. For example, if Mary invited John, you can say either *Mary John invited* or *John Mary invited* in Japanese. Like I said, as long as the verb is at the end, the order of other phrases doesn't matter.

Although it sounds great, a smart person like you may be saying, "Wait a minute! How do you know who invited whom?" The secret is that Japanese use a little tag called a particle right after each noun phrase. The particle for the action performer is **ga** (gah), and the particle for the action receiver is **o** (oh). So, both of the following sentences mean Mary invited John:

> メアリーがジョンを誘いました。**Mearī ga Jon o sasoimashita.** (meh-ah-reee gah john oh sah-soh-ee-mah-shee-tah.)

> ジョンをメアリーが誘いました。**Jon o Mearī ga sasoimashita.** (john oh meh-ah-reee gah sah-soh-ee-mah-shee-tah.)

In other words, **ga** is the subject-marking particle, and **o** is the direct object-marking particle. They can't be translated into English. Sorry, it's just Japanese.

Other Japanese particles include **kara** (kah-rah), **made** (mah-deh), **ni** (nee), **de** (deh), **to** (toh), and **ka** (kah). Luckily, they can be translated into English words like *from, until, to, with, by, at, in, on, and,* and *or*. But each particle is translated differently depending on the context. For example, the particle **de** corresponds to *in*, *by*, or *with* in English, depending on the context:

ボストンで勉強します。**Bosuton de benkyō shimasu.** (boh-soo-tohn deh behn-kyohh shee-mah-soo.) (*I'll study in Boston.*)

タクシーで行きます。**Takushī de ikimasu.** (tah-koo-sheee deh ee-kee-mah-soo.) (*I'll go by taxi.*)

フォークで食べます。**Fōku de tabemasu.** (fohh-koo deh tah-beh-mah-soo.) (*I eat with a fork.*)

TIP

Translation isn't always the best way to figure out a foreign language, so remember the particles in terms of their general functions, not their exact English translations. Table 3-2 presents Japanese particles and their various meanings. I provide translations where I can.

TABLE 3-2   **Particles**

Particle	English	General Function	Example
が **ga** (gah)	No English equivalent	Specifies the subject of the sentence.	ジョンが来た。 **Jon ga kita.** (john gah kee-tah.) (*John came.*)
を **o** (oh)	No English equivalent	Specifies the direct object of the sentence.	メアリーがジョンを誘った。 **Mearī ga Jon o sasotta.** (meh-ah-reee gah john oh sah-soht-tah.) (*Mary invited John.*)
から **kara** (kah-rah)	*from*	Specifies the starting point of the action.	9時から勉強した。 **Ku-ji kara benkyō shita.** (koo-jee kah-rah behn-kyohh shee-tah.) (*I studied from 9:00.*)
まで **made** (mah-deh)	*until*	Specifies the ending point of the action.	3時まで勉強した。 **San-ji made benkyō shita.** (sahn-jee mah-deh behn-kyohh shee-tah.) (*I studied until 3:00.*)

Particle	English	General Function	Example
に **ni** (nee)	*to, on, at, in*	Specifies the target of the action. Specifies the location of existence. Specifies the time of the event.	日本に行った。 **Nihon ni itta.** (nee-hohn nee eet-tah.) (*I went to Japan*.) 弟に本をあげた。 **Otōto ni hon o ageta.** (oh-tohh-toh nee hohn oh ah-geh-tah.) (*I gave the book to my little brother*.) 兄は東京にいる。 **Ani wa Tōkyō ni iru.** (ah-nee wah tohh-kyohh nee ee-roo.) (*My brother is in Tokyo*.) 3時に着いた。 **San-ji ni tsuita.** (sahn-jee nee tsoo-ee-tah.) (*I arrived at 3:00*.)
へ **e** (eh)	*to, toward*	Specifies the direction of the action.	東京へ行った。 **Tōkyō e itta.** (tohh-kyohh eh eet-tah.) (*I went to/toward Tokyo*.)
で **de** (deh)	*in, by, with, at*	Specifies the location, the manner, or the background condition of the action.	ボストンで勉強した。 **Bosuton de benkyō shita.** (boh-soo-tohn de behn-kyohh shee-tah.) (*I studied in Boston*.) タクシーで行った。 **Takushī de itta.** (tah-koo-sheee deh eet-tah.) (*I went there by taxi*.) フォークで食べた。 **Fōku de tabeta.** (fohh-koo deh tah-beh-tah.) (*I ate with a fork*.)
の **no** (noh)	*'s*	Creates a possessive phrase or a modifier phrase.	メアリーの本 **Mearī no hon** (meh-ah-reee noh hohn) (*Mary's book*) 日本語の本 **nihongo no hon** (nee-hon-goh noh hohn) (*a Japanese language book*)

(continued)

TABLE 3-2 *(continued)*

Particle	English	General Function	Example
と **to** (toh)	*and, with*	Lists items. Specifies an accompanying person or a reciprocal relationship.	すしと刺身とてんぷらを食べた。 **Sushi to sashimi to tenpura o tabeta.** (soo-shee toh sah-shee-mee to tehn-poo-rah oh tah-beh-tah.) (*I ate sushi, sashimi, and tempura.*) ジョンがメアリーと歌った。 **Jon ga Mearī to utatta.** (john gah meh-ah-reee toh oo-taht-tah.) (*John sang with Mary.*) トムはマイクと似ている。 **Tomu wa Maiku to nite iru.** (toh-moo wah mah-ee-koo toh nee-teh ee-roo.) (*Tom resembles Mike.*)
は **wa** (wah)	*speaking of*	Marks the topic of the sentence.	東京は去年行った。 **Tōkyō wa kyonen itta.** (tohh-kyohh wah kyoh-nehn eet-tah.) (*Speaking of Tokyo, I went there last year.*)

REMEMBER

If you're going to be writing Japanese particles, use the **hiragana** を (oh) rather than the **hiragana** お (oh) for representing the particle **o** (oh). The **hiragana** を is used only as the particle for direct objects. Also, use the **hiragana** へ (heh) for representing the particle **e** (eh). It's just a convention of the Japanese language.

You can have a bunch of particles in a sentence, as the following sentences illustrate:

メアリーが車で東京へ行った。**Mearī ga kuruma de Tōkyō e itta.** (meh-ah-reee gah koo-roo-mah deh tohh-kyohh eh eet-tah.) (*Mary went to Tokyo by car.*)

ジョンのお父さんからビールとお酒とワインをもらった。**Jon no otōsan kara bīru to osake to wain o moratta.** (john noh oh-tohh-sahn kah-rah beee-roo toh oh-sah-keh toh wah-een oh moh-raht-tah.) (*I received beer, sake, and wine from John's dad.*)

REMEMBER

Japanese nouns don't need articles like *a* and *the* in English. Furthermore, you don't need to specify singular or plural. **Tamago** (tah–mah–goh) is either *an egg* or *eggs*.

Telling the topic

English doesn't have a topic phrase, but if you put a topic phrase at the beginning of whatever you say in Japanese, you can sound a lot more like a native Japanese speaker. Japanese just love to mention topics at the beginning of their sentences.

At the very beginning of a statement, clarify what you're talking about — in other words, state the topic of the sentence. You need to provide the listener with a heads up: *What I'll say from now is about* [topic], *As for* [topic], or *Speaking of* [topic]. Use the particle **wa** (wah) to mark the topic word. Sorry, but use the **hiragana** は (hah) and not わ (wah) to represent the particle **wa** (wah).

Suppose you're talking about what you did yesterday. You start with the word for yesterday, **kinō** (kee-nohh), and add **wa** after the word to alert the listener that yesterday is your topic and that you're going to say something about it in the rest of the sentence.

The following sentences differ in what the speaker is talking about. The statement can be about what happened yesterday, about what happened to the teacher, or about what happened to John, depending on what precedes **wa**:

> 昨日は先生がジョンを叱った。**Kinō wa sensei ga Jon o shikatta.** (kee-nohh wah sehn-sehh gah john oh shee-kaht-tah.) (*As for yesterday, what happened is that the teacher scolded John.*)

> 先生は昨日ジョンを叱った。**Sensei wa kinō Jon o shikatta.** (sehn-sehh wah kee-nohh john oh shee-kaht-tah.) (*As for the teacher, what he did yesterday was to scold John.*)

> ジョンは先生が昨日叱った。**Jon wa sensei ga kinō shikatta.** (john wah sehn-sehh gah kee-nohh shee-kaht-tah.) (*As for John, what happened to him was that the teacher scolded him yesterday.*)

Any noun can be the topic. The subject noun can be the topic, and the object noun can be the topic, too. When a noun is both the subject of the sentence and the topic of the sentence, use only the topic particle **wa** — never **ga wa** — to mark the noun as both the subject and the topic. In the same way, when a noun is the direct object as well as the topic, mark it with just **wa** — never with both **o** and **wa**. However, **wa** can follow other particles, as in **ni wa** and **de wa**.

Dropping understood words

You may have the impression that Japanese people are diligent and hard working — and that is certainly true in many areas — but when it comes to speaking, the Japanese use the minimum number of words necessary to convey their meaning. Minimalist speaking is the Japanese way.

One way to pare down sentences is to drop pronouns and words that are understood in the context, and Japanese drop both almost all the time. As a result, you often hear sentences without a subject, a direct object, a time phrase, or a location phrase. A sentence that consists of just the verb or a question that consists of just the topic isn't uncommon. For example, you don't need to say the words and phrases in the parentheses in the following mini-dialogues.

> *Speaker A:* 昨日はテニスをしましたか。**Kinō wa tenisu o shimashita ka.** (kee-nohh wah teh-nee-soo oh shee-mah-shee-tah kah.) (*Did you play tennis yesterday?*)

> *Speaker B:* はい、(私は昨日テニスを)しました。**Hai, (watashi wa kinō tenisu o) shimashita.** (hah-ee, [wah-tah-shee wah kee-nohh teh-nee-soo oh] shee-mah-shee-tah.) (*Yes, I played tennis yesterday.*)

> *Speaker A:* (今日私の)うちに来ますか。**(kyō watashi no) uchi ni kimasu ka.** ([kyohh wah-tah-shee noh] oo-chee nee kee-mah-soo kah.) (*Will you come to my house today?*)

> *Speaker B:* はい。**Hai.** (hah-ee.) (*Yes.*)

> *Speaker A:* 宿題(をしていますか)。**Shukudai (o shite imasu ka).** (shoo-koo-dah-ee [oh shee-the-ee-mah-soo kah.]) (*Are you doing your homework?*)

> *Speaker B:* はい、そうです。**Hai sō desu.** (hah-ee, soh-deh-soo.) (*Yes, that's right.*)

Asking Questions

If you can form a sentence, you can easily form a question in Japanese. Unlike in English, you don't have to invert the subject and the verb when you ask a question in Japanese. And you don't use question marks, either.

How you form a question depends on whether you're expecting a yes or no answer or a specific piece of information such as a name, place, date, or person. I discuss each case in the following subsections.

Yes/no questions

REMEMBER

To form a question that you expect a *yes* or *no* answer to, just add the question particle **ka** (kah) at the end of the statement sentence and use a rising intonation, just as you do in English. For example, **Jon wa kimasu.** (john wah kee-mah-soo.) means *John will come.*, and **Jon wa kimasu ka.** (john wah kee-mah-soo kah.) means *Will John come?*

Content questions

To ask a question that expects specific information or content as an answer, use a question word in addition to the question particle **ka** at the end of the sentence. Just like in English, you use different question words depending on what you're asking. Table 3-3 provides more information on question words.

TABLE 3-3 **Typical Question Words**

Question Word	Pronunciation	English
だれ **dare**	dah-reh	*who*
どこ **doko**	doh-koh	*where*
どなた **donata**	doh-nah-tah	*who (polite form)*
どれ **dore**	doh-reh	*which one*
どう **dō**	dohh	*how*
いくら **ikura**	ee-koo-rah	*how much*
いつ **itsu**	ee-tsoo	*when*
何 **nani**	nah-nee	*what*

Here are a few examples of content questions so you can see question words in action:

パーティーにはだれと行きますか。**Pātī ni wa dare to ikimasu ka.** (pahh-teee nee wah dah-reh toh ee-kee-mah-soo kah.) (*Who will you go to the party with?*)

昨日は何をしましたか。**Kinō wa nani o shimashita ka.** (kee-nohh wah nah-nee oh shee-mah-shee-tah kah.) (*What did you do yesterday?*)

そのバッグはいくらですか。**Sono baggu wa ikura desu ka.** (soh-noh bahg-goo wah ee-koo-rah deh-soo kah.) (*How much is that bag?*)

Talkin' the Talk

Yoko is asking Ken who came to yesterday's party.

Yoko: **Kinō no pātī wa dare ga kimashita ka.**
         kee-nohh noh pahh-teee wah dah-reh gah
         kee-mah-shee-tah ka.
         Who came to yesterday's party?

Ken: **Jon to Mearī ga kimashita.**
         john toh meh-ah-reee gah kee-mah-shee-tah.
         John and Mary came.

Yoko: **Ā, sō desu ka.**
         Ahh, sohh deh-soo kah.
         Oh, really?

Getting a Handle on Pronouns

Pronouns are convenient shorthand for nouns that both English and Japanese make good use of. Check out the following instruction, where I italicized all the pronouns:

> Mix *those* together like *this,* leave *it* right *there* for a while, and then give *it* to *him* with *that.*

Makes you realize how convenient pronouns are, doesn't it? And take it from me, they become even more useful when your short-term memory worsens as you age and you start referring to everything as "that," "it," and "her."

Demonstrative pronouns

Demonstrative pronouns seems like much too big a phrase to talk about four little words: *this, that, these,* and *those.* Think about the donut shop. You point at all the goodies and say, "I want six of these, two of those, and that big one right there." You use demonstrative pronouns to point verbally. In Japanese, things are just a little more complicated than they are in English.

Suppose you're the speaker and your girlfriend is the listener, and just the two of you are sitting face to face at a cozy table in a fancy restaurant. How romantic! In this case, the half of the table on your side is your territory, and the other half on your girlfriend's side is her territory. "Territory" is a strange word in this context, but it gives you a clear idea. Any other tables in the restaurant are outside of both your territories. With these boundaries drawn, you can use the following pronouns when referring to various foods throughout the restaurant.

» これ **kore** (koh-reh): Things in your territory

» それ **sore** (soh-reh): Things in her territory

» あれ **are** (ah-reh): Things outside of both your territories

Do you get the idea? If you do, you can understand who is eating **tako** (tah-koh) (*octopus*), who is eating **ika** (*ee-kah*) (squid), and who is eating **awabi** (ah-wah-bee) (*abalone*) at the Japanese restaurant in the following Talkin' the Talk dialogue. (Note that abalone is a type of shellfish.)

Talkin' the Talk

Michelle and Brandon are sitting at a table in a fancy Japanese restaurant eating *sashimi,* which is sliced raw seafood. Seafood can look similar when sliced, which may account for Michelle and Brandon's confusion.

Brandon: **Sore wa ika desu ka.**
soh-reh wah ee-kah deh-soo kah.
Is that squid?

Michelle: **Ie, kore wa tako desu. Sore wa ika desu ka.**
eee-eh, koh-ree wah tah-koh deh-soo. soh-ree wah ee-kah deh-soo kah.
No, this one is octopus. Is that one squid?

Brandon:	**Hai, kore wa ika desu.**
	hah-ee, koh-reh wah ee-kah deh-soo.
	Yes, this one is squid.

Michelle:	**Jā, are wa nan desu ka.**
	jahh, ah-reh wah nahn deh-soo kah.
	Then what is that one over there?

Brandon:	**Are wa awabi desu.**
	ah-reh wah ah-wah-bee deh-soo.
	That one over there is abalone.

WORDS TO KNOW

sore	soh-reh	that one (near you)
ika	ee-kah	squid
desu	deh-soo	to be
kore	koh-reh	this one
tako	tah-koh	octopus
are	ah-reh	that one (over there)
awabi	ah-wah-bee	abalone (a type of shellfish)

Personal pronouns

The first-person singular pronoun in Japanese is **watashi** (wah-tah-shee), and it corresponds to the English *I* and *me*. Japanese does have other personal pronouns, which you can check out in Table 3-4.

Note: Although the first-person singular pronoun is typically **watashi,** you can say *I/me* more than one way. The formal version is **watakushi** (wah-tah-koo-shee). Men say **boku** (boh-koo) in informal and neutral contexts. In informal contexts, some men say **ore** (oh-reh), some older men say **washi** (wah-shee), and some young women say **atashi** (ah-tah-shee).

TABLE 3-4   **Personal Pronouns**

Pronoun	Pronunciation	English
私 **watashi**	wah-tah-shee	*I, me*
私たち **watashitachi**	wah-tah-shee-tah-chee	*we, us*
あなた **anata**	ah-nah-tah	*you* (singular)
あなたたち **anatatachi**	ah-nah-tah-tah-chee	*you* (plural)
彼 **kare**	kah-reh	*he, him*
彼ら **karera**	kah-reh-rah	*they, them* (male and mixed genders)
彼女 **kanojo**	kah-noh-joh	*she, her*
彼女ら or 彼女たち **kanojora** *or* **kanojotachi**	kah-noh-joh-rah *or* kah-noh-joh-tah-chee	*they, them* (female)

WARNING

Never use **ore, washi,** and **atashi** when talking with your teacher, boss, customer, or client. **Boku** isn't that bad, but **watashi** is safer in formal situations. Some people may say **jibun (jee-boon),** which literally means "self."

GRAMMAR CHAT

Japanese use the first-person pronouns repeatedly in conversations, but they often don't use other pronouns. In fact, the use of **anata** is almost forbidden. The person who says **anata** sounds snobby, arrogant, or just foreign. So how can you ask a question like *Will you go there?* without using **anata?** One strategy is to drop the pronoun (see the "Dropping understood words" section earlier in this chapter). Just use the verb and the question particle: **Ikimasu ka.** (ee-kee-mah-soo kah.) (*Will [you] go [there]?*) Another strategy to avoid **anata** is to repeatedly use the person's name. You can ask Yōko this question: **Yōko-san, Yōko-san wa ikimasu ka.** (yohh-koh-sahn, yohh-koh-sahn wah ee-kee-mah-soo kah.) (*Yoko, are you going there?* [Literally: *Yoko, is Yoko going?*])

Working with Verbs

The Japanese language places a lot of emphasis on verbs. Verbs not only express certain actions or states of being but also indicate social status, respect, and humility. You can often tell whether Japanese are talking to an esteemed guest, a colleague, a spouse, or even a dog just by the verb they use. Throughout this book, I use examples of plain/informal verbs, polite/neutral verbs, and formal verbs. However, the most common verbs are in the plain/informal and polite/neutral categories. (Head to the earlier section "Using Appropriate Speech Styles" for information on these designations.)

"So how do I conjugate these verbs?" you ask. Good news! You don't need to conjugate verbs based on person, gender, or number in Japanese. You use the same form of a verb regardless of who's performing the action. For example, you use the verb taberu (tah-beh-roo) whether you want to say *I eat, you eat, he eats, she eats,* or *they eat.* "That's great," you're thinking — no conjugation tables to memorize. Not so fast. I'm not saying that Japanese verbs don't conjugate at all; they do. In this section, I walk you through the various conjugations, showing you how to create present, past, negative, and polite verbs (and combinations of these). If you get confused, you can always check out the verb tables in Appendix B.

Understanding basic verb forms

Japanese speakers use four basic verb forms frequently: the *dictionary form,* the *nai-form,* the *stem form,* and the *te-form.* The other forms of a verb can be easily created by making a minor adjustment to one of these forms.

REMEMBER

Throughout the book, when I introduce a new verb, I give you these four forms in this order — dictionary, **nai-,** stem, and **te-**forms — along with the pronunciation. After the stem form, I add ます **masu** because you'll be hearing this form with ます **masu** all the time. The following is an example with **taberu** (tah-beh-roo) (*to eat*):

Japanese Script	Rōmaji	Pronunciation
食べる	taberu	tah-beh-roo
食べない	tabenai	tah-beh-nah-ee
食べ(ます)	tabe(masu)	tah-beh(-mah-soo)
食べて	tabete	tah-beh-the

I describe each form in greater detail in the sections that follow.

Dictionary form

The dictionary form, or *plain present affirmative,* is kind of like an infinitive in English, but without the *to.* You see this verb form when you look up words in the dictionary.

All dictionary forms end in one of the syllables ぶ **bu** (boo), む **mu** (moo), ぬ **nu** (noo), ぐ **gu** (goo), く **ku** (koo), る **ru** (roo), す **su** (soo), つ **tsu** (tsoo), and う **u** (oo). Did you notice that they all include the vowel **u?**

You use the dictionary form when the verb is placed before a noun or some particle as well as before some grammatical items listed in the "Turning to sentence-like adverbs" and "Expressing Moods and Attitudes" sections later in this chapter. Just watch out. Using the dictionary form at the end of a sentence makes you sound rude in a formal context. You can use it without worry in an informal context, like when you're talking with your family, friends, or pet.

Nai-form

The **nai**-form, or *plain present negative*, is the negative counterpart of the dictionary form. For example, if the dictionary form means *I do*, the **nai**-form means *I don't*. All **nai**-forms end in **nai** (nah-ee).

Stem form

The stem form is the shortest pronounceable form of a verb, and it can be tightly combined with grammatical items such as **masu, nagara, ni,** and **tai** and with words such as **nikui, sugiru, tsuzukeru,** and **yasui** (just to name a few) to form a compound verb or adjective. To show you what they mean, check out the following examples featuring **tabe** (tah-beh), the stem form of the verb **taberu:**

食べます **tabe-masu** (tah-beh-mah-soo) (*to eat* [polite])

食べながら **tabe-nagara** (tah-beh-nah-gah-rah) (*while eating*)

食べに **tabe ni** (tah-beh nee) (*in order to eat*)

食べたい **tabe-tai** (tah-beh-tah-ee) (*to want to eat*)

食べにくい **tabe-nikui** (tah-beh-nee-koo-ee) (*to be difficult to eat*)

食べすぎる **tabe-sugiru** (tah-beh-soo-gee-roo) (*to eat too much*)

食べつづける **tabe-tsuzukeru** (tah-beh-tsoo-zoo-keh-roo) (*to continue to eat*)

食べやすい **tabe-yasui** (tah-beh-yah-soo-ee) (*to be easy to eat*)

Because the stem form is used right before the most frequently used verb suffix, **masu,** it's also called the *pre-masu* form. See the "Speaking politely with -masu" section in this chapter for more about **masu.**

Te-form

Called the **te**-form because it ends in **te** (teh) or its variant, **de** (deh), this verb form means *do . . . and*, and is used to connect the verb with other verbs and adjectives. For example, to connect the three verbs **taberu, nomu** (noh-moo) (*to drink*), and **neru** (neh-roo) (*to sleep*) to mean to eat, drink, and go to bed, you make all verbs except for the last one the **te**-forms as in **tabete, nonde, neru** (tah-beh-teh, nohn-deh, neh-roo).

Te-forms are also necessary right before many auxiliary verbs, such as **kudasai, iru, miru, oku,** and **shimau,** which refine what the speaker wants to express. See how these auxiliary verbs can follow **tabete,** the **te**-form of the verb **taberu:**

食べてください。 **Tabete kudasai.** (tah-beh-teh koo-dah-sah-ee) (*Please eat.*)

食べている **tabete iru** (tah-beh-teh ee-roo) (*to be eating*)

食べてみる **tabete miru** (tah-beh-teh mee-roo) (*to try eating*)

食べておく **tabete oku** (tah-beh-teh oh-koo) (*to eat in advance*)

食べてしまう **tabete shimau** (tah-beh-teh shee-mah-oo) (*to eat up*)

Doing the conjugation thing

As in English, Japanese has regular and irregular verbs. All regular verbs conjugate according to a predictable pattern, whereas irregular verbs deviate from the pattern to a greater or lesser extent. Luckily, most verbs are regular. The following sections help you conjugate various kinds of verbs in the past and present, as well as form negative verbs.

Conjugating verbs

REMEMBER

Regular verbs come in two basic types: **ru**-verbs and **u**-verbs. Before you can conjugate any regular verb, you have to determine which type you're dealing with.

» If you don't see **eru** or **iru** at the end of the dictionary form of a verb, you can relax and trust that it's an **u**-verb.

» If the verb ends in **eru** or **iru**, you need to be on alert because it can be either a **ru**-verb or an **u**-verb.

For example, **kaeru** (kah-eh-roo) is either a **ru**-verb (meaning *change*) or an **u**-verb (meaning *go home*). Similarly, **kiru** (kee-roo) is either a **ru**-verb (meaning *wear*) or an **u**-verb (meaning *cut*). The distinction is important because these verbs conjugate differently depending on the form. **Ru**-verbs are sort of more stable verbs conjugation-wise because the stem-form appears in every form. U-verbs are a bit more complex: They add one more sound or one more syllable in the **nai-**, stem, and **te**-forms.

Table 3-5 lists representative **ru**-verbs, **u**-verbs, and irregular verbs and includes these tricky **eru/iru** verbs (**kaeru** and **kiru** pairs), so you can check them out!

TABLE 3-5 **Verb Forms**

	Meaning	Dictionary Form	Nai-Form	Stem Form	Te-Form
Ru-verbs	*to eat*	たべる **taberu**	たべない **tabenai**	たべ **tabe**	たべて **tabete**
	to change	かえる **kaeru**	かえない **kaenai**	かえ **kae**	かえて **kaete**
	to wear	きる **kiru**	きない **kinai**	き **ki**	きて **kite**
U-verbs	*to speak*	はなす **hanasu**	はなさない **hanasanai**	はなし **hanashi**	はなして **hanashite**
	to write	かく **kaku**	かかない **kakanai**	かき **kaki**	かいて **kaite**
	to swim	およぐ **oyogu**	およがない **oyoganai**	およぎ **oyogi**	およいで **oyoide**
	to drink	のむ **nomu**	のまない **nomanai**	のみ **nomi**	のんで **nonde**
	to jump	とぶ **tobu**	とばない **tobanai**	とび **tobi**	とんで **tonde**
	to die	しぬ **shinu**	しなない **shinanai**	しに **shini**	しんで **shinde**
	to buy	かう **kau**	かわない **kawanai**	かい **kai**	かって **katte**
	to cut	きる **kiru**	きらない **kiranai**	きり **kiri**	きって **kitte**
	to take	とる **toru**	とらない **toranai**	とり **tori**	とって **totte**
	to go home	かえる **kaeru**	かえらない **kaeranai**	かえり **kaeri**	かえって **kaette**

(continued)

TABLE 3-5 *(continued)*

	Meaning	Dictionary Form	Nai-Form	Stem Form	Te-Form
	to wait	まつ **matsu**	またない **matanai**	まち **machi**	まって **matte**
Irregular verbs	*to exist (inanimate things)*	ある **aru**	ない **nai**	あり **ari**	あって **atte**
	to come	くる **kuru**	こない **konai**	き **ki**	きて **kite**
	to do	する **suru**	しない **shinai**	し **shi**	して **shite**
	to go	いく **iku**	いかない **ikanai**	いき **iki**	いって **itte**

To conjugate a **ru**-verb, you drop the **ru** (roo) at the end of its dictionary form and add something or nothing. By contrast, to conjugate an **u**-verb, you drop the **u** (oo) and always add something. (Maybe I should call them **ru**-dropping verbs and **u**-dropping verbs. First drop something and then add something or nothing!)

For conjugating a verb, check the ending syllable and the type of the verb, and then follow the pattern of one of the verbs in Table 3-5. But which one? Pick the one with the same ending syllable and the same verb type. By the ending syllable, I mean the last syllable, not the last sound. That is, the last consonant and vowel combination. If no consonant precedes the last vowel (for example, as in the word **kau**), the last vowel by itself is the ending syllable of the verb.

TIP

Nai-forms and stem forms are pretty easy to make, but **te**-forms aren't if the verb is an **u**-verb, right? Here are some rules of thumb that can make Japanese verb conjugations easier:

>> For **u**-verbs whose dictionary forms end in う**u**, る **ru**, or つ **tsu**, replace these ending syllables with って **tte**.

>> For **u**-verbs whose dictionary forms end in む **mu**, ぬ **nu**, or ぶ **bu**, replace these ending syllables with んで **nde**.

>> For **u**-verbs whose dictionary forms end in す **su**, replace す **su** with して**shite**.

>> For **u**-verbs whose dictionary forms end in く **ku** or ぐ **gu**, replace them with いて **ite** and いで **ide**, respectively.

>> For the two major irregular verbs, くる **kuru** (*to come*) and する **suru** (*to do*), as well as the verb いく **iku** (*to go*), simply remember their **te**-forms, which are きて **kite**, して **shite**, and いって **itte**.

>> For **ru**-verbs, just replace the る **ru** at the end of the dictionary form with て **te**.

Deciding between present and past tense

REMEMBER

Japanese verbs have just two tenses: present and past. However, these grammar terms are misleading. *Present tense* in Japanese refers to actions that regularly take place or will take place in the future, which makes the verb **taberu** not just *I eat* but also *I will eat.* For this reason, some people call the present tense the *non-past* tense. Usually, the context tells you which meaning the verb is expressing. As in English, the present tense often doesn't refer to this very moment, but to some habitual action, such as *I eat dinner every day at 6:00.*

Forming the present and past tenses

Creating the present tense of a Japanese verb is a no-brainer: It's just the dictionary form. If you know a verb's **te**-form, expressing that verb in the past tense is still pretty easy. You simply change the final vowel; because you're working with the **te**-form, you're always changing an **e** to an **a**. For example, **tabete** becomes **tabeta** (tah-beh-tah) (*ate*), and **nonde** (nohn-deh) becomes **nonda** (nohn-dah) (*drank*).

Creating negative past tense verbs

In order to say that you didn't do something in the past, you need to be able to fashion verbs into their negative past forms. No problem. It's easy. Simply take the **nai**-form, drop the final vowel **i**, and add **-katta**. For example, **tabenai** (tah-beh-nah-ee) (*don't eat*) becomes **tabenakatta** (tah-beh-nah-kaht-tah) (*didn't eat*). Cool, huh?

Speaking politely with –masu

In Japanese, the verbs you choose to use say a lot about you. Using the plain/ informal verb forms — specifically, dictionary forms, **nai**-forms, and their past counterparts (which I discuss in the earlier "Doing the conjugation thing" section) — is sufficient when you talk with close friends or family members. However, using them in a business situation or with strangers may make the listener think you're unsophisticated or even rude. The ability to judge the situation and know what level of formality is appropriate is an integral part of speaking

Japanese. That's why it's worth knowing another set of conjugation patterns that use the polite suffix **masu** to make the polite/neutral verb forms.

Conjugating with -**masu** is easy if you know the stem form of verbs (I tell you about this verb form in the earlier related section). You just have to remember four verb endings (one each for affirmative present, negative present, affirmative past, and negative past), and add one of them to the end of the verb in the stem form.

» For affirmative present verbs, add -**masu**. For example, 食べます **tabemasu** (tah-beh-mah-soo) (*eats*) or 飲みます **nomimasu** (noh-mee-mah-soo) (*drinks*).

» For negative present verbs, add -**masen**. For example, 食べません **tabemasen** (tah-beh-mah-sehn) (*doesn't eat*) or 飲みません **nomimasen** (noh-mee-mah-sehn) (*doesn't drink*).

» For affirmative past verbs, add -**mashita**. For example, 食べました **tabemashita** (tah-beh-mah-shee-tah) (*ate*) or 飲みました **nomimashita** (noh-mee-mah-shee-tah) (*drank*).

» For negative past verbs, add -**masen deshita**. For example, 食べませんでした **tabemasen deshita** (tah-beh-mah-sehn deh-shee-tah) (*didn't eat*), 飲みません でした **nomimasen deshita** (noh-mee-mah-sehn deh-shee-tah) (*didn't drink*).

Introducing the Verb Desu, to Be

Like the English verb *to be*, **desu** (deh-soo) expresses the identity or state of people and things. **Desu** is used in the construction **X wa Y desu.** (X wah Y deh-soo.) (*X is Y.*) (As I note earlier in the chapter, the conventional Japanese sentence order is *X Y is*, not *X is Y*. The particle **wa** [wah] is the topic particle I discuss in the earlier section "Telling the topic.")

Desu follows either a noun or an adjective. For example, **Otōto wa gakusei desu.** (oh-tohh-toh wah gah-koo-sehh deh-soo.) means *My little brother is a student.* **Watashi wa genki desu.** (wah-tah-shee wah gehn-kee deh-soo.) means *I am fine.* Now you know why many Japanese sentences end in **desu**. And like the English verb *to be*, **desu** can also express the location of people and things. For example, **Jon wa Bosuton desu.** (john wah boh-soo-tohn deh-soo.) means *John is in Boston.* Just be aware that you can also express the location of things and people using the verbs **aru** and **iru.** To find out more about **aru** and **iru,** see Chapter 7.

Conjugation-wise, **desu** doesn't look like any other verb. (That's because **desu** didn't start out as a stand-alone verb; it was the combination of the particle **de,** the verb **aru** [ah-roo] [*to exist*], and the polite suffix -**masu**.) Table 3-6 shows you the patterns of **desu.** To help you see the point easily, I use the same noun **gakusei** (gah-koo-sehh) (*student*) in each example. If you want to know how to use **desu** after an adjective, see the following section.

TABLE 3-6 **Polite/Neutral Form of Noun plus Desu**

Japanese	Pronunciation	English
学生です **gakusei desu**	gah-koo-sehh deh-soo	*is a student*
学生じゃありません **gakusei ja arimasen**	gah-koo-sehh jah ah-ree-mah-sehn	*isn't a student*
学生でした **gakusei deshita**	gah-koo-sehh deh-shee-tah	*was a student*
学生じゃありませんでした **gakusei ja arimasen deshita**	gah-koo-sehh jah ah-ree-mah-sehn deh-shee-tah	*wasn't a student*

In an informal context, you can use the shorter version of **desu,** as Table 3-7 demonstrates.

TABLE 3-7 **Informal Form of Noun plus Desu**

Japanese	Pronunciation	English
学生だ **gakusei da**	gah-koo-sehh dah	*is a student*
学生じゃない **gakusei ja nai**	gah-koo-sehh jah nah-ee	*isn't a student*
学生だった **gakusei datta**	gah-koo-sehh daht-tah	*was a student*
学生じゃなかった **gakusei ja nakatta**	gah-koo-sehh jah nah-kaht-tah	*wasn't a student*

TIP

Ja (jah), which you see in the negative forms in Tables 3-6 and 3-7, is the contraction of **de wa** (deh wah). Most Japanese use **ja** in everyday conversation, but occasionally, they use **de wa,** which sounds a bit more formal. Just be ready to hear either of them.

Talkin' the Talk

Susan asks Ken some questions.

Susan: **Ano otoko no hito wa gakusei desu ka.**
ah-noh oh-toh-koh noh hee-toh wah gah-koo-sehh deh-soo ka.
Is that man a student?

Ken: **Īe, gakusei ja arimasen. Watashi no karate no sensei desu.**
eee-eh, gah-koo-sehh jah ah-ree-mah-sehn. wah-tah-shee noh kah-rah-teh noh sehn-sehh deh-soo.
No, he's not a student. He is my karate teacher.

Susan: **Ā, sō desu ka. Chotto kowasō desu ne.**
ahh, sohh deh-soo kah. choht-toh koh-wah-sohh deh-soo neh.
Oh, I see. He looks a little scary.

WORDS TO KNOW		
otoko no hito	oh-toh-koh noh hee-toh	man
gakusei	gah-koo-sehh	student
sensei	sehn-sehh	teacher
kowasō	koh-wah-sohh	scary-looking

Describing People and Things with Adjectives

As in English, you can place Japanese adjectives either before a noun as a noun modifier (an *expensive* book, for example) or at the end of a sentence (The book is *expensive*.).

Believe it or not, all Japanese adjectives end in either **i** or **na** when they're placed before a noun (except some categories of adjectives, namely no adjectives, which I don't cover here because they pattern like nouns). Adjectives that end in **i** are called *i-type adjectives,* and those that end in **na** are called *na-type adjectives.* **I**-type adjectives are pure adjectives, but **na**-type adjectives are a sort of "noun" followed by **na.** There's really no clear-cut distinction between the two groups in terms of meaning. For example, **takai** (tah-kah-ee) and **kōka na** (kohh-kah nah) both mean *expensive,* but one is an **i**-type adjective and the other is a **na**-type adjective.

Look at some adjectives that modify the noun **hon** (hohn) (*book*):

» 高い本 **takai hon** (tah-kah-ee hohn) (*an expensive book*)

» おもしろい本 **omoshiroi hon** (oh-moh-shee-roh-ee hohn) (*an interesting book*)

» 高価な本 **kōka na hon** (kohh-kah nah hohn) (*a high-priced book*)

» 便利な本 **benri na hon** (behn-ree nah hohn) (*a useful book*)

» きれいな本 **kirei na hon** (kee-rehh nah hohn) (*a beautiful book*)

REMEMBER

Japanese adjectives consist of a *stem* (the part that remains the same) and an *inflection* part (the part that changes depending on the context). The endings **i** and **na** are inflection parts.

English adjectives conjugate based on whether they're comparative or superlative, like *tall, taller,* and *tallest,* but Japanese adjectives conjugate based on different factors. For example, when the adjectives appear at the end of a sentence rather than before a noun, the **i** and **na** change or disappear, and an extra item like the verb **desu** (deh-soo) (*to be*) shows up in various forms, all of which depend on the tense, the *polarity* (whether the statement is affirmative or negative), or the speech style.

Look at the following sentences, all of which either include **takai,** an **i**-type adjective, or **kōka na,** a **na**-type adjective:

あれは高価じゃありません。**Are wa kōka ja arimasen.** (ah-reh wah kohh-kah jah ah-ree-mah-sehn.) (*That isn't high-priced.*)

ハンバーガーは高くありません。**Hanbāgā wa takaku arimasen.** (hahn-bahh-gahh wah tah-kah-koo ah-ree-mah-sehn.) (*Hamburgers aren't expensive.*)

高価なネックレスを買いました。**Kōka na nekkuresu o kaimashita.** (kohh-kah nah nehk-koo-reh-soo oh kah-ee-mah-shee-tah.) (*I bought an expensive necklace.*)

これは高かったです。**Kore wa takakatta desu.** (koh-reh wah tah-kah-kaht-tah deh-soo.) (*This was expensive.*)

高い本を買いました。**Takai hon o kaimashita.** (tah-kah-ee hohn oh kah-ee-mah-shee-tah.) (*I bought an expensive book.*)

Table 3-8 summarizes the patterns for **i**-type and **na**-type adjectives.

TABLE 3-8   Adjective Patterns

	Tense/Polarity	I-type	Na-type
Plain/informal style			
	Present affirmative (is)	高い **takai**	高価だ **kōka da**
	Present negative (isn't)	高くない **takaku nai**	高価じゃない **kōka ja nai**
	Past affirmative (was)	高かった **takakatta**	高価だった **kōka datta**
	Past negative (wasn't)	高くなかった **takaku nakatta**	高価じゃなかった **kōka ja nakatta**
Polite/neutral style			
	Present affirmative (is)	高いです **takai desu**	高価です **kōka desu**
	Present negative (isn't)	高くありません **takaku arimasen** 高くないです **takaku nai desu**	高価じゃありません **kōka ja arimasen** *or* 高価じゃないです **kōka ja nai desu**
	Past affirmative (was)	高かったです **takakatta desu**	高価でした **kōka deshita**
	Past negative (wasn't)	高くありませんでした **takaku arimasen deshita** 高くなかったです **taka-ku nakatta desu**	高価じゃありませんでした **kōka ja arimasen deshita** *or* 高価じゃなかったです **kōka ja nakatta desu**

Of course, some Japanese adjectives are irregular. The most-frequently used irregular adjective is **ii** (ee-ee) (*good*). Its stem part is the initial **i,** and its inflection part is the second **i**. The stem part **i** becomes **yo** in all the forms except the present affirmative form, regardless of whether the adjective appears at the end of a sentence or right before a noun. Here are some examples:

いい本です **ii hon desu** (ee-ee hohn deh-soo) (*is a good book*)

いいです **ii desu** (ee-ee deh-soo) (*is good*)

よかったです **yokatta desu** (yoh-kaht-tah deh-soo) (*was good*)

よくありませんでした **yoku arimasendeshita** (yoh-koo ah-ree-mah-sehn deh-shee-tah) (*wasn't good*)

よくありません **yoku arimasen** (yoh-koo ah-ree-mah-sen) (*isn't good*)

REMEMBER

In this book, when I list an adjective in the Words to Know section, I list **i**-type adjectives and **na**-type adjectives in the form you see before a noun, but I put **na** in the parentheses. When you use a Japanese dictionary, **na**-type adjectives often appear in their stem form, without **na**.

Using Adverbs to Describe Your Actions

Just as adjectives describe how people and things are, adverbs describe how actions are performed. Japanese adverbs fall into two categories: the ones that are created from adjectives and the ones that aren't. I tell you about both types of adverbs, as well as adverbial clauses, in the next sections.

Creating adverbs from adjectives

Notice anything special about the words *slowly, quickly, pleasantly, neatly,* and *quietly?* They're all adverbs created from adjectives by adding *–ly!* In Japanese, you can also create adverbs from adjectives. Just add **ku** (koo) and **ni** (nee) to the stem of an **i**-type adjective and a **na**-type adjective, respectively. (I tell you about **i**-type adjectives and **na**-type adjectives in the earlier "Describing People and Things with Adjectives" section.) Table 3-9 shows you what I mean.

TABLE 3-9   **Adverbs Created from Adjectives**

	Japanese Adjective	English	Japanese Adverb	English
I-type adjective	楽しい **tanoshii** (tah-noh-shee)	*pleasant, fun*	楽しく **tanoshiku** (tah-noh-shee-koo)	*pleasantly*
Adjectival Noun	静か(な) **shizuka (na)** (shee-zoo-kah [nah])	*quiet*	静かに **shizuka ni** (shee-zoo-kah nee)	*quietly*

Perusing pure adverbs

Unlike the adverbs that are created from adjectives (see the preceding section), some adverbs are just born as adverbs. For example

>> ちょっと **chotto** (choht-toh) (*slightly, a little*)

>> いつも **itsumo** (ee-tsoo-moh) (*always*)

>> もう **mō** (mohh) (*already*)

>> たいてい **taitei** (tah-ee-tehh) (*usually*)

>> ときどき **tokidoki** (toh-kee-doh-kee) (*sometimes*)

>> ゆっくり **yukkuri** (yook-koo-ree) (*slowly*)

The adverb–version of **ii** (ee–ee) (*good*) is **yoku** (yoh–koo) (*well*).

Turning to sentence-like adverbs

You can describe the action or state by using a sentence–like adverb, or an *adverbial clause*, to express its circumstances. For example, **kara** designates reasons for an action, and **toki ni** states the time of an action. Reasons can be stated by a sentence, such as *because I will go to Japan.* The time of an action can also be stated by a sentence, such as *when I take an exam.*

日本に行きますから, 日本語を勉強します。**Nihon ni ikimasu kara, Nihongo o benkyō shimasu.** (nee-hohn nee ee-kee-mah-soo kah-rah, nee-hohn-goh oh behn-kyohh shee-mah-soo.) (*Because I'll go to Japan, I'll study Japanese.*)

日本が好きですから, 日本語を勉強します。**Nihon ga suki desu kara, Nihongo o benkyō shimasu.** (nee-hohn gah soo-kee deh-soo kah-rah, nee-hohn-goh oh behn-kyohh shee-mah-soo.) (*Because I like Japan, I'll study Japanese.*)

試験を受けるときに, 勉強します。**Shiken o ukeru toki ni, benkyō shimasu.** (shee-kehn oh oo-keh-roo toh-kee nee, behn-kyohh shee-mah-soo.) (*When I take an exam, I study.*)

静かなときに, 勉強します。**Shizuka na toki ni, benkyō shimasu.** (shee-zoo-kah nah toh-kee nee, behn-kyohh shee-mah-soo.) (*When it's quiet, I study.*)

These are only a couple of the many kinds of adverbial clauses, but I show you the others throughout the book as they become relevant so you can get a better idea of how to use them in context.

Spicing Up Your Japanese with Onomatopoeia

The Japanese language includes a lot of *onomatopoeic* expressions, which describe sounds, actions, or states of things. *Bow-wow* and *meow* describe the sounds of dogs and cats in English, respectively. In Japanese, these sounds are **wanwan** (wahn–wahn) and **nyānyā** (nyahh–nyahh). Each onomatopoeic expression is composed of a sound repeated twice in many cases. There are sound symbolic words that describe not only sounds but also actions or states of things that can be depicted in verbs or adjectives in English. For example, *fluffy* can be translated into **fuwafuwa** (foo–wah–foo–wah) as in **fuwafuwa no kēki** (*fluffy cake*). **Dara dara** means someone *stagnates* or *is lazy*. You can imagine a student mindlessly watching TV all day during summer break. A good portion of onomatopoeic words do not have English equivalents. There are too many onomatopoeic expressions to list here, but following are some examples that you can have fun with!

ニコニコ する **nikoniko suru** (nee-koh-nee-ko soo-roo) (*smiling, beaming*)

たろうはいつもニコニコしています。**Taro wa itsumo nikoniko shiteimasu.** (Tarō wah ee-tsoo-moh nee-koh-nee-ko shee-the-ee-mah-soo.) (*Taro is always smiling.*)

ドキドキする **dokidoki suru** (doh-kee-doh-kee soo-roo) (*feeling excited, nervous, one's heart is beating fast*)

あした、プレゼンテーションがありますから、ドキドキします。**Ashita purezentēshon ga arimasu kara, dokidoki shimasu.** (Ah-shee-tah, poo-reh-zehn-teh-shohn gah ah-ree-mah-soo-kah-rah, doh-kee-doh-kee shee-mah-soo.) (*Because I have a presentation tomorrow, I am nervous.*)

ペラペラはなす **perapera hanasu** (peh-rah-peh-rah hah-nah-soo) (*speak fluently*)

ジョンは日本語をペラペラ話します。**Jon wa nihongo o perapera hanashimasu.** (John wah nee-hohn-goh o peh-rah-peh-rah hah-nah-shee-mah-soo.) (*John speaks Japanese fluently.*)

ピカピカ **pikapika** (pee-kah-pee-kah) (describes something shiny that has a smooth surface)

この車はピカピカです。**Kono kuruma wa pikapika desu.** (Koo-noh koo-roo-mah wah pee-kah-pee-kah deh-soo.) (*This car is shiny.*)

ペコペコ **pekopeko** (peh-koh-peh-koh) (*hungry, starving*)

おなかがペコペコです。**Onaka ga pekopeko desu.** (Oh-nah-kah gah peh-koh-peh-koh deh-soo.) (*I'm starving!*)

Expressing Moods and Attitudes

To express your attitude toward your statement, you add some little elements at the end of your sentence (like you'd add *right?* or *you know?* to an English sentence). Here, I list the most useful ones, with example sentences so you'll know how to use them.

» ね **ne** (neh) (used for confirming; *all right?; right?; isn't it?*):

- 食べますね。**Tabemasu ne.** (tah-beh-mah-soo neh.) (*I'll eat it, all right?*)

- 高いですね。**Takai desu ne.** (tah-kah-ee deh-soo neh.) (*It's expensive, isn't it?*)

- きれいですね。**Kirei desu ne.** (kee-rehh deh-soo neh.) (*It's pretty, isn't it?*)

- 学生ですね。**Gakusei desu ne.** (gah-koo-sehh deh-soo neh.) (*He is a student, right?*)

» よ **yo** (yoh) (used for emphasis; *I tell you; you know?*):

- 食べますよ。**Tabemasu yo.** (tah-beh-masu yoh.) (*I'll eat it!*)

- 高いですよ。**Takai desu yo.** (tah-kah-ee deh-soo yoh.) (*It's expensive!*)

- きれいですよ。**Kirei desu yo.** (kee-rehh deh-soo yoh.) (*It's pretty, I tell you!*)

- 学生ですよ。**Gakusei desu yo.** (gah-koo-sehh deh-soo yoh.) (*He is a student, you know?*)

» でしょう **deshō** (deh-shohh) (*probably*)

- 食べるでしょう。**Taberu deshō.** (tah-beh-roo deh-shohh.) (*He'll probably eat it.*)

- 高いでしょう。**Takai deshō.** (tah-kah-ee deh-shohh.) (*It's probably expensive.*)

- きれいでしょう。**Kirei deshō.** (kee-rehh deh-shohh.) (*It's probably pretty.*)

- 学生でしょう。**Gakusei deshō.** (gah-koo-sehh deh-shohh.) (*He is probably a student.*)

» かもしれません **ka mo shiremasen** (kah moh shee-reh-mah-sehn) (*may; possibly*)

- 食べるかもしれません。**Taberu ka mo shiremasen.** (tah-beh-roo kah moh shee-reh-mah-sehn.) (*He may eat it.*)

- 高いかもしれません。**Takai ka mo shiremasen.** (tah-kah-ee kah moh shee-reh-mah-sehn.) (*It may be expensive.*)

- きれいかもしれません。**Kirei ka mo shiremasen.** (kee-rehh kah moh shee-reh-mah-sehn.) (*It may be pretty.*)

- 学生かもしれません。**Gakusei ka mo shiremasen.** (gah-koo-sehh kah moh shee-reh-mah-sehn.) (*He may be a student.*)

FUN & GAMES

Try your hand at the following activities based on the concepts in this chapter. Flip to Appendix C for the answers.

Activity 1: Pick the most appropriate item in the parentheses.

1. 昨日は (a. お酒を飲みました / b. 飲みましたお酒を)。

Kinō wa (a. **osake o nomimashita** / b. **nomimashita osake o**).

2. 東京 (a. で / b. に) 行きます。

Tōkyō (a. **de** / b. **ni**) **ikimasu.**

3. タクシー(a. で / b. に)行きます。

Takushī (a. **de** / b. **ni**) **ikimasu.**

4. 私は学生(a. ます / b. です)。

Watashi wa gakusei (a. **masu** / b. **desu**).

5. あの人は(a. いつ / b. だれ)ですか。

Ano hito wa (a. **itsu** / b. **dare**) **desu ka.**

6. この本は(a. 高価な / b. 高価)です。

Kono hon wa (a. **kōka na** / b. **kōka**) **desu.**

Activity 2: Susan and Ken are at a Japanese restaurant. Fill in the blanks.

Susan: それは_____ですか。

Sore wa _____ desu ka.

Ken: _____ はてんぷらです。

_____ wa tenpura desu.

Susan: じゃあ、あれは何ですか。

Jā, are wa nan desu ka.

Ken: _____ はすきやきです。

_____ wa sukiyaki desu.

Susan: ああ、そうですか。

Ā, sō desu ka.

SUKIYAKI

TENPURA

Illustration by Elizabeth Kurtzman

Chapter **4**

Getting Your Numbers, Times, and Measurements Straight

Y ou probably count and measure a variety of items every day, so quantities and amounts are essential for doing almost everything in your life. Apples, coffee, people, time, distance, temperature — you name it, and it likely requires counting or measuring. In this chapter, you find out all about Japanese numbers. You also discover how to express times and dates in Japanese so you can describe, for example, when you're going to meet with your business partners or when your date should pick you up.

REMEMBER

You can listen to all the Talkin' the Talk dialogues featured in this chapter. Go to www.dummies.com/go/japanesefd and click on the dialogue you want to hear.

Ichi, Ni, San: Counting in Japanese

In this section, I will show you numbers from 1 to 100,000 in Japanese. Think of it — you can increase your vocabulary by 100,000 words!

Numbers from 1 to 10

You can master the art of counting from one to ten right now. It'll be handy as you earn your belts at a **karate dōjō** (kah-rah-teh dohh-johh) (*karate training hall*). At a **karate dōjō,** they never start from **rei** (rehh) (*zero*). They always start from **ichi** (ee-chee) (*one*) when they punch and kick. **Ichi, ni** (nee) (*two*), **san** (sahn) (*three*)!

Japanese usually write numbers by using Arabic numerals, but they also write them in **kanji.** Here's how Japanese write and say the numbers from 1 to 10:

>> *1:* 一 **ichi** (ee-chee)

>> *2:* 二 **ni** (nee)

>> *3:* 三 **san** (sahn)

>> *4:* 四 **yon** (yohn) *or* **shi** (shee)

>> *5:* 五 **go** (goh)

>> *6:* 六 **roku** (roh-koo)

>> *7:* 七 **nana** (nah-nah) *or* **shichi** (shee-chee)

>> *8:* 八 **hachi** (hah-chee)

>> *9:* 九 **kyū** (kyooo) *or* **ku** (koo)

>> *10:* 十 **jū** (jooo)

GETTING A BLACK BELT IN COUNTING

Japanese usually use the pronunciations し **shi** (shee), しち **shichi** (shee-chee), and く **ku** (koo) — for *four, seven,* and *nine,* respectively — only for reciting numbers or doing arithmetic and not for actually counting things. Students of martial arts may be familiar with these numbers from counting while practicing kicks, punches, and so on. In martial-type language, syllables are often cut short, making counting practice sound like **ich, ni, san, shi, go, rok, shich, hach, ku, jū.** It also makes war movies hard to understand!

Numbers from 11 to 99

To make any number from 11 to 99, you just combine the numbers from 1 to 10. For example, *11* is **jū-ichi** (jooo-ee-chee) — 10 **(jū)** plus 1 **(ichi)**. How about *12*? Same thing: *12* is **jū-ni** (jooo-nee). *Twenty* is two sets of ten, so you say "two-tens," **ni-jū** (nee-jooo). It may help you to think of 20 as 2 times 10. *Twenty-one* is **ni-jū-ichi** (nee-jooo-ee-chee). Do you see the logic? You can use this pattern to count up to **kyū-jū-kyū** (kyooo-jooo-kyooo) (*99*), or nine tens plus nine.

Numbers from 100 to 9,999

To count over 100, keep using the pattern for numbers up to 99 (which I describe in the preceding section). *One hundred* is **hyaku** (hyah-koo). So *200* is **ni-hyaku** (nee-hyah-koo). *One thousand* is **sen** (sehn); therefore, *2,000* is **ni-sen** (nee-sehn). I'm sure you can't wait to say *9,999*. Yes. It's **kyū-sen kyū-hyaku kyū-jū kyū** (kyooo-sehn kyooo-hyah-koo kyooo-jooo kyooo).

REMEMBER

This counting business sounds easy, but be aware of some irregular sound changes. When the words for *100* **(hyaku)** and *1,000* **(sen)** are preceded by the number *3* **(san)**, they become **byaku** (byah-koo) and **zen** (zehn), respectively. So *300* is **san-byaku** and *3,000* is **san-zen**. Other irregular sound changes are found in *600* **(rop-pyaku)** (rohp-pyah-koo), *800* **(hap-pyaku)** (hahp-pyah-koo), and *8,000* **(has-sen)** (hahs-sehn). See the following list:

- » *100:* 百 **hyaku** (hyah-koo)
- » *200:* 二百 **ni-hyaku** (nee-hyah-koo)
- » *300:* 三百 **san-byaku** (sahn-byah-koo)
- » *400:* 四百 **yon-hyaku** (yohn-hyah-koo)
- » *500:* 五百 **go-hyaku** (goh-hyah-koo)
- » *600:* 六百 **rop-pyaku** (rohp-pyah-koo)
- » *700:* 七百 **nana-hyaku** (nah-nah-hyah-koo)
- » *800:* 八百 **hap-pyaku** (hahp-pyah-koo)
- » *900:* 九百 **kyū-hyaku** (kyooo-hyah-koo)
- » *1,000:* 千 **sen** (sehn)
- » *2,000:* 二千 **ni-sen** (nee-sehn)
- » *3,000:* 三千 **san-zen** (sahn-zehn)
- » *4,000:* 四千 **yon-sen** (yohn-sehn)

>> *5,000:* 五千 **go-sen** (goh-sehn)

>> *6,000:* 六千 **roku-sen** (roh-koo-sehn)

>> *7,000:* 七千 **nana-sen** (nah-nah-sehn)

>> *8,000:* 八千 **has-sen** (hahs-sehn)

>> *9,000:* 九千 **kyū-sen** (kyooo-sehn)

Numbers from 10,000 to 99,999

Unlike English, Japanese has a special digit name for *10,000:* **man** (mahn). So *50,000* isn't **go-jū-sen**, which is **go-jū** (*50*) of **sen** (*1,000*), but **go-man** (goh-mahn) (*50,000*). As you can see from the following list, there's no annoying sound change when you combine numbers and **man**:

>> *10,000:* 一万 **ichi-man** (ee-chee-mahn)

>> *20,000:* 二万 **ni-man** (nee-mahn)

>> *30,000:* 三万 **san-man** (sahn-mahn)

>> *40,000:* 四万 **yon-man** (yohn-mahn)

>> *50,000:* 五万 **go-man** (goh-mahn)

>> *60,000:* 六万 **roku-man** (roh-koo-mahn)

>> *70,000:* 七万 **nana-man** (nah-nah-mahn)

>> *80,000:* 八万 **hachi-man** (hah-chee-mahn)

>> *90,000:* 九万 **kyū-man** (kyooo-mahn)

Now, can you say *99,999?* It's **kyū-man kyū-sen kyū-hyaku kyū-jū kyū.**

Numbers over 100,000

Japanese doesn't have a digit name for million. *One million* in Japanese is **100 man**, or more correctly, **hyaku man** (hyah-koo mahn). However, Japanese does have a richly special digit name for *100 million*, which is **1 oku** (oh-koo), or more correctly, **ichi oku** (ee-chee oh-koo). Now, can you say *999,999,999?* It's **kyū-oku kyū-sen kyū-hyaku kyū-jū kyū-man kyū-sen kyū-hyaku kyū-jū kyū.**

COMPARING ENGLISH AND JAPANESE DIGIT NAMES

You may find it helpful to see a side-by-side comparison of the English and Japanese names for different digits. If that's the case, you're in the right place.

Number	English	Japanese
10	*ten*	十 **jū** (jooo)
100	*hundred*	百 **hyaku** (hyah-koo)
1,000	*thousand*	千 **sen** (sehn)
10,000	*N/A*	万 **man** (mahn)
100,000	*N/A*	**N/A**
1,000,000	*million*	**N/A**
10,000,000	*N/A*	**N/A**
100,000,000	*N/A*	億 **oku** (oh-koo)

Expressing amount or quantity with counters

Words like *piece*, *sheet*, and *pair* (as in a *piece* of cake, a *sheet* of paper, and a *pair* of shoes) express the amount or quantity unit. Depending on the shape, size, and type of the item, you use different *counters* (short suffixes following numerals). Table 4-1 lists some frequently used counters along with their uses.

TABLE 4-1   ## Counters and Their Uses

Counter	Use	Examples
台 **-dai** (dah-ee)	Mechanical items	Cars, computers, refrigerators
匹 **-hiki** (hee-kee)	Animals (small or medium size)	Mosquitoes, dogs, cats, frogs, fish

(continued)

TABLE 4-1 *(continued)*

Counter	Use	Examples
本 **-hon** (hohn)	Cylindrical items	Pens, pencils, bananas, sticks, umbrellas
枚 **-mai** (mah-ee)	Flat items	Bedsheets, paper, stamps
人 **-nin** (neen)	People	Students, children, women
つ **-tsu** (tsoo)	Various inanimate items	Furniture, apples, bags, traffic lights

Of course, to use counters, you have to pair them with numbers. Table 4-2 shows you how to combine the numbers one to ten with the frequently used counters shown in Table 4-1.

TABLE 4-2 ## Counting with Counters

Number	Counters					
	台 -dai	匹 -hiki	本 -hon	枚 -mai	人 -nin	つ -tsu
1	**ichi-dai** (ee-chee-dah-ee)	**ip-piki** (eep-pee-kee)	**ip-pon** (eep-pohn)	**ichi-mai** (ee-chee-mah-ee)	**hitori** (hee-toh-ree)	**hito-tsu** (hee-toh-tsoo)
2	**ni-dai** (nee-dah-ee)	**ni-hiki** (nee-hee-kee)	**ni-hon** (nee-hohn)	**ni-mai** (nee-mah-ee)	**futari** (foo-tah-ree)	**futa-tsu** (foo-tah-tsoo)
3	**san-dai** (sahn-dah-ee)	**san-biki** (sahn-bee-kee)	**san-bon** (sahn-bohn)	**san-mai** (sahn-mah-ee)	**san-nin** (sahn-neen)	**mit-tsu** (meet-tsoo)
4	**yon-dai** (yohn-dah-ee)	**yon-hiki** (yohn-hee-kee)	**yon-hon** (yohn-hohn)	**yon-mai** (yohn-mah-ee)	**yo-nin** (yoh-neen)	**yot-tsu** (yoht-tsoo)
5	**go-dai** (goh-dah-ee)	**go-hiki** (goh-hee-kee)	**go-hon** (goh-hohn)	**go-mai** (goh-mah-ee)	**go-nin** (goh-neen)	**itsu-tsu** (ee-tsoo-tsoo)
6	**roku-dai** (roh-koo-dah-ee)	**rop-piki** (rohp-pee-kee)	**rop-pon** (rohp-pohn)	**roku-mai** (roh-koo-mah-ee)	**roku-nin** (roh-koo-neen)	**mut-tsu** (moot-tsoo)

Number	Counters					
	台 -dai	匹 -hiki	本 -hon	枚 -mai	人 -nin	つ -tsu
7	nana-dai (nah-nah-dah-ee)	nana-hiki (nah-nah-hee-kee)	nana-hon (nah-nah-hohn)	nana-mai (nah-nah-mah-ee)	nana-nin (nah-nah-neen)	nana-tsu (nah-nah-tsoo)
8	hachi-dai (hah-chee-dah-ee)	hap-piki (hahp-pee-kee)	hap-pon (hahp-pohn)	hachi-mai (hah-chee-mah-ee)	hachi-nin (hah-chee-neen)	yat-tsu (yaht-tsoo)
9	kyū-dai (kyooo-dah-ee)	kyū-hiki (kyooo-hee-kee)	kyū-hon (kyooo-hohn)	kyū-mai (kyooo-mah-ee)	kyū-nin (kyooo-neen)	kokono-tsu (koh-koh-noh-tsoo)
10	jū-dai (jooo-dah-ee)	jup-piki (joop-pee-kee)	jup-pon (joop-pohn)	jū-mai (jooo-mah-ee)	jū-nin (jooo-neen)	tō (tohh)

Notice how the counter **-tsu** is a little bit different from the other counters in the table? First off, it's written in **kana** (つ) rather than **kanji**. What does that tell you? That **-tsu** is a native Japanese counter, whereas the other counters in the table are originally from Chinese. As a result, the numbers used with **-tsu** aren't **ichi, ni, san,** and so on, which are originally from Chinese, but **hito, futa, mi,** and so on, which are native Japanese vocabulary.

GRAMMAR
CHAT

The counter for people (人) is written using the native Japanese counter only for the first two numbers, but a Chinese counter should be used for three and greater, as you can see in Table 4-2. The counter 人 is pronounced as **ri** and used with native Japanese numbers for the first two, but it's pronounced as **nin** and used with numbers of Chinese origin for three and greater. At any rate, when you write, you can write the numbers in Arabic numerals or in **kanji**. In either case, the number will be followed by the counter written in **kanji**. When you use つ **tsu**, つshould be written in **hiragana**. For example, **ichi-dai** will be written 1台 or 一台. One person, **hitori,** will be written in 1人 or 一人, but **hitotsu** will be written in 1つ or 一つ.

Using some counters causes sound changes in the numbers and in the counter itself. And the Japanese native word for the number ten, **tō** (tohh) (*ten*), can't be followed by the counter **-tsu.** Don't be too concerned about these irregular changes. Even if you make a mistake here, you'll be understood perfectly by Japanese.

REMEMBER

Native Japanese numbers are available only from one to ten. If you have 11 or more apples, use the counter **-ko.** For example, to say 9 when counting apples, you can say either **kokono-tsu** or **kyū-ko.** However, to say 12 for apples, you need to say **jūni-ko.**

TIP

If you forget which counter to use and you're counting no more than ten of something, the number phrases in the last column of Table 4-2 (the **-tsu** column) work for counting pretty much anything except for people and animals.

Indicating ordinal numbers with -me

Ordinal-number phrases such as *the first* and *the second* are essential for pinpointing things and people in a sequence. To form an ordinal-number phrase in Japanese, you take one of the Japanese counters (see the preceding section) and add **-me** after it. For example, **san-nin-me** means *third person* and **mit-tsu-me** means *third thing*. Following are some additional examples of ordinal-number phrases:

3人目の息子 **san-nin-me no musuko** (sahn-neen-meh noh moo-soo-koh) (*my third son*)

右側の5つ目の家 **migi gawa no itsu-tsu-me no ie** (mee-gee gah-wah noh ee-tsoo-tsoo-meh noh ee-eh) (*the fifth house on the right-hand side*)

2杯目のコーヒー **ni-hai-me no kōhī** (nee-hah-ee-meh noh kohh-heee) (*second cup of coffee*)

4つ目の信号 **yot-tsu-me no shingō** (yot-tsoo-meh noh sheen-gohh) (*the fourth traffic light*)

2番目の息子 **ni-ban-me no musuko** (nee-bahn-meh noh moo-soo-koh) (*my second son*)

TIP

If you want to say *number X*, just add **ban** (bahn) after the number — for example, **ichi-ban.** So to tell someone that *Mike is number 1 in the class,* you'd say **Maiku wa kurasu de ichi-ban desu.** (mah-ee-koo wah koo-rah-soo deh ee-chee-bahn deh-soo.).

Telling Time

If someone asks you **Nan-ji.** (nahn-jee.) (*What time?*), can you respond quickly by looking at your **tokei** (toh-kehh) (*watch, clock*)? You can after reviewing the next sections, which tell you how to refer to time both generally and in terms of hours and minutes.

Noting hours and minutes

You can express time in Japanese by using the counters **–ji** (jee) (*o'clock*) and **–fun** (foon) (*minutes*), as shown in Tables 4-3 and 4-4. *Note:* When talking about minutes, **–fun** sometimes changes to **–pun** (poon), so watch out.

TABLE 4-3

Stating the Hour

Time Expression	Pronunciation	English
1時 **1-ji**	ee-chee-jee	*1:00*
2時 **2-ji**	nee-jee	*2:00*
3時 **3-ji**	sahn-jee	*3:00*
4時 **4-ji**	yoh-jee	*4:00*
5時 **5-ji**	goh-jee	*5:00*
6時 **6-ji**	roh-koo-jee	*6:00*
7時 **7-ji**	shee-chee-jee	*7:00*
8時 **8-ji**	hah-chee-jee	*8:00*
9時 **9-ji**	koo-jee	*9:00*
10時 **10-ji**	jooo-jee	*10:00*
11時 **11-ji**	jooo-ee-chee-jee	*11:00*
12時 **12-ji**	jooo-nee-jee	*12:00*

TABLE 4-4

Stating Minutes

Time Expression	Pronunciation	English
1分 **1-pun**	eep-poon	*1 minute*
2分 **2-fun**	nee-foon	*2 minutes*
3分 **3-pun**	sahn-poon	*3 minutes*
4分 **4-pun**	yohn-poon	*4 minutes*
5分 **5-fun**	goh-foon	*5 minutes*
6分 **6-pun**	rohp-poon	*6 minutes*
7分 **7-fun**	nah-nah-foon	*7 minutes*
8分 **8-pun**	hahp-poon	*8 minutes*
9分 **9-fun**	kyooo-foon	*9 minutes*
10分 **10-pun**	joop-poon	*10 minutes*
11分 **11-pun**	jooo-eep-poon	*11 minutes*
12分 **12-fun**	jooo-nee-foon	*12 minutes*

You can use the convenient phrase **han** (hahn) (*half*) for *half an hour* or *30 minutes*. **Mae** (mah-eh) (*before*) and **sugi** (soo-gee) (*after*) are also convenient for telling time. Sorry, but there's no simple phrase for *a quarter of an hour* or *15 minutes* in Japanese. So, if you want to say *a quarter past 2:00*, you need to say **2-ji 15-fun sugi**. To specify **gozen** (goh-zehn) (*a.m.*) or **gogo** (goh-goh) (*p.m.*), put the appropriate word in front of the number, as in **gogo 8-ji** (*8 p.m.*). Check how people say what time it is now:

今, 何時ですか。**Ima, nan-ji desu ka.** (ee-mah, nahn-jee deh-soo kah.) (*What time is it now?*)

今, 3時5分です。**Ima, 3-ji 5-fun desu.** (ee-mah, sahn-jee goh-foon deh-soo.) (*It's 3:05 now.*)

今、3時5分すぎです。**Ima, 3-ji 5-fun sugi desu.** (ee-mah, sahn-jee goh-foon soo-gee deh-soo.) (*It's 5 minutes past 3:00 now.*)

今、12時3分前です。**Ima, 12-ji 3-pun mae desu.** (ee-mah, jooo-nee-jee sahn-poon mah-eh deh-soo.) (*It's 3 minutes before 12:00.*)

今、日本は午前2時です。**Ima, Nihon wa gozen 2-ji desu.** (ee-mah, nee-hohn wa goh-zehn nee-jee deh-soo.) (*It's 2:00 a.m.in Japan.*)

Japanese train schedules usually follow the 24-hour system. For example, **1-ji** (ee-chee-jee) means only *1:00 a.m.*, and **13-ji** (jooo-sahn-jee) means only *1:00 p.m.* This system eliminates a.m./p.m. ambiguity, and you don't need to say **gozen** or **gogo.**

Talking about time

To express *at what time, from what time, until what time,* and *by what time,* you need the particles **ni** (nee) (*at*), **kara** (kah-rah) (*from*), **made** (mah-deh) (*until*), and **made ni** (mah-deh nee) (*by*). Make sure to place the particle after, not before, the time phrase. Chapter 3 gives you the lowdown on using particles. Here are some examples:

コンサートは何時に始まりますか。3時に始まります。**Konsāto wa nan-ji ni hajimari-masu ka. 3-ji ni hajimarimasu.** (kohn-sahh-toh wah nahn-jee nee hah-jee-mah-ree-mah-soo kah. sahn-jee nee hah-jee-mah-ree-mah-soo.) (*What time does the concert start? It starts at 3:00.*)

ランチサービスは午前11時半から午後2時までです。**Ranchi sābisu wa gozen 11-ji han kara gogo 2-ji made desu.** (rahn-chee sahh-bee-soo wah goh-zehn jooo-ee-chee-jee hahn kah-rah goh-goh nee-jee mah-deh deh-soo.) (*Lunch special is from 11:30 a.m. to 2 p.m.*)

3時5分前までに来てください。**3-ji 5-fun mae made ni kite kudasai.** (sahn-jee goh-foon mah-eh mah-deh nee kee-teh koo-dah-sah-ee.) (*Please come by five minutes before 3:00.*)

KNOWING WHEN TO USE –FUN AND –PUN

-Fun changes to **-pun** depending on the preceding sound. When the numbers are いち **ichi,** ろく **roku,** はち hachi, and じゅう **jū,** replace the last **hiragana** with っ, which is basi-cally a moment of silence, and add ぷん **pun.** That is, you get いっぷん **ippun,** ろっぷん **roppun,** はっぷん **happun,** and じゅっぷん **juppun.** In addition, after ん **n,** just add ぷん **pun.** So, you'll get さんぷん **sanpun** and よんぷん **yonpun.** For other numbers, just add ふん **fun.**

Instead of giving the exact time, you can vaguely specify the part of the day or use relative time expressions:

>> 朝 **asa** (ah-sah) (*morning*)

>> 昼 **hiru** (hee-roo) (*noon, middle of the day*)

>> 晩 **ban** (bahn) (*evening*)

>> 夜中 **yonaka** (yoh-nah-kah) (*the middle of the night*)

>> 今 **ima** (ee-mah) (*now*)

>> さっき **sakki** (sahk-kee) (*a little while ago*)

To tell the length of time, just add –**kan** (kahn) after –**ji** or –**fun**. However, –**kan** is usually omitted after –**fun** in conversations. Check out these examples:

2時間勉強しました。**2-jikan benkyō shimashita.** (nee-jee-kahn behn-kyohh shee-mah-shee-tah.) (*I studied for two hours.*)

8時間かかりました。**8-jikan kakarimashita.** (hah-chee-jee-kahn kah-kah-ree-mah-shee-tah.) (*It took eight hours.*)

15分かかります。**15-fun kakarimasu.** (jooo-goh-foon kah-kah-ree-mah-soo.) (*It takes 15 minutes.*)

It's a Date! Delving into the Calendar

Making plans with others in Japanese requires having a basic grasp of the terms used for days of the week, months, years, and so on. With the information in the following sections, you'll be prepared to mark your **karendā** (kah-rehn-dahh) (*calendar*) for all kinds of fun activities.

Talking about the days of the week

Both American and Japanese weeks only have seven days. An American week — at least on the calendar — starts on **nichiyōbi** (nee-chee-yohh-bee) (*Sunday*) and ends on **doyōbi** (doh-yohh-bee) (*Saturday*), but a Japanese week starts on **getsuyōbi** (geh-tsoo-yohh-bee) (*Monday*) and ends on **nichiyōbi** (nee-chee-yohh-bee) (*Sunday*). Japanese work first and rest later. Here are all the terms you need to know to talk about days of the week:

- » 月曜日 **getsuyōbi** (geh-tsoo-yohh-bee) (*Monday*)

- » 火曜日 **kayōbi** (kah-yohh-bee) (*Tuesday*)

- » 水曜日 **suiyōbi** (soo-ee-yohh-bee) (*Wednesday*)

- » 木曜日 **mokuyōbi** (moh-koo-yohh-bee) (*Thursday*)

- » 金曜日 **kin'yōbi** (keen-yohh-bee) (*Friday*)

- » 土曜日 **doyōbi** (doh-yohh-bee) (*Saturday*)

- » 日曜日 **nichiyōbi** (nee-chee-yohh-bee) (*Sunday*)

So if someone were to ask you **Kyō wa nan'yōbi desu ka.** (kyohh wah nahn-yohh-bee deh-soo kah.) (*What day is it today?*), you may respond with **Kyō wa doyōbi desu.** (kyohh wah doh-yohh-bee deh-soo.) (*Today is Saturday.*) Following are some additional statements featuring days of the week so you can see them in action:

> 月曜日から金曜日まで働きます。 **Getsuyōbi kara kin'yōbi made hatarakimasu.**
> (geh-tsoo-yohh-bee kah-rah keen-yohh-bee mah-deh hah-tah-rah-kee-mah-soo.)
> (*I work from Monday to Friday.*)

> コンサートは土曜日です。 **Konsāto wa doyōbi desu.** (kohn-sahh-toh wa doh-yohh-bee deh-soo.) (*The concert is on Saturday.*)

> 日曜日はゆっくりします。 **Nichiyōbi wa yukkuri shimasu.** (nee-chee-yohh-bee wah yook-koo-ree shee-mah-soo.) (*I relax on Sundays.*)

Naming the months and counting them up

The Japanese word for *moon* is **tsuki** (tsoo-kee), which also means *month*. Japanese doesn't have a separate name for each month — it uses a number paired with the counter **-gatsu** (gah-tsoo). So, *January* is **ichi-gatsu** (eeh-chee-gah-tsoo) and *December* is **jū-ni-gatsu** (jooo-nee-gah-tsoo). Here's how to write and say all 12 months in Japanese:

- » 1月 **ichi-gatsu** (ee-chee-gah-tsoo) (*January*)

- » 2月 **ni-gatsu** (nee-gah-tsoo) (*February*)

- » 3月 **san-gatsu** (sahn-gah-tsoo) (*March*)

- » 4月 **shi-gatsu** (shee-gah-tsoo) (*April*)

- » 5月 **go-gatsu** (goh-gah-tsoo) (*May*)

- » 6月 **roku-gatsu** (roh-koo-gah-tsoo) (*June*)

» 7月 **shichi-gatsu** (shee-chee-gah-tsoo) (*July*)

» 8月 **hachi-gatsu** (hah-chee-gah-tsoo) (*August*)

» 9月 **ku-gatsu** (koo-gah-tsoo) (*September*)

» 10月 **jū-gatsu** (jooo-gah-tsoo) (*October*)

» 11月 **jū-ichi-gatsu** (jooo-ee-chee-gah-tsoo) (*November*)

» 12月 **jū-ni-gatsu** (jooo-nee-gah-tsoo) (*December*)

To express a number of months, like *one month* and *two months,* use the counter **-kagetsu** (kah-geh-tsoo) or **-kagetsukan** (kah-geh-tsoo-kahn).

» 1ヶ月 **ik-kagetsu** (eek-kah-geh-tsoo) (*1 month*)

» 2ヶ月 **ni-kagetsu** (nee-kah-geh-tsoo) (*2 months*)

» 3ヶ月 **san-kagetsu** (sahn-kah-geh-tsoo) (*3 months*)

» 4ヶ月 **yon-kagetsu** (yohn-kah-geh-tsoo) (*4 months*)

» 5ヶ月 **go-kagetsu** (goh-kah-geh-tsoo) (*5 months*)

» 6ヶ月 **rok-kagetsu** (rohk-kah-geh-tsoo) (*6 months*)

» 7ヶ月 **nana-kagetsu** (nah-nah-kah-geh-tsoo) (*7 months*)

» 8ヶ月 **hachi-kagetsu** (hah-chee-kah-geh-tsoo) (*8 months*)

» 9ヶ月 **kyū-kagetsu** (kyooo-kah-geh-tsoo) (*9 months*)

» 10ヶ月 **juk-kagetsu** (jook-kah-geh-tsoo) (*10 months*)

» 11ヶ月 **jū-ik-kagetsu** (jooo-eek-kah-geh-tsoo) (*11 months*)

» 12ヶ月 **jū-ni-kagetsu** (jooo-nee-kah-geh-tsoo) (*12 months*)

TIP

In conversation, **-kagetsu** is more common than **-kagetsukan,** so you can just use **-kagetsu,** but it's good to know both of them because you may hear either one.

Counting the days

In this section, I will show you how you say *the first, the second,* and so on, for dates. (To find out how you say these types of words in relation to other items, such as buildings, coffee, and people, see the earlier "Indicating ordinal numbers with -me" section.)

The way that dates are pronounced in Japanese isn't very systematic; it's full of irregularities. I know that's not very encouraging — sorry — so your best bet is to memorize Table 4-5.

TABLE 4-5

What's Today's Date?

Date	Japanese	Pronunciation
1st	1日 **tsuitachi**	tsoo-ee-tah-chee
2nd	2日 **futsuka**	foo-tsoo-kah
3rd	3日 **mikka**	meek-kah
4th	4日 **yokka**	yohk-kah
5th	5日 **itsuka**	ee-tsoo-kah
6th	6日 **muika**	moo-ee-kah
7th	7日 **nanoka**	nah-noh-kah
8th	8日 **yōka**	yohh-kah
9th	9日 **kokonoka**	koh-koh-noh-kah
10th	10日 **tōka**	tohh-kah
11th	11日 **jū-ichi-nichi**	jooo-ee-chee-nee-chee
12th	12日 **jū-ni-nichi**	jooo-nee-nee-chee
13th	13日 **jū-san-nichi**	jooo-sahn-nee-chee
14th	14日 **jū-yokka**	jooo-yohk-kah
15th	15日 **jū-go-nichi**	jooo-goh-nee-chee
16th	16日 **jū-roku-nichi**	jooo-roh-koo-nee-chee
17th	17日 **jū-shichi-nichi**	jooo-shee-chee-nee-chee

(continued)

TABLE 4-5 *(continued)*

Date	Japanese	Pronunciation
18th	18日 **jū-hachi-nichi**	jooo-hah-chee-nee-chee
19th	19日 **jū-ku-nichi**	jooo-koo-nee-chee
20th	20日 **hatsuka**	hah-tsoo-kah
21st	21日 **ni-jū-ichi-nichi**	nee-jooo-ee-chee-nee-chee
22nd	22日 **ni-jū-ni-nichi**	nee-jooo-nee-nee-chee
23rd	23日 **ni-jū-san-nichi**	nee-jooo-sahn-nee-chee
24th	24日 **ni-jū-yokka**	nee-jooo-yohk-kah
25th	25日 **ni-jū-go-nichi**	nee-jooo-goh-nee-chee
26th	26日 **ni-jū-roku-nichi**	nee-jooo-roh-koo-nee-chee
27th	27日 **ni-jū-shichi-nichi**	nee-jooo-shee-chee-nee-chee
28th	28日 **ni-jū-hachi-nichi**	nee-jooo-hah-chee-nee-chee
29th	29日 **ni-jū-ku-nichi**	nee-jooo-koo-nee-chee
30th	30日 **san-jū-nichi**	sahn-jooo-nee-chee
31st	31日 **san-jū-ichi-nichi**	sahn-jooo-ee-chee-nee-chee

REMEMBER

You can also use the dates shown in Table 4-5 for expressing the number of days in a given span. For example, **futsuka** can mean either *the second* or *two days.* To make it crystal clear that you're talking about the *number of days*, just add **-kan** (kahn) to this form — **futsukakan** (foo-tsoo-kah-kahn) *(two days)* — to eliminate any ambiguity. The only exception to these rules is **tsuitachi. Tsuitachi** means only *the first* and not *one day.* To say *one day*, use **ichi-nichi** (ee-chee-nee-chee).

Counting the weeks

You can specify the weeks in a month, or the weeks in any cycle, by saying **dai** (dah-ee), the number, and then **-shū** (shooo). For example:

» 第1週 **dai is-shū** (dah-ee ees-shooo) (*the first week*)

» 第2週 **dai ni-shū** (dah-ee nee-shooo) (*the second week*)

» 第3週 **dai san-shū** (dah-ee sahn-shooo) (*the third week*)

» 第4週 **dai yon-shū** (dah-ee yohn-shoo) (*the fourth week*)

To count weeks, use the counter **-shūkan**, as in **is-shūkan** (ees-shooo-kahn) (*one week*), **ni-shūkan** (nee-shooo-kahn) (*two weeks*), and so on.

Reeling off the years

To specify the **toshi** (toh-shee) (*year*), just add the counter **-nen** after the number that expresses the year — **1998-nen** (sehn-kyooo-hyah-koo-kyooo-jooo-hah-chee-nehn) (*1998*) and **2012-nen** (nee-sehn-jooo-nee-nehn) (*2012*), for example.

Follow this advice, and you'll be understood perfectly in Japan. But be ready to hear a year referred to with a unique **nengō** (nehn-gohh) (*era name*), as in **Heisei 30-nen** (hehh-sehh nee-jooo-yoh-nehn), which is equivalent to 2018. Check out the nearby "Era names in Japan" sidebar for information on this system.

If you want to count years, use either **-nenkan** or **-nen** as counters. So, *one year* is **ichi-nen** (ee-chee-nehn) or **ichi-nenkan** (ee-chee-nehn-kahn), and *two years* is **ni-nen** (nee-nehn) or **ni-nenkan** (nee-nehn-kahn). *Note:* In conversation, the shorter version, **-nen**, is used more frequently than **-nenkan**, but again, being aware of both forms is a good idea.

Specifying dates and times

When specifying a full date the Japanese way, start from the largest unit of time, the **toshi,** and then move to successively smaller units: the **tsuki,** the **hi,** and the **yōbi,** in that order. For example, *Thursday, October 25, 2012* is

» 2018年10月25日木曜日 **nisenjūni-nen jū-gatsu nijūgo-nichi Mokuyōbi** (nee-sehn joo-nee-nehn jooo-gah-tsoo nee-jooo-goh-nee-chee moh-koo-yohh-bee)

» 平成30年10月25日木曜日 **Heisei nijūyo-nen jū-gatsu nijūgo-nichi Mokuyōbi** (hehh-sehh nee-jooo-yoh-nehn jooo-gah-tsoo nee-jooo-goh-nee-chee moh-koo-yohh-bee)

ERA NAMES IN JAPAN

You can express years in two ways in Japan. You can use the Western system with the counter 年 **-nen** (nehn), as in 2018年 **2018-nen** (nee-sehn-jooo-nee-nehn) (*2018*). Or you can use the Japanese system with the 年号 **nengō** (nehn-gohh) (*era name*) and the counter **-nen**, as in 平成30年 **Heisei 30-nen** (hehh-sehh nee-jooo-yoh-nehn) (*2018*).

A new **nengō** is created every time a new emperor ascends the throne in Japan and continues to be used until a different emperor takes his place. The first year of any era is called 元年 **gan-nen** (gahn-nehn). For example, Emperor Showa passed away on January 7 in 1989 and Emperor Heisei ascended the throne next day on January 8. Starting on January 8, the year was called 平成元年 **Heisei gan-nen** (hehh-sehh gahn-nehn) in the Japanese system. And the following year (1990) was called 平成2年 **Heisei 2-nen** (hehh-sehh nee-nehn).

Government officials tend to use only the Japanese system, but many companies and institutions use the Western systems. My daughter was born in **Heisei** era, my mother and I were born in 昭和 **Shōwa** (shohh-wah) era, and my grandmother was born in **Meiji** (mehh-jee) era. There was a short era, 大正 **Taishō** (tah-ee-shohh) era, between the **Meiji** era and **Shōwa** eras. Let me list these eras of modern Japan chronologically:

- 明治 **Meiji** (mehh-jee) 1868–1912
- 大正 **Taishō** (tah-ee-shohh) 1912–1926
- 昭和 **Shōwa** (shohh-wah) 1926–1989
- 平成 *Heisei* (heh-ee-sehh) 1989–Present

Instead of using a specific date on the calendar, you can also use relative time expressions based on the concepts of *before* and *after* or *previous* and *following*. See what I mean in Table 4-6.

You can expect to hear alternative terms such as these when you're in a slightly formal context:

» 本日 **honjitsu** (hohn-jee-tsoo) (*today*)

» 明日 **asu** (ah-soo) (*tomorrow*)

» 昨日 **sakujitsu** (sah-koo-jee-tsoo) (*yesterday*)

» 昨年 **sakunen** (sah-koo-nehn) (*last year*)

TABLE 4-6

Relative Time Expressions with Translations

Previous	Current	Future
昨日 **kinō** (kee-nohh) (*yesterday*)	今日 **kyō** (kyohh) (*today*)	あした **ashita** (ah-shee-tah) (*tomorrow*)
先週 **senshū** (sehn-shooo) (*last week*)	今週 **konshū** (kohn-shooo) (*this week*)	来週 **raishū** (rah-ee-shooo) (*next week*)
先月 **sengetsu** (sehn-geh-tsoo) (*last month*)	今月 **kongetsu** (kohn-geh-tsoo) (*this month*)	来月 **raigetsu** (rah-ee-geh-tsoo) (*next month*)
去年 **kyonen** (kyoh-nehn) (*last year*)	今年 **kotoshi** (koh-toh-shee) (*this year*)	来年 **rainen** (rah-ee-nehn) (*next year*)

TIP

The following additional terms for referring to the future are always useful:

» あさって **asatte** (ah-saht-teh) (*the day after tomorrow*)

» 再来週 **saraishū** (sah-rah-ee-shooo) (*the week after next*)

» 再来月 **saraigetsu** (sah-rah-ee-geh-tsoo) (*the month after next*)

» 再来年 **sarainen** (sah-rah-ee-nehn) (*the year after next*)

GRAMMAR CHAT

To specify *when* something happens or happened, insert a time phrase into the sentence. You can place the time phrase anywhere in a sentence, as long as it's before the verb. If you're dealing with a *specific time*, place the particle **ni** (nee) after the time phrase. If you're dealing with a *relative time*, you don't need to use the particle **ni**. I illustrate the differences in the following list of examples:

12月28日に東京に行きます。**12-gatsu 28-nichi ni Tōkyō ni ikimasu.** (jooo-nee-gah-tsoo nee-jooo-hah-chee-nee-chee nee tohh-kyohh nee ee-kee-mah-soo.) (*I'll go to Tokyo on December 28th.*)

あした買い物をします。**Ashita kaimono o shimasu.** (ah-shee-tah kah-ee-moh-noh oh shee-mah-soo.) (*I'll go shopping tomorrow.*)

1998年に生まれました。**1998-nen ni umaremashita.** (sehn-kyooo-hyah-koo-kyooo-jooo-hah-chee-nehn nee oo-mah-reh-mah-shee-tah.) (*I was born in 1998.*)

先週家賃を払いました。**Senshū yachin o haraimashita.** (sehn-shooo yah-cheen oh hah-rah-ee-mah-shee-tah.) (*I paid the rent last week.*)

To list a number of activities in the same sentence, put all the verbs, except the last one, into the **te**-form (I cover **te**-forms in Chapter 3). You don't need to use any particle that would correspond to *and* in English — converting all the verbs, except the last one, into the **te**-form handles the *and* concept. The last verb expresses the tense of all the activities.

> 昨日は9時に銀行に行って10時にデパートに行って5時に帰りました。**Kinō wa ku-ji ni ginkō ni itte jū-ji ni depāto ni itte go-ji ni kaerimashita.** (kee-nohh wah koo-jee nee geen-kohh nee eet-teh jooo-jee nee deh-pahh-toh nee eet-teh goh-jee nee kah-eh-ree-mah-shee-tah.) (*Yesterday, I went to the bank at 9:00, went to the department store at 10:00, and went home at 5:00.*)

> あしたは買い物をして映画を見ます。**Ashita wa kaimono o shite eiga o mimasu.** (ah-shee-tah wah kah-ee-moh-noh oh shee-teh ehh-gah oh mee-mah-soo.) (*I will go shopping and watch a movie tomorrow.*)

In the nearby Talkin' the Talk dialogue, Eleanor talks about her vacation plans for Hawaii. Notice that her first sentence ends with **-n-desu** (n-deh-soo).

In Japanese, you often form a statement by using **-n-desu** (n-deh-soo) in conversation, especially when you provide some information or explanations. The effect of **-n-desu** is to encourage your partner to respond to your statements. You'll sound much more inviting and friendly if you use this ending. It shows your willingness to listen to your partner's comments and opinions. Therefore, use **-n-desu** in conversations, but not in written form or public speech where you don't expect your audience to respond to you after each statement. When a verb is followed by **-n-desu,** it must be in the informal/plain form.

Eleanor in the dialogue talks about when she'll leave and when she'll return from her trip. The Japanese verbs *to go* and *to return* are **iku** (ee-koo) and **kaeru** (kah-eh-roo). Both of them are **u**-verbs. Practice conjugating them.

Japanese Script	Rōmaji	Pronunciation
行く	iku	ee-koo
行かない	ikanai	ee-kah-nah-ee
行き(ます)	iki (masu)	ee-kee (mah-soo)
行って	itte	eet-teh
帰る	kaeru	kah-eh-roo
帰らない	kaeranai	kah-eh-rah-nah-ee
帰り(ます)	kaeri (masu)	kah-eh-ree (mah-soo)
帰って	kaette	kah-eht-the

Talkin' the Talk

Eleanor is planning to go to Hawaii next month. She talks about it with Kevin.

Eleanor:	**Raigetsu Hawai ni iku-n-desu.**
	rah-ee-geh-tsoo hah-wah-ee nee ee-koon-deh-soo.
	I'm going to Hawaii next month.
Kevin:	**Hontō. Nan-nichikan.**
	hohn-tohh. nahn-nee-chee-kahn.
	Really? For how many days?
Eleanor:	**Mikkakan.**
	meek-kah-kahn.
	Three days.
Kevin:	**Mijikai desu ne.**
	mee-jee-kah-ee deh-soo neh.
	That's short, isn't it?
Eleanor:	**Ē, 15-nichi ni itte 18-nichi ni kaeru-n-desu.**
	ehh, jooo-goh-nee-chee nee eet-teh jooo-hah-chee-nee-chee nee kah-eh-roon-deh-soo.
	Uh-huh. I'll go there on the 15th, and I'll be back on the 18th.

WORDS TO KNOW		
hontō	hohn-tohh	true
iku	ee-koo	to go
kaeru	kah-eh-roo	to return
mijikai	mee-jee-kah-ee	short

Familiarizing Yourself with the Metric System

Japanese use the metric system for taking and discussing measurements. So if you go to Japan, expect to hear about liters, grams, meters, and kilometers rather than gallons, pounds, feet, and miles. Here are the terms you need to know to speak about measurements in Japanese:

» ミリ **miri (mētoru)** (mee-ree [mehh-toh-roo]) (*millimeter*)

» センチ **senchi (mētoru)** (sehn-chee [mehh-toh-roo]) (*centimeter*)

» メートル **mētoru** (mehh-toh-roo) (*meter*)

» キロ (メートル) **kiro (mētoru)** (kee-roh [mehh-toh-roo]) (*kilometer*)

» グラム **guramu** (goo-rah-moo) (*gram*)

» キロ (グラム) **kiro (guramu)** (kee-roh [goo-rah-moo]) (*kilogram*)

» トン **ton** (tohn) (*ton*)

» リットル **rittoru** (reet-toh-roo) (*liter*)

» 平方メートル **heihō mētoru** (hehh-hohh mehh-toh-roo) (*square meter*)

» 立法メートル **rippō mētoru** (reep-pohh mehh-toh-roo) (*cubic meter*)

FUN & GAMES

Match the illustrations with the correct Japanese phrases. Turn to Appendix C for the answers.

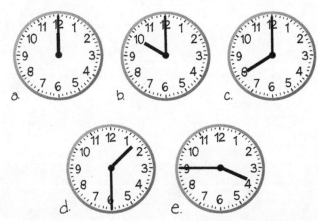

Illustration by Elizabeth Kurtzman

1. いちじはん **ichi-ji han**
2. はちじ **hachi-ji**
3. じゅうじ **jū-ji**
4. じゅうにじ **jū-ni-ji**
5. さんじよんじゅうごふん **san-ji yonjū-go-fun**

Chapter **5**

Speaking Japanese at Home

There is no better place than your **uchi** (oo–chee) (*home*). What do you have in your **uchi?** What do you eat at **uchi?** What do you do at **uchi?** This chapter helps you answer these questions in Japanese.

REMEMBER

You can listen to all the Talkin' the Talk dialogues featured in this chapter. Go to www.dummies.com/go/japanesefd and click on the dialogue you want to hear.

Taking a Tour of Your Home

Whether you live in a *house* (**ie**) (ee–eh) or an *apartment* (**apāto**) (ah–pahh–toh), your **uchi** probably has these rooms and structures:

>> 玄関 **genkan** (gehn-kahn) (*entryway*)

>> キッチン **kitchin** (keet-cheen) *or* 台所 **daidokoro** (dah-ee-doh-koh-roh) (*kitchen*)

>> ダイニング **dainingu** (dah-ee-neen-goo) *or* 食堂 **shokudō** (shoh-koo-dohh) (*dining room*)

>> リビング **ribingu** (ree-been-goo) *or* 居間 **ima** (ee-mah) (*living room*)

- » 寝室 **shinshitsu** (sheen-shee-tsoo) (*bedroom*)

- » 書斎 **shosai** (shoh-sah-ee) (*office*)

- » バスルーム **basurūmu** (bah-soo-rooo-moo) or 風呂場 **furoba** (foo-roh-bah) (*bathroom*)

- » 洗濯場 **sentakuba** (sehn-tah-koo-bah) (*laundry room*)

- » 床 **yuka** (yoo-kah) (*floor*)

- » 天井 **tenjō** (tehn-johh) (*ceiling*)

- » 壁 **kabe** (kah-beh) (*wall*)

- » クローゼット **kurōzetto** (koo-rohh-zeht-toh) (*Western-style closet*)

- » 窓 **mado** (mah-doh) (*window*)

- » 押入れ **oshiire** (oh-shee-ee-reh) (*oshiire—closet for futon and other items*)

CULTURAL WISDOM

When you enter Japanese homes, make sure you take off your **kutsu** (koo-tsoo) (*shoes*) after you're in the **genkan** (not outside it). In Japanese houses, the **genkan** has two levels. The area you step in first is the lower level or ground level, and it's made of concrete, tile, or stone. You're allowed to step into this lower area while wearing your shoes. The second, upper, level is a part of the house, and you're not allowed to step up to it with your shoes on. Take off your shoes on the lower level and then immediately step up to the upper level, where you'll typically be asked to wear **surippa** (soo-reep-pah) (*slippers*). You can wear slippers anywhere inside the house except in rooms with **tatami** (tah-tah-mee) (*straw mat*) floors. When you go to a toilet room, another pair of slippers are waiting for you. Change into those slippers for your time in that room and then back into your other slippers to return to the rest of the house. (In other words, don't come back to the living room with your toilet slippers on.)

The kitchen

The **kitchin** must be the most heavily used room in any house (unless you're really big on takeout). Here are the Japanese terms for some of the major appliances and fixtures in your kitchen:

- » 電子レンジ **denshi-renji** (dehn-shee-rehn-jee) (*microwave oven*)

- » 冷凍庫 **reitōko** (rehh-tohh-koh) or フリーザー **furīzā** (foo-reee-zahh) (*freezer*)

- » 椅子 **isu** (ee-soo) (*chair*)

- » コンロ **konro** (kohn-roh) (*stove*)

- » キャビネット **kyabinetto** (kyah-bee-neht-toh) (*cabinet*)

- » オーブン **ōbun** (ohh-boon) (*oven*)

- » 冷蔵庫 **reizōko** (rehh-zohh-koh) (*refrigerator*)

- » 食器洗い機 **shokki-arai-ki** (shohk-kee ah-rah-ee kee) (*dishwasher*)

- » 流し台 **nagashidai** (nah-gah-shee-dah-ee) *or* シンク **shinku** (sheen-koo) (*sink*)

- » テーブル **tēburu** (tehh-boo-roo) (*table*)

Not many Japanese have a big oven or a dishwasher in their kitchens, so when in Japan, be prepared to bake smaller cakes and do your dishes by hand.

What do you have in your kitchen drawers and cabinets? If you're like most people, you probably have various implements and gadgets:

- » ボール **bōru** (*mixing bowl*)

- » フードプロセッサー **fūdo purosessā** (fooo-doh poo-roh-sehs-sahh) (*food processor*)

- » フライパン **furaipan** (foo-rah-ee-pahn) (*frying pan*)

- » 包丁 **hōchō** (hohh-chohh) (*chef's knife*)

- » 泡立て器 **awatateki** (ah-wah-tah-teh-kee) (*whisk*)

- » 計量カップ **keiryō kappu** (kehh-ryohh kahp-poo) (*measuring cup*)

- » 計量スプーン **keiryō supūn** (kehh-ryohh soo-pooon) (*measuring spoon*)

- » コーヒーメーカー **kōhīmēkā** (kohh-heee-mehh-kahh) (*coffee maker*)

- » まな板 **manaita** (mah-nah-ee-tah) (*cutting board*)

- » ミキサー **mikisā** (mee-kee-sahh) (*blender*)

- » 鍋 **nabe** (nah-beh) (*pot*)

- » トースター **tōsutā** (tohh-soo-tahh) (*toaster*)

- » ざる **zaru** (zah-roo) (*colander*)

The dining room

Most houses have a dining table in the kitchen, but you certainly need these items wherever you eat:

- » フォーク **fōku** (fohh-koo) (*fork*)

- » コップ **koppu** (kohp-poo) (*glass, cup*)

» ナイフ **naifu** (nah-ee-foo) (*table knife*)

» ナプキン **napukin** (nah-poo-keen) (*napkin*)

» 皿 **sara** (sah-rah) (*plate*)

» スパチュラ **supachura** (soo-pah-choo-rah) (*spatula*)

» スプーン **supūn** (soo-pooon) (*spoon*)

» テーブルクロス **tēburukurosu** (tehh-boo-roo koo-roh-soo) (*tablecloth*)

» 器 **utsuwa** (oo-tsoo-wah) (*bowl*)

CULTURAL WISDOM

Dining in Japanese homes can be quite different from what you're probably used to. For one, Japanese often eat meals in a Japanese-style room, sitting on the floor at a low table and using **hashi** (hah-shee) (*chopsticks*), **chawan** (chah-wahn) (*Japanese rice bowl*), and **o-wan** (oh-wahn) (*Japanese lacquered soup bowl*). Additionally, the Japanese table often features **shōyu** (shohh-yoo) (*soy sauce*).

The living room

Whether your living room is a formal entertaining space or just where the family hangs out, it probably has many of the following items:

» アームチェアー **āmucheā** (ahh-moo-cheh-ahh) (*armchair*)

» 電気スタンド **denki-sutando** (dehn-kee-soo-tahn-doh) (*desk lamp, floor lamp*)

» 絵 **e** (eh) (*painting*)

» エアコン **eakon** (eh-ah-kohn) (*air-conditioner*)

» エンドテーブル **endo tēburu** (ehn-doh tehh-boo-roo) (*end table*)

» 電話 **denwa** (dehn-wah) (*phone*)

» ヒーター **hītā** or ストーブ **sutōbu** (heee-tahh or soo-tohh-boo) (*space heater*)

» 本棚 **hondana** (hohn-dah-nah) (*bookshelf, bookcase*)

» コーヒーテーブル **kōhī tēburu** (kohh-heee tehh-boo-roo) (*coffee table*)

» ソファー **sofā** (soh-fahh) (*sofa*)

» テレビ **terebi** (teh-reh-bee) (*TV*)

The bedroom

Worn out from all your Japanese studying? Before you hit the sack for a nap, look at some common bedroom furnishings:

- » ベッド **beddo** (behd-doh) (*bed*)
- » ふとん **futon** (foo-tohn) (*futon*)
- » カーテン **kāten** (kahh-tehn) (*curtains*)
- » 枕 **makura** (mah-koo-rah) (*pillow*)
- » 目覚まし時計 **mezamashi-dokei** (meh-zah-mah-shee-doh-kehh) (*alarm clock*)
- » 毛布 **mōfu** (mohh-foo) (*blanket*)
- » ナイトスタンド **naitosutando** (nah-ee-toh-soo-tahn-doh) (*nightstand*)
- » シーツ **shītsu** (sheee-tsoo) (*sheet*)
- » たんす **tansu** (tahn-soo) (*chest of drawers*)

CULTURAL WISDOM

Japanese sleep on beds or on **futon,** depending on their preferences and how big the room is. (Beds take up more permanent space; check out the nearby sidebar "Futon: Not just for college students" for more on the futon sleeping option.)

The bathroom

Most bathrooms typically contain the following items:

- » バスタオル **basu-taoru** (bah-soo-tah-oh-roo) (*bath towel*)
- » ブラシ **burashi** (boo-rah-shee) (*brush*)
- » ドライヤー **doraiyā** (doh-rah-ee-yahh) (*hair dryer*)
- » 歯ブラシ **ha-burashi** (hah-boo-rah-shee) (*toothbrush*)
- » 歯磨き粉 **hamigakiko** (hah-mee-gah-kee-koh) (*toothpaste*)
- » 鏡 **kagami** (kah-gah-mee) (*mirror*)
- » シャワー **shawā** (shah-wahh) (*shower*)
- » 石鹸 **sekken** (sehk-kehn) (*soap*)
- » トイレットペーパー **toiretto pēpā** (toh-ee-reht-toh pehh-pahh) (*toilet tissue*)

FUTON: NOT JUST FOR COLLEGE STUDENTS

Futons have become a trendy piece of furniture in the West. Like most cultural imports, however, the real thing is quite a bit different. For starters, the Japanese word ふとん **futon** isn't pronounced foo-tahn, as you may be accustomed to, but rather foo-tohn, with an oh sound in the second syllable.

A Western *futon* is just the mattress you sleep on — the comforter or blankets you use to keep warm are separate items. In Japan, however, both the mattress and covering make up a **futon.** At night, you lay out your **futon** on the floor, and in the morning, you fold it up and put it in 押入れ **oshiire** (oh-shee-ee-reh) (*oshiire—closet for futon and other items*). The same room can serve as a bedroom at night and as a living room during the day — quite convenient in a country where space is at a premium.

If sleeping on the floor seems a little awkward, rest assured that a Japanese **futon** is actually quite comfortable and gives you a good night's rest. On top of that, sleeping on a **futon** is good for your back because a **futon** contains no spring, and your back has to be straight!

In most Japanese houses, the **furoba** (foo-roh-bah) (*bathing room*) and **toire** (toh-ee-reh) (*toilet room*) are separate rooms. In cities where the space is limited, some apartments have a **yunitto basu** (yoo-neet-toh bah-soo) (*unit bath*) — a compact combination of a bathtub, a sink, a toilet, and the surrounding wall and floor. It's preassembled at a factory before installation and looks like a sheet of molded plastic. The **yunitto basu** is extremely space-saving and economical, but still has everything you expect to find in a bathroom.

Japanese love to use English in general, so they also use the term **basurūmu** to mean *bathroom*. Most **basurūmu** in Japan still have only bathing areas, but the term is relatively new and a bit vague. By contrast, the term **furoba** refers strictly to a bathing room.

The laundry room

The Japanese often hang their washed clothes in their backyards or on their balconies. It saves energy and kills germs! If airing your (clean) laundry isn't your style, you can throw it in the dryer, iron, and explain the whole thing in Japanese with the following words:

- アイロン **airon** (ah-ee-rohn) (*iron*)

- アイロン台 **airondai** (ah-ee-rohn-dah-ee) (*ironing board*)

- 漂白剤 **hyōhakuzai** (hyohh-hah-koo-zah-ee) (*bleach*)

- ハンガー **hangā** (hahn-gahh) (*clothes hanger*)

- 柔軟剤 **jūnanzai** (jooo-nahn-zah-ee) (*fabric softener*)

- 乾燥機 **kansōki** (kahn-sohh-kee) (*dryer*)

- 洗濯機 **sentakuki** (sehn-tah-koo-kee) (*washing machine*)

- 洗剤 **senzai** (sehn-zah-ee) (*detergent*)

The storage room

If you're lucky, your home has a spacious **shako** (shah-koh) (*garage*), **yaneura-beya** (yah-neh-oo-rah-beh-yah) (*attic*), or **chikashitsu** (chee-kah-shee-tsoo) (*basement*) where you can store all kinds of things such as the following:

- 道具箱 **dōgubako** (dohh-goo-bah-koh) (*toolbox*)

- 延長コード **enchō kōdo** (ehn-chohh kohh-doh) (*extension cord*)

- 金槌 **kanazuchi** (kah-nah-zoo-chee) *or* ハンマー **hanmā** (hahm-mahh) (*hammer*)

- 肥料 **hiryō** (hee-ryohh) (*fertilizer*)

- ホース **hōsu** (hohh-soo) (*garden hose*)

- 釘 **kugi** (koo-gee) (*nail*)

- 自転車 **jitensha** (jee-tehn-shah) (*bicycle*)

- 巻き尺 **makijaku** (mah-kee-jah-koo) (*tape measure*)

- ねじ **neji** (neh-jee) (*screw*)

- のこぎり **nokogiri** (noh-koh-gee-ree) (*saw*)

- レンチ **renchi** (rehn-chee) (*wrench*)

- 芝刈り機 **shibakariki** (shee-bah-kah-ree-kee) (*lawnmower*)

- ドライバー **doraibā** (doh-rah-ee-bahh) (*screwdriver*)

CULTURAL WISDOM

Most Japanese, especially in the city, are a bit more storage–challenged than you may be used to; they just have a small space near the foyer, a part of their closet, an area under the **kaidan** (kah–ee–dahn) (*staircase*), or a space in the back of the house to stash their extra stuff in.

GRAMMAR CHAT

If you aren't so sure about something, but you think *maybe* or *possibly*, say it with **kamoshiremasen.** Add it at the end of a verb or an adjective in the plain/informal form, but just drop **da** that appears in the plain present affirmative form of the linking verb, **desu,** or a **na**–type adjective. For example

釘は道具箱の中にあるかもしれません。 **Kugi wa dōgubako no naka ni aru kamoshiremasen.** (koo-gee wah dohh-goo-bah-koh noh nah-kah nee ah-roo-kah-moh-shee-reh-mah-sehn.) (*Nails may be in the toolbox.*)

ミキサーはあまり使わないかもしれません。 **Mikisā wa amari tsukawanai kamoshiremasen.** (mee-kee-sahh wah ah-mah-ree tsoo-kah-wah-nah-ee kah-moh-shee-reh-mah-sehn.) (*We may not use the blender very often.*)

このシーツは大きいかもしれません。 **Kono shītsu wa ōkii kamoshiremasen.** (koh-noh sheee-tsoo wah ohh-keee kah-moh-shee-reh-mah-sehn.) (*This sheet may be big.*)

あの部屋は静かかもしれません。 **Ano heya wa shizuka kamoshiremasen.** (ah-noh heh-yah wah shee-zoo-kah kah-moh-shee-reh-mah-sehn.) (*That room may be quiet.*)

···········Talkin' the Talk···········

Marge is looking for an apartment and has just entered the second one with a Realtor.

Realtor: **Koko ga ribingu; asoko ga kitchin. Koko ga furoba desu.**
              koh-koh gah ree-been-goo; ah-soh-koh gah keet-cheen. koh-koh gah foo-roh-bah deh-soo.
              This is the living room; the kitchen is over there. Here's the bathroom.

Marge: **Ii desu ne.**
              eee deh-soo neh.
              It's good.

Realtor: **Kore ga kurōzetto desu.**
              koh-reh gah koo-rohh-zeht-toh deh-soo.
              This is the closet.

Marge:	**Kono kurōzetto wa chotto chīsai kamoshiremasen.**
	koh-noh koo-rohh-zeht-toh wah choht-toh cheee-sah-ee kah-moh-shee-reh-mah-sehn.
	This closet may be a bit small.
Realtor:	**Demo, oshiire mo arimasu yo.**
	deh-moh, oh-shee-ee-reh moh ah-ree-mah-soo yoh.
	But there's an oshiire closet, too.

● ●

WORDS TO KNOW

koko	koh-koh	here
asoko	ah-soh-koh	over there
chotto	choht-toh	a bit
chīsai	cheee-sah-ee	small
mo	moh	also
aru	ah-roo	to exist

Home Is Where the Food Is

Nothing is tastier than the dishes your mom makes at home. (That's one of the reasons there's no place like home.) While you're stuffing yourself with home-made goodies, check out some terminology for various eating times:

» 朝ごはん **asagohan** (ah-sah-goh-hahn) *or* 朝食 **chōshoku** (chohh-shoh-koo) (*breakfast*)

» 昼ごはん **hirugohan** (hee-roo-goh-hahn) *or* 昼食 **chūshoku** (chooo-shoh-koo) (*lunch*)

» 晩ごはん **bangohan** (bahn-goh-hahn) *or* 夕食 **yūshoku** (yooo-shoh-koo) (*supper*)

» おやつ **oyatsu** (oh-yah-tsoo) (*snack*)

» 夜食 **yashoku** (yah-shoh-koo) (*midnight snack*)

The following sections help you talk about eating. Just don't practice with your mouth full.

Getting cooking

The general verb *to cook* in Japanese is **ryōri suru** (ryohh-ree soo-roo). In fact, **ryōri** is a noun that means *cooking*, and **suru** is the verb that means *to do*. You know that cooking involves a variety of actions. The following verbs will help you enjoy cooking at home!

» 揚げる **ageru** (ah-geh-roo) (*to deep fry*)

» 炒める **itameru** (ee-tah-meh-roo) (*to stir-fry*)

» 蒸す **musu** (moo-soo) (*to steam*)

» 煮る **niru** (nee-roo) (*to stew*)

» 焼く **yaku** (yah-koo) (*to bake, to broil, to grill, to sauté fry*)

» ゆでる **yuderu** (yoo-deh-roo) (*to boil*)

Using two verbs at the table

What do you do at the table? You **taberu** (tah-beh-roo) (*to eat*) and **nomu** (noh-moo) (*to drink*), of course! Actually, **taberu** is the first verb I teach in my Japanese class. It's a **ru**-verb. Here's the conjugation:

Japanese Script	Rōmaji	Pronunciation
食べる	taberu	tah-beh-roo
食べない	tabenai	tah-beh-nah-ee
食べ(ます)	tabe(masu)	tah-beh(-mah-soo)
食べて	tabete	tah-beh-the

By contrast, **nomu** is obviously an **u**-verb because it has no **eru** or **iru** sequence at the end. Here's its conjugation:

Japanese Script	Rōmaji	Pronunciation
飲む	nomu	noh-moo
飲まない	nomanai	noh-mah-nah-ee
飲み(ます)	nomi(masu)	noh-mee(-mah-soo)
飲んで	nonde	nohn-deh

GRAMMAR CHAT

Whatever you eat or drink is marked by the particle **o** (oh). This particle marks the direct object of the verb, so you can use **o** with other verbs like *to read, to buy, to make, to invite, to write,* and so on. In all cases, **o** marks the direct object of the verb: the book read, the thing bought, the pizza made, the person invited, the letter written, and so on, regardless of who performed these actions. Here are a couple of examples of **o** with **taberu** and **nomu**.

> ピザを食べました。**Piza o tabemashita.** (pee-zah oh tah-beh-mah-shee-tah.)
> (*I ate pizza.*)

> コーラを飲みました。**Kōra o nomimashita.** (kohh-rah oh noh-mee-mah-shee-tah.)
> (*I drank cola.*)

Considering proper table manners

What qualifies as proper table manners depends on the culture and customs of your hosts. Japanese drink soup directly from an **o-wan** without using a spoon. And that's polite. Japanese slurp **ramen** noodles in soup. That's polite too.

WARNING

When you start eating, always say **itadakimasu** (ee-tah-dah-kee-mah-soo). It's a very humble word for *receive,* but in this context, there's really no good translation. Just remember that it's a set phrase used to express humble gratitude to those who made the meal that you're about to receive possible. Even young kids say it in Japan. If they forget, their moms scold them. So never forget **itadakimasu**. And when you're done with your meal, say **gochisōsama** (goh-chee-sohh-sah-mah). It's another word of gratitude that has no English equivalent, but you never want to leave the table without saying it.

Enjoying foods of all kinds

How often do you eat at home? If you eat at home three times per week, you can save a lot of money and stay healthier. The following sections introduce a variety of foods that you can enjoy at home.

Eating breakfast in two cultures

A Japanese breakfast can be downright exquisite — if you have the eyes (and palate) to see it that way. Following are some foods you can expect to find in a traditional Japanese breakfast:

>> ご飯 **gohan** (goh-hahn) (*cooked rice*)

>> ほうれん草のおひたし **hōrensō no ohitashi** (hohh-rehn-sohh noh oh-hee-tah-shee) (*boiled spinach seasoned with soy sauce*)

» みそ汁 **misoshiru** (mee-soh-shee-roo) (*soybean-paste soup*)

» 生たまご **nama tamago** (nah-mah tah-mah-goh) (*raw egg*)

» 納豆 **nattō** (naht-tohh) (*fermented soybeans*)

» のり **nori** (noh-ree) (*seaweed*)

» 漬け物 **tsukemono** (tsoo-keh-moh-noh) (*pickled vegetables*)

» 焼き魚 **yakizakana** (yah-kee-zah-kah-nah) (*grilled/broiled fish*)

If a Western-style breakfast is more your speed, you can enjoy the following items, at least until you're feeling more adventurous:

» バター **batā** (bah-tahh) (*butter*)

» ベーコン **bēkon** (behh-kohn) (*bacon*)

» ハム **hamu** (hah-moo) (*ham*)

» ジャム **jamu** (jah-moo) (*jam*)

» クロワッサン **kurowassan** (koo-roh-wahs-sahn) (*croissant*)

» 紅茶 **kōcha** (kohh-chah) (*black tea*)

» 目玉焼き **medamayaki** (meh-dah-mah-yah-kee) (*fried egg*)

» 牛乳 **gyūnyū** (gyooo-nyooo) (*milk*)

» オレンジジュース **orenji jūsu** (oh-rehn-jee jooo-soo) (*orange juice*)

» シリアル **shiriaru** (shee-ree-ah-roo) (*cereal*)

» スクランブルエッグ **sukuranburu eggu** (soo-koo-rahn-boo-roo ehg-goo) (*scrambled eggs*)

» ソーセージ **sōsēji** (sohh-sehh-jee) (*sausage*)

» トースト **tōsuto** (tohh-soo-toh) (*toast*)

Munching your lunch

In Japan, noodles are always popular lunchtime meals. The thick, white noodles that you may have seen in soups are **udon** (oo-dohn), and *buckwheat noodles* are **soba** (soh-bah). And don't forget **rāmen** (rahh-mehn) noodles, which the Japanese adopted from China.

Rice dishes in big bowls are also very popular for lunch. These meals are called 丼物 **donburimono** (dohn-boo-ree-moh-noh) (*big bowl dishes*) and feature a bowl of rice with different toppings. If you have cooked chicken and egg over the rice, it's called **oyako donburi** (oh-yah-koh dohn-boo-ree). **Oyako** literally means *parent-child*; it describes the chicken and the egg.

Here are some lunch options you may be more familiar with:

» チーズ **chīzu** (cheee-zoo) (*cheese*)

» ハンバーガー **hanbāgā** (hahn-bahh-gahh) (*hamburger*)

» ピザ **piza** (pee-zah) (*pizza*)

» サンドイッチ **sandoicchi** (sahn-doh-eet-chee) (*sandwich*)

» サラダ **sarada** (sah-rah-dah) (*salad*)

» スパゲッティー **supagettī** (soo-pah-geht-teee) (*spaghetti*)

» スープ **sūpu** (sooo-poo) (*soup*)

You can use these items to give your **sandoicchi** a little kick:

» ケチャップ **kechappu** (keh-chahp-poo) (*ketchup*)

» マスタード **masutādo** (mah-soo-tahh-doh) (*mustard*)

» マヨネーズ **mayonēzu** (mah-yoh-nehh-zoo) (*mayonnaise*)

» ピクルス **pikurusu** (pee-koo-roo-soo) (*pickle*)

Savoring dinner dishes

Japanese eat all kinds of ethnic foods, but here are some of the popular homemade dinner dishes:

» カレーライス **karēraisu** (kah-rehh-rah-ee-soo) (*curry sauce served over cooked rice*)

» マーボー豆腐 **mābōdōfu** (mahh-bohh-dohh-foo) (*bean curd cooked with ground beef and chili peppers*)

» 肉じゃが **nikujaga** (nee-koo-jah-gah) (*meat, potatoes, and onion stewed in sweetened soy sauce*)

» さしみ **sashimi** (sah-shee-mee) (*sliced raw fish*)

» ステーキ **sutēki** (soo-tehh-kee) (*steak*)

» てんぷら **tenpura** (tehn-poo-rah) (*seafood, vegetables, and mushrooms with batter and deep fried*)

» とんかつ **tonkatsu** (tohn-kah-tsoo) (*breaded deep-fried pork cutlets served with shredded cabbage*)

Sampling party foods

For a friendly and easy home party, Japanese often serve dishes that they cook right at the table, using a portable stove or electric hot plate. Instead of being stuck in the kitchen and missing the fun, the hosts can cook, eat, and chat with their friends at the same time. Common Japanese party offerings include the following:

>> しゃぶしゃぶ **shabushabu** (shah-boo-shah-boo): Beef and vegetables cooked in a pot of boiling broth

>> すき焼き **sukiyaki** (soo-kee-yah-kee): Beef and vegetables cooked in **warishita** (wah-ree-shee-tah), which is a mixture of soy sauce, sugar, broth, and liquor

>> 寄せ鍋 **yosenabe** (yoh-seh-nah-beh): Japanese casserole of vegetables, fish, or meat

>> 焼き肉 **yakiniku** (yah-kee-nee-koo): Korean-style barbecue

Talking about foods you like and dislike

GRAMMAR
CHAT

When you talk about your preferences in English, you use verbs such as *to like, to love,* and *to hate.* In Japanese, though, you use adjectives to express your likes and dislikes. For example, **suki** (soo-kee) (*to like*) is an adjective. If you want to say that you like pizza, you say **Watashi wa piza ga suki desu.** (wah-tah-shee wah pee-zah gah soo-kee deh-soo.) (*I like pizza.*) The translation becomes misleading here, so watch out: The item you like, *pizza* in this case, is marked by the subject-marking particle **ga.** You can't use the direct object–marking particle **o** because you use **o** with a verb only.

If you know **suki,** you also have to know **kirai** (kee-rah-ee) (*to hate*). To say that you like or hate something a lot, add **dai-** (dah-ee), which means *big,* before **suki** or **kirai,** as in **daisuki** (dah-ee-soo-kee) (*to like it a lot*), and **daikirai** (dah-ee-kee-rah-ee) (*to hate it a lot*). Now you have four adjectives that you can use to express your likes and dislikes, you picky eater, you. Check out some examples of these adjectives in action:

私は魚が好きです。**Watashi wa sakana ga suki desu.** (wah-tah-shee wah sah-kah-nah gah soo-kee deh-soo.) (*I like fish.*)

妹はチーズケーキが大好きです。**Imōto wa chīzu kēki ga daisuki desu!** (ee-mohh-toh wah cheee-zoo kehh-kee gah dah-ee-soo-kee deh-soo!) (*My little sister loves cheesecake a lot!*)

妹は野菜が嫌いです。**Imōto wa yasai ga kirai desu.** (ee-mohh-toh wah yah-sah-ee gah kee-rah-ee deh-soo.) (*My little sister hates vegetables.*)

私は納豆が大嫌いです！**Watashi wa nattō ga daikirai desu!** (wah-tah-shee wah naht-tohh gah dah-ee-kee-rah-ee deh-soo!) (*I hate fermented soybeans a lot!*)

Engaging in Common Household Activities

Your house is the nicest place to be, but keeping your house just the way you like it requires a lot of responsibilities. The next sections give you the Japanese words and phrases you need for keeping your home clean and safe.

Keeping your home clean

Keeping your home clean can make life a lot more comfortable. You may use these phrases as you do your weekly or yearly **sōji** (sohh–jee) (*cleaning*):

>> 部屋を掃除する **heya o sōji suru** (heh-yah oh sohh-jee soo-roo) (*to clean the room*)

>> 部屋をかたづける **heya o katazukeru** (heh-yah oh kah-tah-zoo-keh-roo) (*to tidy up the room*)

>> 埃をとる **hokori o toru** (hoh-koh-ree oh toh-roo) (*to dust*)

>> 窓をふく **mado o fuku** (mah-doh oh foo-koo) (*to clean the windows*)

>> 掃除機をかける **sōjiki o kakeru** (sohh-jee-kee oh kah-keh-roo) (*to vacuum*)

>> 床をふく **yuka o fuku** (yoo-kah oh foo-koo) (*to mop the floor*)

Performing a safety check

You don't want to have a **kaji** (kah–jee) (*fire*) while you're sleeping or have a **dorobō** (doh–roh–bohh) (*thief*) break into your home when you're on vacation. Go over the following checklist when you go out or go to bed:

>> 暖房を切る **danbō o kiru** (dahn-bohh oh kee-roo) (*to shut off the heat*)

>> 電源を切る **dengen o kiru** (dehn-gehn oh kee-roo) (*to shut off the power supply*)

>> ドアの鍵をかける **doa no kagi o kakeru** (doh-ah noh kah-gee oh kah-keh-roo) (*to lock the door*)

>> 電気を消す **denki o kesu** (dehn-kee oh keh-soo) (*to turn off the light*)

>> ガスの元栓をしめる **gasu no motosen o shimeru** (gah-soo noh moh-toh-sehn oh shee-meh-roo) (*to close the main gas valve*)

>> 窓をしめる **mado o shimeru** (mah-doh oh shee-meh-roo) (*to close the window*)

Talking about What You Do Regularly

Different people have different daily habits. Do you always jog in the morning? Drink beer with dinner? Watch YouTube? Check emails? All the above?

GRAMMAR CHAT

To express that you do something regularly, such as run, play tennis, go to work, brush your teeth, and so on, you can use the verb that expresses the activity and the verb **iru** (ee-roo) (*to exist*), in that order. Make sure to conjugate the verb that expresses the action in the **te**-form. (See Chapter 3 for the details on the **te**-form.) You can leave the verb **iru** as it is or use the polite form, **imasu** (ee-mah-soo).

For example, you can combine the verbs **hashiru** (hah-shee-roo) (*to run*) and **iru** to get **hashitte iru** (hah-sheet-teh ee-roo) or **hashitte imasu** (hah-sheet-teh ee-mah-soo). Both phrases mean that someone runs regularly. It's sort of like saying, "I run and exist every day." Just be careful: **Hashitte iru** also has an ongoing-action connotation that translates to *I'm in the middle of running*. The context helps determine which meaning is intended. If you say **mainichi** (mah-ee-nee-chee) (*every day*) before saying **hashitte imasu**, it obviously means a habitual activity — *I run every day*. If you say **ima** (ee-mah) (*now*) instead, the sentence means *I'm in the middle of running now*, which is a progressive action. The following sentences use the **te**-form plus **iru** and express habitual actions:

お父さんはいつも寝ているよ! **Otōsan wa itsumo nete iru yo!** (oh-tohh-sahn wah ee-tsoo-moh neh-teh ee-roo yoh!) (*My dad is always sleeping!*)

ケンは毎日ピザを食べています。 **Ken wa mainichi piza o tabete imasu.** (kehn wah mah-ee-nee-chee pee-zah oh tah-beh-teh ee-mah-soo.) (*Ken eats pizza every day.*)

The alternative to using the **te**-form–plus–**iru** combination is to use the simple present tense:

毎朝新聞を読みます。 **Maiasa shinbun o yomimasu.** (mah-ee-ah-sah sheen-boon oh yoh-mee-mah-soo.) (*I read the newspaper every morning.*)

週末は掃除をします。 **Shūmatsu wa sōji o shimasu.** (shooo-mah-tsoo wah sohh-jee oh shee-mah-soo.) (*I clean [the house] every weekend.*)

.........Talkin' the Talk.................

David is talking with his friend Michiko.

David: **Michiko-san wa maiasa nan-ji ni okimasu ka.**
mee-chee-koh-sahn wah mah-ee-ah-sah nahn-jee
nee oh-kee-mah-soo kah.
Michiko, what time do you wake up every morning?

Michiko: **6-ji ni okimasu.**
roh-koo-jee nee oh-kee-mah-soo.
I wake up at 6:00.

David: **Hayai desu ne.**
hah-yah-ee deh-soo neh.
It's very early, isn't it?

Michiko: **Ē. Maiasa 1-jikan hashitte imasu.**
ehh. mah-ee-ah-sah ee-chee-jee-kahn hah-sheet-
teh ee-mah-soo.
I run for one hour every morning.

David: **Sugoi!**
soo-goh-ee!
Great!

WORDS TO KNOW		
okiru	oh-kee-roo	to wake up
maiasa	mah-ee-ah-sah	every morning
hayai	hah-yah-ee	early
hashiru	hah-shee-roo	to run
sugoi	soo-goh-ee	great

FONDUE, JAPANESE STYLE

Japanese often serve a sort of fondue called しゃぶしゃぶ **shabushabu** (shah-boo-shah-boo) — a big pot of kelp broth placed on a portable stove on the dining table. You pick up a thin slice of beef with chopsticks, immerse it in the boiling broth, and swish it around for several seconds. You eat it right away with the dip of your choice (such as sesame paste dip or soy sauce and lime dip). Other ingredients include Chinese cabbage, garland chrysanthemum leaves, mushrooms, soybean curds, and gelatin noodles. Some people add thick white noodles called うどん **udon** (oo-dohn), leeks, and other ingredients.

Japanese beef is very expensive, but it's also very tender and delicious. To produce this quality beef, farmers feed the cows beer and massage them with big brushes. So the next time you meet a well-groomed cow with beer on its breath, you'll know that it has recently been to Japan.

FUN & GAMES

Match the rooms in the house with the Japanese words. Check Appendix C for the answers.

Illustration by Elizabeth Kurtzman

1. __
2. __
3. __
4. __
5. __
6. __
a. リビング **ribingu**
b. 寝室 **shinshitsu**
c. キッチン **kitchin**
d. バスルーム **basurūmu**
e. 書斎 **shosai**
f. ダイニング **dainingu**

2

Japanese in Action

Strike up a conversation when you want to get to know new people.

Ask for directions to get to places.

Figure out how to deal with money, shop, and go out on the town.

Practice using Japanese in business settings.

Find out how to "speak technology" in Japanese business and daily life.

Chapter **6**

Icebreakers and Conversation Starters

Konnichiwa! (kohn-nee-chee-wa!) (*Good afternoon!/Hi!*) Greetings like this one are basic expressions you can use to kick off conversations with people you know. For people you don't know, you can introduce yourself and find out more about them by engaging in light conversation. This chapter shows you how to form greetings, introductions, and goodbyes in Japanese. It also describes how to interact politely with new people and how to tell someone *Thank you* or *Sorry.*

REMEMBER

You can listen to all the Talkin' the Talk dialogues featured in this chapter. Go to www.dummies.com/go/japanese and click on the dialogue you want to hear.

Beginning (and Ending) Conversations

Aisatsu (ah-ee-sah-tsoo) (*greetings*) are the most important communication tools. Start your day with a friendly and cheerful greeting to your family, friends, colleagues, teachers, bosses, and even strangers on the street. In the following sections, you find out how to greet all kinds of people throughout the day. And because you inevitably have to say goodbye to the people you encounter during your day, you will also discover how to do just that.

Addressing friends and strangers

In English, you address others by their first names ("Hi, Robert!"), by their nicknames ("Hey, Bobby!"), by their positions ("Excuse me, professor"), or by their family names with appropriate titles ("Hello, Mr. Right"), depending on your relationship and how close you are to that person. You don't want to sound too formal or distant, but you don't want to sound too friendly or presumptuous, either.

WARNING

In Japanese society, addressing people is something that you don't want to mess up. When you meet someone new at work and you know the person's occupational title (such as company president, professor, or division manager), use the title along with his family name — for example, **Sumisu-shachō** (soo-mee-soo-shah-chohh) (*President Smith*). Following are some examples of occupational titles:

- » 部長 **buchō** (boo-chohh) (*division manager*)
- » 学長 **gakuchō** (gah-koo-chohh) (*university president*)
- » 校長 **kōchō** (kohh-chohh) (*school principal*)
- » 先生 **sensei** (sehn-sehh) (*teacher, doctor*)
- » 社長 **shachō** (shah-chohh) (*company president*)
- » 店長 **tenchō** (tehn-chohh) (*store manager*)

If you don't know the person's occupational title, the safest way to address him is to use his family name plus the respectful title **-san** (sahn) — **Sumisu-san** (soo-mee-soo-sahn) (*Mr. Smith* or *Ms. Smith*). The more polite version of **-san** is **-sama** (sah-mah), but it's too formal and businesslike for most social situations. Other respectful titles include **-chan** (chahn) and **-kun** (koon), but you must use them very carefully. Check out Table 6-1 to see which titles are appropriate for your friends and acquaintances. The table contains examples of various ways you may address Robert (**Robāto**) and Susan (**Sūzan**) Smith (**Sumisu**).

TABLE 6-1 **Respectful Titles**

Title	Function	Example
一ちゃん **-chan** (chahn)	Mainly for children; used after a boy's or girl's given name.	スーザンちゃん **Sūzan-chan** (sooo-zahn-chahn) ロバートちゃん **Robāto-chan** (roh-bahh-toh-chahn)
一君 **kun** (koon)	Used after a boy's given name. Also used after a subordinate's family name, regardless of gender.	ロバート君 **Robāto-kun** (roh-bahh-toh-koon) スミス君 **Sumisu-kun** (soo-mee-soo-koon)
一様 **sama** (sah-mah)	Used after a superior's or customer's name, regardless of gender. Also used when addressing letters (*Dear. . .*).	スミス様 **Sumisu-sama** (soo-mee-soo-sah-mah) スーザン様 **Sūzan-sama** (sooo-zahn-sah-mah) ロバート・スミス様 **Robāto Sumisu-sama** (roh-bahh-toh soo-mee-soo-sah-mah)
一さん **-san** (sahn)	Used with anyone if other titles are unavailable.	スミスさん **Sumisu-san** (soo-mee-soo-sahn) スーザンさん **Sūzan-san** (sooo-zahn-sahn) ロバート・スミスさん **Robāto Sumisu-san** (roh-bahh-toh soo-mee-soo-sahn)

CULTURAL WISDOM

When introducing themselves, Japanese (as well as Chinese and Koreans) give their family names first and given names last. Most Japanese realize that Western names aren't in the same order, and they won't expect you to reverse the order of your own name to match the Japanese pattern of giving names. Many Japanese also realize that Westerners tend to use their given names a lot, but you should use the family name for all but your closest friends and family.

If you use the Japanese word for *you* — **anata** (ah-nah-tah) — you'll sound boastful or rude. Japanese people try not to say **anata;** instead, they just drop pronouns or use names or titles (whereas English uses *you*). If you visit a Japanese store, you'll notice that the store representatives address you with **okyaku-sama** (oh-kyah-koo-sah-mah) (*customer*) in order to avoid saying **anata.** Instead of *you*, you can use interesting age- and gender-sensitive terms when addressing strangers in friendly contexts. For example, **ojisan** (oh-jee-sahn) literally means *uncle*, but you can use it to casually address any unfamiliar middle-aged man. The following list shows other general descriptions of strangers and the Japanese terms you can use to address them:

>> おばさん **obasan** (oh-bah-sahn) (*middle-aged woman* [Literally: *aunt*])

>> おじいさん **ojīsan** (oh-jeee-sahn) (*old man* [Literally: *grandfather*])

>> おばあさん **obāsan** (oh-bahh-sahn) (*old woman* [Literally: *grandmother*])

>> 坊や **bōya;** お坊ちゃん **obocchan** (bohh-yah; oh-boht-chahn) (*young boy* [Literally: *son*])

>> お嬢さん **ojōsan** (oh-johh-sah) (*young girl* [Literally: *daughter*])

>> お兄さん **onīsan** (oh-neee-sahn) (*young man* [Literally: *big brother*])

>> お姉さん **onēsan** (oh-nehh-sahn) (*young woman* [Literally: *big sister*])

Greetings throughout the day

In Japanese, as in every other language, what you say and do to greet people depends on the time of the day and the person you're greeting.

>> In the morning, as you greet family and friends, say **ohayō** (oh-hah-yohh), the informal version of *good morning*. As you greet your boss or teacher, or even your colleagues, use the formal **ohayō gozaimasu** (oh-hah-yohh goh-zah-ee-mah-soo) — and don't forget to bow as you say it. Check out the nearby sidebar "Bowing" for more on this custom.

>> In the afternoon, say **konnichiwa** (kohn-nee-chee-wah) (*good afternoon*) to everyone, regardless of the person's position and status.

>> When you can see the stars or the moon in the sky, say **konbanwa** (kohn-bahn-wah), regardless of whom you greet. It means *good evening*.

CULTURAL WISDOM

If you haven't seen someone in a while, ask him or her **O-genki desu ka.** (oh-gehn-kee deh-soo kah.) (*Are you well?* or *How are you?*) as well. When others ask you **O-genki desu ka,** you can say **Hai, genki desu.** (hah-ee, gehn-kee deh-soo.) (*I'm fine.*), but if you want to sound a bit more sophisticated, say **Hai, okagesama de.** (hah-ee oh-kah-geh-sah-mah-deh.) (*Yes, I'm fine, thanks to you and all beings.*) or **Nantoka.** (nahn-toh-kah.) (*I'm barely managing things in my life* or *I'm barely coping.*). Those two expressions sound very modest and mature to Japanese, even though the last one sounds pretty negative to American ears.

WARNING

English speakers make a habit of asking everyone, "*How are you?*" even if they have seen the person the day before. **O-genki desu ka** is a serious question about a person's mental and physical health, so don't use it when greeting someone you saw yesterday. Say it when you mean it.

Saying goodbye

When you leave a friend, say **jā, mata** (jahh, mah-tah) (*see you again*). You can also say **sayōnara** (sah-yohh-nah-rah) (*goodbye*) if you're parting for a longer period of time, but don't use this option if you'll see the person later that same day. Otherwise, you can use either phrase or both of them together. When taking leave of your boss or teacher, say **shitsurei shimasu** (shee-tsoo-rehh shee-mah-soo). **Shitsurei shimasu** literally means *I'll be rude.* How do you get *goodbye* out of *I'll be rude?* It's as if you're saying *I'm being rude by leaving your presence.*

REMEMBER

Don't say **sayōnara** or **shitsurei shimasu** to your family members when you leave home for school or work. Instead, say **ittekimasu** (eet-teh-kee-mah-soo) (Literally: *I'll go and come back*) — a set phrase for this occasion. Your family will respond to you with **itterasshai** (eet-teh-rahs-shah-ee) (Literally: *You go and come back!*). Just in case, when you get home, say **tadaima** (tah-dah-ee-mah) (Literally: *just now*), which actually means *I'm home!* Then, your family will respond to you with **okaeri** (oh-kah-eh-ree) (Literally: *You got home.*). If you have trouble memorizing these four phrases, try not to think about their literal meanings and instead focus on which phrase applies when leaving home and which phrase applies when returning.

Talkin' the Talk

Jessica runs into her professor in the morning while rushing to another class.

Jessica: **Sensei, ohayō gozaimasu!**
sen-sehh, oh-hah-yohh goh-zah-ee-mah-soo!
Professor, good morning!

Professor: **Ā, Jeshika-san. Ohayō.**
ahh, jeh-shee-kah-sahn. oh-hah-yohh.
Oh, Jessica. Good morning.

Jessica: **Jā, mata kurasu de. Shitsurei shimasu.**
jahh, mah-tah koo-rah-soo deh. shee-tsoo-rehh
shee-mah-soo.
I'll see you again in class. Goodbye.

Professor: **Hai. Jā, mata.**
hah-ee. jahh, mah-tah.
Yes. See you later.

WORDS TO KNOW		
sensei	sehn-sehh	teacher
Ohayō.	oh-hah-yohh.	Good morning.
Shitsurei shimasu.	shee-tsoo-rehh shee-mah-soo.	Goodbye. (formal)
Jā, mata.	jahh, mah-tah.	See you later.
kurasu	koo-rah-soo	class

Initiating Small Talk

You can initiate small talk with others in a number of ways. Saying "Excuse me" is always a good option. If you're traveling, you can talk to your fellow passengers about where they're going. If you're at home, you can strike up a conversation with your neighbor about the day's weather. So be open and initiate a conversation whenever you can by using the vocabulary I provide in the next sections.

Breaking the ice with "excuse me"

Small talk often starts with **Sumimasen.** (soo-mee-mah-sehn.) (*Excuse me.*) You use this phrase to break the ice. But afterward, you usually need to ask a few questions to strike up a conversation. Depending on the type of information you're looking for, you need to use different question words like **doko** (doh-koh) (*where*), **dore** (doh-reh) (*which one*), and **nan-ji** (nahn-jee) (*what time*). Chapter 3 summarizes the types of questions and provides a list of question words, but you can use these simple icebreaking questions to make small talk:

>> バス停はどこですか。**Basutē wa doko desu ka.** (bah-soo-tehh wah doh-koh deh-soo kah.) (*Where is the bus stop?*)

>> 今,何時ですか。**Ima, nan-ji desu ka.** (ee-mah, nahn-jee deh-soo kah.) (*What time is it now?*)

Talking about where you're going

When you're traveling and feel like talking to the person seated next to you on the plane, bus, or train, why not begin a conversation by asking **Dochira made desu ka.** (doh-chee-rah mah-deh deh-soo kah.) (*Where are you heading to?*) **Dochira** (doh-chee-rah) means *which one* or *which way*, but it can function as the polite version of **doko** (doh-koh) (*where*). **Made** (mah-deh) is a particle that means *up to*. To answer the question **Dochira made desu ka,** just replace **dochira** with the place name and drop the question particle **ka** (kah), as in **Tōkyō made desu.** (tohh-kyohh mah-deh deh-soo.) (*I'm heading to Tokyo.*)

Talkin' the Talk

Richard is sitting in a bullet train in Japan. He wants to know what time it is but doesn't have a watch, so he asks a woman who is sitting next to him.

Richard: **Sumimasen. Ima nan-ji desu ka.**
             soo-mee-mah-sehn. ee-mah nahn-jee deh-soo kah.
             Excuse me. What time is it now?

Woman: **4-ji 17-fun desu.**
             yoh-jee joo-nah-nah-foon deh-soo.
             It's 4:17.

Richard:	**Ā, sō desu ka. Dōmo.**
	ahh, sohh deh-soo-ka. dohh-mo.
	Oh, really. Thank you.

Woman:	**Īe. Dochira made desu ka.**
	eee-eh. doh-chee-rah mah-deh deh-soo kah.
	Don't mention it. Where are you heading to?

Richard:	**Hiroshima made desu.**
	hee-roh-shee-mah mah-deh deh-soo.
	To Hiroshima.

Woman:	**Ā, sō desu ka. Watashi mo desu!**
	ahh, sohh deh-soo kah. wah-tah-shee moh deh-soo!
	Oh, really? Me, too!

WORDS TO KNOW

Sumimasen.	soo-mee-mah-sehn.	Excuse me.
ima	ee-mah	now
nan-ji	nahn-jee	what time
Dochira made desu ka.	doh-chee-rah mah-deh deh-soo kah.	Where are you going?

Discussing the weather

Discussing **tenki** (tehn-kee) (*weather*) is a tried-and-true way of making casual conversation because **tenki** seems to be a universally neutral topic. On a nice, clear day, try starting a conversation with **Ii tenki desu ne.** (eee tehn-kee deh-soo neh.) (*It's nice today, isn't it?*) The following adjectives describe temperature and humidity:

» 暖かい **atatakai** (ah-tah-tah-kah-ee) (*warm*)

» 暑い **atsui** (ah-tsoo-ee) (*hot*)

» 蒸し暑い **mushi-atsui** (moo-shee-ah-tsoo-ee) (*muggy*)

>> 寒い **samui** (sah-moo-ee) (*cold*)

>> 涼しい **suzushii** (soo-zoo-sheee) (*cool*)

GRAMMAR CHAT

You can use these adjectives by themselves in informal contexts. For example, when you're at home and feeling uncomfortable on a hot day, you can exclaim: **Atsui!** (ah-tsoo-ee!) (*Hot!*) If you want to mention to your mom that it's hot, assuming that she'll agree with you, you can add the particle **ne** (neh), as in **Atsui, ne.** (ah-tsoo-ee, neh.) (*It's hot, isn't it?*) The sentence-ending particle **ne** is for confirmation. It invites your partner's agreement and makes your conversation flow more smoothly. If you feel hot, say it with **ne** because your conversation partner probably feels hot too — unless he or she is a cyborg.

GRAMMAR CHAT

In a polite/neutral or formal context, make sure to add **desu** (deh-soo) (*to be*) to the adjective you're using to describe the weather. Adjectives always sound polite if they end in **desu**. (See Chapter 3 for more about **desu**.) For example, you can say **Atsui desu.** (ah-tsoo-ee deh-soo.) (*It's hot.*) or **Atsui desu ne.** (ah-tsoo-ee deh-soo neh.) (*It's hot, isn't it?*) to your teacher, colleague, and boss.

Making Introductions

Nothing is more exciting than getting to know new people at a **pātī** (pahh-teee) (*party*), **kaigi** (kah-ee-gee) (*conference*), **atarashii shokuba** (ah-tah-rah-sheee shoh-koo-bah) (*new job*), or even on the **tōri** (tohh-ree) (*street*). Tomorrow, you may meet someone who will be very important in your life! The next sections show you how to make a good first impression. Yes, the first 30 seconds may decide the rest of your life!

CULTURAL WISDOM

HERE'S MY CARD

Businesspeople frequently exchange cards when meeting fellow businesspeople, but in Japan, a good deal of etiquette goes along with this exchange. First, you must exchange cards with just one person at a time, focusing all your attention on that person. Make sure to give and receive with both hands and present the card so that the lettering faces the receiver. Also, don't put the card you receive in your wallet right away. You should handle and treat other people's business cards with respect, for the card is like the face of the person; it's their honor and should be handled in the most respectful manner.

Introducing yourself

The first word to say as you introduce yourself to someone is **hajimemashite** (hah-jee-meh-mah-shee-teh). This word literally means *beginning,* and it clarifies the fact that you're meeting that person for the very first time. After saying **hajimemashite,** say your name, and then say **yoroshiku** (yoh-roh-shee-koo). **Yoroshiku** is a set phrase that shows your modest attitude and asks the other party to be friendly and nice to you. No English translation exists for it.

CULTURAL WISDOM

English speakers just say *Pleased to meet you* or *I'm very happy to meet you* when they meet someone. They don't beg people to be nice to them as **yoroshiku** does. But when speaking Japanese, do as the Japanese do and say **yoroshiku.** The response to **yoroshiku** is usually **kochira koso** (koh-chee-rah koh-soh) **yoroshiku,** meaning *It's I who should say that.* So, if you beg someone to be friendly, they beg you right back. After all that begging, you're friends!

The complete formal version of **yoroshiku,** which is **yoroshiku onegai itashimasu** (yoh-roh-shee-koo oh-neh-gah-ee ee-tah-shee-mah-soo), is frequently used in any context where formality is due. So in a business context, you can expect to hear **yoroshiku onegai itashimasu** at the end of every conversation.

Introducing your friends to each other

Your friend can become another friend's friend if you introduce them to each other. When you want to introduce your friend to someone, say **kochira wa** (koh-chee-rah wah) (*as for this person*), your friend's name, and the verb **desu** (deh-soo) (*is*). For example, if you want to say *This is John,* say **Kochira wa Jon-san desu.** (koh-chee-rah wah john-sahn deh-soo.). (The short suffix **-san** (sahn) after the name **Jon** (john) (*John*) is a respectful title; see the "Addressing friends and strangers" section earlier in this chapter.)

BOWING

CULTURAL WISDOM

Bowing plays a very important role in Japanese communication. Bows almost always accompany phrases expressing gratitude, apology, and greeting. Japanese also bow when meeting someone for the very first time. Occasionally, they shake hands, but most of the time, they just bow as they say 宜しく **yoroshiku.** You don't need to bow very deeply in this context. Just slowly tilt your head and upper back slightly forward, and hold the position for two seconds. The deep, long bow is only needed when you make a horrible mistake, receive overwhelming kindness, or associate with people to whom you have to show a great deal of respect. Westerners aren't expected to bow to be polite, but if they do, they'll certainly receive appreciation from Japanese. Just make sure not to put your hands in your pockets, behind your back, or in a fist when bowing.

REMEMBER

As long as I'm talking about introductions, here's one more tip: Always introduce the person with the lower social status to the person with the higher social status.

Talkin' the Talk

Jun is introducing his friends Lisa and Robert to each other.

Jun: **Robāto-san, kochira wa Risa-san desu. Risa-san, kochira wa Robāto-san desu.**
roh-bahh-toh-sahn, koh-chee-rah wah ree-sah-sahn deh-soo. ree-sah-sahn, koh-chee-rah wah roh-bahh-toh-sahn deh-soo.
Robert, this is Lisa. Lisa, this is Robert.

Lisa: **Hajimemashite. Risa Jonson desu. Yoroshiku onegai shimasu.**
hah-jee-meh-mah-shee-teh. ree-sah john-sohn deh-soo. yoh-roh-shee-koo oh-neh-gah-ee shee-mah-soo.
How do you do? I'm Lisa Johnson. I'm pleased to meet you.

Robert: **Hajimemashite. Robāto Rosu desu. Kochira koso yoroshiku.**
hah-jee-meh-mah-shee-teh. roh-bahh-toh roh-soo deh-soo. koh-chee-rah koh-soh yoh-roh-shee-koo.
How do you do? I'm Robert Roth. I'm pleased to meet you, too.

WORDS TO KNOW		
kochira	koh-chee-rah	this person
Hajimemashite.	hah-jee-meh-mah-shee-teh.	How do you do?
Yoroshiku onegai shimasu.	yoh-roh-shee-koo oh-neh-gah-ee shee-mah-soo.	Pleased to meet you.
koso	koh-soh	(emphasis particle)

Asking people their names

Usually, the more people you know, the happier you are. So start asking people their names and make friends! As in English, telling someone your name when speaking Japanese is more or less a cue for that person to tell you her name. If it doesn't turn out that way (suggestion: if the other person doesn't offer her name), you can just ask by saying **Shitsurei desu ga, o-namae wa.** (shee-tsoo-rehh deh-soo gah, oh-nah-mah-eh wah.) (*This may be rude, but what's your name?*)

REMEMBER

Your own name is **namae,** but someone else's name is **o-namae,** as I explain in the following section.

Being polite with o-

The polite (honorific) prefix **o-** is used optionally to show respect to others and their things. This prefix can add some softness or politeness to words. Attaching **o-** is very common for certain words, regardless of whether you're talking about yourself or about others. For example, the word for *money* is **kane** (kah-neh), but people almost always call it **okane** (oh-kah-neh), even if they're talking about their own money. If you say just **kane,** you may sound vulgar and even a little bit scary. Likewise, *tea* and *souvenir* should be **ocha** (oh-chah) and **omiyage** (oh-mee-yah-geh), respectively, no matter what. Some differences with this concept exist, depending on the geographic area of Japan you're in, but I won't go into those here.

Expressing Gratitude and Regret

Phrases of gratitude and apology are the most important and essential phrases in any language. Suppose a stranger holds a door open for you when you're entering a building. What do you say? Suppose you accidentally step on someone's foot on a crowded train. How do you say *I'm sorry*? The next sections answer these questions.

Showing gratitude

You may know the word **arigatō** (ah-ree-gah-tohh) (*thanks*), but it's only one way to express gratitude. However, you should use **arigatō** with only family, friends, co-workers, and subordinates, plus strangers who look easygoing and younger than you. For everyone else (or when in doubt about whether **arigatō** is appropriate), say one of the following instead to mean *thank you:*

>> ありがとうございます。**Arigatō gozaimasu.** (ah-ree-gah-tohh goh-zah-ee-mah-soo.)

>> どうもありがとうございます。**Dōmo arigatō gozaimasu.** (dohh-moh ah-ree-gah-tohh goh-zah-ee-mah-soo.)

>> どうも。**Dōmo.** (dohh-moh.)

GRAMMAR CHAT

The easiest phrase of gratitude is **dōmo** — an adverb that literally means *indeed* or *very much* but can be understood as *thank you.* It's a short, convenient, and yet polite phrase of gratitude that you can use in any context. If you want to express a greater-than-normal degree of gratitude, you can use one of the longer, more fully spelled-out phrases, like **Arigatō gozaimasu** or **Dōmo arigatō gozaimasu.**

Apologizing

To apologize for something you've done or for causing someone pain or inconvenience, say **Dōmo sumimasen.** (dohh-moh soo-mee-mah-sehn.) (*I'm very sorry.*) or just **Sumimasen. Dōmo** is an interesting adverb. Its function is to make you sound serious, and you can use it with either **Arigatō gozaimasu.** (*Thank you.*) or **Sumimasen.** (*I'm sorry.*) (If you just say **dōmo** by itself, it's interpreted as *thank you* but not as *sorry.*) So watch out! In an informal context, **Gomennasai.** (goh-mehn-nah-sah-ee.) (*Sorry.*) is just fine for apologizing.

REMEMBER

Just remember that **sumimasen** can also be used for getting someone's attention. **Sumimasen** means both *I'm sorry* and *Excuse me*, but the context and your facial expression help clarify which one you mean. Japanese even say **sumimasen** in contexts where English speakers would say *Thank you*, as if to say *Excuse me for making you feel that you had to go through all that trouble.*

Speaking about Speaking: The Verb Hanasu

How do you feel about starting to speak Japanese? To answer this question, you need to know how to say *speak* in Japanese! Use the verb **hanasu** (hah-nah-soo) to mean *to speak.* Because **hanasu** doesn't end in **iru/eru**, it's surely an **u-verb**! (I cover the verb types in Chapter 3.) Here's how you conjugate it.

Japanese Script	Rōmaji	Pronunciation
話す	**hanasu**	hah-nah-soo
話さない	**hanasanai**	hah-nah-sah-nah-ee
話し(ます)	**hanashi (masu)**	hah-nah-shee (mah-soo)
話して	**hanashite**	hah-nah-shee-teh

The following examples show you how to use **hanasu** in context:

日本語を話しますか。 **Nihongo o hanashimasu ka.** (nee-hohn-goh oh hah-nah-shee-mah-soo kah.) (*Do you speak Japanese?*)

あの人とは話しません。 **Ano hito to wa hanashimasen.** (ah-noh hee-toh toh wah hah-nah-shee-mah-sehn.) (*I don't speak with that person.*)

人の前で話すのが下手です。 **Hito no mae de hanasu no ga heta desu.** (hee-toh noh mah-eh deh hah-nah-soo noh gah heh-tah deh-soo.) (*I'm not good at speaking in front of people.*)

FUN & GAMES

Match the situation with the appropriate expression. You can find the answers in Appendix C.

1. You accidentally break your neighbor's window.
2. You're about to leave (part with) your friend.
3. You meet someone for the very first time at your friend's house.
4. Your teacher gives you a present.
5. You see your boss in the morning.

a. おはようございます。**Ohayō gozaimasu.**

b. どうもありがとうございます。**Dōmo arigatō gozaimasu.**

c. どうもすみません。**Dōmo sumimasen.**

d. さようなら。**Sayōnara.**

e. はじめまして。**Hajimemashite.**

IN THIS CHAPTER

» **Conversing about your job and family**

» **Understanding the verbs for *to exist* and *to possess***

» **Using the verb *sumu* to relay where you live**

» **Discussing hobbies: sports, art, music, and games**

» **Expressing *to do* with suru and showing off what you can do**

Chapter **7**

Getting to Know You

O ften, the conversations you have when you first meet people consist of statements about what you do, your family, and where you're from. This small talk helps you get to know new people. In this chapter, I show you how to talk about all these topics so you can start making new Japanese connections. I also explain how to share your contact information so that you can keep in touch with your new friends.

REMEMBER

You can listen to all the Talkin' the Talk dialogues featured in this chapter. Go to www.dummies.com/go/japanese and click on the dialogue you want to hear.

Chatting about Your Life

After starting a conversation with the person seated next to you on a train or airplane, you can talk about what you do for a living. If you want, you can also talk about your family.

Your job

To ask other people about their **shigoto** (shee-goh-toh) (*jobs*), you say **O-shigoto wa nan desu ka.** (oh-shee-goh-toh wah nahn deh-soo kah.) (*What's your job?*), or you can use the abbreviated version, **O-shigoto wa.** (oh-shee-goh-toh wah.) (*How about your job?*). Following are some occupations you or your conversational partner may hold:

» 弁護士 **bengoshi** (behn-goh-shee) (*lawyer*)

» デザイナー **dezainā** (deh-zah-ee-nahh) (*designer*)

» 医者 **isha** (ee-shah) (*medical doctor*)

» 事務員 **jimuin** (jee-moo-een) (*secretary*)

» 看護師 **kangoshi** (kahn-goh-shee) (*nurse*)

» 経理士 **keirishi** (kehh-ree-shee) (*accountant*)

» 研究員 **kenkyūin** (kehn-kyooo-een) (*researcher*)

» コック **kokku** (kohk-koo) (*chef*)

» 教師 **kyōshi** (kyohh-shee) (*teacher*)

» 音楽家 **ongakuka** (ohn-gah-koo-kah) (*musician*)

» プログラマー **puroguramā** (poo-roh-goo-rah-mahh) (*programmer*)

» ウエーター **uētā** (oo-ehh-tahh) (*waiter*)

» ウエートレス **uētoresu** (oo-ehh-toh-reh-soo) (*waitress*)

These terms express specific roles and functions. If you just want to say that you work for a **kaisha** (kah-ee-shah) (*company*) or that you're an *office worker*, you can use the term **kaishain** (kah-ee-shah-een) (*company employee*). In fact, Japanese typically identify themselves as **kaishain** without specifying their specific job titles or roles in the **kaisha**.

Your family

Japanese has two terms for every one English word used to talk about one's family — a polite term and a plain term. Which version you use depends on the context. In this case, you choose from three possible contexts:

» When you refer to someone else's family, use the polite term.

» To talk about your own family members to nonfamily, use the plain term.

>> When you talk to any one of your older family members other than your spouse, or when you talk about them in an informal way, you should use the polite term. For example, you can call out for your mother by saying **Okāsan! Doko.** (oh-kahh-sahn! doh-koh.) (*Mom! Where are you?*)

Table 7-1 lists several terms you may want to use when talking about your family.

TABLE 7-1

Family Terms

English	Polite Term	Plain Term
family	ご家族 **go-kazoku** (goh-kah-zoh-koo)	家族 **kazoku** (kah-zoh-koo)
siblings	ご兄弟 **go-kyōdai** (goh-kyohh-dah-ee)	兄弟 **kyōdai** (kyohh-dah-ee)
parents	ご両親 **go-ryōshin** (goh-ryohh-sheen)	両親 **ryōshin** (ryohh-sheen)
father	お父さん **otōsan** (oh-tohh-sahn)	父 **chichi** (chee-chee)
mother	お母さん **okāsan** (oh-kahh-sahn)	母 **haha** (hah-hah)
older brother	お兄さん **onīsan** (oh-neee-sahn)	兄 **ani** (ah-nee)
older sister	お姉さん **onēsan** (oh-nehh-sahn)	姉 **ane** (ah-neh)
younger brother	弟さん **otōto-san** (oh-tohh-toh-sahn)	弟 **otōto** (oh-tohh-toh)
younger sister	妹さん **imōto-san** (ee-mohh-toh-sahn)	妹 **imōto** (ee-mohh-toh)
husband	ご主人 **go-shujin** (goh-shoo-jeen)	主人 or 夫 **otto** (oht-toh) *or* **shujin** (shoo-jeen)

(continued)

TABLE 7-1 *(continued)*

English	Polite Term	Plain Term
wife	奥さん **okusan** (oh-koo-sahn)	家内 or 妻 **tsuma** (tsoo-mah) *or* **kanai** (kah-nah-ee)
child	お子さん **okosan** (oh-koh-sahn)	子ども **kodomo** (koh-doh-moh)
son	息子さん **musuko-san** (moo-soo-koh-sahn)	息子 **musuko** (moo-soo-koh)
daughter	お嬢さん **ojōsan** (oh-johh-sahn)	娘 **musume** (moo-soo-meh)
grandfather	おじいさん **ojīsan** (oh-jeee-sahn)	祖父 **sofu** (soh-foo)
grandmother	おばあさん **obāsan** (oh-bahh-sahn)	祖母 **sobo** (soh-boh)
grandchild	お孫さん **omagosan** (oh-mah-goh-sahn)	孫 **mago** (mah-goh)
uncle	おじさん **ojisan** (oh-jee-sahn)	おじ **oji** (oh-jee)
aunt	おばさん **obasan** (oh-bah-sahn)	おば **oba** (oh-bah)
nephew	甥御さん **oigosan** (oh-ee-goh-sahn)	甥 **oi** (oh-ee)
niece	姪御さん **meigosan** (meh-ee-goh-sahn)	姪 **mei** (meh-ee)
cousin	おいとこさん **oitokosan** (oh-ee-toh-koh-sahn)	いとこ **itoko** (ee-toh-koh)

Additionally, you can refer to your in-laws by using 義理の **giri no** (gee-ree noh) before the terms in Table 7-1. For example

義理の母 **giri no haha** (gee-ree noh hah-hah) (*one's mother-in-law*)

義理のお母さん **giri no okāsan** (gee-ree noh oh-kahh-sahn) (*someone else's mother-in-law*)

義理の兄 **giri no ani** (gee-ree noh ah-nee) (*one's older brother-in-law*)

Existing and Possessing: The Verbs Iru and Aru

To tell someone that you have or possess something, have something to do, or have some relationship, use the verbs **iru** (ee-roo) and **aru** (ah-roo). They both mean *to exist*. That is, you use the verb *to exist* to mean *to have* in Japanese. I know it sounds strange, but it's just one of those things. Another strange concept is that you choose the verb according to whether the item you possess or that exists is animate or inanimate:

>> いる **Iru** is for animate items — things that can move by themselves, such as people and animals.

>> ある **Aru** is for inanimate items — things that don't move by themselves, such as books, money, plants, and houses.

So *I have a boyfriend.* is **Watashi wa kareshi ga iru.** (wah-tah-shee wah kah-reh-shee gah ee-roo.), which literally means *As for me, a boyfriend exists.* Similarly, *Alison has money.* is **Arison wa o-kane ga aru.** (ah-ree-sohn wah oh-kah-neh gah ah-roo.), which literally means *As for Alison, money exists.* Getting used to the *exist* business?

Now you can talk about what you have or don't have, using the verbs **iru** and **aru**. When you're speaking in a polite/neutral context, use the polite forms of the verbs — **imasu** (ee-mah-soo) and **arimasu** (ah-ree-mah-soo), respectively — which are both conjugated here. **Iru** is a **ru**-verb, but **aru** is an **u**-verb with a slight irregularity, so pay close attention to the negative form.

Japanese Script	Rōmaji	Pronunciation
いる	iru	ee-roo
いない	inai	ee-nah-ee
い(ます)	i (masu)	ee (-mah-soo)
いて	ite	ee-teh

Japanese Script	Rōmaji	Pronunciation
ある	aru	ah-roo
ない	nai	nah-ee
あり(ます)	ari (masu)	ah-ree (-mah-soo)
あって	atte	aht-the

REMEMBER

Don't forget to put the particle **ga** at the end of the object or animal you're claiming exists — the particle tells your listener what the subject of your sentence is.

Look at the following examples and think about what you have and what you don't have:

暇がありません。 **Hima ga arimasen.** (hee-mah gah ah-ree-mah-sehn.) (*I don't have free time.*)

ペットがいます。 **Petto ga imasu.** (peht-toh gah ee-mah-soo.) (*I have a pet.*)

私は兄弟がいません。 **Watashi wa kyōdai ga imasen.** (wah-tah-shee wah kyohh-dah-ee gah ee-mah-sehn.) (*I don't have siblings.*)

父はお金があります。 **Chichi wa o-kane ga arimasu.** (chee-chee wah oh-kah-neh gah ah-ree-mah-soo.) (*My father has money.*)

宿題があります。 **Shukudai ga arimasu.** (shoo-koo-dah-ee gah ah-ree-mah-soo.) (*I have homework.*)

The verbs **iru** and **aru** can also express the existence or the location of people and things. Just mark the item with the particle **wa** (wah) rather than **ga** (gah) and notice that the location is marked by **ni** (nee). For example

母はうちにいます。 **Haha wa uchi ni imasu.** (hah-hah wah oo-chee nee ee-mah-soo.) (*My mom is at home.*)

郵便局はあそこにあります。 **Yūbinkyoku wa asoko ni arimasu.** (yooo-been-kyoh-koo wah ah-soh-koh nee ah-ree-mah-soo.) (*The post office is over there.*)

Talkin' the Talk

Jason, a high-school student, visits the house of his classmate Ken for the first time. Ken's mother asks about Jason's family members.

Ken's mother: **Go-kyōdai wa.**
goh-kyohh-dah-ee wah.
Do you have any siblings?

Jason: **Ane ga imasu.**
ah-neh gah ee-mah-soo.
I have an older sister.

Jason shows a picture of his family to Ken's mother.

Jason: **Kore ga ane desu.**
koh-reh gah ah-neh deh-soo.
This one is my sister.

Ken's mother: **Ā, Jēson-san no onēsan desu ka. Kirei desu ne.**
ahh, jehh-sohn-sahn noh oh-nehh-sahn deh-soo kah. kee-rehh deh-soo ne.
Oh, this is your older sister. She is pretty, isn't she?

Jason: **Īe, zenzen.**
eee-eh, zehn-zehn.
No, not at all.

Ken's mother: **Onēsan no o-shigoto wa.**
oh-nehh-sahn noh oh-shee-goh-toh wah.
What is your sister's job?

Jason: **Opera kashu desu. Ima Igirisu ni sunde imasu.**
oh-peh-rah kah-shoo deh-soo. ee-mah ee-gee-ree-soo nee soon-deh ee-mah-soo.
She is an opera singer. She now lives in England.

Ken's mother: **Ā, sō desu ka. Ii desu ne!**
ahh, sohh deh-soo kah. eee deh-soo neh!
Oh, really? That's great!

WORDS TO KNOW

go-kyōdai	goh-kyohh-dah-ee	someone else's siblings
ane	ah-neh	one's own older sister
iru	ee-roo	to exist
onēsan	oh-nehh-sahn	someone else's older sister
kirei (na)	kee-rehh (nah)	pretty
shigoto	shee-goh-toh	job
opera kashu	oh-peh-rah kah-shoo	opera singer
sumu	soo-moo	to live
Igirisu	ee-gee-ree-soo	England
Ii desu ne!	eee deh-soo neh!	That's great!

**CULTURAL
WISDOM**

Japanese always praise others' family members, houses, clothes, and even pets, but when Japanese receive a compliment, they deny it no matter what. It's a part of Japanese modesty, but these responses sometimes puzzle non-Japanese who are used to saying or hearing *My mom is pretty* and *I love my house.* So when you speak with Japanese, say nice things about them, but be ready to hear them reject your compliments.

Specifying Where You Live with the Verb Sumu

To express where you live, use the verb **sumu** (soo-moo) (*to live*) and the particle **ni** (nee). Using this verb can be a little tricky. Remember to take the **te**-form of this verb and add the verb **iru** (ee-roo) (*to exist*) right after it, as in **sunde iru.** Of course, you can also use its polite counterpart, **imasu** (ee-mah-soo), as in **sunde imasu.** For example, **Tōkyō ni sunde imasu.** (tohh-kyohh nee soon-deh ee-mah-soo.) means *I live in Tokyo.* If you simply say **Tōkyō ni sumu** or **Tōkyō ni sumimasu**, it means *I will live in Tokyo.* rather than *I currently live in Tokyo.*

Here's the conjugation of the verb **sumu** (soo-moo) (*to live/reside*). It's an **u**–verb.

Japanese Script	Rōmaji	Pronunciation
住む	sumu	soo-moo
住まない	sumanai	soo-mah-nah-ee
住み(ます)	sumi (masu)	soo-mee (-mah-soo)
住んで	sunde	soon-deh

Finding Out about Your New Friend

After an introduction, chat a little so that you and your new acquaintance can get to know each other better. You can talk about where you're from and perhaps make a connection on that basis. A small conversation can mark the beginning of a friendship. The following sections show you how to ask where one is from and how to comment on someone's language skills — two topics that you can most likely talk about with your new friend.

REMEMBER

When someone is telling you something, you can't just stare at the person. You should nod to indicate that you are attentively listening! You can also say **Ā, sō desu ka.** (ahh, sohh deh-soo kah.), which means *Oh, is that so? Oh, really?* or *Oh, I see.* Or you can just say **Ā** (ahh), as you nod, to convey the same message. By doing so, you acknowledge the information given to you by your conversational partner. If you don't do it, your partner may start to think that you're feeling upset, being rude, or daydreaming.

Asking people where they're from

When you meet someone, a natural question is *Where are you from?* Pose this question by saying **Dochira kara desu ka.** (doh-chee-rah kah-rah deh-soo kah.) **Dochira** is the polite form of **doko** (doh-koh) (*where*). The particle **kara** means *from.* (I cover particles in Chapter 3.) To answer the question **Dochira kara desu ka,** you just replace **dochira** with a place name and drop the question particle **ka,** as Ken and Susan do in the nearby Talkin' the Talk dialogue.

GRAMMAR CHAT

Doesn't it make you feel that the world is small when you find out the person you've just met is from the same city or graduated from the same high school? In such contexts, you need to know how to say *Me too!* To say *too* or *also*, use the particle **mo** (moh). For example, **Watashi mo Tōkyō kara desu.** (wah-tah-shee moh tohh-kyohh kah-rah deh-soo.) (*I'm from Tokyo, too.*)

Talkin' the Talk

Ken Yamada has just introduced himself to Susan Brennan at their mutual friend's house. Ken asks Susan where she's from.

Ken: **Sūzan-san, Sūzan-san wa dochira kara desu ka.**
sooo-zahn-sahn, sooo-zahn-sahn wah doh-chee-rah kah-rah deh-soo kah.
Susan, where are you from?

Susan: **Watashi wa San Furanshisuko kara desu.**
wah-tah-shee wah sahn-foo-rahn-shee-soo-koh kah-rah deh-soo.
I'm from San Francisco.

Ken: **Hontō ni.**
hohn-tohh nee.
Really?

Susan: **Ē. Yamada-san wa.**
ehh. yah-mah-dah-sahn wah.
Yes. How about you, Mr. Yamada?

Ken: **Boku mo San Furanshisuko kara desu.**
boh-koo moh sahn-foo-rahn-shee-soo-koh kah-rah deh-soo.
I'm also from San Francisco.

Susan: **Ā, sō desu ka.**
ahh, sohh deh-soo kah.
Oh, really?

WORDS TO KNOW

dochira	doh-chee-rah	which way, where
kara	kah-rah	from
Hontō ni.	hohn-tohh nee.	Really?
Mo	moh	also
Ā, sō desu ka.	ahh, sohh deh-soo kah.	Oh, really?

In the preceding Talkin' the Talk, Ken uses **boku** (boh-koo) when referring to himself instead of saying **watashi** (wah-tah-shee). Men and boys often substitute **boku** for **watashi,** which is neither very formal nor very informal. (Turn to Chapter 3 to read about formal and informal speech styles.) Ken also says **Sūzan-san** twice, which may sound strange to you. The first **Sūzan-san** is to get Susan's attention, and the second **Sūzan-san** is used to mean *you*. See Chapter 3 for more on avoiding the pronoun **anata** (ah-nah-tah) (*you*).

Talking about your language skills

Whenever you speak **Nihongo** (nee-hohn-goh) (*the Japanese language*) to **Nihonjin** (nee-hohn-jeen) (*Japanese people*), they'll say **Nihongo ga jōzu desu ne!** (nee-hohn-goh gah johh-zoo deh-soo neh!) (*Your Japanese is great!*). Because Japan is a society where being bilingual is considered very special and admirable, Japanese people are always impressed if you speak Japanese. They appreciate your effort to study and use their language.

As a reply to a compliment on your Japanese skills, you can say **dōmo** (dohh-moh) (*thank you*), or you can choose one of the following modest phrases. It's up to you.

>> いいえ, 下手です。 **Īe, heta desu.** (eee-eh, heh-tah deh-soo.) (*No, I'm bad.*)

>> いいえ, まだまだです。 **Īe, madamada desu.** (eee-eh, mah-dah-mah-dah deh-soo.) (*No, not yet, not yet.*)

>> いいえ, ぜんぜん。 **Īe, zenzen.** (eee-eh, zehn-zehn.) (*No, not at all.*)

If you reply modestly using one of these expressions, the Japanese person will be further impressed by your ability and will praise your Japanese again. Don't feel like you need to keep denying your compliment forever, though. Try not to deny your compliment too many times. If you don't, your conversation partner will be exhausted! After a few times of denying, you can just smile and stop denying. These expressions are applicable for sports, artistic endeavors, music instruments, and other skill-based activities.

Even Japanese people who possess a very high degree of English proficiency often still say such modest phrases when they're complimented.

Talkin' the Talk

David has been studying Japanese for two years. He sits at the counter in a Japanese restaurant and chats with a Japanese waitress.

Waitress: **Nihongo ga jōzu desu ne!**
              nee-hohn-goh gah johh-zoo deh-soo neh!
              Your Japanese is excellent!

David: **Īe, madamada desu.**
              eee-eh, mah-dah-mah-dah deh-soo.
              No, not yet, not yet.

Waitress: **Nihonjin-mitai.**
              nee-hohn-jeen-mee-tah-ee.
              You're like a Japanese person.

David: **Sō desu ka.**
              sohh deh-soo kah.
              Is that so?

WORDS TO KNOW

Nihongo	nee-hohn-goh	Japanese language
jōzu (na)	johh-zoo (nah)	skilled
Nihonjin	nee-hohn-jeen	Japanese person
. . . mitai	mee-tah-ee	just like . . .

GRAMMAR
CHAT

When describing someone or something by saying (comparing) what he, she, or it is like, use **mitai** (mee–tah–ee) (*just like*), as in the following examples:

マイクさんは日本人みたいです。 **Maiku-san wa Nihonjin mitai desu.** (mah-ee-koo-sahn wa nee-hohn-jeen mee-tah-ee deh-soo.) (*Mike is just like a Japanese person.*)

このまんじゅうは花みたいです。 **Kono manjū wa hana mitai desu.** (koh-noh mahn-jooo wah hah-nah mee-tah-ee deh-soo.) (*This steamed bun looks like a flower.*)

私の彼氏はスーパーマンみたいです。 **Watashi no kareshi wa Sūpāman mitai desu!** (wah-tah-shee noh kah-reh-shee wah sooo-pahh-mahn mee-tah-ee deh-soo!) (*My boyfriend is like Superman!*)

Living the Sporting Life

Do you like to participate in **supōtsu** (soo-pohh-tsoo) (*sports*)? Or maybe you prefer to sit back and watch. **Yakyū** (yah-kyooo) (*baseball*) and **sakkā** (sahk-kahh) (*soccer*) are very popular sports in Japan. But Japanese also enjoy a wide variety of other sports. Here are some examples:

» バレーボール **barēbōru** (bah-rehh-bohh-roo) (*volleyball*)

» バスケットボール **basukettobōru** (bah-soo-keht-toh-bohh-roo) (*basketball*)

» フットボール **futtobōru** (foot-toh-bohh-roo) (*football*)

» ゴルフ **gorufu** (goh-roo-foo) (*golf*)

» 空手 **karate** (kah-rah-teh) (*karate*)

Using Your Artistic Talent

Don't be afraid of expressing your feelings and ideas artistically. Use your creativity. Which of the following art forms interests you?

» 油絵 **aburae** (ah-boo-rah-eh) (*oil painting*)

» 彫刻 **chōkoku** (chohh-koh-koo) (*sculpting/engraving*)

» 生け花 **ikebana** (ee-keh-bah-nah) (*flower arranging*)

» キルティング **kirutingu** (kee-roo-teen-goo) (*quilting*)

» クラフト **kurafuto** (koo-rah-foo-toh) (*crafting*)

» 折り紙 **origami** (oh-ree-gah-mee) (*origami*)

» 茶道 **sadō** *or* **chadō** (sah-dohh *or* chah-dohh) (*tea ceremony*)

» 書道 **shodō** (shoh-dohh) (*calligraphy*)

>> 水彩画 **suisaiga** (soo-ee-sah-ee-gah) (*watercolor painting*)

>> 墨絵 **sumie** (soo-mee-eh) (*ink painting*)

>> 陶芸 **tōgei** (tohh-gehh) (*pottery*)

Making Music with Instruments

Many Japanese kids take piano and violin lessons because being able to play classical music is considered sophisticated and desirable. But when they become teenagers, they may play the electric guitar in rock bands. That's fun, too! Do you play any of these musical instruments?

>> バイオリン **baiorin** (bah-ee-oh-reen) (*violin*)

>> チェロ **chero** (cheh-roh) (*cello*)

>> ドラム **doramu** (doh-rah-moo) (*drums*)

>> エレキギター **erekigitā** (eh-reh-kee gee-tahh) (*electric guitar*)

>> フルート **furūto** (foo-rooo-toh) (*flute*)

>> ギター **gitā** (gee-tahh) (*guitar*)

>> ピアノ **piano** (pee-ah-noh) (*piano*)

>> サクソフォン **sakusofon** (sah-koo-soh-fohn) (*saxophone*)

>> トランペット **toranpetto** (toh-rahn-peht-toh) (*trumpet*)

If you've seen old Japanese films or visited a traditional Japanese town, you've probably heard one of these Japanese musical instruments:

>> 琴 **koto** (koh-toh) (*long Japanese zither*)

>> 尺八 **shakuhachi** (shah-koo-hah-chee) (*Japanese end-blown flute*)

>> 三味線 **shamisen** (shah-mee-sehn) (*three-stringed Japanese banjo*)

>> 太鼓 **taiko** (tah-ee-koh) (*Japanese drums*)

>> 横笛 **yokobue** (yoh-koh-boo-eh) (*Japanese transverse flute*)

WARNING

Telling someone you play a specific instrument in Japanese isn't as simple as it is in English. Different types of musical instruments use different verbs to mean *to play*. For wind instruments, you use the verb **fuku** (foo-koo). So to *say I play the flute*, you'd say **furūto o fuku** (foo–rooo–toh oh foo–koo). For a stringed instrument or a keyboard, you use the verb **hiku** (hee-koo). So to say *I play the piano and the violin*, you'd say **piano o hiku** (pee-ah-noh oh hee-koo) and **baiorin o hiku** (bah-ee-oh-reen oh hee-koo), respectively. For drums, use the verb **tataku** (tah-tah-koo).

TIP

If you aren't sure or don't remember which verb to use for a musical instrument, you can use the verb **suru** (soo-roo). It's not perfect, but others will understand what you mean. For more information about the verb suru, see the upcoming section "Using the Verb Suru (to Do)."

GRAMMAR CHAT

Did your mother make you practice violin or piano when you were younger, like many Japanese moms do? If so, she probably forced you to. Express a command or give an order by using a verb in its stem form plus **-nasai**. For example, the stem form of the verb **suru** is **shi** (shee). So **Shinasai!** (shee-nah-sah-ee!) means *Do it!* It's an order. Now you're the boss and can order your child to do the following:

>> バイオリンを練習しなさい。**Baiorin o renshū shinasai!** (bah-ee-oh-reen oh rehn-shooo shee-nah-sah-ee!) (*Practice your violin!*)

>> 勉強しなさい。**Benkyō shinasai!** (behn-kyohh shee-nah-sah-ee!) (*Study!*)

>> 聞きなさい。**Kikinasai!** (kee-kee-nah-sah-ee!) (*Listen!*)

>> 掃除しなさい。**Sōji shinasai!** (sohh-jee shee-nah-sah-ee!) (*Clean!*)

Just don't use such commands with your spouse if you want to stay happily married.

Playing Games

You can always play a game when you have some free time. These games can make you forget about the real world for a while:

>> ボードゲーム **bōdo gēmu** (bohh-doh gehh-moo) (*board game*)

>> チェス **chesu** (cheh-soo) (*chess*)

>> 碁 **go** (goh) (*go [a kind of Japanese chess]*)

>> マージャン **mājan** (mahh-jahn) (*mahjong*)

>> パチンコ **pachinko** (pah-cheen-koh) (*a Japanese pinball game*)

>> トランプ **toranpu** (toh-rahn-poo) (*cards*)

When you want to say *to play a game*, use the verb **suru**, as in **chesu o suru** (cheh-soo oh soo-roo) (*to play chess*), and just conjugate **suru**.

CULTURAL WISDOM

Do you play games? Many people enjoy games on consoles such as PlayStation, Xbox, Switch, and even on smartphones. These games are generally called **gēmu** (ghee-mu) as in *game*. If someone says **gēmu-suru**, that's probably about video or computer games.

Using the Verb Suru (to Do)

The verb **suru** (soo-roo) (*to do*) is the most frequently used verb in Japanese. You can use **suru** for talking about doing many different types of recreational activities discussed in this chapter. To start with, conjugate the irregular verb **suru** as follows:

Japanese Script	Rōmaji	Pronunciation
する	suru	soo-roo
しない	shinai	shee-nah-ee
し(ます)	shi (masu)	shee (-mah-soo)
して	shite	shee-teh

You can use **suru** to express many recreational activities, from sports to sightseeing:

>> 電話をする **denwa o suru** (dehn-wah oh soo-roo) (*to telephone someone*)

>> 買い物をする **kaimono o suru** (kah-ee-moh-noh oh soo-roo) (*to do the shopping*)

>> 観光をする **kankō o suru** (kahn-kohh oh soo-roo) (*to go sightseeing*)

>> 空手をする **karate o suru** (kah-rah-teh oh soo-roo) (*to do karate*)

>> 料理をする **ryōri o suru** (ryohh-ree oh soo-roo) (*to cook*)

>> テニスをする **tenisu o suru** (teh-nee-soo oh soo-roo) (*to play tennis*)

>> トランプをする **toranpu o suru** (toh-rahn-poo oh soo-roo) (*to play cards*)

>> 釣りをする **tsuri o suru** (tsoo-ree oh soo-roo) (*to fish*)

>> 山登りをする **yamanobori o suru** (yah-mah-noh-boh-ree oh soo-roo) (*to mountain climb*)

The verb **suru** also follows some English loan words. These words are pretty easy to understand even without the translation.

» チェックする **chekku suru** (chehk-koo soo-roo) (*to check*)

» キャンセルする **kyanseru suru** (kyahn-seh-roo soo-roo) (*to cancel*)

» リラックスする **rirakkusu suru** (ree-rahk-koo-soo soo-roo) (*to relax*)

Saying "I Can"

GRAMMAR CHAT

Japanese doesn't have a convenient word like *can*. To say that you *can do* something rather than that you *do* something, add a suffix (**-eru** or **-rareru**) to the verb. You need to do a little surgery on the verb to securely attach the suffix. (Don't worry; verbs don't bleed.) The particular suffix and the amount of verb surgery necessary both depend on the class of the verb.

» If the verb is an **u**-verb, remove the **u** at the end of the verb in the dictionary form and add **-eru**. For example, **aruku** (ah-roo-koo) (*to walk*) is an **u**-verb. Removing the final **u** and adding **-eru** gives you **arukeru** (ah-roo-keh-roo). **Aruku** means *I walk,* but **arukeru** means *I can walk.*

» If the verb is a **ru**-verb, remove the **ru** at the end of the verb in the dictionary form and add **-rareru**. For example, the verb **okiru** (oh-kee-roo) (*to sit up*) is a **ru**-verb. Removing the **ru** and adding **-rareru** gives you **okirareru** (oh-kee-rah-reh-roo). **Okirareru** means *I can sit up.*

The only necessary sound adjustment in this whole process is to change **ts** to **t** before adding **-eru** in verbs ending in **tsu (tsoo).** So the *can* form of the verb **motsu** (moh-tsoo) (*to hold*) is **moteru** (moh-teh-roo) (*can hold*), not **motseru** (moh-tseh-roo). That doesn't mean that **motsu** is an irregular verb; it's actually regular. **Tse** (tseh) just isn't an authentic Japanese sound, so it gets simplified to **te** (teh). That's a reasonable and minor sound adjustment, right?

Two of the major irregular verbs, **suru** (see the preceding section) and **kuru** (koo-roo) (*to come*), undergo major changes in the *can* situation. The *can* form of the verb **suru** is actually a substitution with the verb **dekiru** (deh-kee-roo) (*can do*) taking its place. The *can* form of **kuru** is **korareru** (koh-rah-reh-roo) (*can come*).

When you use the *can* form of a verb in a sentence, replace the direct object particle **o** (oh) with the particle **ga** (gah). (See Chapter 3 for more on the particles **o** and **ga**.) I know — it's not a subject, but you mark it with the particle **ga** anyway. Strange, isn't it? So **Sushi o tsukuru.** (soo-shee oh tsoo-koo-roo.) means *You make sushi.*, but **Sushi ga tsukureru.** (soo-shee gah tsoo-koo-reh-roo.) means *You can make sushi.* After you create a can-form, such as **tsukureru**, treat it as an independent verb and conjugate it as a **ru**-verb. Right, **tsukureru, tsukurenai, tsukure (masu),** and **tsukurete!** (For a refresher on how to conjugate **ru**-verbs, check out Chapter 3.) These examples help you express who can and can't do what:

> アダムは空手ができます。**Adamu wa karate ga dekimasu.** (ah-dah-moo wah kah-rah-teh gah deh-kee-mah-soo.) (*Adam can do karate.*)

> 私は箸が使えません。**Watashi wa hashi ga tsukaemasen.** (wah-tah-shee wah hah-shee gah tsoo-kah-eh-mah-sehn.) (*I can't use chopsticks.*)

> 父は日本語が話せません。でも, 中国語が話せます。**Chichi wa Nihongo ga hanasemasen. Demo, Chūgokugo ga hanasemasu.** (chee-chee wah nee-hohn-goh gah han-nah-seh-mah-sehn. deh-moh, chooo-goh-koo-goh gah hah-nah-seh-mah-soo.) (*My father can't speak Japanese. However, he can speak Chinese.*)

What? You can only speak English? To say *only* in Japanese, you add the particle **shika** (shee-kah) to the end of the noun and make the verb negative. (Don't forget to make the verb negative because **shika** and the negative verb work together to mean *only*.) Also, if **shika** follows the subject particle **ga** or the object particle **o**, you drop the particle; other particles stay, as the following examples show:

> 私は英語しか話せません。**Watashi wa eigo shika hanasemasen.** (wah-tah-shee wah ehh-goh shee-kah hah-nah-seh-mah-sehn.) (*I can only speak English.*)

> 田中さんしか来られませんでした。**Tanaka-san shika koraremasendeshita.** (tah-nah-kah-sahn shee-kah koh-rah-reh-mah-sehn-deh-shee-tah.) (*Only Mr. Tanaka could come.*)

> 明子さんは野菜しか食べられません。**Akiko-san wa yasai shika taberaremasen.** (ah-kee-koh-sahn wah yah-sah-ee shee-kah tah-beh-rah-reh-mah-sehn.) (*Akiko can only eat vegetables.*)

> ふぐはレストランでしか食べません。**Fugu wa resutoran de shika tabemasen.** (foo-goo wah reh-soo-toh-rahn deh shee-kah tah-beh-mah-sehn.) (*I eat blowfish at a restaurant only.*)

> テニスは父としかしません。**Tenisu wa chichi to shika shimasen.** (teh-nee-soo wah chee-chee toh shee-kah shee-mah-sehn.) (*I play tennis with my father only.*)

FUN & GAMES

Match these family members with the words that identify them. Refer to Appendix C for the answers.

Illustration by Elizabeth Kurtzman

a. お母さん **okāsan**

b. お姉さん **onēsan**

c. おばあさん **obāsan**

d. お父さん **otōsan**

Chapter **8**

Asking for Directions

I f you can ask for directions in Japanese, you're ready to go anywhere in Japan. Japanese will enjoy talking to you and offering their help. This chapter gives you the words and phrases necessary for receiving directions.

You can listen to all the Talkin' the Talk dialogues featured in this chapter. Go to www.dummies.com/go/japanese and click on the dialogue you want to hear.

REMEMBER

Figuring Out Where Places Are Located

One of the most basic questions to help you get where you need to go is *where*. If you can't ask "where" questions and understand the answers, you'll probably be spending a lot of time at home. That's no good, so the following sections help you ask where things are located so that you aren't stuck in the house.

Asking "where" questions

Suppose you want to go to the city hall. You know it's near the subway station, but you can't see it. What do you do? Suppose you want to go City Hall. You know it's near the subway station, but you can't see it. What would you do? Well, let's find a kind stranger and ask for directions!

Where in Japanese is **doko** (doh-koh). But you can't just say **doko**. You'll sound like you have a very bad concussion and don't know where you are. Mention what you're looking for first — for example, **shiyakusho** (shee-yah-koo-shoh) (*city hall*).

Put the topic particle **wa** after the place you're looking for. Then add **doko desu ka** (doh-koh deh-soo kah) (*where is*) or **doko ni arimasu ka** (doh-koh nee ah-ree-mah-soo kah) (*where is it located*). You can use either one, but **doko desu ka** is shorter and probably easier for you to say. Here are a couple of examples of how to form "where" questions:

病院はどこですか。**Byōin wa doko desu ka.** (byohh-een wah doh-koh deh-soo kah.) (*Where is the hospital?*)

銀行はどこにありますか。**Ginkō wa doko ni arimasu ka.** (geen-kohh wah doh-koh nee ah-ree-mah-soo kah.) (*Where is the bank located?*)

The places you want to look for may include the following:

>> アメリカ大使館 **Amerika taishikan** (ah-meh-ree-kah tah-ee-shee-kahn) (*American embassy*)

>> バス停 **basu-tei** (bah-soo-tehh) (*bus stop*)

>> 病院 **byōin** (byohh-een) (*hospital*)

>> 映画館 **eigakan** (ehh-gah-kahn) (*movie theater*)

>> 駅 **eki** (eh-kee) (*train/subway station*)

>> 学校 **gakkō** (gahk-kohh) (*school*)

>> ガソリンスタンド **gasorin sutando** (gah-soh-reen soo-tahn-doh) (*gas station*)

>> 銀行 **ginkō** (geen-kohh) (*bank*)

>> 博物館 **hakubutsukan** (hah-koo-boo-tsoo-kahn) (*museum*)

>> コンビニ **konbini** (kohn-bee-nee) (*convenience store*)

>> ドラッグストアー **doraggu sutoā** (doh-rahg-goo soo-toh-ahh) (*drugstore*)

>> 市役所 **shiyakusho** (shee-yah-koo-shoh) (*city hall*)

>> 図書館 **toshokan** (toh-shoh-kahn) (*library*)

>> 役場 **yakuba** (yah-koo-bah) (*town hall*)

>> 郵便局 **yūbinkyoku** (yooo-been-kyoh-koo) (*post office*)

Getting basic location/position answers

REMEMBER

The easiest way to answer "where" questions is to point and say "there," so many Japanese whom you ask for directions will simply point their index fingers while saying **Asoko desu.** (ah-soh-koh deh-soo.) (*It's over there.*). Other location words you may hear in conjunction with pointing are **koko** (koh-koh) and **soko** (soh-koh). (Notice how they all end in **oko?**) Table 8-1 shows you what each word means in English and the location it refers to.

TABLE 8-1

Pronouns for Location

Japanese	Pronunciation	English	Location
ここ **koko**	koh-koh	*here*	*near the speaker*
そこ **soko**	soh-koh	*there; near you*	*near the listener but far from the speaker*
あそこ **asoko**	ah-soh-koh	*over there*	*far from both the speaker and the listener*

If pointing and the short location words in Table 8-1 aren't sufficient, your helper may describe the location with some of the position words in Table 8-2.

WARNING

You use **tonari** (toh-nah-ree) (*next to*) only if you're dealing with two similar things like two buildings, two people, or two seats. For two different things that are close to each other, you use **yoko** (yoh-koh) to express *next to*. For example, if you want to say *There is a police officer next to the museum.* in Japanese, say **Keisatsukan ga hakubutsukan no yoko ni imasu.** (kehh-sah-tsoo-kahn gah hah-koo-boo-tsoo-kahn noh yoh-koh nee ee-mah-soo.).

GRAMMAR CHAT

You can't use one of the position words in Table 8-2 all by itself to describe the location of something. If you say *My house is on the left,* no one will understand you. You have to indicate what your house is to the left of as a reference point. Use the particle **no** to create a modifier phrase that gives the reference point, and place it right before one of the position words from Table 8-2. For example, **ginkō no hidari** means *the bank's left,* or *to the left of the bank.* Remember: The position **aida** (*between*) requires two reference points; connect them with the particle **to.**

TABLE 8-2

Position Words

Position Phrase	Pronunciation	English
間 **aida**	ah-ee-dah	*between*
近く **chikaku**	chee-kah-koo	*near*
反対(側) **hantai (gawa)**	hahn-tah-ee (gah-wah)	*opposite (side)*
左(側) **hidari (gawa)**	hee-dah-ree (gah-wa)	*left (side)*
前 **mae**	mah-eh	*front*
右(側) **migi (gawa)**	mee-gee (gah-wah)	*right (side)*
向かい(側) **mukai (gawa)**	moo-kah-ee (gah-wah)	*across the street from/facing to*
そば **soba**	soh-bah	*right near*
後ろ **ushiro**	oo-shee-roh	*behind*
横 **yoko**	yoh-koh	*side*

The following phrases put some of these modifiers in context:

図書館は学校の後ろです。**Toshokan wa gakkō no ushiro desu.** (toh-shoh-kahn wah gahk-kohh noh oo-shee-roh deh-soo.) (*The library is behind the school.*)

郵便局は図書館と市役所の間です。**Yūbinkyoku wa toshokan to shiyakusho no aida desu.** (yooo-been-kyoh-koo wah toh-shoh-kahn toh shee-yah-koo-shoh noh ah-ee-dah deh-soo.) (*The post office is between the library and the city hall.*)

学校は病院の前です。**Gakkō wa byōin no mae desu.** (gah-kohh wah byohh-een noh mah-eh deh-soo.) (*The school is in front of the hospital.*)

銀行は病院の隣です。**Ginkō wa byōin no tonari desu.** (geen-kohh wah byohh-een noh toh-nah-ree deh-soo.) (*The bank is next to the gas station.*)

Specifying how far or how near you are to a location is often very helpful information. The word for *far* is **tōi** (tohh-ee), and the word for *near* is **chikai** (chee-kah-ee). To be more informative, you can use adverbs such as **chotto** (choht-toh) (*a little bit*), **sugu** (soo–goo) (*right, just*), or **totemo** (toh-teh–moh) (*very much*). Take a look at these examples:

> ちょっと遠いですよ。 **Chotto tōi desu yo.** (choht-toh tohh-ee deh-soo yoh.) (*It's a bit far.*)

> すぐそこです。 **Sugu soko desu.** (soo-goo soh-koh deh-soo.) (*It's right there.*)

> とても近いです。 **Totemo chikai desu.** (toh-teh-moh chee-kah-ee deh-soo.) (*It's very close.*)

REMEMBER

Desu is used a lot for expressing locations, but it also expresses the identity, property, characteristics, or the state of people and things. To see how to conjugate **desu,** turn to Chapter 3. For examples of **desu** in action, check out the following list:

> 私は学生です。 **Watashi wa gakusei desu.** (wah-tah-shee wah gah-koo-sehh deh-soo.) (*I'm a student.*)

> 恵美さんは優しいです。 **Emi-san wa yasashii desu.** (eh-mee-sahn wah yah-sah-sheee deh-soo.) (*Emi is kind.*)

> すしはおいしいです。 **Sushi wa oishii desu.** (soo-shee wah oh-ee-sheee deh-soo.) (*Sushi is delicious.*)

> 今日は寒いです。 **Kyō wa samui desu.** (kyohh wah sah-moo-ee deh-soo.) (*It is cold today.*)

Talkin' the Talk

Ben is looking for a subway station. He asks a woman where it is.

Ben:	**Sumimasen. Chikatetsu no eki wa doko desu ka.** soo-mee-mah-sehn. chee-kah-teh-tsoo noh eh-kee wah doh-koh deh-soo kah. *Excuse me. Where is the subway station?*
Woman:	**Chikatetsu no eki wa asoko desu.** chee-kah-teh-tsoo noh eh-kee wah ah-soh-koh deh-soo. *The subway station is over there.*
Ben:	**Ano hon'ya no tonari desu ka.** ah-noh hohn-yah noh toh-nah-ree deh-soo kah. *The one next to the bookstore?*

Woman:	**Hai.**
	hah-ee.
	Right.

Ben:	**Arigatō gozaimashita.**
	ah-ree-gah-tohh goh-zah-ee-mah-shee-tah.
	Thank you very much.

Woman:	**Īe.**
	eee-eh.
	No problem.

WORDS TO KNOW

chikatetsu no eki	chee-kah-teh-tsoo noh eh-kee	subway station
doko	doh-koh	where
asoko desu	ah-soh-koh deh-soo	over there
hon'ya	hohn-yah	bookstore
tonari	toh-nah-ree	next to

Pinpointing an exact location

Having someone tell you that the bank is "over there" is all well and good, but it's not effective when you can't easily tell where "over there" is. To be really helpful, directions have to pinpoint specific locations unambiguously. Words and phrases such as *north*, *the third building*, and *five minutes' walk* all help to clarify where something is located. I give you the words you need in the sections that follow.

Using cardinal points

Migi (mee-gee) (*right*) and **hidari** (hee-dah-ree) (*left*) are great. However, after you turn 180 degrees or make a couple of lefts and rights, you may get confused. To avoid any confusion, your helper may specify *cardinal points* such as north and east and *ordinal points* such as northwest and southwest.

>> 東 **higashi** (hee-gah-shee) (*east*)

>> 北 **kita** (kee-tah) (*north*)

>> 南 **minami** (mee-nah-mee) (*south*)

>> 西 **nishi** (nee-shee) (*west*)

>> 北西 **hokusei** (hoh-koo-sehh) (*northwest*)

>> 北東 **hokutō** (hoh-koo-tohh) (*northeast*)

>> 南西 **nansei** (nahn-sehh) (*southwest*)

>> 南東 **nantō** (nahn-tohh) (*southeast*)

Specifying the order

Ordinal–number phrases such as *the first* and *the second* are essential for pin-pointing houses, buildings, intersections, and streets. Remember that you can convert quantity phrases into ordinal–number phrases just by adding **-me** (meh) after them. (Go to Chapter 4 for more information on ordinal numbers.)

2つ目の交差点 **futa-tsu-me no kōsaten** (foo-tah-tsoo-meh noh kohh-sah-tehn) (*the second intersection*)

1つ目の建物 **hito-tsu-me no tatemono** (hee-toh-tsoo-meh noh tah-teh-moh-noh) (*the first building*)

右側の3つ目の家 **migi gawa no mit-tsu-me no ie** (mee-gee gah-wah noh meet-tsoo-meh noh ee-eh) (*the third house on the right-hand side*)

4本目の道 **yon-hon-me no michi** (yohn-hohn-meh noh mee-chee) (*the fourth street*)

Stating how far

You can express how far away a location is by specifying either the time it takes to get somewhere or the actual distance. In urban areas in Japan, many people use public transportation instead of automobiles. As a result, directions often include an estimate of the number of minutes it would take to walk from the nearest station. Japanese use the counters **-fun** (foon) for *minutes* and **-jikan** (jee-kahn) for *hours*. Following are a few examples:

ここから駅まで10分です。 **Koko kara eki made 10-pun desu.** (koh-koh kah-rah eh-kee mah-deh joop-poon deh-soo.) (*The train station is ten minutes away from here.*)

歩いて30分です。 **Aruite 30-pun desu.** (ah-roo-ee-teh sahn-joop-poon deh-soo.) (*Thirty minutes on foot.*)

空港までバスで1時間です。 **Kūkō made basu de ichi-jikan desu.** (kooo-kohh mah-deh bah-soo deh ee-chee-jee-kahn deh-soo.) (*It's an hour to the airport by bus.*)

東京から新幹線で2時間です。 **Tōkyō kara shinkansen de ni-jikan desu.** (tohh-kyohh kah-rah sheen-kahn-sehn deh nee-jee-kahn deh-soo.) (*It takes two hours from Tokyo by Shinkansen [bullet train].*)

Of course, you can also specify the actual distance. For example, **Eki made ni-kiro desu.** (eh-kee mah-deh nee-kee-roh deh-soo.) means *It's two kilometers to the railway station.*

To say *approximately* or *about*, you add **gurai** (goo-rah-ee) after the time or distance expression, as in the following examples:

> ここから車で5分ぐらいです。**Koko kara kuruma de go-fun gurai desu.** (koh-koh kah-rah koo-roo-mah deh goh-foon goo-rah-ee deh-soo.) (*It's about five minutes from here by car.*)

> ここから1マイルぐらいです。**Koko kara ichi-mairu gurai desu.** (koh-koh kah-rah ee-chee mah-ee-roo goo-rah-ee deh-soo.) (*It's about one mile from here.*)

Some people say **kurai** (koo-rah-ee) rather than **gurai,** but younger people tend to say **gurai** more frequently than they say **kurai.**

Talkin' the Talk

Masako is looking for the post office. She asks a man on the street to help her.

Masako:	**Sumimasen. Yūbinkyoku wa chikaku ni arimasu ka.**
	soo-mee-mah-sehn. yooo-been-kyoh-koo wah chee-kah-koo nee ah-ree-mah-soo kah.
	Excuse me. Is there a post office nearby?
Man	**Ē. Aruite 5-fun desu yo.**
	ehh. ah-roo-ee-teh goh-foon deh-soo yoh.
	Yes. Just a 5-minute walk.
Masako:	**Ā, sō desu ka.**
	ahh, sohh deh-soo kah.
	Oh, really?
Man:	**Koko kara mittsu-me no kōsaten desu.**
	koh-koh kah-rah meet-tsoo-meh noh kohh-sah-tehn deh-soo.
	It's at the third intersection from here.
Masako:	**Higashi gawa desu ka.**
	hee-gah-shee gah-wah deh-soo kah.
	Is it on the east side?

Man:	**Īe. Nishi gawa desu.**
	eee-eh. nee-shee gah-wah deh-soo.
	No, it's on the west side.
Masako:	**Ā, dōmo.**
	ahh, dohh-moh.
	Oh, thanks.
Man:	**Īe.**
	eee-eh.
	No problem.

WORDS TO KNOW

yūbinkyoku	yooo-been-kyoh-koo	post office
chikaku	chee-kah-koo	nearby
ni arimasu	nee ah-ree-mah-soo	to be located at
mittsu-me	meet-tsoo-meh	third
kōsaten	kohh-sah-tehn	intersection
koko kara	koh-koh kah-rah	from here
higashi gawa	hee-gah-shee gah-wah	east side
nishi gawa	nee-shee gah-wah	west side

Finding Your Way to Your Destination

"Where" questions are great, but after you know the where, you probably also want to know how to get there. In the following sections, I help you get the information you need to get where you're going.

Requesting travel instructions

You can ask a fellow traveler at the bus stop or in the train or subway station for directions. Chances are you'll find someone who is heading in the same direction as you. If so, your journey will become easier and more fun. Just follow your new best friend (cautiously, of course).

To ask "how do I get to . . ." questions, use the question word **dōyatte** (dohh-yaht-teh) (*how*). Place it right after the destination phrase and the particle **wa** (wah) in the question. You can see it in the following examples:

アメリカ大使館はどうやって行くんですか。**Amerika taishikan wa dōyatte iku-n-desu ka.** (ah-meh-ree-kah tah-ee-shee-kahn wah dohh-yaht-teh ee-koon-deh-soo kah.) (*How do I get to the American embassy?*)

市役所はどうやって行くんですか。**Shiyakusho wa dōyatte iku-n-desu ka.** (shee-yah-koo-shoh wah dohh-yaht-teh ee-koon-deh-soo kah.) (*How do I get to city hall?*)

TIP

You may be asking about a very specific location, like a restaurant called Fuji. Before asking *How can I get to Fuji?*, you may want to ask *Do you know the restaurant called Fuji?* This way, the person knows you aren't talking about the famous mountain but rather a restaurant. To ask *do you know*, say **shitte imasu ka** (sheet-teh ee-mah-soo kah). To say *. . . called . . .*, say the proper name, followed by **to iu** (toh ee-oo *or* toh yooo) and the kind of location (in this case, a restaurant), as in **Fuji to iu resutoran** (foo-jee toh ee-oo reh-soo-toh-rahn) (*a restaurant called Fuji*). You can use this construction for asking about things other than directions, too:

由紀さんという人を知っていますか。**Yuki-san to iu hito o shitte imasu ka.** (yoo-kee sahn toh ee-oo hee-toh oh sheet-teh ee-mah-soo kah.) (*Do you know the person called Yuki?*)

岡崎というところを知っていますか。**Okazaki to iu tokoro o shitte imasu ka.** (oh-kah-zah-kee toh ee-oo toh-koh-roh oh sheet-teh ee-mah-soo kah.) (*Do you know the place called Okazaki?*)

たこ焼きという食べ物を知っていますか。**Takoyaki to iu tabemono o shitte imasu ka.** (tah-koh-yah-kee toh ee-oo tah-beh-moh-noh oh sheet-teh ee-mah-soo kah.) (*Do you know the food called takoyaki?*)

Finding out whether you need transportation to get to your destination is always a good idea. Ask whether your destination is within walking distance. Use the **u**-verb **aruku** (ah-roo-koo) (*to walk*) in the "can" form in this case. (Check out Chapter 7 for a discussion of this verb form.)

ここから秋葉原まで歩けますか。**Koko kara Akihabara made arukemasu ka.** (koh-koh kah-rah ah-kee-hah-bah-rah mah-deh ah-roo-keh-mah-soo kah.) (*Can I walk to Akihabara from here?*)

市役所は歩いて行けますか。**Shiyakusho wa aruite ikemasu ka.** (shee-yah-koo-shoh wah ah-roo-ee-teh ee-keh-mah-soo kah.) (*Can I get to city hall on foot?*)

If your destination isn't within walking distance, ask which transportation method to use. Chapter 14 shows you how to ask "which" questions and has an extensive inventory of transportation terms.

Referring to landmarks

When giving directions, people often include several landmarks that the traveler has to pass to get to his destination. In Japan, many streets do not have names, so landmarks and buildings (such as banks, department stores, convenience stores, parks, and other noticeable places) are important points of reference. Table 8-3 provides some common visible and semi-permanent landmarks.

TABLE 8-3

Landmarks

Landmark	Pronunciation	English
踏み切り **fumikiri**	foo-mee-kee-ree	*railway crossing*
橋 **hashi**	hah-shee	*bridge*
go **ichiji teishi** *or* 止まれ **tomare**	ee-chee-jee tehh-shee *or* toh-mah-reh	*stop sign*
角 **kado**	kah-doh	*corner*
交差点 **kōsaten**	kohh-sah-tehn	*intersection*
道 **michi**	mee-chee	*road*
信号 **shingō**	sheen-gohh	*traffic light*
通り **tōri**	tohh-ree	*street*
突き当り **tsukiatari**	tsoo-kee-ah-tah-ree	*end of the street*

TIP

As in English, **michi** (mee-chee) (*road*) and **tōri** (tohh-ree) (*street*) are subtly different. They both have two functions — to connect locations and to accommodate stores and houses. And though they each perform both functions, the emphasis of **michi** is on the connection and the emphasis of **tōri** is on the accommodation of shops or homes.

REMEMBER

You can combine landmarks with the ordinal numbers introduced in Chapter 4 to give pretty specific directions, such as **mit-tsu-me no shingō** (meet-tsoo-meh noh sheen-gohh) (*the third traffic light*) or **itsu-tsu-me no kado** (ee-tsoo-tsoo-meh noh kah-doh) (*the fifth corner*).

Providing actions with directions

Most people use an imperative like *Go straight on this street for five minutes* or a request sentence such as *Please make a turn at the second intersection.* In Japanese, directions use a *request sentence* that consists of a verb in the **te**-form and **kudasai** (koo-dah-sah-ee). **Kudasai** literally means *Give it to me* (or *to us*), but when used right after a verb in the **te**-form, it basically means *Do [such and such], please.* (Literally: *Do [such and such] and give that to me as a favor.*) It creates a polite request sentence.

Conjugating verbs to the **te**-form is the first step of making a request sentence. You can look at Chapter 3 to find out how to get the **te**-form, but for your convenience, I list the dictionary forms and the **te**-forms of the verbs that you need for giving directions in Table 8-4.

TABLE 8-4

Verbs for Giving Directions

Dictionary Form	Te-Form	English
歩く **aruku** (ah-roo-koo)	歩いて **aruite** (ah-roo-ee-teh)	*to walk*
行く **iku** (ee-koo)	行って **itte** (eet-teh)	*to go*
くだる **kudaru** (koo-dah-roo)	くだって **kudatte** (koo-daht-teh)	*to go down*
曲がる **magaru** (mah-gah-roo)	曲がって **magatte** (mah-gaht-teh)	*to make a turn*
のぼる **noboru** (noh-boh-roo)	のぼって **nobotte** (noh-boht-teh)	*to go up*
乗る **noru** (noh-roo)	乗って **notte** (noht-teh)	*to get on*
降りる **oriru** (oh-ree-roo)	降りて **orite** (oh-ree-teh)	*to get off, to go down*
過ぎる **sugiru** (soo-gee-roo)	過ぎて **sugite** (soo-gee-teh)	*to pass*
渡る **wataru** (wah-tah-roo)	渡って **watatte** (wah-taht-teh)	*to cross*

Of course, a person giving you directions needs to be able to tell you exactly where to go and how. Where do you make a turn? What kind of place do you cross? Which street do you take? The Japanese language specifies these locations by marking them with the particle **o** directly following the word for the location or landmark. (A smart person like you may wonder why you need the direct object particle **o** here, but let the scholars of grammar wonder about that.)

交差点を曲がる **kōsaten o magaru** (kohh-sah-tehn oh mah-gah-roo) (*to make a turn at the intersection*)

橋を渡る **hashi o wataru** (hah-shee oh wah-tah-roo) (*to cross the bridge*)

この道を歩く **kono michi o aruku** (koh-noh mee-chee oh ah-roo-koo) (*to walk along this road*)

銀行を過ぎる **ginkō o sugiru** (geen-kohh oh soo-gee-roo) (*to pass the bank*)

Specify the direction of your movement by marking it with the particle **ni**.

右に曲がる **migi ni magaru** (mee-gee nee mah-gah-roo) (*to make a right turn*)

東に行く **higashi ni iku** (hee-gah-shee nee ee-koo) (*to go east*)

Here are a few sample directions that put all these concepts together:

三番通りを南に行ってください。 **San-ban-dōri o minami ni itte kudasai.** (sahn-bahn-dohh-ree oh mee-nah-mee nee eet-teh koo-dah-sah-ee.) (*Go south on Third Street, please.*)

あの角を右に曲がってください。 **Ano kado o migi ni magatte kudasai.** (ah-noh kah-doh oh mee-gee nee mah-gaht-teh koo-dah-sah-ee.) (*Please make a right at that corner.*)

駅まで歩いてください。 **Eki made aruite kudasai.** (eh-kee mah-deh ah-roo-ee-teh koo-dah-sah-ee.) (*Walk to the railway station, please.*)

新橋から浅草線に乗ってください。 **Shinbashi kara Asakusa-sen ni notte kudasai.** (sheen-bah-shee kah-rah ah-sah-koo-sah-sehn nee noht-teh koo-dah-sah-ee.) (*Take Asakusa-line from Shinbashi, please.*)

Making directions flow

To make directions flow, Japanese connect them with the word **sorekara** (soh-reh-kah-rah) (*and then*), as in these examples:

この道をまっすぐ行ってください。それから, 三つ目の角を右に曲がってください。 **Kono michi o massugu itte kudasai. Sorekara, mit-tsu-me no kado o migi ni magatte kudasai.** (koh-noh mee-chee oh mahs-soo-goo eet-teh koo-dah-sah-ee.

soh-reh-kah-rah, meet-tsoo-meh noh kah-doh oh mee-gee-nee mah-gaht-teh koo-dah-sah-ee.) (*Go straight on this street and then make a right at the third corner.*)

橋を渡ってください。それから, 交番を過ぎてください。**Hashi o watatte kudasai. Sorekara, kōban o sugite kudasai.** (hah-shee oh wah-taht-teh koo-dah-sah-ee. soh-reh-kah-rah, kohh-bahn oh soo-gee-teh koo-dah-sah-ee.) (*Cross the bridge and then pass the kōban [police box].*)

They may also say **sōsuruto** (sohh-soo-roo-toh) (*then*, Literally: *if you do so*) to show what you will see afterward. For example, **Fumikiri o watatte kudasai; sōsuruto, hidari ni resutoran ga arimasu.** (foo-mee-kee-ree oh wah-taht-teh koo-dah-sah-ee; sohh-soo-roo-toh, hee-dah-ree nee reh-soo-toh-rahn gah ah-ree-mah-soo.) translates to *Please cross the railroad crossing; then you'll see a restaurant on your left.*

............Talkin' the Talk............

Ben is looking for a restaurant called Shiro. He asks a stranger on the street for directions.

Ben:	**Sumimasen. Shiro to iu resutoran o shitte imasu ka.** soo-mee-mah-sehn. shee-roh toh ee-oo reh-soo-toh-rahn oh sheet-teh ee-mah-soo kah. *Excuse me. Do you know the restaurant called Shiro?*
Woman:	**Hai.** hah-ee. *Yes.*
Ben:	**Dōyatte iku-n-desu ka.** dohh-yaht-teh ee-koon-deh-soo kah. *How can I get there?*
Woman:	**Tsugi no kōsaten o hidari ni magatte kudasai.** tsoo-gee noh kohh-sah-tehn oh hee-dah-ree nee mah-gaht-teh koo-dah-sah-ee. *Make a left turn at the next intersection.*

Ben:	**Ano shingō no kōsaten desu ne.**
	ah-noh sheen-gohh noh kohh-sah-tehn deh-soo neh.
	The one with the traffic light over there, right?
Woman:	**Hai. Sorekara, fumikiri o watatte kudasai. Sōsuruto, Shiro wa hidari gawa ni arimasu.**
	hah-ee. sohh-reh-kah-rah, foo-mee-kee-ree oh wah-taht-teh koo-dah-sah-ee. sohh-soo-roo-toh, shee-roh wah hee-dah-ree gah-wah nee ah-ree-mah-soo.
	Yes. And then cross the railway crossing. Then you'll see Shiro on your left.
Ben:	**Ā, sō desu ka. Dōmo.**
	ahh, sohh deh-soo kah. dohh-moh.
	Oh, I see. Thank you.
Woman:	**Īe.**
	eee-eh.
	No problem.

WORDS TO KNOW

tsugi	tsoo-gee	next
kōsaten	kohh-sah-tehn	intersection
shingō	sheen-gohh	traffic light
sorekara	soh-reh-kah-rah	and then
fumikiri	foo-mee-kee-ree	railroad crossing
sōsuruto	sohh-soo-roo-toh	then

FUN & GAMES

Match the pictures to the descriptions. Check the answers in Appendix C.

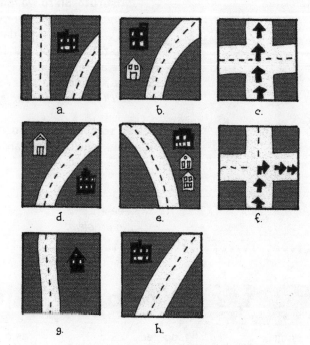

Illustration by Elizabeth Kurtzman

1. 向かい側にあります。**Mukai gawa ni arimasu.**

2. 道の右側です。**Michi no migi gawa desu.**

3. 道の右側の三つ目です。**Michi no migi gawa no mit-tsu-me desu.**

4. この道をまっすぐ行きます。**Kono michi o massugu ikimasu.**

5. 道の左側です。**Michi no hidari gawa desu.**

6. 隣にあります。**Tonari ni arimasu.**

7. 交差点を右に曲がります。**Kōsaten o migi ni magarimasu.**

8. 道と道の間にあります。**Michi to michi no aida ni arimasu.**

IN THIS CHAPTER

» Obtaining Japanese yen

» Visiting the bank

» Withdrawing money from the ATM

» Paying with cold, hard cash

» Burning up the plastic

Chapter 9

Dealing with Money in a Foreign Land

Kane wa tenka no mawari mono. (kah-neh wah tehn-kah noh mah-wah-ree-moh-noh.) (*Money goes around the world.*) This Japanese proverb means that the **o-kane** (oh-kah-neh) (*money*) you spend today will come back to you in the future. You buy other people's products, but they also buy yours. Use your money to make yourself, your family, and your friends happy.

In this chapter, I will give you important words and phrases for handling money. I also explain how to talk about acquiring and spending money in Japanese.

REMEMBER

You can listen to all the Talkin' the Talk dialogues featured in this chapter. Go to www.dummies.com/go/japanesefd and click on the dialogue you want to hear.

Getting Money

Spending money is fun, especially when you are visiting a foreign land. But you will need to get money somehow. In this section, I will introduce you to the ways you can access it. You can get your money from an ATM, a foreign-currency exchange counter, or a bank. I know you have some under your mattress, too. Oh, it's not under your mattress? Then where is it? Can you tell me in Japanese?

Exchanging money

If you're in Japan, the **en** (ehn) (*yen*) is the only acceptable currency. Don't say *yen*; say **en**. Drop that *y* sound. As you can see, the yen sign, ¥, looks like an uppercase Y with two horizontal lines. (Note that ¥ is the currency sign, not a **kanji**. The **kanji** for **yen** is 円, which is read as **en** [ehn].) You can exchange your money for **en** at the airport or at major banks. Check out Table 9-1 and find the foreign currency that you have in your pocket.

TABLE 9-1

Currencies

Currency	Pronunciation	English
アメリカドル **Amerika doru**	ah-meh-ree-kah doh-roo	*U.S. dollar*
中国元 **Chūgoku gen**	chooo-goh-koo gehn	*Chinese yuan*
イギリスポンド **Igirisu pondo**	ee-gee-ree-soo pohn-doh	*British pound*
カナダドル **Kanada doru**	kah-nah-dah doh-roo	*Canadian dollar*
メキシコペソ **Mekishiko peso**	meh-kee-shee-koh peh-soh	*Mexican peso*
オーストラリアドル **Ōsutoraria doru**	ohh-soo-toh-rah-ree-ah doh-roo	*Australian dollar*
ユーロ **Yūro**	yooo-roh	*European Union euro*

The following words are essential for exchanging currency:

>> 円 **en** (ehn) (*yen*)

>> 外貨 **gaika** (gah-ee-kah) (*foreign currency*)

>> 銀行 **ginkō** (geen-kohh) (*bank*)

» 為替レート **kawase rēto** (kah-wah-seh rehh-toh) (*exchange rate*)

» 両替 **ryōgae** (ryohh-gah-eh) (*exchange*)

Ask for the current exchange rate and exchange your currency for yen. The following phrases may be helpful:

» 外貨の両替はできますか。**Gaika no ryōgae wa dekimasu ka.** (gah-ee-kah noh ryohh-gah-eh wah deh-kee-mah-soo kah.) (*Can you exchange foreign currency?*)

» 今1ドル何円ですか。**Ima ichi-doru nan-en desu ka.** (ee-mah ee-chee-doh-roo nahn-ehn deh-soo kah.) (*How many for a dollar now?*)

» 今日の為替レートを教えてください。**Kyō no kawase rēto o oshiete kudasai.** (kyohh noh kah-wah-seh rehh-toh oh oh-shee-eh-teh koo-dah-sah-ee.) (*Please let me know today's exchange rate.*)

» アメリカドルを円に両替したいんですが。**Amerika doru o en ni ryōgae shi-tai-n-desu ga.** (ah-meh-ree-kah doh-roo oh ehn nee ryohh-gah-eh shee-tah-een-deh-soo gah.) (*I'd like to exchange some U.S. dollars for yen [but could you help me?].*)

» 500ドルを円に両替してください。**500-doru o en ni ryōgae shite kudasai.** (goh-hyah-koo-doh-roo oh ehn nee ryohh-gah-eh shee-teh koo-dah-sah-ee.) (*Please exchange $500 for yen.*)

Some of the responses you may get when you exchange currency are as follows:

» 買いは1ドル80円, 売りは1ドル81円です。**Kai wa ichi-doru 80-en; uri wa ichi-doru 81-en desu.** (kah-ee wa ee-chee-doh-roo hah-chee-jooo-ehn; oo-ree wah ee-chee-doh-roo hah-chee-jooo-ee-chee-ehn deh-soo.) (*The rate for exchanging dollars for yen is 80 yen to the dollar; the rate for exchanging yen for dollars is 81 yen to the dollar.*)

» 手数料は含まれています。**Tesūryō wa fukumarete imasu.** (teh-sooo-ryohh wah foo-koo-mah-reh-teh ee-mah-soo.) (*The fee is already included.*)

» 今日の為替レートは昨日と同じです。**Kyō no kawase rēto wa kinō to onaji desu.** (kyohh noh kah-wah-seh rehh-toh wah kee-nohh toh oh-nah-jee deh-soo.) (*Today's exchange rate is the same as yesterday's.*)

Talkin' the Talk

Natalie has just arrived at Narita Airport in Tokyo, and she's about to exchange her U.S. dollars for Japanese yen at the exchange counter.

Natalie:
Sumimasen. Amerika doru kara en no ryōgae wa dekimasu ka.
soo-mee-mah-sehn. ah-meh-ree-kah doh-roo kah-rah ehn noh ryohh-gah-eh wah deh-kee-mah-soo kah.
Excuse me. Can I change U.S. dollars for yen?

Clerk:
Hai.
hah-ee.
Sure.

Natalie:
Kyō no kawase rēto wa ikura desu ka.
kyohh noh kah-wah-seh rehh-toh wah ee-koo-rah deh-soo kah.
What is today's exchange rate?

Clerk:
Ichi-doru 81-en desu.
ee-chee-doh-roo hah-chee-jooo-ee-chee-ehn deh-soo.
81 for $1.

Natalie:
Jā, 200-doru onegaishimasu.
jahh, nee-hyah-koo-doh-roo oh-neh-gah-ee-shee-mah-soo.
Then I'd like to exchange $200, please.

Clerk:
Pasupōto wa gozaimasu ka.
pah-soo-pohh-toh wah goh-zah-ee-mah-soo kah.
Do you have your passport?

Natalie:
Hai. Dōzo.
hah-ee. dohh-zoh.
Yes. Here you are.

WORDS TO KNOW

ryōgae suru	ryohh-gah-eh soo-roo	to exchange
wa dekimasu ka	wah deh-kee-mah-soo kah	Can you do . . .?
amerika doru	ah-meh-ree-kah doh-roo	U.S. dollar
kawase rēto	kah-wah-seh rehh-toh	exchange rate
pasupōto	pah-soo-pohh-toh	passport

Opening a bank account

Bank is **ginkō** (geen-kohh) in Japanese. It sounds like the popular dietary supplement *ginko biloba,* which is supposed to increase your brainpower, but it has nothing to do with that. I know a lot of people who don't use their brains at all when they withdraw money from the **ginkō.**

CULTURAL WISDOM

When you enter a bank in Japan, you'll hear this right away: **Irasshaimase.** (ee-rahs-shah-ee-mah-sehh.) (*Welcome.*). The bank tellers dress in uniforms, and they treat you almost like a god. After you enter the bank, pick up a ticket and wait until your number is called. Most Japanese banks have comfy couches, current magazines, and TVs that make your wait almost enjoyable. When your number is called, go to the designated **madoguchi** (mah-doh-goo-chee) (*window*). Japanese banks have low windows so that customers can sit down while they perform their transactions.

CULTURAL WISDOM

When you open a Japanese bank account, the bank clerk asks you to fill out a form and present your identification. When opening a bank account, bring your **inkan** (een-kahn) (*seal*) along with your identification. **Inkan** is a seal stamp of your name; it's used in lieu of signatures in Japan. You can get a custom-made **inkan** pretty cheaply, although some **inkan** can be very expensive depending on the material that they use. Some banks let foreigners open an account with their signatures without requiring an **inkan,** but be sure to confirm your bank's policy before you go in to open an account.

To open a bank account, you need your identification as well as some money for your initial **yokin** (yoh-keen) (*deposit*). You also need the **u**-verb **hiraku** (hee-rah-koo) (*to open*). Check out its conjugated forms, and notice the **k** in all the forms except the **te**-form.

Japanese Script	Rōmaji	Pronunciation
開く	hiraku	hee-rah-koo
開かない	hirakanai	hee-rah-kah-nah-ee
開き(ます)	hiraki (masu)	hee-rah-kee (mah-soo)
開いて	hiraite	hee-rah-ee-teh

Here are some terms you need for banking in Japan:

>> 電信送金する **denshin sōkin suru** (dehn-sheen sohh-keen soo-roo) (*to wire money*)

>> 普通預金口座 **futsū yokin kōza** (foo-tsoo yoh-keen kohh-zah) (*savings account*)

>> 現金 **genkin** (gehn-keen) (*cash*)

>> 口座 **kōza** (kohh-za) (*account*)

>> 身分証明書 **mibun shōmeisho** (mee-boon shohh-mehh-shoh) (*identification*)

>> 利息 **risoku** (ree-soh-koo) (*interest*)

>> 定期預金口座 **teiki yokin kōza** (tehh-kee yoh-keen kohh-zah) (*fixed-term deposit account/CD*)

>> 預金する **yokin suru** (yoh-keen soo-roo) (*to make a deposit*)

>> 用紙 **yōshi** (yohh-shee) (*form*)

CULTURAL WISDOM

Personal checks are unheard of in Japan. Most companies and institutions have **tōza yokin kōza** (tohh-zah yoh-keen kohh-zah) (*checking accounts*), but individuals usually don't. People often pay bills online, through a special postal service, or at a convenience store.

GRAMMAR CHAT

Bank clerks speak to customers by using super-polite words and phrases. To make their requests very polite, bank clerks may use a verb in the stem form and place it between **o** (oh) and **kudasai** (koo-dah-sah-ee), as in **O-kaki kudasai.** (oh-kah-kee koo-dah-sah-ee.) (*Please write it.*) and **O-mise kudasai.** (oh-mee-seh koo-dah-sah-ee.) (*Please show it to me.*). In addition, many words that bank tellers use start with the polite prefix **go** or **o. Go** should be used for words from Chinese and **o** for native Japanese words, but this guideline has so many exceptions that you really have to just consider each word one by one. (See Chapters 6 and 12 for more information about these polite prefixes.) Be ready for the following super-polite requests from people at the bank:

» ご住所とお電話番号をお願いします。**Go-jūsho to o-denwa-bangō o onegaishi-masu.** (goh-jooo-shoh toh oh-dehn-wah-bahn-gohh oh oh-neh-gah-ee-shee-mah-soo.) (*Your address and your telephone number, please.*)

» 身分証明書をお見せください。**Mibun shōmeisho o o-mise kudasai.** (mee-boon shohh-mehh-shoh oh oh-mee-seh koo-dah-sah-ee.) (*Please show me your identification.*)

» お名前をお書きください。**O-namae o o-kaki kudasai.** (oh-nah-mah-eh oh oh-kah-kee koo-dah-sah-ee.) (*Please write your name.*)

» こちらにご捺印をお願いいたします。**Kochira ni go-natsuin o onegai itashi-masu.** (koh-chee-rah nee goh-nah-tsoo-een oh oh-neh-gah-ee ee-tah-shee-mah-soo.) (*Please stamp your name seal here.*)

Making withdrawals from your account

The most convenient way of withdrawing money from your bank is to find a nearby ATM. If you use the machine at your own bank, you can insert your pass-book in addition to your card, so the transaction details can be printed on your passbook on the spot (meaning no need to keep the slip). If you want to withdraw your money at the window, you'll have to bring your passbook and your **inkan** and fill out a withdrawal slip. (I tell you all about **inkan** in the preceding section.) Actually, bring your identification along as well when you withdraw your money manually.

Regardless of how you choose to withdraw your money, here are the words you need:

» 引き出す **hikidasu** (hee-kee-dah-soo) (*to withdraw*)

» 自動引き落とし **jidō hikiotoshi** (jee-dohh hee-kee-oh-toh-shee) (*automatic payment*)

» 口座番号 **kōza bangō** (kohh-zah bahn-gohh) (*account number*)

Note that if you withdraw your money at the window, you'll need to state your request along these lines:

» 10万円引き出したいんですが。**Jū-man-en hikidashi-tai-n-desu ga.** (jooo-mahn-ehn hee-kee-dah-shee-tah-een-deh-soo gah.) (*I'd like to withdraw 100,000 yen [but is it possible?].*)

» 残高を調べてくださいませんか。**Zandaka o shirabete kudasai masen ka.** (zahn-dah-kah oh shee-rah-beh-teh koo-dah-sah-ee mah-sehn kah.) (*Could you please check the balance?*)

Using an ATM

An **ATM** (ehh–teee–eh–moo) (*ATM*) makes getting cash easy: All you need is your **kyasshu kādo** (kyahs–shoo kahh–doh) (*ATM card*). You can select from the following functions displayed on the ATM:

>> お預け入れ **o-azukeire** (oh-ah-zoo-keh-ee-reh) (*deposit*)

>> お振込み **o-furikomi** (oh-foo-ree-koh-mee) (*transfer*)

>> お引き出し **o-hikidashi** (oh-hee-kee-dah-shee) (*withdrawal*)

>> 残高照会 **zandaka shōkai** (zahn-dah-kah shohh-kah-ee) (*balance inquiry*)

ATMs in Japan often give you instructions verbally, but some only show the instructions in Japanese script on their screens. Pay attention to the **kana** and **rōmaji** in the following list of common ATM instructions, and you'll be good to go either way:

>> カードをお入れください。**Kādo o o-ire kudasai.** (kahh-doh oh oh-ee-reh koo-dah-sah-ee.) (*Insert your card, please.*)

>> 暗証番号をどうぞ。**Anshō bangō o dōzo.** (ahn-shohh bahn-gohh oh dohh-zoh.) (*Enter your PIN.*)

>> しばらくお待ちください。**Shibaraku o-machi kudasai.** (shee-bah-rah-koo oh-mah-chee koo-dah-sah-ee.) (*Please wait.*)

>> 金額をどうぞ。**Kingaku o dōzo.** (keen-gah-koo oh dohh-zoh.) (*Enter the amount please.*)

>> 確認してください。**Kakunin shite kudasai.** (kah-koo-neen shee-teh koo-dah-sah-ee.) (*Confirm the amount.*)

>> 現金をお受け取りください。**Genkin o o-uketori kudasai.** (gehn-keen oh oh-oo-keh-toh-ree koo-dah-sah-ee.) (*Take the cash.*)

>> カードをお取りください。**Kādo o o-tori kudasai.** (kahh-doh oh oh-toh-ree koo-dah-sah-ee.) (*Remove your card.*)

>> ありがとうございました。**Arigatō gozaimashita.** (ah-ree-gah-tohh goh-zah-ee-mah-shee-tah.) (*Thank you very much.*)

Conjugate the important **u**-verb **toru** (toh–roo) (*to take*). Notice that the **r** appears in all the forms except the **te**-form. Just swallow the **r** in the **te**-form. How did it taste? Not bad, right?

Japanese Script	Rōmaji	Pronunciation
取る	toru	toh-roo
取らない	toranai	toh-rah-nah-ee
取り(ます)	tori (masu)	toh-ree (-mah-soo)
取って	totte	toht-the

TIP

You can withdraw money in yen from ATMs at convenience stores like 7-Eleven and Japanese post offices. Some ATMs offered by Japanese banks may not allow you to withdraw cash, using credit cards or debit cards issued outside Japan.

Spending Money

Spending money shouldn't always be a pain; it should be a rewarding experience as well. What's the point in saving all your cash until you can no longer use it? As the saying goes, "You can't take it with you." Whether you believe in spending only cash or you're a **kurejitto kādo** (koo-reh-jeet-toh kahh-doh) (*credit card*) worshipper, the next sections have the information you need to get that money spent.

Ka-ching! Shelling out cash

Cash is convenient for buying little things like a cup of coffee, a magazine, or a snack from the vending machine. Most countries' currencies include both **shihei** (shee-hehh) (*bills*) and **kōka** (kohh-kah) (*coins*).

REMEMBER

Satsu (sah-tsoo) is also used instead of **shihei** when following an amount, as in **sen-en satsu** (sehn-ehn sah-tsoo) (¥1,000 bill). Similarly, **dama** (dah-mah) is also used instead of **kōka** when following an amount, as in **jū-en dama** (jooo-ehn dah-mah) (¥10 coin).

Following are all the bills and coins used in Japan:

>> 一万円紙幣 **ichi-man-en shihei** (ee-chee-mahn-ehn shee-hehh) (*¥10,000 bill*)

>> 五千円紙幣 **go-sen-en shihei** (goh-sehn-ehn shee-hehh) (*¥5,000 bill*)

>> 二千円紙幣 **ni-sen-en shihei** (nee-sehn-ehn shee-hehh) (*¥2,000 bill*)

>> 千円紙幣 **sen-en shihei** (sehn-ehn shee-hehh) (*¥1,000 bill*)

- » 五百円硬貨 **go-hyaku-en kōka** (goh-hyah-koo-ehn kohh-kah) (*¥500 coin*)

- » 百円硬貨 **hyaku-en kōka** (hyah-koo-ehn kohh-kah) (*¥100 coin*)

- » 五十円硬貨 **go-jū-en kōka** (goh-jooo-ehn kohh-kah) (*¥50 coin*)

- » 十円硬貨 **jū-en kōka** (jooo-ehn kohh-kah) (*¥10 coin*)

- » 五円硬貨 **go-en kōka** (goh-ehn kohh-kah) (*¥5 coin*)

- » 一円硬貨 **ichi-en kōka** (ee-chee-ehn kohh-kah) (*¥1 coin*)

CULTURAL WISDOM

The ¥2,000 bill note was issued in the year 2000 with limited quantity. If you have it, I recommend keeping it instead of using it! There's also an old-fashioned supplementary currency unit called **sen** (sehn), which is 1/100 of ¥1, and 厘 **rin** (reen), which is 1/1,000 of ¥1. Currencies based on **sen** and **rin** were taken out of circulation in 1953, but these units are still used in some contexts, including stock markets.

To count coins and bills, use the counter **-mai**, as in **ichi-mai** (eeh-chee-mah-ee), **ni-mai** (nee-mah-ee), **san-mai** (sahn-mah-ee), and so on. (See Chapter 4 for more about **-mai** and other counters.) Now, you're ready to count, spend, borrow, or lend your **genkin**. Conjugate the **ru**-verb **kariru** (kah-ree-roo) (*to borrow*) and the **u**-verb **kasu** (kah-soo) (*to lend*).

Japanese Script	Rōmaji	Pronunciation
借りる	kariru	kah-ree-roo
借りない	karinai	kah-ree-nah-ee
借り(ます)	kari (masu)	kah-ree (-mah-soo)
借りて	karite	kah-ree-teh
貸す	kasu	kah-soo
貸さない	kasanai	kah-sah-nah-ee
貸し(ます)	kashi (masu)	kah-shee (-mah-soo)
貸して	kashite	kah-shee-teh

Following are a few phrases that you can use to talk about **genkin**:

父から5万円借りました。**Chichi kara go-man-en karimashita.** (chee-chee kah-rah goh-mahn-ehn kah-ree-mah-shee-tah.) (*I borrowed ¥50,000 from my father.*)

500円貸してください。**Go-hyaku-en kashite kudasai.** (goh-hyah-koo-ehn kah-shee-teh koo-dah-sah-ee.) (*Please loan me ¥500.*)

千円札3枚ありますか。**Sen-en-satsu san-mai arimasu ka.** (sehn-ehn-sah-tsoo sahn-mah-ee ah-ree-mah-soo kah.) (*Do you have three ¥1,000 bills?*)

一万円札しかありません。**Ichi-man-en-satsu shika arimasen.** (ee-chee-mahn-ehn-sah-tsoo shee-kah ah-ree-mah-sehn.) (*I have only ¥10,000 bills.*)

REMEMBER

To say *only*, place the particle **shika** (shee-kah) at the end of the noun and make the verb negative, as in the last example. You can read more on **shika** in Chapter 7.

Charge! Paying with plastic

A credit card is almost a must-have in today's world, particularly when you're traveling, because you need a credit card for renting a car and reserving a hotel room. In Japan, credit cards are accepted in many stores, hotels, and restaurants, but just in case, check first to see whether you can use them in a given establishment. For example, credit card acceptance is still limited in rural areas of Japan.

Conjugate the **u**-verb **tsukau** (tsoo-kah-oo) (*to use*). Just watch out for the **w** sound that appears only in the negative.

Japanese Script	Rōmaji	Pronunciation
使う	tsukau	tsoo-kah-oo
使わない	tsukawanai	tsoo-kah-wah-nah-ee
使い(ます)	tsukai (masu)	tsoo-kah-ee (-mah-soo)
使って	tsukatte	tsoo-kaht-teh

REMEMBER

To ask whether you can use your credit card, you first need to know how to say *can.* For example, **tsukau** (tsoo-kah-oo) means *to use,* but **tsukaeru** (tsoo-kah-eh-roo) means *to be able to use* or *can use.* Then, you take this verb, **tsukaeru,** and conjugate it — for example, **Kurejitto kādo wa tsukaemasu ka.** (koo-reh-jeet-toh kahh-doh wa tsoo-kah-eh-mah-soo kah.) (*Can I use a credit card?*). Turn to Chapter 7 to find out exactly how to make the *can* form of various verbs.

GRAMMAR
CHAT

If you have multiple credit cards and you want to know which one is accepted at a particular shop or restaurant, use the particle **ka** (kah), which means *or.* You can use **ka** to list two or more choices. When listing more than two choices, simply place **ka** after each noun except the last one. A few examples may be helpful:

ビザかマスターカードは使えますか。**Biza ka Masutā kādo wa tsukaemasu ka.** (bee-zah kah mah-soo-tahh kahh-doh wah tsoo-kah-eh-mah-soo kah.) (*Can I use a Visa or MasterCard?*)

アメリカンエキスプレスかディスカバーかJCBは使えます。**Amerikan Ekisupuresu ka Disukabā ka JCB wa tsukaemasu.** (ah-meh-ree-kahn eh-kee-soo-poo-reh-soo kah dee-soo-kah-bahh ka jehh-sheee-beee wa tsoo-kah-eh-mah-soo.) (*If it's American Express, Discover, or JCB, you can use it.*)

空港か銀行で両替をします。**Kūkō ka ginkō de ryōgae o shimasu.** (kooo-kohh kah geen-kohh deh ryohh-gah-eh oh shee-mah-soo.) (*I'll exchange money at the airport or at the bank.*)

Perhaps you would like to use your **debitto kādo** (deh–beet–toh kahh–doh) (*debit card*) to pay for everyday expenses. **Debitto kādo** have one advantage over **kurejitto kādo:** Because the money is deducted directly from your bank account, you can't spend more than you have.

GRAMMAR CHAT

To explain that you use your debit card to pay for purchases, say **Debitto kādo de haraimasu.** (d deh–beet–toh kahh–doh deh hah–rah–ee–mah–soo.) (*I'll pay by debit card.*). Remember that the particle **de** (deh) marks the location of activity. It also specifies the tools and means for the action, as in the following examples:

箸で食べます。**Hashi de tabemasu.** (hah-shee deh tah-beh-mah-soo.) (*I eat with chopsticks.*)

鉛筆で書きます。**Enpitsu de kakimasu.** (ehn-pee-tsoo deh kah-kee-mah-soo.) (*I write with a pencil.*)

FUN & GAMES

Identify the total amount of bills and coins in each of the following sets. Answers are in Appendix C.

1.

2.

3.

4.

5.

Illustration by Elizabeth Kurtzman

IN THIS CHAPTER

» **Specifying what you're searching for**

» **Going to a grocery or convenience store**

» **Knowing what's where in the department store**

» **Trying and buying clothes**

» **Comparing items**

» **Spending money**

Chapter **10**

Shopping Made Easy

I love **kaimono** (kah-ee-moh-noh) (*shopping*). When I feel great, I shop. When I feel depressed, I shop. And when I get a raise — you guessed it — I shop. If you love shopping too, this chapter is for you. It's full of the information and vocabulary you need to know if you're going to go shopping. Specifically, you discover how to explain what you're looking for, how to compare both prices and quality in Japanese, and how to pay for your merchandise.

REMEMBER

You can listen to all the Talkin' the Talk dialogues featured in this chapter. Go to www.dummies.com/go/japanesefd and click on the dialogue you want to hear.

Naming Shops and Stores

You can refer to some types of shops and stores using the suffix **ya** (yah) (*shop*) in a friendly manner. For example:

» 花屋 **hana-ya** (hah-nah-yah) (*flower shop*)

» 本屋 **hon-ya** (hohn-yah) (*bookstore*)

» 自転車屋 **jitensha-ya** (jee-tehn-shah-yah) (*bicycle shop*)

» 薬屋 **kusuri-ya** (koo-soo-ree-yah) (*drugstore*)

» 靴屋 **kutsu-ya** (koo-tsoo-yah) (*shoe store*)

» おもちゃ屋 **omocha-ya** (oh-moh-cha-yah) (*toy store*)

» パン屋 **pan-ya** (pahn-yah) (*bakery*)

» 酒屋 **saka-ya** (sah-kah-yah) (*liquor shop*)

Some stores are conventionally referred to by English loan words with some modifications. Here are a few examples:

» ブティック **butikku** (boo-teek-koo) (*boutique*)

» デパート **depāto** (deh-pahh-toh) (*department store*)

» ホームセンター **hōmusentā** (hohh-moo-sehn-tahh) (*home center, home improvement store*)

» コンビニ **konbini** (kohn-bee-nee) (*convenience store*)

» スーパー **sūpā** (sooo-pahh) (*supermarket*)

Going Grocery Shopping

Restaurants are great, but if you want to save time and money, go shopping for your food. If you go to a supermarket, you can get most of the items you need in one trip, including the following:

» アイスクリーム **aisukurīmu** (ah-ee-soo-koo-reee-moo) (*ice cream*)

» バター **batā** (bah-tahh) (*butter*)

» チーズ **chīzu** (cheee-zoo) (*cheese*)

» 牛乳 **gyūnyū** (gyooo-nyooo) (*milk*)

» ジュース **jūsu** (jooo-soo) (*juice*)

» 米 **kome** (koh-me) (*uncooked rice*)

» 果物 **kudamono** (koo-dah-moh-noh) (*fruits*)

» 肉 **niku** (nee-koo) (*meat*)

» パン **pan** (pahn) (*bread*)

» 魚 **sakana** (sah-kah-nah) (*fish*)

>> たまご **tamago** (tah-mah-goh) (*eggs*)

>> 野菜 **yasai** (yah-sah-ee) (*vegetables*)

Going to a butcher

Whether your butcher has a special shop or just works behind the counter at a regular grocery store, he can be a meat-eater's best friend. Here are some of the meats you can get from a butcher:

>> 豚肉 **butaniku** (boo-tah-nee-koo) (*pork*)

>> 牛肉 **gyūniku** (gyooo-nee-koo) (*beef*)

>> マトン **maton** (mah-tohn) (*mutton*)

>> 七面鳥 **shichimenchō** (shee-chee-mehn-chohh) (*turkey*)

>> 鶏肉 **toriniku** (toh-ree-nee-koo) (*chicken*)

Processed, cured, and cooked meats are very convenient. If you need to whip up a quick dinner, you may want to buy one of these:

>> ベーコン **bēkon** (behh-kohn) (*bacon*)

>> ハム **hamu** (hah-moo) (*ham*)

>> コーンビーフ **kōn bīfu** (kohhn beee-foo) (*corned beef*)

>> ローストビーフ **rōsuto bīfu** (rohh-soo-toh beee-foo) (*roast beef*)

>> ソーセージ **sōsēji** (sohh-sehh-jee) (*sausage*)

Purchasing fresh fish

Japanese people are big fish-eaters. If you're also a fish lover, the fish market is the place for you. The names of fish are often written in **katakana** at the fish market (and in the following list), but some are also written in **kanji** or **hiragana**. Remember the names of your favorite fish when you make the trip:

>> ハマチ **hamachi** (hah-mah-chee) (*yellowtail*)

>> ヒラメ **hirame** (hee-rah-meh) (*flounder*)

>> マグロ **maguro** (mah-goo-roh) (*tuna*)

>> マス **masu** (mah-soo) (*trout*)

>> サバ **saba** (sah-bah) (*mackerel*)

>> サケ **sake** (sah-keh) (*salmon*)

>> スズキ **suzuki** (soo-zoo-kee) (*Japanese sea bass*)

>> タイ **tai** (tah-ee) (*red snapper*)

>> タラ **tara** (tah-rah) (*cod*)

CULTURAL WISDOM

If you go to Japan, try buying fresh fish at the **Toyosu** (toh-yoh-soo) Market. It's the new fish market in Tokyo which replaced the famous Tsukiji (tsoo-kee-jee) Market. Tsukiji closed in October 2018 after 83 years of service. The new fish market is larger and closer to a train station called "Shijyomaeeki" (shee-jyohh-mah-eh-eh-kee) on the Yurikamome line (yoo-ree-kah-moh-meh). If you want to see the famous early morning tuna auctions, get up early! They start at 4:30 a.m.!

Buying vegetables and fruit

Include some of the following vegetables and fruits on your shopping list. Some are always written in **katakana** (as I've done in the following list), but others are written in **katakana, hiragana,** or **kanji.** Regardless of the Japanese script used, these items are good for you:

>> バナナ **banana** (bah-nah-nah) (*bananas*)

>> ブドウ **budō** (boo-dohh) (*grapes*)

>> ダイコン **daikon** (dah-ee-kohn) (*Japanese daikon radish*)

>> イチゴ **ichigo** (ee-chee-goh) (*strawberries*)

>> ジャガイモ **jagaimo** (jah-gah-ee-moh) (*potatoes*)

>> カキ **kaki** (kah-kee) (*persimmons*)

>> キャベツ **kyabetsu** (kyah-beh-tsoo) (*cabbage*)

>> ミカン **mikan** (mee-kahn) (*tangerines*)

>> ナシ **nashi** (nah-shee) (*pears*)

>> ナス **nasu** (nah-soo) (*eggplant*)

>> ネギ **negi** (neh-gee) (*green onions*)

>> ニンジン **ninjin** (neen-jeen) (*carrots*)

>> ピーマン **pīman** (peee-mahn) (*green peppers*)

>> レモン **remon** (reh-mohn) (*lemons*)

» レタス **retasu** (reh-tah-soo) (*lettuce*)

» リンゴ **ringo** (reen-goh) (*apples*)

» サツマイモ **satsumaimo** (sah-tsoo-mah-ee-moh) (*sweet potatoes*)

» スイカ **suika** (soo-ee-kah) (*watermelon*)

» タマネギ **tamanegi** (tah-mah-neh-gee) (*round onions*)

» トマト **tomato** (toh-mah-toh) (*tomatoes*)

Shopping at a Konbini (Convenience Store)!

When you visit Japan, you should definitely check out a **konbini** (kohn-bee-nee). **Konbini** play a critical role in Japanese society. They typically carry almost anything you need in your daily life from **onigiri** (oh-neh-gee-ree) (*rice balls*) to toothpaste to an umbrella to shampoo to underwear, and almost any basic necessities. They sell foods that can be meals such as **obentō** (oh-beh-n-tohh) (*boxed meals*), bread, side dishes, soups, and desserts. But that's not all. People can fax, make copies, purchase tickets for busses or events, pay utility bills, print photos, and send/receive packages through delivery services. Some places offer an ATM and Wi-Fi as well! Some stores offer a nice cozy corner where you can sit and enjoy a quick bite. A lot of things are nicely organized at a **konbini**. Yes, it is convenient! Here are daily necessities you may look for at a **konbini** in addition to the vocabulary introduced in the preceding grocery section.

» チョコレート **chokorēto** (choh-koh-rehh-toh) (*chocolates*)

» ガム **gamu** (gah-moo) (*gum*)

» ケーキ **kēki** (kehh-kee) (*cake*)

» コンディショナー **kondhishonā** (koh-n-dhee-shoh-nahh) (*conditioner*)

» クッキー **kukkī** (kook-keee) (*cookie*)

» おべんとう **obentō** (oh-beh-n-tohh) (*boxed meals*)

» おにぎり **onigiri** (oh-neh-gee-ree) (*rice balls*)

» サンドイッチ **sandoicchi** (sah-n-doh-eehc-chee) (*sandwich*)

» シャンプー **shanpū** (shah-n-puu) (*shampoo*)

» スイーツ **suītsu** (soo-ee-tsoo) (*sweets*)

Telling a Salesperson What You're Looking For

If you have a particular item in mind, step into a store and say the name of the item and **wa arimasu ka** (wah ah-ree-mah-soo kah) (*do you have*). Or you can use the **u**-verb **sagasu** (sah-gah-soo) (*to look for*) to state that you're looking for, for example, **furoshiki** (foo-roh-shee-kee). (These big, smooth, square Japanese wrapping cloths have beautiful patterns and colors.) Here's how to conjugate **sagasu**:

Japanese Script	Rōmaji	Pronunciation
探す	sagasu	sah-gah-soo
探さない	sagasanai	sah-gah-sah-nah-ee
探し(ます)	sagashi (masu)	sah-gah-shee (-mah-soo)
探して	sagashite	sah-gah-shee-teh

GRAMMAR CHAT

If you say **sagasu** or **sagashimasu**, it means you *will* look for something or you *regularly* look for something. In order to mean that you *are* looking for something, conjugate the verb **sagasu** to the **te**-form, which is **sagashite** (sah-gah-shee-teh), and then add the verb **iru** (ee-roo) or its polite form **imasu** (ee-mah-soo) (*to exist*). **Sagashite iru** or **sagashite imasu** means you are looking for something. (For more on basic verb forms such as the **te**-form, see Chapter 3.)

CULTURAL WISDOM

If you're traveling in Japan, perhaps you have some specific souvenirs in mind that you know you want to pick up. Visit the fun and friendly souvenir shops in **Kyōto** (kyohh-toh), **Nara** (nah-rah), and **Asakusa** (ah-sah-koo-sah), where you can say that you're looking for the following popular souvenirs:

» 茶碗 **chawan** (chah-wahn) (*rice bowl, teacup that's wider than it is tall and used for tea ceremonies*)

» 風呂敷 **furoshiki** (foo-roh-shee-kee) (*wrapping cloths*)

» 下駄 **geta** (geh-tah) (*type of wooden clogs*)

» 箸 **hashi** (hah-shee) (*chopsticks*)

» 花瓶 **kabin** (kah-been) (*vase*)

» 傘 **kasa** (kah-sah) (*umbrella*)

» 着物 **kimono** (kee-moh-noh) (*kimono*)

» くし **kushi** (koo-shee) (*comb*)

» 人形 **ningyō** (neen-gyohh) (*doll [for display only]*)

» お茶 **o-cha** (oh-chah) (*green tea*)

» 折り紙 **origami** (oh-ree-gah-mee) (*origami*)

» お皿 **o-sara** (oh-sah-rah) (*plate*)

» せんべい **senbei** (sehn-behh) (*rice cracker*)

» 扇子 **sensu** (sehn-soo) (*fan*)

» 湯飲み **yunomi** (yoo-noh-mee) (*teacup that's taller than it is wide and used for drinking regular green tea*)

GRAMMAR CHAT

Express your request by using a verb in the **te**-form (see Chapter 3) and **kudasai** (koo-dah-sah-ee) as in the following examples:

その花瓶を見せてください。**Sono kabin o misete kudasai.** (soh-noh kah-been oh mee-seh-teh koo-dah-sah-ee.) (*Please show me that vase.*)

この茶碗を包んでください。**Kono chawan o tsutsunde kudasai.** (koh-noh chah-wahn oh tsoo-tsoon-deh koo-dah-sah-ee.) (*Please wrap this teacup.*)

.... Talkin' the Talk ....

Joan wants to buy a Japanese souvenir and steps into a souvenir store in Asakusa.

Joan:	**Sumimasen. Furoshiki wa arimasu ka.** soo-mee-mah-sehn. foo-roh-shee-kee wah ah-ree-mah-soo kah. *Excuse me. Do you have furoshiki?*
Clerk:	**Furoshiki wa arimasen.** foo-roh-shee-kee wah ah-ree-mah-sehn. *Furoshiki? We don't have it.*
Joan:	**Ā, sō desu ka. Jā, sono sensu o chotto misete kudasai.** ahh, sohh deh-soo kah. jahh, soh-noh sehn-soo oh choht-toh mee-seh-teh koo-dah-sah-ee. *Oh, I see. Then could you show me that fan please?*
Clerk:	**Kore desu ka.** koh-reh deh-soo kah. *This one?*

Joan:	**Hai.**
	hah-ee.
	Yes.
Clerk:	**Dōzo.**
	dohh-zo.
	Here you are.

. . . .

WORDS TO KNOW

furoshiki	foo-roh-shee-kee	wrapping cloths
(X) wa arimasu ka	(X) wah ah-ree-mah-soo kah	do you have (X)
sono	soh-noh	that
sensu	sehn-soo	fan
Misete kudasai.	mee-seh-teh koo-dah-sah ee.	Please show it to me.
kore	koh-reh	this one

Exploring the Variety of a Department Store

Depāto (deh-pahh-toh) (*department stores*) are fascinating. Their **nedan** (neh-dahn) (*prices*) are a little high, but they offer a variety of quality items and **burandohin** (boo-rahn-doh-heen) (*designer-brand items*). They also offer good **sābisu** (sahh–bee-soo) (*service*), I suppose. You can find the following items in a **depāto**:

>> 婦人服 **fujinfuku** (foo-jeen-foo-koo) (*women's clothes*)

>> 楽器 **gakki** (gahk-kee) (*musical instruments*)

>> 宝石 **hōseki** (hohh-seh-kee) (*jewelry*)

>> 鞄 **kaban** (kah-bahn) (*luggage*)

>> 家具 **kagu** (kah-goo) (*furniture*)

>> 化粧品 **keshōhin** (keh-shohh-heen) (*cosmetics*)

- » 子供服 **kodomofuku** (koh-doh-moh-foo-koo) (*children's clothes*)

- » 靴 **kutsu** (koo-tsoo) (*shoes*)

- » 紳士服 **shinshifuku** (sheen-shee-foo-koo) (*men's clothes*)

- » 書籍 **shoseki** (shoh-seh-kee) (*books*)

- » スポーツ用品 **supōtsu yōhin** (soo-pohh-tsoo yohh-heen) (*sporting goods*)

GRAMMAR CHAT

Which floor do you want to go to? To answer this question, use the counter **-kai**. For example, **2-kai** (nee-kah-ee) means *second floor*. For more info on Japanese counters, see Chapter 4.

REMEMBER

Store clerks speak very politely. One of the polite phrases that they often use is **de gozaimasu** (deh goh-zah-ee-mah-soo). It's a polite version of the verb **desu** (deh-soo) (*to be*). So instead of saying **Hōseki wa nana-kai desu.** (hohh-seh-kee wah nah-nah-kah-ee deh-soo.) (*Jewelry is on the seventh floor.*), they say **Hōseki wa nana-kai de gozaimasu.** (hohh-seh-kee wah nah-nah-kah-ee deh goh-zah-ee-mah-soo.).

Department stores have fixed business hours. Before you head out shopping, you can find out a department store's hours by asking **Eigyō jikan wa nan-ji kara nan-ji made desu ka.** (ehh-gyohh jee-kahn wah nahn-jee kah-rah nahn-jee mah-deh deh-soo kah.) (*From what time to what time are your business hours?*). If you're already at the store and you want to ask *What time does your store close?* say **Heiten wa nan-ji desu ka.** (hehh-tehn wah nahn-jee deh-soo kah.)

CULTURAL WISDOM

BASEMENTS OF DEPARTMENT STORES

The basements of department stores are dedicated to offering good (and upscale) foods. These basements are informally called **depachika** (deh-pah-chee-kah), which literally means *department basement*. **Depachika** often showcase an upgraded grocery section, obentō, elegant sweets, a nice bakery (or nice bakery items), upscale tea and coffee, gourmet salads, sushi, side dishes, expensive wine and sake, and many other attractive foods. If you love eating like I do, this is an alluring space! When you go to a basement of a department store after 6:30 p.m. or so, you will see many people getting dishes for their dinner tables. Many freshly made foods are discounted just around the time when people are on their way home. Another interesting time to visit a department store basement is during the Valentine's Day season. You will be amazed by beautifully packaged chocolates by many chocolate venders! I hope you enjoy shopping in a basement of a department store.

Going Clothes Shopping

When you go shopping for **yōfuku** (yohh-foo-koo) (*clothes*), do you look for quality items that you can wear for years, or do you buy cheap items that you just wear for one season? Whatever your approach, check out the following sections to make sure you get just what you want.

Considering the clothing and accessories you need

Some pieces of clothing are staples. For example, you pretty much always need **shitagi** (shee-tah-gee) (*underwear*). Other clothing items and accessories, such as a **nekkuresu** (nehk-koo-reh-soo) (*necklace*), are fun to have but won't cause your wardrobe to fall apart if you don't own them. Check out the following list of clothes and accessories:

>> ベルト **beruto** (beh-roo-toh) (*belt*)

>> 帽子 **bōshi** (bohh-shee) (*cap, hat*)

>> ブラジャー **burajā** (boo-rah-jahh) (*bra*)

>> ブリーフ **burīfu** (boo-reee-foo) (*briefs, men's underwear*)

>> ドレス **doresu** (doh-reh-soo) (*dress*)

>> ジャケット **jaketto** (jah-keht-toh) (*jacket*)

>> ジーンズ **jīnzu** (jeeen-zoo) (*jeans*)

>> コート **kōto** (kohh-toh) (*coat*)

>> 靴 **kutsu** (koo-tsoo) (*shoes*)

>> 靴下 **kutsushita** (koo-tsoo-shee-tah) (*socks*)

>> ネクタイ **nekutai** (neh-koo-tah-ee) (*necktie*)

>> サングラス **sangurasu** (sahn-goo-rah-soo) (*sunglasses*)

>> セーター **sētā** (sehh-tahh) (*sweater*)

>> シャツ **shatsu** (shah-tsoo) (*shirt*)

>> スカート **sukāto** (soo-kahh-toh) (*skirt*)

>> スニーカー **sunīkā** (soo-neee-kahh) (*sneakers*)

>> スーツ **sūtsu** (sooo-tsoo) (*suit*)

>> トランクス **torankusu** (toh-rahn-koo-soo) (*boxers, men's underwear*)

>> ズボン **zubon** (zoo-bohn) (*pants*)

Examining the color

What's your favorite **iro** (ee-roh) (*color*)? When you buy clothes, check out all the colors and pick the one that looks best on you.

>> 赤 **aka** (ah-kah) (*red*)

>> 青 **ao** (ah-oh) (*blue*)

>> 茶色 **chairo** (chah-ee-roh) (*brown*)

>> 黄色 **kiiro** (keee-roh) (*yellow*)

>> 黒 **kuro** (koo-roh) (*black*)

>> 緑 **midori** (mee-doh-ree) (*green*)

>> 紫 **murasaki** (moo-rah-sah-kee) (*purple*)

>> オレンジ **orenji** (oh-rehn-jee) (*orange*)

>> ピンク **pinku** (peen-koo) (*pink*)

>> 白 **shiro** (shee-roh) (*white*)

GRAMMAR CHAT

You can just add the particle **no** (noh) after nouns and adjectives to mean *a . . . one*. For example, **aka no** (ah-kah noh) means *a red one*.

茶色のはありますか。**Chairo no wa arimasu ka.** (chah-ee-roh noh wah ah-ree-mah-soo kah.) (*Do you have a brown one?*)

色がきれいなのを探しています。**Iro ga kirei na no o sagashite imasu.** (ee-roh gah kee-rehh na noh oh sah-gah-shee-teh ee-mah-soo.) (*I'm looking for something with a pretty color.*)

Trying something on

When you need to get permission to do something, start with **chotto** (choht-toh), a word with far more uses than a dictionary can suggest. The English translation is usually *a little*, but you hear it in situations where no literal translation works. You can think of the phrase **chotto kite mite mo ii desu ka** (choht-toh kee-teh mee-teh moh eee deh-sooo kah) as having a meaning close to *Can I try it on for a minute?* (Literally: *Can I try it on a little?*). In this context, **chotto** makes it sound as if you'll be done as soon as possible.

When you want to try doing something, use the verb in the **te**-form and add **miru**. For example, **tabete miru** (tah-beh-teh mee-roo) means *to try eating.* **Kite miru** (kee-teh mee-roo) means *to try wearing* or *to try on.*

Ask for permission by using the verb in the **te**-form (see Chapter 3) with the phrase **mo ii desu ka** (moh eee deh-soo kah). For example, **Kite mite mo ii desu ka.** (kee-teh mee-teh moh eee deh-soo kah.) means *Is it okay to try it on?*

After you have the okay to try on a piece of clothing, head to the **shichakushitsu** (shee-chah-koo-shee-tsoo) (*fitting room*). Use the following phrases to express what you think of the outfit:

>> 丁度いいです。 **Chōdo ii desu.** (chohh-doh eee deh-soo.) (*It's just right.*)

>> ちょっと小さいです。 **chotto chīsai desu** (choht-toh cheee-sah-ee deh-soo) (*a little small*)

>> ちょっと大きいかな。 **Chotto ōkii kana.** (choht-toh ohh-keee kah-nah.) (*Is it a little big for me?*)

>> 長いです。 **Nagai desu.** (nah-gah-ee deh-soo.) (*It's long.*)

>> 少し短いです。 **sukoshi mijikai desu** (soo-koh-shee mee-jee-kah-ee deh-soo) (*a little short*)

Note that the verb **kiru** (kee-roo), which means *to wear,* is a **ru**-verb. Here's how to conjugate it:

Japanese Script	Rōmaji	Pronunciation
着る	kiru	kee-roo
着ない	kinai	kee-nah-ee
着(ます)	ki (masu)	kee (-mah-soo)
着て	kite	kee-teh

Although **kiru** is the most general verb that means *to wear,* you can't use it for everything you wear. It's good only for items you put above your waist, such as sweaters and shirts, or on your entire body, such as long dresses or coats. For items you wear below your waist (think skirts, pants, socks, and shoes), use the verb **haku** (hah-koo). For items you put over your head, such as caps and hats, use **kaburu** (kah-boo-roo). For eyeglasses or sunglasses, use the verb **kakeru** (kah-keh-roo) or **suru** (soo-roo), which means *to do.* For other accessories, use **suru** or **tsukeru** (tsoo-keh-roo) (*to attach*).

Talking about sizing

Trying on clothing is important, but shopping for a T-shirt is pretty easy. You can often avoid going to the fitting room if you know your **saizu** (sah-ee-zoo) (*size*).

» S サイズ **S saizu** (eh-soo sah-ee-zoo) (*small*)

» M サイズ **M saizu** (eh-moo sah-ee-zoo) (*medium*)

» L サイズ **L saizu** (eh-roo sah-ee-zoo) (*large*)

» XL サイズ **XL saizu** (ehk-koo-soo eh-roo sah-ee-zoo) (*extra large*)

Buying a dress is more complicated than shopping for a T-shirt. Use the counter **-gō** (gohh) when sizing up your choices. (For more info on using Japanese counters and Japanese numbers, check out Chapter 4.)

Women's dress sizes in Japan are three sizes less than they are in America. Here are the rough equivalents for women's dress sizes:

American Size	Japanese Size
4	7
6	9
8	11
10	13
12	15
14	17
16	19

Men's suit and coat sizes are expressed in letters in Japan. Compare American sizes and Japanese sizes:

American Size	Japanese Size
34	S
36	S
38	M
40	M
42	L
44	L
46	LL

In Japan, length is specified in metric units. If your waist is **30 inchi** (sahn–jooo een–chee) (*30 inches*), it's **76.2 senchi** (nah–nah–jooo–roh–koo tehn nee sehn–chee) (*76.2 centimeters*). To find your size in centimeters, just multiply your size in inches by 2.54 (1 inch = 2.54 centimeters). Carry a little **dentaku** (dehn–tah–koo) (*calculator*) with you if you shop in Japan.

The particle **ga** (gah) (*but*), as it's used in the following Talkin' the Talk dialogue, connects two contrasting or conflicting sentences. Simply add the particle **ga** (gah) (*but*) at the end of the first sentence as in the following examples.

ジャケットはありますが、ロングコートはありません。**Jaketto wa arimasu ga, rongu kōto wa arimasen.** (jah-keht-toh wa ah-ree-mah-soo gah, rohn-goo kohh-toh wah ah-ree-mah-sehn.) (*We have jackets, but we don't have long coats.*)

私はアメリカ人ですが、日本語を話します。**Watashi wa Amerikajin desu ga, Nihongo o hanashimasu.** (wah-tah-shee wah ah-meh-ree-kah-jeen deh-soo gah, nee-hohn-goh oh hah-nah-shee-mah-soo.) (*I'm American, but I speak Japanese.*)

Talkin' the Talk

Lori has found a nice-looking jacket in a store, but she doesn't like the color. She's about to ask the clerk if the store has the same jacket in a different color.

Lori:	**Chigau iro wa arimasu ka.** chee-gah-oo ee-roh wa ah-ree-mah-soo kah. *Do you have a different color?*
Clerk:	**Aka wa arimasu ga, saizu wa S dake desu.** ah-kah wah ah-ree-mah-soo gah, sah-ee-zoo wah eh-soo dah-keh deh-soo. *We have red ones, but only small sizes.*
Lori:	**Chotto kite mite mo ii desu ka.** choht-toh kee-teh mee-teh moh eee deh-soo kah. *Can I try it on?*
Clerk:	**Dōzo.** dohh-zo. *Go ahead.*

Lori tries on the red jacket.

Lori: **Yappari chotto chīsai desu.**
          yahp-pah-ree choht-toh cheee-sah-ee deh-soo.
          As I expected, it's a little small.

Clerk: **Jā, midori wa. Midori wa M saizu to L saizu ga
          arimasu yo.**
          jahh, mee-doh-ree wah. mee-doh-ree wah eh-moo
          sah-ee-zoo toh eh-roo sah-ee-zoo gah ah-ree-
          mah-soo yoh.
          *Then how about green? We have medium and
          large in green.*

Lori tries on a green jacket.

Lori: **Ā, kore wa chōdo ii. Kore o kudasai.**
          ahh, koh-reh wah chohh-doh eee. koh-reh oh
          koo-dah-sah-ee.
          Wow, this one fits just right. I'll take this one, please.

Clerk: **Hai.**
          hah-ee.
          Okay.

WORDS TO KNOW

chigau	chee-gah-oo	different, wrong
Kite mite mo ii desu ka.	kee-teh mee-teh moh eee deh-soo kah.	Can I try it on?
yappari	yahp-pah-ree	expectedly
chīsai	cheee-sah-ee	small
chōdo ii	chohh-doh eee	exact fit

Deciding What You Want to Buy

Finding a good deal is impossible without carefully comparing the **shōhin** (shohh-heen) (*merchandise*). When you shop, look at the quality and the functions of the product closely and compare several similar items you're interested in. Ask yourself which one is better/best.

Making comparisons, grammar-wise, is much easier in Japanese than in English. In English, you need to conjugate the adjective, like *pretty-prettier-prettiest*, but in Japanese, you don't have to! **Kirei** (kee-reh-ee) (*pretty*), remains **kirei;** you use other words to make the comparison. The following sections show you how to make different comparisons and get you comfortable using demonstrative adjectives.

Using demonstrative adjectives

GRAMMAR CHAT

If you see a nice item in a store window, ask the clerk to show it to you. How do you specify the item that you want to see? Most of the time, you can point at it with your finger and use the demonstrative pronoun **kore** (koh-reh) (see Chapter 3). But what if a **yunomi** (yoo-noh-mee) (*teacup*) and a **kyūsu** (kyooo-soo) (*teapot*) are right next to each other in the store window, and your finger doesn't have a laser pointer attached to it? If you say **kore**, the clerk will ask **dore** (doh-reh) (*which one?*), and you'll have to say **kore** again, and the clerk will have to say **dore** again. To end this frustrating and repetitious conversation, change **kore** to **kono** and add the common noun you're referring to — in this case, **kono yunomi** (koh-noh yoo-noh-mee) (*this teacup*) or **kono kyūsu** (koh-noh kyooo-soo) (*this teapot*).

Similarly, **sore** (soh-reh) (*that one near you*) and **are** (ah-reh) (*that one over there*) become **sono** (soh-noh) and **ano** (ah-noh), respectively, when followed by a common noun. (If you want to know more about **sore** and **are,** check out Chapter 3.) Even the question word **dore** (doh-reh) (*which one*) must become **dono** when followed by a common noun. Wow, too many forms? If you think about it, the change is very systematic: The ending **re** becomes **no. Kono, sono,** and **ano** are all demonstrative adjectives. **Dono** is their question counterpart. That's why they're used with a common noun. Check out Table 10-1's breakdown of the Japanese demonstrative pronouns and demonstrative adjective as well as the following examples to straighten everything out.

TABLE 10-1

This, That, and Which

Term Used Independently	Term Followed by a Common Noun
これ **kore** (koh-reh) *this one*	この **kono** (koh-noh) *this . . .*
それ **sore** (soh-reh) *that one near you*	その **sono** (soh-noh) *that . . . near you*

Term Used Independently	Term Followed by a Common Noun
あれ **are** (ah-reh) *that one over there*	あの **ano** (ah-noh) *that . . . over there*
どれ **dore** (doh-reh) *which one*	どの **dono** (doh-noh) *which . . .*

あのビルは何ですか。**Ano biru wa nan desu ka.** (ah-noh bee-roo wah nahn deh-soo kah.) (*What is that building?*)

あれはデパートです。**Are wa depāto desu.** (ah-reh wah deh-pahh-toh deh-soo.) (*That one is a department store.*)

そのネックレスは高いですか。**Sono nekkuresu wa takai desu ka.** (soh-noh nehk-koo-reh-soo wah tah-kah-ee deh-soo kah.) (*Is that necklace expensive?*)

どれを買いますか。**Dore o kaimasu ka.** (doh-reh oh kah-ee-mah-soo kah.) (*Which one will you buy?*)

静岡のお茶はどれですか。**Shizuoka no o-cha wa dore desu ka.** (shee-zoo-oh-kah noh oh-chah wah doh-reh deh-soo kah.) (*Which one is the tea produced in Shizuoka?*)

REMEMBER

The particle **wa** (wah) marks the topic the speaker wants to talk about, so the item in question must already be familiar to both the speaker and the listener. As a result, a question word like **dore** (doh-reh) (*which one*) or **dono o-cha** (doh-noh oh-chah) (*which tea*) can't be marked by the topic particle **wa.**

Comparing two items

GRAMMAR CHAT

To make a comparison between two items in Japanese, you just need the Japanese equivalent of *than,* which is the particle **yori** (yoh-ree). Place **yori** right after the second item in the comparison. Take a look at a few examples to see this concept in action:

古い家具は新しい家具よりいいです。**Furui kagu wa atarashii kagu yori ii desu.** (foo-roo-ee kah-goo wah ah-tah-rah-sheee kah-goo yoh-ree eee deh-soo.) (*Old furniture is better than new furniture.*)

私の車はあなたの車より高いです。**Watashi no kuruma wa anata no kuruma yori takai desu.** (wah-tah-shee noh koo-roo-mah wah ah-nah-tah noh koo-roo-mah yoh-ree tah-kah-ee deh-soo.) (*My car is more expensive than your car.*)

この店はあの店よりサービスがいいです。**Kono mise wa ano mise yori sābisu ga ii desu.** (koh-noh mee-seh wah ah-noh mee-seh yoh-ree sahh-bee-soo gah eee deh-soo.) (*This store has better service than that store.*)

To ask a friend or sales clerk *Which one is better*, remember that *which one* in Japanese is **dore** (doh-reh) or **dochira** (doh-chee-rah) and that you only use **dochira** when the question is about two items. (I tell you how to ask a question about three or more items in the following section.) Here are the steps for constructing an out-of-two comparison question:

1. **List the two items being compared at the beginning of the sentence.**

2. **Add the particle** to **(toh)** (*and*) **after each item, just to make it look like a list.**

3. **Insert the question word** dochira, **followed by the subject-marking particle** ga **(gah).**

    You can't use the topic particle **wa** (wah) after **dochira**. Actually, you can't use **wa** after any question word. So your choice is limited to **ga** in this case.

4. **Add the adjective with the question particle** ka **(kah).**

Did you get lost? If you did, these examples will hopefully help clear things up:

これと、あれと、どちらがいいですか。**Kore to, are to, dochira ga ii desu ka.** (koh-reh toh, ah-reh toh, doh-chee-rah gah eee deh-soo kah.) (*Which one is better, this one or that one?*)

ジェシカと、私と、どちらが好きですか。**Jeshika to, watashi to, dochira ga suki desu ka.** (jeh-shee-kah toh, wah-tah-shee toh, doh-chee-rah gah soo-kee deh-soo kah.) (*Who do you like, Jessica or me?*)

お金と、名声と、どちらが大事ですか。**O-kane to, meisei to, dochira ga daiji desu ka.** (oh-kah-neh toh, mehh-sehh toh, doh-chee-rah gah dah-ee-jee deh-soo kah.) (*Which one is more important, money or reputation?*)

You can answer these comparison questions a few different ways, but here's the simplest one: Just say the item of your choice with the verb **desu** (deh-soo) (*to be*). For example, if someone asks you **Piza to, sushi to, dochira ga suki desu ka.** (pee-zah toh, soo-shee toh, doh-chee-rah gah soo-kee deh-soo kah.) (*Which one do you like better, pizza or sushi?*), you can answer with **piza desu** (pee-zah deh-soo) (*pizza*) or **sushi desu** (soo-shee deh-soo) (*sushi.*), depending on which one you like better.

Comparing three or more items

GRAMMAR CHAT

To express *the best* or *the most* in Japanese, just use the adverb **ichiban** (ee-chee-bahn) (*the most/the best*), which literally means *number one*. Simply place **ichiban** right before the adjective. Look at the following examples and see how easy forming *-est* and *most* sentences in Japanese is:

この車は一番大きいです。**Kono kuruma wa ichiban ōkii desu.** (koh-noh koo-roo-mah wah ee-chee-bahn ohh-keee deh-soo.) (*This car is the biggest.*)

この車は一番高級です。**Kono kuruma wa ichiban kōkyū desu.** (koh-noh koo-roo-mah wah ee-chee-bahn kohh-kyooo deh-soo.) (*This car is the most luxurious.*)

トムは一番まじめです。**Tomu wa ichiban majime desu.** (toh-moo wah ee-chee-bahn mah-jee-meh deh-soo.) (*Tom is the most serious.*)

If you want to specify the domain in which an item is *the most* or *the best*, such as "in the class," "in the United States," or "in the world," insert a noun that specifies the domain, along with the particle **de** (deh), right before **ichiban**.

この車はアメリカで一番大きいです。**Kono kuruma wa Amerika de ichiban ōkii desu.** (koh-noh koo-roo-mah wah ah-meh-ree-kah deh ee-chee-bahn ohh-keee deh-soo.) (*This car is the biggest in America.*)

この車は世界で一番高級です。**Kono kuruma wa sekai de ichiban kōkyū desu.** (koh-noh koo-roo-mah wah seh-kah-ee deh ee-chee-bahn kohh-kyooo deh-soo.) (*This car is the most luxurious in the world.*)

トムはクラスで一番まじめです。**Tomu wa kurasu de ichiban majime desu.** (toh-moo wah koo-rah-soo deh ee-chee-bahn mah-jee-meh deh-soo.) (*Tom is the most serious in the class.*)

GRAMMAR CHAT

To ask which item is the best among three or more items, list them by using the particle **to** (toh); add two particles, **de** (deh) and **wa** (wah); and use the question words **dare** (dah-reh), **doko** (doh-koh), or **dore** (doh-reh). Use **dare** for people, **doko** for places, and **dore** for other items, including foods, cars, animals, plants, games, and academic subjects. All three words mean *which one*. (As I explain in the preceding section, you can't use **dochira** to mean *which one* in this context because you use **dochira** only for asking a question about two items.) Then add **ichiban**. Take a look:

ベスと、メアリーと、ケンと、ジョンでは、だれが一番優しいですか。**Besu to, Mearī to, Ken to, Jon de wa, dare ga ichiban yasashii desu ka.** (beh-soo toh, meh-ah-reee toh, kehn toh, john deh wah, dah-reh gah ee-chee-bahn yah-sah-sheee deh-soo kah.) (*Among Beth, Mary, Ken, and John, who is the kindest?*)

ボストンと、東京と、シカゴでは、どこが一番寒いですか。**Bosuton to, Tōkyō to, Shikago de wa, doko ga ichiban samui desu ka.** (boh-soo-tohn toh, tohh-kyohh toh, shee-kah-goh deh wah, doh-koh gah ee-chee-bahn sah-moo-ee deh-soo kah.) (*Among Boston, Tokyo, and Chicago, which one is the coldest?*)

ハンバーガーと、ホットドッグと、ピザでは、どれが一番好きですか。**Hanbāgā to, hotto doggu to, piza de wa, dore ga ichiban suki desu ka.** (hahn-bahh-gahh toh, hoht-toh dohg-goo toh, pee-zah deh wah, doh-reh gah ee-chee-bahn soo-kee deh-soo kah.) (*Among hamburgers, hot dogs, and pizza, which one do you like the best?*)

Sometimes you want to specify the category of the items among which the comparison is made, like *out of foods, out of the students in the class,* or *among the cities in the country.* If so, specify the category at the beginning of the question and place two particles, **de** (deh) and **wa** (wah), right after it. Remember that you have to use **nani** (nah-nee) (*what*) rather than **dore** (doh-reh) (*which one*). So, if you're specifying a category rather than giving a list, use **dare** (dah-reh) (*who*) for people, **doko** (doh-koh) (*where*) for locations, and **nani** (nah-nee) (*what*) for other items. Switching **dore** and **nani** is a bit cumbersome, isn't it? You deserve a table to help you sort things out, so check out Table 10-2.

TABLE 10-2   **Japanese Question Words for Various Comparisons**

Category	Out of Two Items	Out of Three or More Items	Out of a Category of Items
People	どちら **dochira**	だれ **dare**	だれ **dare**
Locations	どちら **dochira**	どこ **doko**	どこ **doko**
Other items	どちら **dochira**	どれ **dore**	何 **nani**

Look at some "which one" questions concerning a category of items:

このクラスではだれが一番まじめですか。**Kono kurasu de wa dare ga ichiban majime desu ka.** (koh-noh koo-rah-soo deh wah dah-reh gah ee-chee-bahn mah-jee-meh deh-soo kah.) (*Who is the serious in this class?*)

日本の町ではどこが一番きれいですか。**Nihon no machi de wa doko ga ichiban kirei desu ka.** (nee-hohn noh mah-chee deh wah doh-koh gah ee-chee-bahn kee-rehh deh-soo kah.) (*Out of Japanese cities, which one is most beautiful?*)

食べ物では何が一番好きですか。**Tabemono de wa nani ga ichiban suki desu ka.** (tah-beh-moh-noh deh wah nah-nee gah ee-chee-bahn soo-kee deh-soo kah.) (*Which food do you like best? [Literally: Among foods, which one do you like the best?]*)

The simplest way to answer these questions is to use **desu.** If someone asks you **Amerika de wa doko ga ichiban samui desu ka.** (ah-meh-ree-kah deh wah doh-koh gah ee-chee-bahn sah-moo-ee deh-soo kah.) (*Which place is the coldest in America?*), you can answer by saying **Arasuka desu!** (ah-rah-soo-kah deh-soo!) (*Alaska!*).

You Gotta Pay to Play: Buying Your Merchandise

At the end of a successful shopping venture, you get to go home with all kinds of new goodies. But first you have to pay for those goodies. The following sections reveal how to discuss prices, state your intention to buy something, and pay for your merchandise.

Identifying prices

In Japan, bargaining isn't a common practice except in a few places, like **Akihabara** (ah-kee-hah-bah-rah), the famous Electric Town (and nowadays it's also known as a Mecca for popular culture). But you do need to have some idea of how to talk about prices. Here's a list of the basic pricing-related vocabulary to help you out:

» ちょっと高いです。 **Chotto takai desu.** (choht-toh tah-kah-ee deh-soo.) (*It's a little expensive.*)

» いくらですか。 **Ikura desu ka.** (ee-koo-rah deh-soo kah.) (*How much is it?*)

» まあまあ安いですね。 **Māmā yasui desu ne.** (mahh mahh yah-soo-ee deh-soo neh.) (*It's relatively cheap.*)

Stating that you want to buy something

When you're ready to make your purchase, you need to be able to say **kau** (kah-oo) (*to buy*). Here's how to conjugate this **u**-verb (remember to watch out for the **w** sound that appears in the negative form):

Japanese Script	Rōmaji	Pronunciation
買う	kau	kah-oo
買わない	kawanai	kah-wah-nah-ee
買い(ます)	kai (masu)	kah-ee (-mah-soo)
買って	katte	kaht-teh

When you decide to buy something at a store, mention the item and say **o kudasai** (oh koo-dah-sah-ee) or **o onegai shimasu** (oh oh-neh-gah-ee shee-mah-soo). **Kudasai** literally means *give/sell it to me*, whereas **onegai shimasu** literally means something like *beg/ask you to do it*. So **onegai shimasu** can be used in a variety of contexts where you want to ask someone to do something — it's not limited to giving or selling. Accordingly, **kudasai** is more straightforward; use it when you want to buy something as opposed to **onegai shimasu**.

これを下さい。 **Kore o kudasai.** (koh-reh oh koo-dah-sah-ee.) (*Please give this one to me.*)

あれをお願いします。 **Are o onegaishimasu.** (ah-reh oh oh-neh-gah-ee-shee-mah-soo.) (*That one, please.*)

あの人形を下さい。 **Ano ningyō o kudasai.** (ah-noh neen-gyohh oh koo-dah-sah-ee.) (*I'll take that doll.*)

Paying for your purchase

Whether you prefer to pay with **genkin** (gehn-keen) (*cash*) or **kurejitto kādo** (koo-reh-jeet-toh kahh-doh) (*credit card*), chances are you'll need the following words and phrases when paying for your purchases in Japanese:

» 円 **en** (ehn) (*yen*)

» 硬貨 **kōka** (kohh-kah) (*coins*)

» お札 **o-satsu** (oh-sah-tsoo) (*bills*)

» お返し **o-kaeshi** (oh-kah-eh-shee) (*return*)

» お釣り **o-tsuri** (oh-tsoo-ree) (*change*)

» レシート **reshīto** (reh-sheee-to) (*receipt*)

» 財布 **saifu** (sah-ee-foo) (*wallet*)

» 消費税 **shōhizei** (shohh-hee-zehh) (*sales tax*)

» 消費税込みで **shōhizei-komi de** (shohh-hee-zehh-koh-mee deh) (*including sales tax*)

Of course, you also need to know how to say *to pay*: **harau** (hah-rah-oo). Following is a conjugation of this **u**-verb. Watch out for the **w** sound that shows up in the negative form.

Japanese Script	Rōmaji	Pronunciation
払う	harau	hah-rah-oo
払わない	harawanai	hah-rah-wah-nah-ee
払い(ます)	harai (masu)	hah-rah-ee (-mah-soo)
払って	haratte	har-raht-teh

..............Talkin' the Talk..............

Michiko is paying for a pair of sneakers and a racket in a sporting-goods store.

Michiko: **Kore to kore o kudasai.**
koh-reh toh koh-reh oh koo-dah-sah-ee.
I want this and this please.

Clerk: **Hai. Shōhizei-komi de — 3,225-en de gozaimasu.**
hah-ee. shohh-hee-zehh koh-mee deh — sahn-zehn-nee-hyah-koo-nee-jooo-goh-ehn deh goh-zah-ee-mah-soo.
Sure. Including the sales tax — 3,225 yen.

Michiko: **Jā, 4,000-en kara onegai shimasu.**
jahh, yohn-sehn-en kah-rah oh-neh-gah-ee shee-mah-soo.
Then please take it out of 4,000 yen.

Clerk: **Hai. Dewa, 775-en no o-kaeshi de gozaimasu. Reshīto wa kochira de gozaimasu. Dōmo arigatō gozaimashita.**
hah-ee. deh-wah, nah-nah-hyah-koo-nah-nah-jooo-goh-ehn noh oh-kah-eh-shee deh goh-zah-ee-mah-soo. reh-sheee-toh wah koh-chee-rah deh goh-zah-ee-mah-soo. dohh-moh ah-ree-gah-tohh goh-zah-ee-mah-shee-tah.
Sure. Your change is 775 yen. Here's the receipt. Thank you very much.

WORDS TO KNOW

(X) o kudasai	(X) oh koo-dah-sah-ee	please give me (X)
shōhizei-komi de	shohh-hee-zehh-koh-mee deh	including sales tax
4,000-en kara	yohn-sehn-ehn kah-rah	from 4,000 yen
o-tsuri	oh-tsoo-ree	change
reshīto	reh-sheee-toh	receipt

FUN & GAMES

You're about to go to the supermarket to get the following items. Match each illustration to one of the Japanese words in the list. Then turn to Appendix C for the answers.

1.   2.   3.

4.   5.

Illustration by Elizabeth Kurtzman

a. チーズ **chīzu**

b. たまご **tamago**

c. バター **batā**

d. パン **pan**

e. 牛乳 **gyūnyū**

Chapter **11**

Going Out on the Town

I bet that your **machi** (mah-chee) (*town*) is full of great opportunities for fun. Read the **shinbun** (sheen-boon) (*newspaper*), pick up a few **zasshi** (zahs-shee) (*magazines*), or surf the **Intānetto** (een-tahh-neht-toh) (*Internet*) to find out what's going on. Perhaps the local museum is hosting an exhibit or a new movie that you're dying to see is playing at the cinema. Maybe you want to head to a club or try out your karaoke skills. Come on; get up off the couch, invite your friends to join you in your adventures, and then go have some fun!

REMEMBER

You can listen to all the Talkin' the Talk dialogues featured in this chapter. Go to www.dummies.com/go/japanesefd and click on the dialogue you want to hear.

Checking Out Entertaining Activities

Pick your favorite type of entertainment. Do you want to dance, sing, play games, or drink? No need to limit yourself here. You can do all four at the same time! You can also visit an art museum or catch a show. The following sections give you the words and phrases you need to know when partaking in a variety of fun activities while you're out on the town.

Getting cultured at museums and galleries

If your daily life is filled with hassles and headaches, your heart deserves to be cleansed, nourished, and rejuvenated with a little culture. Why not check out one of these places?

>> 美術館 **bijutsukan** (bee-joo-tsoo-kahn) (*art museums*)

>> 画廊 **garō** (gah-rohh) (*art galleries*)

>> 博物館 **hakubutsukan** (hah-koo-boo-tsoo-kahn) (*museums*)

>> 図書館 **toshokan** (toh-shoh-kahn) (*libraries*)

Of course, you need to be aware of when these institutions open and close for the day if you're going to visit them. Conjugate the **u**–verbs **aku** (ah–koo) (*to open*) and **shimaru** (shee–mah–roo) (*to close*).

Japanese Script	Rōmaji	Pronunciation
開く	aku	ah-koo
開かない	akanai	ah-kah-nah-ee
開き(ます)	aki (masu)	ah-kee (-mah-soo)
開いて	aite	ah-ee-teh
閉まる	shimaru	shee-mah-roo
閉まらない	shimaranai	shee-mah-rah-nah-ee
閉まり(ます)	shimari (masu)	shee-mah-ree (-mah-soo)
閉まって	shimatte	shee-maht-teh

Now that you know how to say those verbs in Japanese, take a look at these helpful sample questions that you may want to ask:

博物館は何時に開きますか。 **Hakubutsukan wa nan-ji ni akimasu ka.** (hah-koo-boo-tsoo-kahn wah nahn-jee nee ah-kee-mah-soo kah.) (*What time does the museum open?*)

何時に閉まりますか。 **Nan-ji ni shimarimasu ka.** (nahn-jee nee shee-mah-ree-mah-soo kah.) (*What time does it close?*)

日曜日はお休みですか。 **Nichiyōbi wa oyasumi desu ka.** (nee-chee-yohh-bee wah oh-yah-soo-mee deh-soo kah.) (*Is it closed on Sundays?*)

Heading to the theater

Visiting theaters lets you really feel the passion of the performers. And just about everyone enjoys going to a movie theater. The following words and phrases are useful when heading to the theater to see a performance or watch a movie:

>> バレー **barē** (bah-rehh) (*ballet*)

>> チケット **chiketto** (chee-keht-toh) (*ticket*)

>> 映画 **eiga** (ehh-gah) (*movie*)

>> 映画館 **eigakan** (ehh-gah-kahn) (*movie theater*)

>> 劇場 **gekijō** (geh-kee-johh) (*theater for performances*)

>> インターミッション **intāmisshon** (een-tahh-mee-shohn) (*intermission*)

>> コンサート **konsāto** (kohn-sahh-toh) (*concert*)

>> ミュージカル **myūjikaru** (myooo-jee-kah-roo) (*musical*)

>> 芝居 **shibai** (shee-bah-ee) (*play*)

Here are some example sentences that help you ask for various kinds of tickets at shows and movies:

シニア一人お願いします。**Shinia hitori onegaishimasu.** (shee-nee-ah hee-toh-ree oh-neh-gah-ee-shee-mah-soo.) (*One senior citizen, please.*)

一万円の席をお願いします。**Ichiman-en no seki o onegaishimasu.** (ee-chee-mahn-ehn noh seh-kee oh oh-neh-gah-ee-shee-mah-soo.) (*A 10,000-yen seat, please.*)

大人二人お願いします。**Otona futari onegaishimasu.** (oh-toh-nah foo-tah-ree oh-neh-gah-ee-shee-mah-soo.) (*Two adults, please.*)

大人二人と子ども一人お願いします。**Otona futari to kodomo hitori onegaishimasu.** (oh-toh-nah foo-tah-ree toh koh-doh-moh hee-toh-ree oh-neh-gah-ee-shee-mah-soo.) (*Two adults and one child, please.*)

REMEMBER

Use the counter **-mai** (mah-ee) for counting tickets because tickets are usually flat. (See Chapter 4 for a discussion on counters.)

CULTURAL WISDOM

KABUKI

歌舞伎 **Kabuki** (kah-boo-kee), which began in the seventeenth century, is one of the most popular types of traditional theater in Japan. All the action takes place on a dynamic, revolving stage.

The actors (all males, even in female roles) wear heavy makeup and colorful, spectacular costumes. Watch how they move their necks and fingers and how they walk and sit down. It's amazing.

The Kabukiza Theater in Tokyo is world famous. The theater has large restaurants where you can grab a quick dinner during intermission. It also rents earphones that provide English commentary and explanations on the play's plot, music, and actors.

Other Japanese traditional theater arts include 能 **Nō** (nohh) (*Noh*), a musical theater developed in the fourteenth century, where actors wear masks, and 文楽 **bunraku** (boon-rah-koo) (*Bunraku*), a puppet theater developed in the seventeenth century.

Eating Out at Fast-Food and Sit-Down Restaurants

Would you like to eat before or after your activity? Whether you're out to eat in Japan or the United States, you're bound to find all kinds of delicious options, from fast-food establishments to more traditional sit-down restaurants.

You need to know how to order food! Practice conjugating the verb **chūmon suru** (chooo-mohn soo-roo) (*to order*). It's actually a combination of the noun **chūmon** (*order*) and the verb **suru** (*to do*), so you can just conjugate the **suru** part. Yes, it's an irregular verb. (See Chapter 3 for more about the verb **suru**.)

Japanese Script	Rōmaji	Pronunciation
注文する	chūmon suru	chooo-mohn soo-roo
注文しない	chūmon shinai	chooo-mohn shee-nah-ee
注文し(ます)	chūmon shi (masu)	chooo-mohn shee (-mah-soo)
注文して	chūmon shite	chooo-mohn shee-teh

In this section, I give you the fast-food words and phrases you need whenever you decide to eat out. You're still responsible for the check, though!

Ordering fast food

In Japan, you can find some of the familiar fast-food restaurants you see in the States. Here are the names of some common fast-food dishes in Japan — or at least in Japanese:

>> アイスティー **aisutī** (ah-ee-soo teee) (*iced tea*)

>> チーズバーガー **chīzu bāgā** (cheee-zoo bahh-gahh) (*cheeseburger*)

>> フライドチキン **furaido chikin** (foo-rah-ee-doh chee-keen) (*fried chicken*)

>> フライドポテト **furaido poteto** (foo-rah-ee-doh poh-teh-toh) (*French fries*)

>> ハンバーガー **hanbāgā** (hahn-bahh-gahh) (*hamburger*)

>> ホットドッグ **hotto doggu** (hoht-toh dohg-goo) (*hot dog*)

>> コーヒー **kōhī** (kohh-heee) (*coffee*)

>> コーラ **kōra** (kohh-rah) (*cola*)

>> オレンジジュース **orenjijūsu** (oh-rehn-jee jooo-soo) (*orange juice*)

>> ピザ **piza** (pee-zah) (*pizza*)

>> シェイク **sheiku** (sheh-ee-koo) (*milkshakes*)

>> テリヤキバーガー **teriyaki bāgā** (teh-ree-yah-kee bahh-gahh) (*teriyaki burger*)

You may have to answer a few questions when you order at a fast-food joint. **O-mochi kaeri desu ka.** (oh-moh-chee kah-eh-ree deh-soo kah.) means *Will you take it home?* or *To go?* **Kochira de omeshiagari desu ka.** (koh-chee-rah deh oh-meh-shee-ah-gah-ree deh-soo kah.) means *Will you eat here?* or *For here?* If you hear one of these questions, just answer with **hai** (hah-ee) (*yes*) or **Īe** (eee-eh) (*no*). If you can't get by with a simple *yes* or *no*, say one of the following:

>> 持って帰ります。 **Motte kaerimasu.** (moht-teh kah-eh-ree-mah-soo.) (*I'll take it home.*)

>> ここで食べます。 **Koko de tabemasu.** (koh-koh deh tah-beh-mah-soo.) (*I'll eat here.*)

If you want to contrast how you treat or feel about two items — for example, *I like fish but hate meat* — you can highlight each term by marking it with **wa** (wah). You can place **wa** after the noun you want to highlight and the particle that's already there. Just remember to drop the original particle if it's the subject–marking particle **ga** (gah) or the object–marking particle **o** (oh). (Chapter 3 gives you more information on using these particles.) Here are some examples:

このレストランはパスタはおいしいです。でも、ピザはまずいです。**Kono resutoran wa pasuta wa oishii desu. Demo, piza wa mazui desu.** (koh-noh reh-soo-toh-rahn wah pah-soo-tah wah oh-ee-sheee deh-soo. deh-moh, pee-zah wah mah-zoo-ee deh-soo.) (*In this restaurant, pasta is delicious. But pizza is bad.*)

レストランにはよく行きます。でも、バーにはあまり行きません。**Resutoran ni wa yoku ikimasu. Demo, bā ni wa amari ikimasen.** (reh-soo-toh-rahn nee wah yoh-koo ee-kee-mah-soo. deh-moh, bahh nee wa ah-mah-ree ee-kee-mah-sehn.) (*I often go to restaurants. However, I don't often go to bars.*)

サラダは食べます。でも、肉は食べません。**Sarada wa tabemasu. Demo, niku wa tabemasen.** (sah-rah-dah wah tah-beh-mah-soo. deh-moh, nee-koo wah tah-beh-mah-sehn.) (*I eat salad. But I don't eat meat.*)

レストランではお酒を飲みます。でも、家ではお酒を飲みません。**Resutoran de wa o-sake o nomimasu. Demo, ie de wa o-sake o nomimasen.** (reh-soo-toh-rahn deh wah oh-sah-keh oh noh-mee-mah-soo. deh-moh, ee-eh deh wah oh-sah-keh oh noh-mee-mah-sehn.) (*I drink sake at restaurants. However, I don't drink sake at home.*)

Talkin' the Talk

Jenna is about to place an order at a fast-food restaurant.

Fast-food worker:	**Irasshaimase! O-mochikaeri desu ka. Kochira de o-meshiagari desu ka.**
	ee-rahs-shah-ee-mah-seh! oh-moh-chee-kah-eh-ree deh-soo kah. koh-chee-rah deh oh-meh-shee-ah-gah-ree deh-soo kah.
	Welcome! Is this to go? Or will you be dining here?
Jenna:	**Motte kaerimasu.**
	moht-teh kah-eh-ree-mah-soo.
	To go, please.
Fast-food worker:	**Kashikomarimashita! Go-chūmon wa.**
	kah-shee-koh-mah-ree-mah-shee-tah! goh-chooo-mohn wah.
	Certainly! And your order?

Jenna:	**Chīzu bāgā to teriyaki bāgā o onegai shimasu.**
	cheee-zoo bahh-gahh toh teh-ree-yah-kee bahh-gahh oh oh-neh-gah-ee shee-mah-soo.
	A cheeseburger and a teriyaki burger, please.

Fast-food worker:	**O-nomimono wa.**
	oh-noh-mee-moh-noh wah.
	Anything to drink?

Jenna:	**Kōra to banira sheiku o onegai shimasu.**
	kohh-rah toh bah-nee-rah sheh-ee-koo oh oh-neh-gah-ee shee-mah-soo.
	A cola and a vanilla shake, please.

Fast-food worker:	**Kashikomarimashita!**
	kah-shee-koh-mah-ree-mah-shee-tah!
	Certainly!

WORDS TO KNOW

Irasshaimase!	ee-rahs-shah-ee-mah-seh!	Welcome!
O-mochikaeri desu ka.	oh-moh-chee-kah-eh-ree deh-soo kah.	Is this to go?
Kochira de o-meshiagari desu ka.	koh-chee-rah deh oh-meh-shee-ah-gah-ree deh-soo kah.	Will you be dining here?
Kashikomarimashita!	kah-shee-koh-mah-ree-mah-shee-tah!	Certainly!
Go-chūmon wa.	goh-chooo-mohn wah.	Your order?
O-nomimono wa.	oh-noh-mee-moh-noh wah.	Anything to drink?

Making a reservation

Japanese often line up in front of the most-popular restaurants, and they don't mind waiting for an hour or more. But if you don't want to wait in line, make a reservation over the phone.

Japanese say *to make a reservation* by saying *to do a reservation*, which is **yoyaku o suru** (yoh-yah-koo oh soo-roo). **Yoyaku** is a noun, so all you have to worry about is the **suru** part. Remember that **suru** is an irregular verb as you check out these conjugations:

Japanese Script	Rōmaji	Pronunciation
予約をする	yoyaku o suru	yoh-yah-koo oh soo-roo
予約をしない	yoyaku o shinai	yoh-yah-koo oh shee-nah-ee
予約をし(ます)	yoyaku o shi (masu)	yoh-yah-koo oh shee (-mah-soo)
予約をして	yoyaku o shite	yoh-yah-koo oh shee-teh

TIP

To say you *want to* make a reservation, add **-tai** (tah-ee) at the end of the stem form of this verb: **yoyaku shi-tai** (yoh-yah-koo shee-tah-ee). See Chapter 12 for information on using **-tai**.

To make a reservation, first let the restaurant's host or hostess know when you want to arrive. Table 11-1 shows you how to pronounce the basic time ranges that you're most likely to need for making your dinner reservation. (For the basics of how to tell time in Japanese, including the concepts of *a.m.*, *p.m.*, and *o'clock*, turn to Chapter 4.)

TABLE 11-1

Reservation Time

Time	Japanese	Pronunciation
6:00	6時 **roku-ji**	roh-koo-jee
6:15	6時15分 **roku-ji jūgo-fun**	roh-koo-jee jooo-goh-foon
6:30	6時半 **roku-ji han**	roh-koo-jee hahn
6:45	6時45分 **roku-ji yonjūgo-fun**	roh-koo-jee yohn-jooo-goh-foon
7:00	7時 **shichi-ji**	shee-chee-jee
8:00	8時 **hachi-ji**	hah-chee-jee
9:00	9時 **ku-ji**	koo-jee

When you talk about an approximate time, add **goro** (goh-roh) after the time phrase. **Roku-ji goro** (roh-koo-jee goh-roh) means *about 6:00*, and **roku-ji han goro** (roh-koo-jee hahn goh-roh) means *about 6:30*.

After you establish a reservation time, let the restaurant know how many people are in your party by using a counter. *Counters* are short suffixes that directly follow numbers. As I explain in Chapter 4, the counter you use depends on the item you're counting. So you can't just say **go** (goh) (*five*) when you have five people in your party. You have to say **go-nin** (goh–neen) because **-nin** (neen) is the counter for people. But watch out for the irregular **hitori** (hee–toh–ree) (*one*), **futari** (foo–tah–ree) (*two*), and **yonin** (yoh–neen) (*four*).

Talkin' the Talk

Makoto Tanaka is trying to make a reservation at Fuguichi, a blowfish restaurant, over the phone.

Hostess:	**Maido arigatō gozaimasu. Fuguichi de gozaimasu.** mah-ee-doh ah-ree-gah-tohh goh-zah-ee-mah-soo. foo-goo-ee-chee deh goh-zah-ee-mah-soo. *Thank you for calling. (Literally: Thank you for your patronage.) This is Fuguichi. (How can I help you?)*
Makoto:	**Anō, konban, yoyaku o shitai-n-desu ga.** ah-nohh, kohn-bahn, yoh-yah-koo oh shee-tah-een-deh-soo gah. *I'd like to make a reservation for tonight.*
Hostess:	**Hai, arigatō gozaimasu. Nan-ji goro.** hah-ee, ah-ree-gah-tohh goh-zah-ee-mah-soo. nahn-jee goh-roh. *Yes, thank you. About what time?*
Makoto:	**Shichi-ji ni onegai shimasu.** shee-chee-jee nee oh-neh-gah-ee shee-mah-soo. *7:00, please.*
Hostess:	**Hai. Nan-nin-sama.** hah-ee. nahn-neen-sah-mah. *Certainly. How many people?*
Makoto:	**Go-nin desu.** goh-neen deh-soo. *Five people.*
Hostess:	**Hai, kashikomarimashita. O-namae wa.** hah-ee, kah-shee-koh-mah-ree-mah-shee-tah. oh-nah-mah-eh wa. *Certainly. Your name?*

Makoto:	**Fuji Bōeki no Tanaka desu.**
	foo-jee bohh-eh-kee noh tah-nah-kah deh-soo.
	I'm Tanaka from Fuji Trade Company.

Hostess:	**Fuji Bōeki no Tanaka-sama de gozaimasu ne.**
	foo-jee bohh-eh-kee noh tah-nah-kah-sah-mah deh goh-zah-ee-mah-soo neh.
	Mr. Tanaka from Fuji Trade Company. Is that correct?

Makoto:	**Hai.**
	hah-ee.
	Yes.

Hostess:	**Dewa, shichi-ji ni o-machi shite orimasu.**
	deh-wah, shee-chee-jee nee oh-mah-chee shee-teh oh-ree-mah-soo.
	Then we'll be expecting you at 7:00.

Makoto:	**Hai. Yoroshiku.**
	hah-ee. yoh-roh-shee-koo.
	Yes. Thank you.

WORDS TO KNOW

Maido arigatō gozaimasu.	mah-ee-doh ah-ree-gah-tohh goh-zah-ee-mah-soo.	Thank you for your patronage.
de gozaimasu	deh goh-zah-ee-mah-soo	to be (honorific)
konban	kohn-bahn	tonight
yoyaku (o) suru	yoh-yah-koo (oh) soo-roo	to make a reservation
Shichi-ji ni o-machi shite orimasu.	shee-chee-jee nee oh-mah-chee shee-teh oh-ree-mah-soo.	We'll be expecting you at 7:00.

TIP

In Japanese, you often form a statement using **-n-desu** (n–deh–soo) in conversation, as Makoto does in the preceding Talkin' the Talk. The effect of **-n-desu** is to encourage your partner to respond to your statements. See Chapter 5 for more about **n-desu**.

EATING BLOWFISH CAREFULLY

For a long time, Japanese have admired ふぐ **fugu** (foo-goo) (*blowfish*) as one of the most delicious fish. The only problem: It's poisonous — or at least the ovaries and liver are especially poisonous. If the person preparing **fugu** accidentally slices into either of those two places, eating the **fugu** can kill you. People in Japan have actually died because of improper preparation of fugu by unlicensed chefs.

That's why only trained and licensed chefs are legally permitted to cut, clean, and serve fugu. They remove the dangerous parts and wash the remaining portion of the fish very carefully, using a tremendous amount of water.

Fugu is one of the most expensive delicacies in Japan and costs about $200 for a single fish. Japanese are truly gourmets. They seek out exquisite tastes, risking their lives and paying a fortune in the process.

CULTURAL WISDOM

Japanese say **yoroshiku** (yoh-roh-shee-koo) after asking a favor of someone or after making a request, such as a reservation at a restaurant. In this context, it means *Please take good care of it for me.* You don't say anything like that in English, so just think of it as *thank you.* **Yoroshiku** is one of those phrases you have to use your intuition and cultural understanding rather than translations to understand. But if you use it appropriately, you'll really sound like a native Japanese speaker!

Ordering in a restaurant

How do you order in a restaurant (that is, the kind where the food comes to your table)? Whether you go to a four-star establishment or the corner pub, your waiter or waitress will ask you questions like the following:

» ご注文は。**Gochūmon wa.** (goh-chooo-mohn wah.) (*Your order?*)

» 何になさいますか。**Nani ni nasaimasu ka.** (nah-nee nee nah-sah-ee-mah-soo kah.) (*What will you have?*)

» お飲み物は。**O-nomimono wa.** (oh-noh-mee-moh-noh wah.) (*Anything to drink?*)

Following are some phrases you can use to help you place your order:

» メニューをお願いします。**Menyū o onegai shimasu.** (meh-nyooo oh oh-neh-gah-ee shee-mah-soo.) (*Menu, please.*)

» ラーメンを三つお願いします。**Rāmen o mittsu onegaishimasu.** (rahh-mehn oh meet-tsoo oh-neh-gah-ee-shee-mah-soo.) (*Can we have three orders of ramen noodles, please?*)

» すしと刺し身と味噌汁をお願いします。**Sushi to sashimi to misoshiru o onegaishimasu.** (soo-shee toh sah-shee-mee toh mee-soh-shee-roo oh oh-neh-gah-ee-shee-mah-soo.) (*Can I have sushi, sashimi, and miso soup, please?*)

» ワインはありますか。**Wain wa arimasu ka.** (wah-een wah ah-ree-mah-soo kah.) (*Do you have wine?*)

» 私はステーキを下さい。**Watashi wa sutēki o kudasai.** (wah-tah-shee wah soo-tehh-kee oh koo-dah-sah-ee.) (*Can I have steak, please?*)

» 私はラザニアをお願いします。**Watashi wa razania o onegaishimasu.** (wah-tah-shee wah rah-zah-nee-ah oh oh-neh-gah-ee-shee-mah-soo.) (*Can I have lasagne, please?*)

» 今日のスペシャルは。**Kyō no supesharu wa.** (kyohh noh soo-peh-shah-roo wah.) (*Today's special?*)

REMEMBER

To list several dishes, use **to** (toh) between each dish to link them. Think of **to** as a verbal comma or the word *and*.

To specify the quantity of each item that you want to order, use **–tsu (tsoo)**, the counter that applies to food items — **hito-tsu** (hee-toh-tsoo) (*one*), **futa-tsu** (foo-tah-tsoo) (*two*), **mit-tsu** (meet-tsoo) (*three*), and so forth. (See Chapter 4 for a more in-depth explanation of counters.)

Are you going to eat some of the following today?

» ビーフステーキ **bīfu sutēki** (beee-foo soo-tehh-kee) (*beef steak*)

» ビーフシチュー **bīfu shichū** (beee-foo shee-chooo) (*beef stew*)

» 牛丼 **gyūdon** (gyooo-dohn) (*a bowl of rice topped with cooked beef and vegetables*)

» マッシュポテト **masshu poteto** (mas-shoo poh-teh-toh) (*mashed potato*)

» ミートローフ **mīto rōfu** (meee-toh rohh-foo) (*meatloaf*)

» 親子丼 **oyako donburi** (oh-yah-koh dohn-boo-ree) (*a bowl of rice topped with cooked chicken and eggs*)

» サラダ **sarada** (sah-rah-dah) (*salad*)

» スープ **sūpu** (sooo-poo) (*soup*)

» スパゲッティ **supagetti** (soo-pah-geht-tee) (*spaghetti*)

» てんぷら **tenpura** (tehn-poo-rah) (*tempura, deep-fried and battered vegetables or seafood*)

>> とんかつ **tonkatsu** (tohn-kah-tsoo) (*pork cutlet*)

>> 鰻 **unagi** (oo-nah-gee) (*eel*)

>> 焼き肉 **yakiniku** (yah-kee-nee-koo) (*Korean-style barbecue*)

TIP

If you want to have a complete meal that comes with rice, soup, and a salad, order a **teishoku** (tehh-shoh-koo) (*set meal*), like **sashimi teishoku** and **tenpura teishoku**.

CULTURAL WISDOM

Wondering what to do if you can't read the Japanese menu at a restaurant? Don't worry. Most restaurants in Japan have colored pictures on the menus or life-sized wax models of the food in their windows. The easiest way to order food is to follow this simple formula: Say **watashi wa** (wah-tah-shee wah) (*as for me*), point to the picture of the dish on the menu, say **kore o** (koh-reh oh) (*this one* plus direct object particle), and say **onegaishimasu** (oh-neh-gah-ee-shee-mah-soo) (*I'd like to ask you*) or **kudasai** (koo-dah-sah-ee) (*please give me*) at the end.

.... Talkin' the Talk ....

Ken and Akiko are going to place an order at a restaurant inside the Tokyo station.

Server:	**Nani ni nasaimasu ka.**
	nah-nee nee nah-sah-ee-mah-soo kah.
	What would you like to have?

Ken:	**Boku wa sashimi teishoku.**
	boh-koo wah sah-shee-mee tehh-shoh-koo.
	I'll have the sashimi set.

Server:	**O-nomimono wa.**
	oh-noh-mee-moh-noh wa.
	How about something to drink?

Ken:	**Bīru.**
	beee-roo.
	Beer.

Server:	**Hai, kashikomarimashita. O-kyaku-sama wa.**
	hah-ee, kah-shee-koh-mah-ree-mah-shee-tah.
	oh-kyah-koo-sah-mah wah.
	Sure, certainly. How about you? (Literally: How about the customer?)

Akiko:	**Watashi wa tenpura teishoku o onegai shimasu.**
	wah-tah-shee wa tehn-poo-rah tehh-shoh-koo oh oh-neh-gah-ee shee-mah-soo.
	I'll have the tempura set.

Server:	**O-nomimono wa.**
	oh-noh-mee-moh-noh wah.
	How about something to drink?

Akiko:	**Īe, ii desu.**
	eee-eh, eee deh-soo.
	No, thank you.

Server:	**Hai, sashimi teishoku ga o-hitotsu, tenpura teishoku ga o-hitotsu, bīru ga o-hitotsu desu ne.**
	hah-ee, sah-shee-mee tehh-shoh-koo gah oh-hee-toh-tsoo, tehn-poo-rah tehh-shoh-koo gah oh-hee-toh-tsoo, beee-roo gah oh-hee-toh-tsoo deh-soo neh.
	Yes, certainly. So, one sashimi set, one tempura set, and one beer, right?

Ken and Akiko:	**Hai.**
	hah-ee.
	Yes.

•••

WORDS TO KNOW

Nani ni nasaimasu ka.	nah-nee nee nah-sah-ee-mah-soo kah.	What would you like to have?
teishoku	tehh-shoh-koo	set menu
O-nomimono wa.	oh-noh-mee-moh-noh wah.	How about something to drink?
o-kyaku-sama	oh-kyah-koo-sah-mah	customer
o-hitotsu	oh-hee-toh-tsoo	one (honorific)

Chatting with the waiter or waitress

At some point, you may need to ask your server questions or give her feedback on your food. Here are some phrases to help you do those very things:

>> ちょっと変な味です。 **Chotto henna aji desu.** (choh-toh hehn-nah ah-jee deh-soo.) (*It tastes sort of strange.*)

>> これは何ですか。 **Kore wa nan desu ka.** (koh-reh wah nahn deh-soo kah.) (*What is this?*)

>> これは焼けていますか。 **Kore wa yakete imasu ka.** (koh-reh wah yah-keh-teh ee-mah-soo kah.) (*Is it cooked through?*)

>> おいしいですね。 **Oishii desu ne.** (oh-ee-sheee deh-soo neh.) (*It's delicious, isn't it?*)

>> お水を下さい。 **O-mizu o kudasai.** (oh-mee-zoo oh koo-dah-sah-ee.) (*Water, please.*)

>> お手洗いはどこですか。 **O-tearai wa doko desu ka.** (oh-teh-ah-rah-ee wah doh-koh deh-soo kah.) (*Where is the bathroom?*)

>> とてもおいしかったです。 **Totemo oishikatta desu!** (toh-teh-moh oh-ee-shee-kaht-tah deh-soo!) (*That was very delicious!*)

TIP

To express what you can and what you can't eat, use the verb **taberu** (tah-beh-roo) (*to eat*) in the potential form: **taberaremasu** (tah-beh-rah-reh-mah-soo) (*I can eat*) and **taberaremasen** (tah-beh-rah-reh-mah-sehn) (*I can't eat*). For example, **Watashi wa ebi ga taberaremasen.** (wah-tah-shee wah eh-bee gah tah-beh-rah-reh-mah-sehn.) (*I can't eat shrimp.*) See Chapter 7 for details on the potential form.

Paying for your meal

When and how you pay for your meal can vary by restaurant. You may have to pay upfront, or you may be able to pay after eating. Most restaurants accept **kurejitto kādo** (koo-reh-jeet-toh kahh-doh) (*credit cards*), but many of them still only accept **genkin** (gehn-keen) (*cash*), especially in smaller cities and rural areas. Clarifying these details before eating is your best bet. Then all you have to do is request your bill. Here are the phrases you need to know:

>> 別々にお願いします。 **Betsubetsu ni onegai shimasu.** (beh-tsoo-beh-tsoo nee oh-neh-gah-ee shee-mah-soo.) (*Please give us separate checks.*)

>> チェックお願いします。 **Chekku onegai shimasu.** (chehk-koo oh-neh-gah-ee shee-mah-soo.) (*Check, please.*)

>> 一緒にお願いします。**Isshoni onegai shimasu.** (ees-shoh-nee oh-neh-gah-ee shee-mah-soo.) (*Please give us one check.*)

>> 領収書お願いします。**Ryōshūsho onegai shimasu.** (ryohh-shooo-shoh oh-neh-gah-ee shee-mah-soo.) (*Receipt, please.*)

CULTURAL WISDOM

You don't have to tip at restaurants in Japan (except for special cases), but you still get very good service about 99 percent of the time. For very expensive meals, the restaurant warns the customers, in writing, that the tip is automatically included in their bill as a **sābisuryō** (sahh-bee-soo-ryohh) (*service fee*). So you still don't have to think about offering a voluntary gratuity.

Drinking and dancing at bars and clubs

Having a drink at home is usually much cheaper than going to a **bā** (bahh) (*bar*), **izakaya** (ee-zah-kah-yah) (*casual Japanese-style bar*), or **kurabu** (koo-rah-boo) (*nightclub*), but where's the fun in that?

All bars and clubs in Japan serve **o-sake** (oh-sah-keh), which means both *Japanese rice wine* and *alcoholic beverages* in general. If you like beer, try some Japanese-brand beers like **Asahi** (ah-sah-hee), **Kirin** (kee-reen), or **Sapporo** (sahp-poh-roh). These beers are sold in many countries throughout the world, including the United States and Canada. Now, take a walk over to the bar and order your favorite **o-sake:**

>> 熱燗 **atsukan** (ah-tsoo-kahn) (*hot sake*)

>> ビール **bīru** (beee-roo) (*beer*)

>> ブランデー **burandē** (boo-rahn-dehh) (*brandy*)

>> チューハイ **chūhai** (chooo-hah-ee) (*shōchū and tonic*)

>> ジン **jin** (jeen) (*gin*)

>> カクテル **kakuteru** (kah-koo-teh-roo) (*cocktail*)

>> 水割り **mizuwari** (mee-zoo-wah-ree) (*whiskey and water*)

>> オンザロック **onzarokku** (ohn-zah-rohk-koo) (*whiskey on the rocks*)

>> ラム酒 **ramushu** (rah-moo-shoo) (*rum*)

>> 冷酒 **reishu** (reh-ee-shoo) (*chilled sake*)

>> 焼酎 **shōchū** (shohh-chooo) (*a Japanese liquor similar to vodka*)

>> ストレート **sutorēto** (soo-toh-rehh-toh) (*whiskey straight*)

>> ウイスキー **uisukī** (oo-ee-soo-keee) (*whiskey*)

>> ウオッカ **uokka** (oo-ohk-kah) (*vodka*)

>> ワイン **wain** (wah-een) (*wine*)

Young people in Japan love to dance the night away in a place referred to as **kurabu.** The popular music in **kurabu** includes **tekuno** (teh-koo-noh) (*techno*), **hippu-hoppu** (heep-poo-hohp-poo) (*hip-hop*), **hausu** (hah-oo-soo) (*house music*), and **jēpoppu** (jehh-pohp-poo) (*J-pop [Japanese pop music]*). You can find many **kurabu** in larger cities such as Tokyo, Osaka, and Nagoya. More and more young Japanese do street dancing, but ballroom dancing is also popular, especially among middle-aged people. (You may want to watch the famous 1996 Japanese film *Shall We Dance?* starring Koji Yakusho. The 2004 American film *Shall We Dance?* starring Richard Gere was a remake of this Japanese film.) Now cut a rug and conjugate the **u**-verb **odoru** (oh-doh-roo) (*to dance*)!

Japanese Script	Rōmaji	Pronunciation
踊る	odoru	oh-doh-roo
踊らない	odoranai	oh-doh-rah-nah-ee
踊り(ます)	odori (masu)	oh-doh-ree (-mah-soo)
踊って	odotte	oh-doht-teh

Talkin' the Talk

Makoto Tanaka goes into an **izakaya** — a casual bar with home-style food — after work.

Cook: **Irasshai! O-hitori.**
ee-rahs-shah-ee! o-hee-toh-ree.
Welcome! Just yourself?

Makoto: **Sō.**
sohh.
Right.

Cook: **Jā, koko dōzo. Nani nomu.**
jahh, koh-koh dohh-zoh. nah-nee noh-moo.
Then please sit here. What will you drink?

Makoto:	**Bīru.**
	beee-roo.
	Beer.

Cook:	**Hai yo.**
	hah-ee yoh.
	Okay.

Makoto looks at the menu on the wall, wondering what to order.

Makoto:	**Kyō wa nani ga oishii.**
	kyohh wah nah-nee gah oh-ee-sheee.
	What's good today?

Cook:	**Kyō wa aji ga oishii yo.**
	kyohh wah ah-jee gah oh-ee-sheee yoh.
	The horse mackerel is delicious today.

Makoto:	**Jā, sore.**
	jahh, soh-reh.
	Then I'll have that.

Cook:	**Hai yo.**
	hah-ee yoh.
	Sure.

WORDS TO KNOW

Irasshai!	ee-rahs-shah-ee!	Welcome!
nomu	noh-moo	to drink
bīru	beee-roo	beer
oishii	oh-ee-shee-ee	delicious
aji	ah-jee	horse mackerel

Singing at a karaoke box

Karaoke is an abbreviation of **kara ōkesutora** (kah-rah ohh-keh-soo-toh-rah), which means *empty orchestra*. So you can think of karaoke as an orchestra in search of a singer.

CULTURAL WISDOM

DINING IN IZAKAYA

Drinking is almost obligatory for Japanese businessmen. Part of their job involves entertaining their clients in bars and nightclubs. But not all bar traffic is work-related. Both Japanese men and women drink with their friends and colleagues in 居酒屋 **izakaya** (ee-zah-kah-yah) (*casual Japanese-style bars*). It's something like the Japanese equivalent of a British pub. In **izakaya**, you don't hear wordy, honorific phrases very much. Waiters and waitresses treat you like you're a member of their families. Sitting at the counter is definitely fun. You can watch the chefs cook, and you can chat with them. Trust me — enjoy several appetizers. You can always share dishes with your friends at the table. Eat some of these foods at **izakaya:**

- 冷やっこ **hiyayakko** (hee-yah-yahk-koh) (*chilled tofu with sauce and spices*)
- 牡蠣フライ **kaki furai** (kah-kee foo-rah-ee) (*deep-fried oysters*)
- 肉じゃが **nikujaga** (nee-koo-jah-gah) (*beef and potatoes*)
- おでん **oden** (oh-dehn) (*hot pot with fish cakes, daikon radish, and so forth in dashi soup*)
- 酢のもの **sunomono** (soo-noh-moh-noh) (*vinegared food*)
- 焼き魚 **yakizakana** (yahk-ee-zah-kah-nah) (*grilled fish*)

Karaoke started in Japan about 30 years ago as a form of after-work entertainment for Japanese businesspeople. Karaoke was viewed as a great way of releasing the daily stress related to work. Today, karaoke is popular among everyone — men and women, young and old. It's an artistic, intelligent, accessible, and healthy entertainment. Nowadays, private rooms for karaoke are more common than a bar style where you sing in front of everyone. Singing at a karaoke room is a fun thing to do for all ages!

Karaoke bars have spread all over the world, but nowadays, karaoke boxes are more popular in Japan. A *karaoke box* is an insulated individual room with a sofa, coffee table, and a karaoke set. You just rent it for a few hours with your friends. It's not expensive, and it's open for all ages, including minors. If you want to enjoy karaoke, make sure you know these words and phrases:

- » 画面 **gamen** (gah-mehn) (*monitor*)
- » 歌詞 **kashi** (kah-shee) (*lyrics*)
- » カラオケ **karaoke** (kah-rah-oh-keh) (*karaoke*)
- » 曲 **kyoku** (kyoh-koo) (*musical pieces*)

» マイク **maiku** (mah-ee-koo) (*microphone*)

» 音痴 **onchi** (ohn-chee) (*tone-deaf*)

» 歌 **uta** (oo-tah) (*song*)

Last, but certainly not least, make sure you know how to say **utau** (oo-tah-oo) (*to sing*). Here's how to conjugate this **u**–verb.

Japanese Script	Rōmaji	Pronunciation
歌う	utau	oo-tah-oo
歌わない	utawanai	oo-tah-wah-nah-ee
歌い(ます)	utai (masu)	oo-tah-ee (-mah-soo)
歌って	utatte	oo-taht-teh

Talking about Entertainment

If your friends or co–workers find out that you visited the museum's latest exhibit or went to the new bar in town, chances are they'll ask you what you thought. Following are some simple phrases you can use to describe what you thought of your entertainment experience. Note that all the sentences are in the past tense and in the informal speech style. (For detailed information on tenses and the difference between the informal style of speech and the polite/neutral style, see Chapter 3.)

» きれいだった。**Kirei datta.** (kee-reh-ee daht-tah.) (*It was beautiful.*)

» ひどかった。**Hidokatta.** (hee-doh-kaht-tah.) (*It was terrible.*)

» 感動した。**Kandō shita.** (kahn-dohh shee-tah.) (*I was moved.*)

» 混んでいた。**Konde ita.** (kohn-deh ee-tah.) (*It was crowded.*)

» 美味しかった。**Oishikatta.** (oh-ee-shee-kaht-tah.) (*It was delicious.*)

» 面白かった。**Omoshirokatta.** (oh-moh-shee-roh-kaht-tah.) (*It was interesting.*)

» 素晴らしかった。**Subarashikatta.** (soo-bah-rah-shee-kaht-tah.) (*It was wonderful.*)

» 高かった。**Takakatta.** (tah-kah-kaht-tah.) (*It was expensive.*)

» 楽しかった。**Tanoshikatta.** (tah-noh-shee-kaht-tah.) (*It was fun.*)

» 安かった。**Yasukatta.** (yah-soo-kaht-tah.) (*It was cheap.*)

» よかった。**Yokatta.** (yoh-kaht-tah.) (*It was good.*)

To make the previous expressions sound polite, do the following:

» For **i**-type adjectives ending in **katta** (kaht-tah), just add **desu** (deh-soo). So instead of saying **Omoshirokatta**, say **Omoshirokatta desu**.

» For **na**-type adjectives ending in **datta** (daht-tah), simply exchange **datta** for **deshita** (deh-shee-tah). So instead of saying **Kirei datta**, say **Kirei deshita**.

» For the verbs, you need to change the ending **ta** (tah) to **mashita** (mah-shee-tah). For example, instead of saying **Kandō shita** and **Konde ita**, say **Kandō shimashita** and **Konde imashita,** respectively.

» For **u**-verbs, refer to the conjugation table in Chapter 3 for precisely how to make additional changes.

Getting Your Friends to Go Out with You

Because going out on the town is often more fun when you're with others, why not invite your significant other, classmate, or colleague to join you? Start by figuring out how to conjugate the **u**-verb **sasou** (sah-soh-oo) (*to invite*).

Japanese Script	Rōmaji	Pronunciation
誘う	sasou	sah-soh-oo
誘わない	sasowanai	sah-soh-wah-nah-ee
誘い(ます)	sasoi (masu)	sah-soh-ee (-mah-soo)
誘って	sasotte	sah-soht-teh

The following sections help you get even more socially active with your Japanese.

Making a suggestion with "Why don't we?"

GRAMMAR
CHAT

If you want to go somewhere with your friend, make a suggestion by saying *Why don't we go there? How about going there?* or *Would you like to go there?* The easiest, most natural, and least pushy way of making a suggestion in Japanese is to ask a question that ends in **-masen ka** (mah-sehn kah). **-masen ka** is the polite negative ending **-masen** plus the question particle **ka**. Why negative? In English, you say things like *Why don't we go to the bar tonight?* That's negative too, so fair is fair.

Make sure the verb before **-masen ka** is in the stem form, as in **Ikimasen ka.** (ee-kee-mah-sehn kah.) (*Why don't we go there?*). The **iki** part is the stem form of the verb **iku** (ee-koo) (*to go*). If you want to do something, use other verbs like **suru** (soo-roo) (*to do*), **utau** (oo-tah-oo) (*to sing*), and **taberu** (tah-beh-roo) (*to eat*). Check out these examples:

映画館に行きませんか。**Eigakan ni ikimasen ka.** (ehh-gah-kahn nee ee-kee-mah-sehn kah.) (*Why don't we go to a movie theater?*)

田中さんと山田さんを誘いませんか。**Tanaka-san to Yamada-san o sasoimasen ka.** (tah-nah-kah-sahn toh yah-mah-dah-sahn oh sah-soh-ee-mah-sehn kah.) (*How about inviting Mr. Tanaka and Mr. Yamada?*)

いつかいっしょにテニスをしませんか。**Itsuka isshoni tenisu o shimasen ka.** (ee-tsoo-kah ees-shoh-nee teh-nee-soo oh shee-mah-sehn kah.) (*Why don't we play tennis together someday?*)

今度いっしょに歌いませんか。**Kondo isshoni utaimasen ka.** (kohn-doh ees-shoh-nee oo-tah-ee-mah-sehn kah.) (*How about singing together next time?*)

今度いっしょにロブスターを食べませんか。**Kondo isshoni robusutā o tabemasen ka.** (kohn-doh ees-shoh-nee roh-boo-soo-tahh oh tah-beh-mah-sehn kah.) (*How about eating lobster together next time?*)

Saying "Let's go" and "Shall we go?"

In English, you can enthusiastically invite your friends to an activity by saying *Let's go there.* or *Let's do it.* How do you say *let's* in Japanese? It's easy: Get a verb in the stem form and add the ending **-mashō** (mah-shohh), as in **ikimashō** (ee-kee-mah-shohh) (*let's go*), **shimashō** (shee-mah-shohh) (*let's do it*), **utaimashō** (oo-tah-ee-mah-shohh) (*let's sing*), and **tabemashō** (tah-beh-mah-shohh) (*let's eat*). Check out the following examples:

いっしょに歌いましょう。**Isshoni utaimashō.** (ees-shoh-nee oo-tah-ee-mah-shohh.) (*Let's sing together.*)

今晩いっしょに飲みましょう。**Konban isshoni nomimashō.** (kohn-bahn ees-sho-nee noh-mee-mah-shohh.) (*Let's drink together tonight.*)

今度いっしょに映画を見ましょう。**Kondo isshoni eiga o mimashō.** (kohn-doh ees-shoh-nee ehh-gah oh mee-mah-shohh.) (*Let's see a movie together next time.*)

If you make a question by using **-mashō**, it means *Shall we?* For example

チェスをしましょうか。**Chesu o shimashō ka.** (cheh-soo oh shee-mah-shohh kah.) (*Shall we play chess?*)

カントリーガーデンに行きましょうか。**Kantorī Gāden ni ikimashō ka.** (kahn-toh-reee gahh-dehn nee ee-kee-mah-shohh kah.) (*Shall we go to Country Garden?*)

TIP

-mashō ka also means *Shall I?* so it's useful when you want to say something like *Shall I bring something?* and *Shall I help you?* Usually, the subject is unspoken, but the context clarifies whether **-mashō ka** means *Shall we?* or *Shall I?* However, you can add **watashi ga** (wah-tah-shee gah) if you want to clarify that you're the only one who is doing the action:

手伝いましょうか。**Tetsudaimashō ka.** (teh-tsoo-dah-ee-mah-shohh kah.) (*Shall I help you?*)

私が予約しましょうか。**Watashi ga yoyaku shimashō ka.** (wah-tah-shee gah yoh-yah-koo shee-mah-shohh kah.) (*Shall I make a reservation?*)

Talkin' the Talk

Allison asks her colleague Yukiko whether she wants to go to a karaoke box together after work.

Allison:	**Konban hima desu ka.** kohn-bahn hee-mah deh-soo kah. *Are you free tonight?*
Yukiko:	**Ē.** ehh. *Yes.*
Allison:	**Karaoke bokkusu ni ikimasen ka.** kah-rah-oh-keh bohk-koo-soo nee ee-kee-mah-sehn kah. *How about going to a karaoke box?*
Yukiko:	**Ii desu ne. Ikimashō.** eee deh-soo neh. ee-kee-mah-shohh. *Sounds good. Let's go there.*
Allison:	**Jēson to Ken mo sasoimasen ka.** jehh-sohn toh kehn moh sah-soh-ee-mah-sehn kah. *How about inviting Jason and Ken, too?*

Yukiko:	**Ii desu yo.**
	eee deh-soo yoh.
	That's fine with me.

Allison:	**Jā, roku-ji ni Karaoke Sebun de.**
	jahh, roh-koo-jee nee kah-rah-oh-keh
	seh-boon deh.
	Then, I'll see you at Karaoke Seven at 6:00.
	(Literally: Then, at 6:00, at Karaoke Seven.)

Yukiko:	**Ē. Jā, mata.**
	ehh. jahh, mah-tah.
	Sure. See you later.

WORDS TO KNOW

konban	kohn-bahn	tonight
hima	hee-mah	free (not busy)
Ii desu ne.	eee deh-soo neh.	Sounds good.
sasou	sah-soh-oo	to invite
sebun	seh-boon	seven (English word)
Ii desu yo.	eee deh-soo yoh.	That's fine (with me).

Inviting Friends Over and Asking Them to Bring Something

Sometimes you just don't feel like going out, but you don't want to be by yourself either. On those occasions, consider inviting your friends over to your house. Use the irregular verb **kuru** (koo-roo) (*to come*) when you call. But before you invite anyone, practice conjugating **kuru**.

Japanese Script	Rōmaji	Pronunciation
来る	kuru	koo-roo
来ない	konai	koh-nah-ee
来(ます)	ki (masu)	kee (-mah-soo)
来て	kite	kee-teh

Now, you're ready to invite your friends over:

うちに来ませんか。 **Uchi ni kimasen ka.** (oo-chee nee kee-mah-sehn kah.) (*Would you like to come to my house?*)

あした私のアパートに来ませんか。 **Ashita watashi no apāto ni kimasen ka.** (ah-shee-tah wah-tah-shee noh ah-pahh-toh nee kee-mah-sehn kah.) (*Would you like to come to my apartment tomorrow?*)

If you're the one who gets invited, ask your friend what you can bring. Japanese hosts and hostesses tend to tell their guests not to bring anything, but go ahead and bring something anyway.

GRAMMAR CHAT

To say *to bring something*, use **motte** (moht-teh), which is the verb **motsu** (moh-tsoo) (*to hold*) in the **te**-form, and add the verb **iku** (ee-koo) (*to go*) or **kuru** (koo-roo) (*to come*). Sounds complex, right? I agree with you. The idea is that bringing something is equivalent to going/coming somewhere while holding it. Of course, you can also understand them as a unit, namely, **mottekuru** and **motteiku**. Check out these examples:

私はビールを持って行きました。 **Watashi wa bīru o motte ikimashita.** (wah-tah-shee wah bee-roo oh moht-teh ee-kee-mah-shee-tah.) (*I brought beer [there]*, or *I took beer.*)

田中さんはビールを持って来ました。 **Tanaka-san wa bīru o motte kimashita.** (tah-nah-kah-sahn wa bee-roo oh moht-teh kee-mah-shee-tah.) (*Mr. Tanaka brought beer [here].*)

To talk about bringing a pet or taking a friend somewhere, use **tsurete** rather than **motte**. **Tsurete** is the **te**-form of the verb **tsureru** (tsoo-reh-roo) (*to take*); see Chapter 3 for more about the **te**-form.

私は友達を連れて行きました。 **Watashi wa tomodachi o tsurete ikimashita.** (wah-tah-shee wah toh-moh-dah-chee oh tsoo-reh-teh ee-kee-mah-shee-tah.) (*I brought my friend [there]*, or *I took my friend.*)

田中さんは友達を連れて来ました。 **Tanaka-san wa tomodachi o tsurete kimashita.** (tah-nah-kah-sahn wa toh-moh-dah-chee oh tsoo-reh-teh kee-mah-shee-tah.) (*Mr. Tanaka brought his friend.*) (My additions may unnecessarily complicate since "bring" and "take" are used interchangeably in English, but offered as suggestions.)

GRAMMAR CHAT

To say *something, someone, somewhere,* and so on, combine a question word and the particle **ka** (kah). The particles **ga** (gah) and **o** (oh) are usually dropped after these words, but other types of particles can appear after them. For example

あそこに何かありますよ。**Asoko ni nanika arimasu yo.** (ah-soh-koh nee nah-nee-kah ah-ree-mah-soo yoh.) (*There is something over there.*)

何か持って行きましょうか。**Nanika motte ikimashō ka.** (nah-nee-kah moht-teh ee-kee-mah-shohh kah.) (*Shall I bring something?*)

誰か来ましたか。**Dareka kimashita ka.** (dah-reh-kah kee-mah-shee-tah kah.) (*Did someone come?*)

どこかに行きませんか。**Dokoka ni ikimasen ka.** (doh-koh-kah nee ee-kee-mah-sehn ka.) (*Shall we go somewhere?*)

いつかいっしょに飲みましょう。**Itsuka isshoni nomimashō.** (ee-tsoo-kah ees-shoh-nee noh-mee-mah-shohh.) (*Let's drink together someday.*)

To say *nothing, no one, nowhere,* and so on, use a question word and the particle **mo** (moh), but make sure to have the verb in the negative form. The particles **ga** and **o** must not occur in this context, but other types of particles need to occur right before **mo.** For example

何も食べませんでした。**Nani mo tabemasen deshita.** (nah-nee moh tah-beh-mah-sehn deh-shee-tah.) (*I ate nothing,* or *I didn't eat anything.*)

何も持って来ないでください。**Nani mo motte konaide kudasai.** (nah-nee moh moht-teh koh-nah-ee-deh koo-dah-sah-ee.) (*Please don't bring anything.*)

誰も来ません。**Dare mo kimasen.** (dah-reh moh kee-mah-sehn.) (*No one will come.*)

昨日はどこにも行きませんでした。**Kinō wa doko ni mo ikimasen deshita.** (kee-nohh wah doh-koh nee moh ee-kee-mah-sehn deh-shee-tah.) (*I went nowhere yesterday,* or *I didn't go anywhere yesterday.*)

See Chapter 3 for a list of question words and particles as well as negative forms of verbs.

............Talkin' the Talk............

Ms. Mori invites George to her house.

Ms. Mori: **Kondo no nichiyōbi, uchi ni kimasen ka.**
kohn-doh noh nee-chee-yohh-bee, oo-chee nee kee-mah-sehn kah.
Would you like to come to my house this Sunday?

George: **Ā, dōmo. Yorokonde.**
ahh, dohh-moh. yoh-roh-kohn-deh.
Oh, thank you. I'd be delighted. (Literally: Delightedly.)

Ms. Mori:	**Isshoni bābekyū o shimashō.** ees-shoh-nee bahh-beh-kyooo oh shee-mah-shohh. *Let's have a barbecue together.*
George:	**Ā, ii desu ne.** ahh, eee deh-soo neh. *That sounds great.*
	Nanika motteikimashō ka. nah-nee-kah moht-teh-ee-kee-mah-shohh kah. *Shall I bring something?*
Ms. Mori:	**Ī e, ii desu. Nani mo motte konaide kudasai.** eee-eh, eee deh-soo. nah-nee moh moht-teh koh- nah-ee-deh koo-dah-sah-ee. *No, thank you. Please don't bring anything.*

WORDS TO KNOW

kondo no nichiyōbi	kohn-doh noh nee-chee-yohh-bee	coming Sunday
yorokonde	yoh-roh-kohn-deh	delightedly
isshoni	ees-shoh-nee	together
bābekyū	bahh-beh-kyooo	barbecue
nanika	nah-nee-kah	something

FUN & GAMES

In the following puzzle, try to find these words in Japanese: *gallery, art museum, movie theater, library, museum, izakaya bar, theater*. The solution is in Appendix C.

ā	w	u	r	y	z	i	d	f	b	f	ō
g	e	k	i	j	ō	z	p	d	i	h	t
a	b	t	h	ī	e	a	a	k	j	p	r
r	h	o	k	o	s	k	z	k	u	r	h
ō	i	s	ī	ō	t	a	ā	h	t	k	e
ū	o	h	b	w	ā	y	ē	f	s	h	ō
k	ā	o	k	m	t	a	z	ē	u	t	u
h	a	k	u	b	u	t	s	u	k	a	n
ē	y	a	n	j	t	z	ā	u	a	u	ī
n	f	n	e	i	g	a	k	a	n	o	ō

Chapter **12**

Taking Care of Business and Telecommunications

Whether you want to find a job in Japan or you simply have Japanese co-workers, knowing some basic office-related terminology is helpful. Consider this chapter your go-to resource for all things regarding Japanese-style business and business communications.

REMEMBER

You can listen to all the Talkin' the Talk dialogues featured in this chapter. Go to www.dummies.com/go/japanesefd and click on the dialogue you want to hear.

Using Japanese at Work

You sent out your **rirekisho** (ree-reh-kee-shoh) (resume), which included your **shokureki** (shoh-koo-reh-kee) (work history), and you were invited to a **mensetsu** (mehn-seh-tsoo) (job interview). And you got a job! Hooray! Now you are embarking on a new job! This section introduces new words and expressions that may be useful at the workplace. First things first, I begin with the conjugation of the u-verb **hataraku** (hah-tah-rah-koo) (be employed at work).

Japanese Script	Rōmaji	Pronunciation
働く	hataraku	hah-tah-rah-koo
働かない	hatarakanai	hah-tah-rah-kah-nah-ee
働き(ます)	hataraki (masu)	hah-tah-rah-kee (-mah-soo)
働いて	hataraite	hah-tah-rah-ee-teh

REMEMBER

You can express a lot of activities you need to do at your workplace by using the verb **suru** (soo-roo) (to do). (See Chapter 7 for a detailed discussion of uses for **suru**.) Here are a few **suru** phrases that may come up in your workplace:

>> チェックする **chekku suru** (chehk-koo soo-roo) (*to check*)

>> ファックスする **fakkusu suru** (fahk-koo-soo soo-roo) (*to fax*)

>> 配達する **haitatsu suru** (hah-ee-tah-tsoo soo-roo) (*to deliver*)

>> 確認する **kakunin suru** (kah-koo-neen soo-roo) (*to confirm*)

>> 計算する **keisan suru** (kehh-sahn soo-roo) (*to calculate*)

>> コピーする **kopī suru** (koh-peee soo-roo) (*to make copies*)

>> メールする **mēru suru** (mehh-roo soo-roo) (*to email*)

>> 出張する **shucchō suru** (shuc-choh soo-roo) (*go on a business trip*)

>> 出勤する **shukkin suru** (shook-kin soo-roo) (*come to work*)

>> 掃除する **sōji suru** (sohh-jee soo-roo) (*to clean*)

>> 早退する **sōtai suru** (soh-tah-ee soo-roo) (*leave work early*)

>> 退社する **taisha suru** (tah-ee-shah soo-roo) (*leave work for the day, retire from a company*)

>> 添付する **tenpu suru** (tehn-poo soo-roo) (*to attach*)

>> 郵送する **yūsō suru** (yooo-sohh soo-roo) (*to mail*)

The benefits offered at a **shokuba** (shoh-koo-bah) (*workplace*) are important information you should certainly have! Make sure you know these words to understand what benefits come with your job:

ADDRESSING SUPERIORS AND SUBORDINATES

Japan is very modern, but a shadow of feudalism still falls on workplaces. Case in point: Subordinates never address their superiors by their first names. If you work in Japan, address your superiors by using their titles and last names. So, if your superior is the company president and his last name is Smith, call him スミス社長 **Sumisu-shachō,** or simply 社長 **shachō** (shah-chohh).

Some titles Japanese companies use are as follows:

- 部長 **buchō** (boo-chohh) (*department chief*)
- 副社長 **fukushachō** (foo-koo-shah-chohh) (*company vice-president*)
- 課長 **kachō** (kah-chohh) (*section chief*)
- 係長 **kakarichō** (kah-kah-ree-chohh) (*subsection chief*)
- 社長 **shachō** (shah-chohh) (*company president*)

Address your subordinates by their last names, plus **-san** or **-kun.** In a business context, both **-san** (sahn) and **-kun** (koon) can be used for women and men. So if Mr. Smith is your assistant, call him **Sumisu-san** (soo-mee-soo-sahn) or **Sumisu-kun** (soo-mee-soo-koon).

- » 健康保険 **kenkō hoken** (kehn-kohh hoh-kehn) (*health insurance*)
- » 交通費 **kōtsūhi** (kohh-tsoo-hee) (*commuting allowance*)
- » 給料 **kyūryō** (kyooo-ryohh) (*salary*)
- » 有給休暇 **yūkyūkyūka** (yooo-kyooo-kyooo-kah) (*paid vacation*)
- » 残業手当 **zangyō teate** (zahn-gyohh teh-ah-teh) (*overtime pay*)

GRAMMAR CHAT

To state a reason, add **node** (noh–deh) (*because*) to a sentence. **Node** is a somewhat formal–sounding connective that combines two sentences into one. It's similar to "since" in English. The structure of a complete sentence will be "sentence 1 **node,** sentence 2," with sentence 1 being the reason for sentence 2. Sentence 1 can end with dictionary forms or **nai**–forms. When you use a **na**–type adjective or noun in your reason sentence, insert **na** before **node.** Take a look at the following examples:

- » 今日は雨が降るので、でかけません。 **Kyō wa ame ga furu node, dekakemasen.** (kyohh wa ahmeh gah foo-roo noh-deh, deh-kah-keh-mah-sehn.) (*Because it will rain today, I will not go out.*)

» このケーキはおいしいので、とても人気があります。**Kono kēki wa oishii node, totemo ninki ga arimasu.** (koh-noh kehh-kee wa oh-ee-sheee noh-deh, toh-teh-moh neen-kee gah ah-ree-mah-soo.) (*Because this cake is delicious, it's very popular.*)

» コンビニは便利なので、よく使います。**Konbini wa benri na node, yoku tsu-kaimasu.** (kohn-bee-nee wa behn-ree nah noh-deh, yoh-koo tsuh-kah-ee-mah-soo.) (*Because a Konbini is very convenient, I often use it.*)

» 私は学生じゃないので、割引がありません。**Watashi wa gakusei janai node, waribiki ga arimasen.** (wah-tah-shee wah gah-koo-seh jah-nah-ee noh-deh, wah-ree-bee-kee gah ah-ree-mah-sehn.) (*Because I'm not a student, I don't get any discount.*)

Talkin' the Talk

John Leigh has a cold today. It's getting worse, and he wants to leave work early. He is talking to his **jyoshi** (jyohh-see) (*boss, superior*), Mr. Tanaka. Mr. Tanaka is his **kachō.**

John:	**Kachō, mōshiwakearimasen ga, guai ga yoku-nai node, sōtai shitemo yoroshii deshō ka.** Kah-choh, moh-shee-wah-keh-ah-ree-mah-sehn gah, goo-gah-ee gah yoh-koo-nah-ee noh-deh, soh-tah-ee shee-teh-moh yoh-roh-sheee deh-shohh kah. *Mr. Tanaka, I'm very sorry, but may I leave early because I'm not feeling well.*
Tanaka:	**Daijōbu desu ka.** Dah-ee-johh-boo deh-soo kah. *Are you okay?*
John:	**Hai, kazeda to omoimasu.** Hah-ee, kah-zeh-dah toh oh-moh-ee-mah-soo. *Yes, I think I have a cold.*
Tanaka:	**Wakarimashita. Odaijini.** Wah-kah-ree-mah-shee-tah. Oh-dah-ee-jee-nee. *I understand. Please take care.*
John:	**Arigatōgozaimasu.** Ah-ree-gah-toh-goh-zah-ee-mah-soo. *Thank you very much.*

WORDS TO KNOW

guai	goo-ah-ee	condition
yokunai	yoh-koo-nah-ee	not good
sōtai suru	soh-tah-ee soo-roo	leave work early
daijōbu	dah-ee-joh-boo	okay, all right
kaze	kah-zeh	a cold (or wind)
odaijini	oh-dah-ee-jee-nee	Please take care

REMEMBER

When you have to miss work or need to leave early, make sure to call your office or talk to your supervisor in person. In general, telling your situation yourself is preferable to emailing about it. But it depends on your workplace, so get to know your work environment!

Making Sense of Your Office Environment

If you're a full-time employee, you probably spend about one-third of your time each week at the office. If you're going to spend so much time at work, you'd better know the terms for basic office equipment, furniture, and supplies, as well as how to get around your office building.

Checking out the supplies

Many workplaces are home to numerous pieces of office equipment and furniture. Check whether you see these items at your workplace:

- 電話 **denwa** (dehn-wah) (*telephone*)
- デスクライト **desuku raito** (deh-soo-koo rah-ee-toh) *or* デスクランプ **desuku ranpu** (deh-soo-koo rahm-poo) (*desk lamp*)
- ゴミ箱 **gomibako** (goh-mee-bah-koh) (*wastebasket*)
- 本棚 **hondana** (hohn-dah-nah) (*bookshelf*)
- 椅子 **isu** (ee-soo) (*chair*)
- カレンダー **karendā** (kah-rehn-dahh) (*calendar*)
- コピー機 **kopīki** (koh-peee-kee) (*copier*)
- 机 **tsukue** (tsoo-koo-eh) (*desk*)

Look inside your desk drawers to see whether you have these office supplies:

>> ボールペン **bōrupen** (bohh-roo-pehn) (*ballpoint pen*)

>> 鉛筆 **enpitsu** (ehn-pee-tsoo) (*pencil*)

>> 封筒 **fūtō** (fooo-tohh) (*envelope*)

>> ホッチキス **hotchikisu** (hoht-chee-kee-soo) (*stapler*)

>> 消しゴム **keshigomu** (keh-shee-goh-moo) (*eraser*)

>> 糊 **nori** (noh-ree) (*glue*)

>> ノート **nōto** (nohh-toh) (*notebook*)

>> シャーペン **shāpen** (shahh-pehn) (*mechanical pencil*)

>> 手帳 **techō** (teh-chohh) (*planner*)

>> セロテープ **setotēpu** (seh-roh-tehh-poo) (*cellophane tape*)

REMEMBER

If you can't find a pen, an eraser, or a stapler, ask a colleague. He probably has one that you can use. Start by mentioning the item you need to borrow and including the topic particle **wa** (wah). Then use the verb **aru** (ah-roo) (*to exist*) to ask *Do you have?* (Using the verb *to exist* seems weird in this case, doesn't it? To see more examples of this strange use of the verb **aru,** flip to Chapter 7.) Add the polite suffix **-masu** (mah-soo) to the stem form of **aru,** as in **arimasu** (ah-ree-mah-soo), and make the phrase into a question by adding the question particle **ka** (kah), as in **arimasu ka** (ah-ree-mah-soo kah). Now you can start bothering your colleagues:

ホッチキスはありますか。 **Hotchikisu wa arimasu ka.** (hoht-chee-kee-soo wah ah-ree-mah-soo kah.) (*Do you have a stapler?*)

消しゴムはありますか。 **Keshigomu wa arimasu ka.** (keh-shee-goh-moo wah ah-ree-mah-soo kah.) (*Do you have an eraser?*)

Touring the rest of the building

Although you may be in the same room in the building every day, knowing the rest of the areas in the building is a good idea in case you need to help other people in the company. Here are helpful words to identify a variety of rooms and areas in your office building:

>> 出口 **deguchi** (deh-goo-chee) (*exit*)

>> エレベーター **erebētā** (eh-reh-behh-tahh) (*elevator*)

>> 入り口 **iriguchi** (ee-ree-goo-chee) (*entrance*)

» 階段 **kaidan** (kah-ee-dahn) (*stairway*)

» 会議室 **kaigishitsu** (kah-ee-gee-shee-tsoo) (*conference room*)

» 警備室 **keibishitsu** (keh-ee-bee-shee-tsoo) (*security room*)

» 工場 **kōjō** (kohh-johh) (*factory*)

» ロビー **robī** (roh-beee) (*lobby*)

» 廊下 **rōka** (rohh-kah) (*hallway*)

» 倉庫 **sōko** (sohh-koh) (*storage*)

» トイレ **toire** (toh-ee-reh) (*toilet*)

TIP

For pointers on referring to specific floors in your building, check out Chapter 10. You can read about using ordinal numbers in general in Chapter 4.

Phoning Made Simple

Telephones are an indispensable part of daily life, particularly in business settings. Emails are also great, but they can't replace the sense of connection that you get from hearing another person's voice. The next sections give you the essential words and phrases that you need to have for telephone conversations in Japanese.

Brushing up on phone-related vocab

Before you get ready to make a call in Japanese, get used to the Japanese words and terms related to telephone equipment, systems, and accessories:

» 電話 **denwa** (dehn-wah) (*telephone*)

» 電話番号 **denwa-bangō** (dehn-wah-bahn-gohh) (*telephone number*)

» 電話帳 **denwachō** (dehn-wah-chohh) (*telephone book*)

» 携帯(電話) **keitai(-denwa)** (kehh-tah-ee[-dehn-wah]) (*cellphone*)

» 留守番電話 **rusuban-denwa** (roo-soo-bahn-dehn-wah) (*answering machine*)

» ヴォイスメール **voisu-mēru** (voh-ee-soo-mehh-roo) (*voice mail*)

After you have a grip on the necessary vocabulary, you're ready to **denwa o kakeru** (dehn-wah oh kah-keh-roo) (*to make a phone call*). Here's how to conjugate the **ru**-verb **kakeru** (kah-keh-roo) (*to make [a phone call]*):

Japanese Script	Rōmaji	Pronunciation
かける	kakeru	kah-keh-roo
かけない	kakenai	kah-keh-nah-ee
かけ(ます)	kake (masu)	kah-keh (-mah-soo)
かけて	kakete	kah-keh-the

TIP

Before you start talking, say **moshimoshi** (moh-shee-moh-shee). In Japanese, **moshimoshi** is a kind of line-testing phrase, like *Hello, are you there?* or *Can you hear me?* If the other party on the phone doesn't speak at all, say **moshimoshi** again. If you still don't hear anything, repeat it more loudly — **MOSHIMOSHI!** If you still don't hear anything, hang up!

Asking to speak with someone

Why do you make a phone call? Because you *want* to talk to someone, right? Oh, you want to talk with Mr. Mori? Here are a couple of different ways to try to get him.

>> 森さんをお願いします。**Mori-san o onegaishimasu.** (moh-ree-sahn oh oh-neh-gah-ee-shee-mah-soo.) (*Mr. Mori, please.*)

>> 森さんはいらっしゃいますか。**Mori-san wa irasshaimasu ka.** (moh-ree-sahn wah ee-rahs-shah-ee-mah-soo kah.) (*Is Mr. Mori available?*)

GRAMMAR CHAT

Suppose you want to phrase your request as *I'd like to speak to Mr. Mori.* I have two confessions to make regarding how to express *to want* in Japanese. First, Japanese usually use an adjective, not a verb, to express *to want*. Second, Japanese use different adjectives to express *to want* depending on whether they want something (such as time, a friend, or a physical object) or want to do something.

To say that you want *something*, use the adjective **hoshii** (hoh-sheee) or its polite/neutral counterpart **hoshii desu** (hoh-sheee deh-soo). Place it at the end of the sentence and place the subject particle **ga** (gah) after the item that you want, as in the following examples:

私は車がほしいです。**Watashi wa kuruma ga hoshii desu.** (wah-tah-shee wah koo-roo-mah gah hoh-sheee deh-soo.) (*I want a car.*)

私はお金がほしいです。**Watashi wa o-kane ga hoshii desu.** (wah-tah-shee wah oh-kah-neh gah hoh-sheee deh-soo.) (*I want money.*)

何が一番ほしいですか。 **Nani ga ichiban hoshii desu ka.** (nah-nee gah ee-chee-bahn hoh-sheee deh-soo kah.) (*What do you want the most?*)

時間が一番ほしいです。 **Jikan ga ichiban hoshii desu.** (jee-kahn gah ee-chee-bahn hoh-sheee deh-soo.) (*I want time the most.*)

いい仕事がほしいです。 **Ii shigoto ga hoshii desu.** (eee shee-goh-toh gah hoh-sheee deh-soo.) (*I want a good job.*)

To say that you want to *do* something, simply add the suffix **-tai** (tah-ee) to the end of the stem form of a verb. For example, if you want to **neru** (neh-roo) (*to sleep*), say **ne-tai** (neh-tah-ee) (*to want to sleep*). Check out these examples:

私は休みたいです。 **Watashi wa yasumi-tai desu.** (wah-tah-shee wah yah-soo-mee-tah-ee deh-soo.) (*I want to take a day off.*)

今日はクラスに行きたくありません。 **Kyō wa kurasu ni ikitaku arimasen.** (kyohh wah koo-rah-soo nee ee-kee-tah-koo ah-ree-mah-sehn.) (*I don't want to go to class today.*)

将来, 何をしたいですか。 **Shōrai, nani o shi-tai desu ka.** (shohh-rah-ee, nah-nee oh shee-tah-ee deh-soo kah.) (*What do you want to do in the future?*)

うちに帰りたいです。 **Uchi ni kaeri-tai desu.** (oo-chee nee kah-eh-ree-tah-ee deh-soo.) (*I want to go home.*)

You can mark the object of the verb with either **o** or **ga** when the verb is combined with -tai. For example, **Kyō wa sutēki o tabe-tai desu.** (kyohh wah soo-tehh-kee oh tah-beh-tah-ee deh-soo.) (*I want to eat a steak today.*) can be **Kyō wa sutēki ga tabe-tai desu.** (kyohh wah soo-tehh-kee gah tah-beh-tah-ee deh-soo.)

TIP

When you tell someone what you want, you should end your statement with **-n-desu ga** (n-deh-soo gah). Doing so injects a nice, friendly, and cooperative attitude into your statement. The function of **-n-desu** is to show your willingness to hear the other person's response to what you're saying. (See Chapter 5 for more on using **-n-desu**.) The last **ga** is actually the sentence-ending particle that means *but*. So, you're literally saying *I want to do such and such, but.* What you actually mean is something like *I want to do such and such, but is it okay with you?*

Suppose you call a hotel to make a reservation. If you say **yoyaku o shitai desu** (yoh-yah-koo oh shee-tah-ee deh-soo), it just means *I want to make a reservation.* But phrasing your statement this way sounds too blunt in Japanese, and you almost sound like you're making a protest or stating a demand. By contrast, if you say **yoyaku o shitai-n-desu ga** (yoh-yah-koo oh shee-tah-een-deh-soo gah), it means something like *I'd like to make a reservation, but could you help me with it?* Now, your statement sounds soft, and you're kindly inviting the hotel clerk's reply.

That's the kind of tone you want to use when asking to talk to your business contact Mr. Mori (remember him?), so you express that request by saying **Mori-san o onegai shi-tai-n-desu ga.** (moh-ree-sahn oh oh-neh-gah-ee shee-tah-een-deh-soo gah.) (*I'd like to talk with Mr. Mori, but is he available?*)

Check out these examples that contain a more realistic translation of three statements that use **-n-desu ga:**

> 予約を確認したいんですが。**Yoyaku o kakunin shi-tai-n-desu ga.** (yoh-yah-koo oh kah-koo-neen shee-tah-een-deh-soo gah.) (*I'd like to confirm the reservation, but is it okay with you?*)

> 営業時間を知りたいんですが。**Eigyō jikan o shiri-tai-n-desu ga.** (ehh-gyohh jee-kahn oh shee-ree-tah-een-deh-soo gah.) (*I'd like to know your business hours, but could you help me with this?*)

> ちょっとお尋ねしたいんですが。**Chotto otazune shi-tai-n-desu ga.** (choht-toh oh-tah-zoo-neh shee-tah-een-deh-soo gah.) (*I'd like to ask you about something, but is it okay?*)

Calling your client

When you call your business clients, remember that you're representing your company. That's the Japanese way to make a business call. Don't forget to mention the name of your company first, before mentioning your own name. Instead of saying *This is Mr. White*, for example, say *This is ABC Technology's Mr. White.*

Greet your client and her secretary with **O-sewa ni natte orimasu.** (oh-seh-wah nee naht-teh oh-ree-mah-soo.) (*Thank you for doing business with us.*) This line is one of the essential set phrases in Japanese business.

TIP

When you ask for your call to be transferred to a specific person, don't forget to specify his title and department. This little tip is important, especially when more than one person in the company has the same last name.

Talkin' the Talk

Patrick White at ABC Technology has just prepared an estimate for his client, Mr. Tanaka, at Yamada Denki, Inc. Patrick is calling Mr. Tanaka to tell him about the quote.

Secretary:	**Yamada Denki de gozaimasu.** yah-mah-dah dehn-kee deh goh-zah-ee-mah-soo. *This is Yamada Denki, Inc.*
Patrick:	**ABC Tekunorojī no Howaito desu. Itsumo o-sewa ni natte orimasu.** ehh-beee-sheee teh-koo-noh-roh-jeee noh hoh-wah-ee-toh deh-soo. ee-tsoo-moh oh-seh-wah nee naht-teh oh-ree-mah-soo. *This is Mr. White from ABC Technology. Thank you for doing business with us.*
Secretary:	**Kochira koso o-sewa ni natte orimasu.** koh-chee-rah koh-soh oh-seh-wah nee naht-teh oh-ree-mah-soo. *Thank you, too.*
Patrick:	**Anō, eigyō-bu no Tanaka buchō-sama wa irasshaimasu ka.** ah-nohh, ehh-gyohh-boo noh tah-nah-kah boo-chohh-sah-mah wah ee-rahs-shah-ee-mah-soo ka. *Umm, is Mr. Tanaka, the head of the sales division, available?*
Secretary:	**Hai, shōshō o-machi kudasai.** hah-ee, shohh-shohh oh-mah-chee koo-dah-sah-ee. *Yes. Could you hold on please?*
Patrick:	**Hai.** hah-ee. *Sure.*
Tanaka:	**Moshimoshi, omatase shimashita. Tanaka desu.** moh-shee-moh-shee, oh-mah-tah-seh shee-mah-shee-tah. tah-nah-kah deh-soo. *Hello, sorry to have kept you waiting. This is Mr. Tanaka speaking.*

Patrick:	**Ā, Tanaka-buchō. Howaito desu. Itsumo o-sewa ni natte orimasu.**
	ahh, tah-nah-kah-boo-chohh. hoh-wah-ee-toh deh-soo. ee-tsoo-moh oh-seh-wah nee naht-teh oh-ree-mah-soo.
	Oh, Division Chief Tanaka. This is Mr. White. I appreciate your doing business with us all this time.
Tanaka:	**Īe, kochira koso.**
	eee-eh, koh-chee-rah koh-soh.
	No, no. It is we who should say that.
Patrick:	**Anō, mitsumorisho ga dekimashita.**
	ah-nohh, mee-tsoo-moh-ree-shoh gah deh-kee-mah-shee-tah.
	Well, the quote is ready.

WORDS TO KNOW

Itsumo o-sewa ni natte orimasu.	ee-tsoo-moh oh-seh-wah nee naht-teh oh-ree-mah-soo.	Thank you for doing business with us.
Shōshō o-machi kudasai.	shohh-shohh oh-mah-chee koo-dah-sah-ee.	Could you hold on please?
Moshimoshi.	moh-shee-moh-shee.	Hello.
Omatase shimashita.	oh-mah-tah-seh shee-mah-shee-tah.	Sorry to have kept you waiting.
mitsumorisho	mee-tsoo-moh-ree-sho	quote
dekiru	deh-kee-roo	to be completed

Leaving a message

Many people's workdays are filled with meetings, deadlines, and can't-miss appointments that keep them from answering their phones — which means you're probably going to have to leave a message for someone at some point in your career. You may leave a message on a voice mail or with a person (such as a secretary or assistant).

To talk about leaving messages, conjugate the **u**–verb **nokosu** (noh–koh–soo), which means *to leave* in the sense of leaving a message or leaving something behind, but not *to leave* in the sense of going away or departing.

Japanese Script	Rōmaji	Pronunciation
残す	nokosu	noh-koh-soo
残さない	nokosanai	noh-koh-sah-nah-ee
残し(ます)	nokoshi (masu)	noh-koh-shee (-mah-soo)
残して	nokoshite	noh-koh-shee-teh

On someone's voice mail

When you leave a message on an answering machine, you need to give the other party all the information necessary to understand your call. Specifically, make sure you clarify which person will call the other back. Here are a few phrases to help you do just that:

» 後ほどお電話を下さい。**Nochihodo o-denwa o kudasai.** (noh-chee-hoh-doh oh-dehn-wah oh koo-dah-sah-ee.) (*Please give me a call later.*)

» またお電話を致します。**Mata o-denwa o itashimasu.** (mah-tah oh-dehn-wah oh ee-tah-shee-mah-soo.) (*I'll call you again.*)

With a person

When you leave a message with a person, be clear about what you want and always use polite phrases such as the following:

» 電話があったことをお伝えください。**Denwa ga atta koto o o-tsutae kudasai.** (dehn-wah gah aht-tah koh-toh oh oh-tsoo-tah-eh koo-dah-sah-ee.) (*Please tell him/her that I called.*)

» またこちらからお電話を致します。**Mata kochira kara o-denwa o itashimasu.** (mah-tah koh-chee-rah kah-rah oh-dehn-wah oh ee-tah-shee-mah-soo.) (*I'll call him/her again.*)

» お電話を頂きたいんですが。**O-denwa o itadakitai-n-desu ga.** (oh-dehn-wah oh ee-tah-dah-kee-tah-een-deh-soo gah.) (*Would you kindly ask him/her to please call me back?*)

» またお電話致しますとお伝え下さい。**Mata o-denwa itashimasu to o-tsutae kudasai.** (mah-tah o-dehn-wah ee-tah-shee-mah-soo toh oh-tsoo-tah-eh koo-dah-sah-ee.) (*Please let him/her know that I'll call again.*)

>> 少し遅れると伝えてください。**Sukoshi okureru to tsutaete kudasai.** (soo-koh-shee oh-koo-reh-roo toh tsoo-tah-eh-teh koo-dah-sah-ee.) (*Please tell him/her that I'll be a little late.*)

GRAMMAR CHAT

The particle **to,** as in **to tsutaete kudasai** in the last example sentence in the preceding list, is a quotation particle. Place it right after your message to indicate what your message is. Use it with the verbs **iu** (ee-oo) (to say), **kaku** (kah-koo) (*to write*), and **tsutaeru** (tsoo-tah-eh-roo) (*to report/tell*), as in the following examples:

一万円借りたと書きました。**10,000-en karita to kakimashita.** (ee-chee-mahn-ehn kah-ree-tah toh kah-kee-mah-shee-tah.) (*I wrote that I borrowed 10,000 yen.*)

田中さんは来ると言いました。**Tanaka-san wa kuru to iimashita.** (tah-nah-kah-sahn wah koo-roo toh eee-mah-shee-tah.) (*Mr. Tanaka said that he'll come.*)

また来ますと伝えてください。**Mata kimasu to tsutaete kudasai.** (mah-tah kee-mah-soo toh tsoo-tah-eh-teh koo-dah-sah-ee.) (*Could you tell him/her that I'll come again?*)

You can also use the quotation particle **to** with the verb **omou** (oh-moh-oo) (*to think*) to mark the content of what a person thinks.

翻訳は来週までにできると思います。**Hon'yaku wa raishū made ni dekiru to omoimasu.** (hohn-yah-koo wah rah-ee-shooo mah-deh nee deh-kee-roo toh oh-moh-ee-mah-soo.) (*I think that the translation can be completed by next week.*)

田中さんは来ないと思います。**Tanaka-san wa konai to omoimasu.** (tah-nah-kah-sahn wah koh-nah-ee toh oh-moh-ee-mah-soo.) (*I think Mr. Tanaka will not come.*)

GRAMMAR CHAT

Go– (goh) is another polite prefix, just like **o**– (oh), which I tell you about in Chapter 6. You can add **go**– to the beginning of a noun to refer respectfully to other people's items. Typically, you use **go**– with words of Chinese origin and **o**– with native Japanese words; however, too many exceptions exist, so you just have to memorize which prefix goes with which nouns. Check out some business-related examples:

>> 御注文 **go-chūmon** (goh-chooo-mohn) (*order*)

>> 御伝言 **go-dengon** (goh-dehn-gohn) (*message*)

>> 御住所 **go-jūsho** (goh-jooo-shoh) (*address*)

>> 御職業 **go-shokugyō** (goh-shoh-koo-gyohh) (*occupation*)

>> 御招待 **go-shōtai** (goh-shohh-tah-ee) (*invitation*)

>> お電話 **o-denwa** (oh-dehn-wah) (*telephone*)

>> お電話番号 **o-denwa-bangō** (oh-dehn-wah-bahn-gohh) (*telephone number*)

>> お客様 **o-kyaku-sama** (oh-kyah-koo-sah-mah) (*customer*)

>> お名前 **o-namae** (oh-nah-mah-eh) (*name*)

GRAMMAR CHAT

As I note in Chapter 10, the particle **ga** means *but* when placed after a sentence. It usually shows contrast, conflict, or contradiction just like *but* does in English, but **ga** can also mean almost nothing, simply marking a transition from one statement to another. The typical situation where you use **ga** as a transition marker is when one person telephones another person. In Japan, you need to say your own name first before asking for someone on the phone, so the particle **ga** is essential for smoothly beginning a telephone conversation. For example, if Mr. Smith wants to talk with Mr. Tanaka, he would first say his name and ask for Mr. Tanaka, as in **Sumisu desu ga, Tanaka-san wa irasshaimasu ka.** (soo-mee-soo deh-soo gah, tah-nah-kah-sahn wah ee-rahs-shah-ee-mah-soo kah.) (*I'm Mr. Smith. Is Mr. Tanaka there?*)

·············· Talkin' the Talk ··············

Jake Brown is a private English tutor. He tries to call his student, Makoto Isobe.

Mrs. Isobe:	**Hai, Isobe desu.** hah-ee, ee-soh-beh deh-soo. *Yes, this is the Isobe residence.*
Jake:	**Buraun desu ga, Makoto-san wa irass-haimasu ka.** boo-rah-oon deh-soo gah, mah-koh-toh-sahn wah ee-rahs-shah-ee-mah-soo ka. *This is Mr. Brown. Is Makoto available?*
Mrs. Isobe:	**Sumimasen. Chotto dekakete imasu. Nanika go-dengon wa.** soo-mee-mah-sehn. choht-toh deh-kah-keh-teh ee-mah-soo. nah-nee-kah goh-dehn-gohn wah. *I'm sorry, but he's out. May I take a message?*
Jake:	**Jā, ashita mata denwa o shimasu to tsutaete kudasai.** jahh, ah-shee-tah mah-tah dehn-wah oh shee-mah-soo toh tsoo-tah-eh-teh koo-dah-sah-ee. *Okay, could you tell him that I'll call him again tomorrow?*

Mrs. Isobe:	**Hai, wakarimashita.**
	hah-ee, wah-kah-ree-mah-shee-tah.
	Sure, certainly.

Jake:	**Jā, yoroshiku onegai shimasu.**
	jahh, yoh-roh-shee-koo oh-neh-gah-ee
	shee-mah-soo.
	Thanks. (Literally: *Thank you for doing me a favor.*)

WORDS TO KNOW

dekakete iru	deh-kah-keh-teh ee-roo	to be out, to have gone out
nanika	nah-nee-kah	something
ashita	ah-shee-tah	tomorrow
wakaru	wah-kah-roo	to understand

Having Meetings in the Workplace

As long as you're engaged in business, you'll be exposed to meetings (regardless of their size and frequency). Here are some words and phrases you need to talk about meetings:

» 議題 **gidai** (gee-dah-ee) (*agenda*)

» 議事録 **gijiroku** (gee-jee-roh-koo) (*minutes*)

» ホワイトボード **howaito bōdo** (hoh-wah-ee-toh bohh-doh) (*whiteboard*)

» 会議 **kaigi** (kah-ee-gee) (*meeting, conference*)

» 会議で話し合う **kaigi de hanashi-au** (kah-ee-gee deh han-nah-shee-ah-oo) (*to discuss at the meeting*)

» 会議で決める **kaigi de kimeru** (kah-ee-gee deh kee-meh-roo) (*to decide at the meeting*)

» 会議に出る **kaigi ni deru** (kah-ee-gee nee deh-roo) (*to attend the meeting*)

» 会議をする **kaigi o suru** (kah-ee-gee oh soo-roo) (*to hold a meeting*)

» コンファレンス **konfarensu** (kohn-fah-rehn-soo) (*conference*)

» コンファレンスコール **konfarensu kōru** (kohn-fah-rehn-soo kohh-roo) (*conference call*)

» プロジェクター **purojekutā** (poo-roh-jeh-koo-tahh) (*projector*)

Navigating Technology: Computer Basics, Mobile Phones, and Social Media

Computers and mobile phones are indispensable communication tools in the business world and in daily life in Japan just like many other countries. This section introduces technology terminology and expressions for you to immerse yourself into the tech world in Japanese. Many technology terms come from English, which means, yes, you will encounter a lot of katakana words!

Familiarizing yourself with basic technology terms

Pasokon (pah–soh–kohn) (*computers*) are essential for many Japanese. **Pasokon** is the abbreviation for personal computers. You need to understand many technology terms to use a **pasokon**. Check out this list for starters:

» CD **CD** (sheee-deee) (*CD*)

» デスクトップパソコン **desukutoppu-pasokon** (deh-soo-koo-tohp-poo-pah-soh-kohn) (*desktop computer*)

» ディスプレイ・モニター **disupurei-monitā** (dee-soo-poo-rehh-moh-nee-tahh) (*display monitor*)

» DVD **DVD** (deee-boo-ee-deee) (*DVD*)

» ドライブ **doraibu** (doh-rah-ee-boo) (*drive*)

» ハードディスク **hādodisuku** (hahh-doh-dee-soo-koo) (*hard disk*)

» キーボード **kībōdo** (keee-bohh-doh) (*keyboard*)

» マウス **mausu** (mah-oo-soo) (*mouse*)

» USBメモリー **USB memorī** (yooo-eh-soo-beee meh-moh-reee) (*flash drive*)

» モデム **modemu** (moh-deh-moo) (*modem*)

» ノートパソコン **nōto-pasokon** (nohh-toh-pah-soh-kohn) (*laptop*)

» パソコン **pasokon** (pah-soh-kohn) (*personal computer*)

» プリンター **purintā** (poo-reen-tahh) (*printer*)

» スキャナー **sukyanā** (soo-kyah-nahh) (*scanner*)

» スピーカー **supīkā** (soo-peee-kahh) (*speakers*)

» タブレット **taburetto** (tah-boo-reht-toh) (*tablet computer*)

» ウェブカメラ **webu-kamera** (weh-boo-kah-meh-rah) (*webcam*)

» 容量 **yōryō** (yoh-ryoh) (*capacity*)

The following words help you talk about the actions you perform and the programs you use on your computer, including Microsoft Word, Excel, and PowerPoint:

» ブラウザ **burauza** (boo-rah-oo-zah) (*browser*)

» エクセル **ekuseru** (eh-koo-seh-roo) (Excel)

» ホームページ **hōmupēji** (hohh-moo-pehh-jee) (*homepage*)

» インターネット **intānetto** (een-tahh-neht-toh) (*Internet*)

» インターフェース **intāfēsu** (een-tah-fehh-soo) (*interface*)

» メール **mēru** (mehh-roo) (*emails*)

» パワーポイント **pawāpointo** (pah-wahh-poh-een-toh) (*PowerPoint*)

» ウェブサイト **webusaito** (weh-boo-sah-ee-toh) (*website*)

» ワード **wādo** (wahh-doh) (*Word*)

Sending email

I love email (**mēru**) (mehh–roo) because I can send or read it whenever I want. Here are basic terms you need to use this convenient tool, both in the workplace and in the comfort of your home:

» 返信する **henshin suru** (hehn-sheen soo-roo) (*to reply to an email*)

» 受信する **jushin suru** (joo-sheen soo-roo) (*to receive an email*)

» 迷惑メール **meiwaku-mēru** (meh-ee-wah-koo-mehh-roo) (*spam mail*)

» メールアドレス **mēru-adoresu** (mehh-roo-ah-doh-reh-soo) (*email address*)

» パスワード **pasuwādo** (pah-soo-wahh-doh) (*password*)

» ログアウト **roguauto** (roh-goo-ah-oo-toh) (*logout*)

» ログイン **roguin** (roh-goo-een) (*login*)

» 送信する **sōshin suru** (sohh-sheen soo-roo) (*to send an email*)

» 添付する **tenpu suru** (tehn-poo soo-roo) (*to attach*)

Using mobile phones and social media

Keitai is the short form of **keitai denwa,** which literally means "portable phone." For the last 15 years or so, smartphones have been the style of **keitai** for many people. Smartphones are called **sumaho** (soo–mah–hoh), which is the abbreviation of "smartphones." **Sumaho** has become a must–have communication and information–gathering device everywhere, especially since social media has become pervasive in Japanese society. Here are some terms you should know to use social media on a **sumaho:**

» **aidyī** (ah-ee-dyee) (*ID*)

» **aifon** (ah-ee-fohn) (*iPhone*)

» アンドロイド **andoroido** (ahn-doh-ro-ee-doh) (*Android*)

» アップロード **appurōdo** (ahp-poo-roh-doh) (*upload*)

» アプリ **apuri** (ah-poo-ree) (*app, the short form of application*)

» アプリケーション **apurikēshon** (ah-poo-ree-kehh-shohn) (*application*)

» ブログ **burogu** (boo-roh-goo) (*blog*)

» チャット **chatto** (chaht-toh) (*chat, chatting*)

» ダウンロード **daunrōdo** (dah-oon-roh-doh) (*download*)

» デバイス **debaisu** (deh-bah-ee-soo) (*device*)

» **esuenuesu** (ee-soo-ee-noo-ee-soo) (*SNS, Social Networking Service*)

» フェイスブック **feisubukku** (feh-ee-soo-book-koo) (*Facebook*)

» インスタグラム **insutaguramu** (een-soo-tah-goo-rah-moo) (*Instagram*)

» **rain** (rah-een) (*LINE*)

» ツイッター **tsuittā** (tsoo-eet-tahh) (*Twitter*)

» フォローする **forō suru** (foh-rohh soo-roo) (*to follow*)

» インストール **insutōru** (een-soo-tohh-roo) (*install*)

» **ōesu** (oh-eh-soo) (*OS*)

» スマホ **sumaho** (soo-mah-hoh) (the short form of *smartphone*)

» スマートフォン **sumātofon** (soo-mah-toh-fohn) (*smartphones*)

» ストリーミング **sutorīmingu** (soo-toh-reee-meen-goo) (*streaming*)

» ユーチューブ **yūchūbu** (yooo-choo-bu) (YouTube)

» ユーザー **yūzā** (yooo-zahh) (*user*)

CULTURAL WISDOM

Facebook, Instagram, and Twitter are very popular among Japanese people. But the social media system called LINE is also widely used as a way to communicate with one another. The Japanese say "LINE **suru** (*do LINE*)." LINE is an application that can be used on computers, tablets, and smartphones. It comes with many features, including text chats, voice chats, and other convenient functions. But the **kawaii** (kah–wah–ee–ee) (*cute*) design of stickers (or stamps) and emojis available in LINE have been especially embraced by users. LINE has original characters that appear on stickers. You can choose an emotive sticker to convey your feeling with a character!

FUN & GAMES

Match each Japanese term with the correct office item marked in the illustration. Flip to Appendix C for the answers.

Illustration by Elizabeth Kurtzman

1. 電話 **denwa**
2. カレンダー **karendā**
3. ホッチキス **hotchikisu**
4. 机 **tsukue**
5. 椅子 **isu**
6. デスクランプ **desuku ranpu**
7. パソコン **pasokon**
8. ペン **pen**
9. 本棚 **hondana**
10. ゴミ箱 **gomibako**
11. 鉛筆削り **enpitsukezuri**

a. chair

b. desk lamp

c. calendar

d. computer

e. telephone

f. pencil sharpener

g. pen

h. bookshelves

i. wastebasket

j. desk

k. stapler

Japanese on the Go

Discover the necessary words and phrases to plan a trip.

Know what to say when you need to find a place to stay.

Find out how to communicate during an emergency.

IN THIS CHAPTER

» **Deciding on a destination**

» **Being prepared with passports and visas**

» **Visiting a travel agent**

» **Packing your bags**

» **Appreciating nature**

Chapter **13**
Planning a Trip

L ife is like a journey, but going on an actual trip once in a while to escape from the pressures of daily life is nice. After all, who doesn't need a little rest and relaxation? This chapter helps you plan where to go and what to bring, using Japanese. It also explains how to deal with travel logistics (namely, passports and visas) and travel agencies. In the last section of this chapter, you discover the words and phrases that let you explore nature. Are you ready for an exciting trip?

REMEMBER

You can listen to all the Talkin' the Talk dialogues featured in this chapter. Go to www.dummies.com/go/japanesefd and click on the dialogue you want to hear.

Picking the Place for Your Trip

After you secure the cash and the time for your **ryokō** (ryoh-kohh) (*trip*), pick the location. Do you want to visit a **gaikoku** (gah-ee-koh-koo) (*foreign country*)? How about one of the following **kuni** (koo-nee) (*countries*)?

>> アイスランド **Aisurando** (ah-ee-soo-rahn-doh) (*Iceland*)

>> 中国 **Chūgoku** (chooo-goh-koo) (*China*)

>> フランス **Furansu** (foo-rahn-soo) (*France*)

>> ギリシャ **Girisha** (gee-ree-shah) (*Greece*)

YOUR TICKET TO RIDE: THE JAPAN RAIL PASS

Many tourists who come to Japan are shocked to find out the high cost of train tickets. A two-hour ride on the 新幹線 **Shinkansen** (sheen-kahn-sehn) (*Bullet Train*) can cost more than 100 dollars. To help foreign travelers in Japan, the Japan Railway Group has been offering ジャパンレールパス **japan rēru pasu** (jah-pahn rehh-roo pah-soo) (*the Japan rail pass*), which short-term visitors to Japan can use for a limited time for sightseeing purposes. All you need to do is purchase a coupon through a travel agency before entering Japan. Then in Japan you exchange the coupon for the pass at a train station when you're ready to start using it. The pass is good for travel on all major forms of transportation provided by the Japan Railway Group, with a few exceptions. ***Note:*** The pass is mainly for non-Japanese passport holders, but some Japanese citizens who live overseas are also eligible; check the qualification criteria carefully.

- » イギリス **Igirisu** (ee-gee-ree-soo) (*England* or *Britain*)
- » インド **Indo** (een-doh) (*India*)
- » イタリア **Italia** (ee-tah-ree-ah) (*Italy*)
- » カナダ **Kanada** (kah-nah-dah) (*Canada*)
- » 韓国 **Kankoku** (kahn-koh-koo) (*South Korea*)
- » オーストラリア **Ōsutoraria** (ohh-soo-toh-rah-ree-ah) (*Australia*)
- » ロシア **Roshia** (roh-shee-ah) (*Russia*)
- » タイ **Tai** (tah-ee) (*Thailand*)

Following are some of the interesting historical buildings you can find in many countries:

- » 教会 **kyōkai** (kyohh-kah-ee) (*churches*)
- » お城 **o-shiro** (oh-shee-roh) (*castles*)
- » お寺 **o-tera** (oh-teh-rah) (*temples*)

In Japan, you may also visit a **jinja** (jeen–jyah) (*shinto shrine*).

You may notice that the sentence–ending particle **yo** (yoh) is used for emphasis in the following Talkin' the Talk dialogue. Depending on the intonation and the context, you may sound very pushy, very helpful, or very enthusiastic when you use **yo**.

So you better not use **yo** when you talk to your teacher or boss until you understand exactly when and how to use it. Often, the feminine ending **wa** occurs right before the emphasis particle **yo**.

GRAMMAR CHAT

The dialogue also features the conjunction word **demo** (deh-moh) (*however*). Use conjunction words such as **demo** to clarify the nature of your statement in relation to the previous statement made by you or someone else. Note that even though **demo** is similar to the particle **ga** (gah), which is placed at the end of a clause (see Chapter 10), **demo** is actually a word, so you place it at the beginning of a sentence.

> 旅行をしたいです。でも, お金がありません。**Ryokō o shitai desu. Demo, okane ga arimasen.** (ryoh-kohh oh shee-tah-ee deh-soo. deh-moh, oh-kah-neh gah ah-ree-mah-sehn.) (*I want to go on a trip. However, I have no money.*)

> サンフランシスコは行きました。でも, ロサンゼルスは行きませんでした。 **Sanfuranshisuko wa ikimashita. Demo, rosanzerusu wa ikimasen deshita.** (sahn-foo-rahn-shee-soo-koh wah ee-kee-mah-shee-tah. deh-moh, roh-sahn-zeh-roo-soo wah ee-kee-mah-sehn deh-shee-tah.) (*I went to San Francisco. However, I didn't go to Los Angeles.*)

> お金はありません。でも, よく旅行をします。**O-kane wa arimasen. Demo, yoku ryokō o shimasu.** (oh-kah-neh wah ah-ree-mah-sehn. deh-moh, yoh-koo ryoh-kohh oh shee-mah-soo.) (*I don't have money. But I often travel.*)

Other conjunction words include **desukara** (deh-soo-kah-rah) (*therefore*), **sorekara** (soh-reh-kah-rah) (*and then*), **soreni** (soh-reh-neee) (*furthermore*), and **sōsuruto** (sohh-soo-roo-toh) (*then*). To see examples of **sorekara** and **sōsuruto** in action, turn to Chapter 8; for examples of **desukara** (*therefore*), check out the following sample sentences:

> お金がありません。ですから, 旅行ができません。**O-kane ga arimasen. Desukara, ryokō ga dekimasen.** (oh-kah-neh gah ah-ree-mah-sehn. deh-soo-kah-rah, ryoh-kohh gah deh-kee-mah-sehn.) (*I don't have any money. Therefore, I can't travel.*)

> 日本に2週間います。ですから, ジャパンレールパスを買いました。**Nihon ni nishūkan imasu. Desukara, japan rēru pasu o kaimashita.** (nee-hohn nee nee-shooo-kahn ee-mah-soo. deh-soo-kah-rah, jah-pahn rehh-roo pah-soo oh kah-ee-mah-shee-tah.) (*I'll be in Japan for two weeks. So I bought a Japan rail pass.*)

REMEMBER

Keep in mind that **aru** (ah-roo) (*to exist*) is slightly irregular — its negative form is **nai**. When you talk about whether you have or don't have something, say **aru** and **nai**, respectively. (For more information on using the verb **aru**, see Chapter 7.)

Talkin' the Talk

Junko and Yuka are co-workers at a company that is going to be closed for one week at the end of the year. They've decided to go on a trip together, and they're debating where to go.

Junko: **Yōroppa wa.**
            yohh-rohp-pah wah.
            How about Europe?

Yuka: **Amerika ga ii yo.**
            ah-meh-ree-kah gah eee yoh.
            America is better.

Junko: **Demo, Amerika wa furui tatemono ga nai kara . . . .**
            deh-moh, ah-meh-ree-kah wah foo-roo-ee tah-teh-moh-noh gah
            nah-ee kah-rah . . . .
            But there are no old buildings in America, so . . . .

Yuka: **Demo, Amerika wa omoshiroi yo.**
            deh-moh, ah-meh-ree-kah wah oh-moh-shee-roh-ee yoh.
            But America is fun.

WORDS TO KNOW

Yōroppa	yohh-rohp-pah	Europe
Amerika	ah-meh-ree-kah	America
demo	deh-moh	but
furui	foo-roo-ee	old
kara	kah-rah	because
tatemono	tah-teh-moh-noh	buildings
omoshiroi	oh-moh-shee-roh-ee	fun

JAPAN: RUNNING HOT AND COLD

If you're planning a trip to Japan, you should know that although the country has four seasons (including a brief rainy season), the climate varies tremendously depending on where in the country you are. Why? Because Japan is a long, narrow country. Japan's north end is at the same latitude as Montreal, and its southern tip is at the same latitude as the Florida Keys. So it snows heavily up north in Hokkaido, but it's warm farther south in Kyushu. Also, know that Japan uses the Celsius scale (°C) rather than the Fahrenheit scale (°F) for indicating temperature. So if you keep your air-conditioning set at 77 degrees Fahrenheit, you'd set it at about 25 degrees Celsius.

Dealing with Passports and Visas

Because the U.S. and Japanese governments have a mutual agreement, American citizens and Japanese citizens can visit each other's countries without a visa for a short sightseeing visit. However, you'll definitely need a passport. My advice? Don't wait until the last minute to obtain a passport or renew one. Following are some vocabulary words and phrases that are bound to come in handy when dealing with passports and visas:

>> ビザ *or* 査証 **biza** *or* **sashō** (bee-zah *or* sah-shohh) (*visa*)

>> 長期滞在 **chōki taizai** (chohh-kee tah-ee-zah-ee) (*long-term visit*)

>> 入国目的 **nyūkoku mokuteki** (nyooo-koh-koo moh-koo-tah-kee) (*purpose of visit*)

>> 入国審査 **nyūkoku shinsa** (nyooo-koh-koo sheehn-sah) (*immigration*)

>> パスポート *or* 旅券 **pasupōto** *or* **ryoken** (pah-soo-pohh-toh *or* ryoh-kehn) (*passport*)

>> 写真 **shashin** (shah-sheen) (*photo*)

>> 申請書 **shinseisho** (sheen-sehh-shoh) (*application form*)

>> 総領事館 **sōryōjikan** (sohh-rhohh-jee-kahn) (*consulate general*)

>> 大使館 **taishikan** (tah-ee-shee-kahn) (*embassy*)

>> 滞在期間 **taizai kikan** (tah-ee-zah-ee kee-kahn) (*duration of stay*)

>> 短期滞在 **tanki taizai** (tahn-kee tah-ee-zah-ee) (*short-term visit*)

>> 税関 **zēkan** (zehh-kahn) (*customs*)

Getting Help from a Travel Agency

If arranging the transportation and accommodations for your trip is too much for you, get help from a **ryokō gaisha** (ryoh–kohh gah–ee–shah) (*travel agency*) and choose the plan that satisfies your needs. To explore the agency's tours and packages, you'll need these words and phrases:

>> ホテル **hoteru** (hoh–teh–roo) (*hotel*)

>> 観光 **kankō** (kahn–kohh) (*sightseeing*)

>> キャンセル **kyanseru** (kyahn–seh–roo) (*cancel*)

>> キャンセル料 **kyanseruryō** (kyahn–seh–roo–ryohh) (*cancellation fee*)

>> 申込書 **mōshikomisho** (mohh–shee–koh–mee–shoh) (*application form*)

>> パッケージツアー **pakkēji tsuā** (pahk–kehh–jee tsoo–ahh) (*package tour*)

>> 添乗員 **tenjōin** (tehn–johh–een) (*tour conductor*)

>> ツアー **tsuā** (tsoo–ahh) (*tour*)

>> 予約 **yoyaku** (yoh–yah–koo) (*reservation*)

Tell the agency where you want to go and how many days and nights you want to spend there. In Japanese, say the number of nights first, and then say the number of days. To specify the number of nights, use the counter **-haku**. Depending on the preceding number, **-haku** alternates with **-paku.** Here's the general pattern (for more help specifying the number of days, flip to Chapter 4).

>> 一泊二日 **ip-paku futsuka** (eep–pah–koo foo–tsoo–kah) (*one night, two days*)

>> 二泊三日 **ni-haku mikka** (nee–hah–koo meek–kah) (*two nights, three days*)

>> 七泊八日 **nana-haku yōka** (nah–nah–hah–koo yohh–kah) (*seven nights, eight days*)

Also, check what the travel agency's packages include. **Tsukimasu** (tsoo–kee–mah–soo) means *to be included.* Its dictionary form is **tsuku** (tsoo–koo). Here's how to conjugate this **u**-verb:

Japanese Script	Rōmaji	Pronunciation
付く	tsuku	tsoo-koo
付かない	tsukanai	tsoo-kah-nah-ee
付き (ます)	tsuki(masu)	tsoo-kee(-mah-soo)
付いて	tsuite	tsoo-ee-teh

You may hear phrases like these after inquiring about what's included in a particular travel package:

» 朝食と夕食が付きます。**Chōshoku to yūshoku ga tsukimasu.** (chohh-shoh-koo toh yooo-shoh-koo gah tsoo-kee-mah-soo.) (*Breakfast and dinner are included.*)

» ホテル付きで3万円です。**Hoteru tsuki de 3-man-en desu.** (hoh-teh-roo tsoo-kee deh sahn-mahn-ehn deh-soo.) (*It costs 30,000 yen including the hotel fee.*)

» 添乗員が同行します。**Tenjōin ga dōkō shimasu.** (tehn-johh-een gah dohh-kohh shee-mah-soo.) (*A tour guide will accompany you.*)

» 東京ディズニーランド一日観光です。**Tōkyō dizunīrando ichi-nichi kankō desu.** (tohh-kyohh dee-zoo-neee-rahn-doh ee-chee-nee-chee kahn-kohh deh-soo.) (*It's a one-day sightseeing trip to Tokyo Disneyland.*)

Stating Your Opinions

If you're planning your trip with others, you may need to make a case for a certain hotel you want to stay at or sight you want to see. To state what you think, use the **u–verb omou** (oh–moh–oo) (*to think*). Practice conjugating the verb **omou**. Don't forget the **w** sound in the negative form.

Japanese Script	Rōmaji	Pronunciation
思う	omou	oh-moh-oo
思わない	omowanai	oh-moh-wah-nah-ee
思い（ます）	omoi(masu)	oh-moh-ee(-mah-soo)
思って	omotte	oh-moht-teh

As I explain in Chapter 12, you use the quotation particle **to** (toh) to mark a sentence that expresses what you think. Just make sure the sentence before the particle **to** ends in a verb or adjective in the plain/informal form.

田中さんも行くと思います。**Tanaka-san mo iku to omoimasu.** (tah-nah-kah-sahn moh ee-koo toh oh-moh-ee-mah-soo.) (*I think Mr. Tanaka will also go there.*)

あの人は添乗員だと思います。**Ano hito wa tenjōin da to omoimasu.** (ah-noh hee-toh wah tehn-johh-een dah toh oh-moh-ee-mah-soo.) (*I think that person is a tour conductor.*)

あのホテルはよくないと思います。**Ano hoteru wa yokunai to omoimasu.** (ah-noh hoh-teh-roo wah yoh-koo-nah-ee toh oh-moh-ee-mah-soo.) (*I think that hotel isn't good.*)

そう思います。**Sō omoimasu.** (sohh oh-moh-ee-mah-soo.) (*I think so.*)

TIP

Both **omou** and **kangaeru** (kahn-gah-eh-roo) mean *to think*, but they're not interchangeable. **Omou** is *to think* in the sense of having an opinion, and **kangaeru** expresses more of a sense of pondering.

これはいいと思います。**Kore wa ii to omoimasu.** (koh-reh wah eee toh oh-moh-ee-mah-soo.) (*I think this is good.*)

それをよく考えてください。**Sore o yoku kangaete kudasai.** (soh-reh oh yoh-koo kahn-gah-eh-teh koo-dah-sah-ee.) (*Please think carefully about that.*)

GRAMMAR CHAT

To indicate that what you think is just a guess, use **deshō** (deh-shohh) at the end of the sentence. The sentence before **deshō** is in the plain/informal style, but just remember to drop the **da** (dah) that appears in the plain present affirmative form of **desu** or a **na**-type adjective. Here are some examples:

あのホテルは高いでしょう。**Ano hoteru wa takai deshō.** (ah-noh hoh-tah-roo wah tah-kah-ee deh-shohh.) (*That hotel is probably expensive.*)

あの人は添乗員でしょう。**Ano hito wa tenjōin deshō.** (ah-noh hee-toh wah tehn-johh-een deh-shohh.) (*I guess that person is a tour conductor.*)

You can use **kamoshiremasen** (kah-moh-shee-reh-mah-sehn) to say *It's possible that . . .* (see Chapter 5 for info on how to use **kamoshiremasen**).

CULTURAL WISDOM

EATING A BOX LUNCH FROM THE TRAIN STATION

駅弁 **Ekiben** (eh-kee-behn) is a box lunch sold at 駅 **eki** (eh-kee) (*train stations*) or on trains. Different **eki** sell different **ekiben** with unique names. The name of my favorite **ekiben** is 峠の釜飯 Tōge no kamameshi (tohh-geh noh kah-mah-meh-shee) (*Mountain Pass Chicken-Vegetable Rice in a Pot*) from Nagano.

Some **ekiben** are famous, and people visit the **eki** or get on the train just to buy one of these lunches. If you travel by train in Japan, buy an **ekiben** and a bottle of hot green tea at the platform. What a fun experience!

Packing for Your Trip

The first step in packing for your trip is to decide on the luggage. Are you going to take a big **sūtsukēsu** (sooo-tsoo-kehh-soo) (*suitcase*) or a smaller **ryokō kaban** (ryoh-kohh kah-bahn) (*travel bag*)?

Whatever bag you choose, be sure to pack clothing staples such as a **sētā** (sehh-tahh) (*sweater*), プルオーバーパーカー **puruōbā pākā** (poo-roo-ohh-bahh pahh-kahh) (*pullover parka*), **sunīkā** (soo-neee-kahh) (*sneakers*), and **jīnzu** (jeeen-zoo) (*jeans*); see Chapter 10 for additional clothing vocabulary words. And if you're traveling to a warm destination, don't forget to pack some weather-appropriate gear, including the following:

» バイザー **baizā** (bah-ee-zahh) (*visor*)

» 帽子 **bōshi** (bohh-shee) (*hat/cap*)

» サンダル **sandaru** (sahn-dah-roo) (*sandals*)

» サングラス **sangurasu** (sahn-goo-rah-soo) (*sunglasses*)

What else do you need? First, conjugate the **u**-verb **iru** (ee-roo) (*to need*) — not to be confused with the verb **iru** (ee-roo) (*to exist*), which is a **ru**-verb.

Japanese Script	Rōmaji	Pronunciation
要る	iru	ee-roo
要らない	iranai	ee-rah-nah-ee
要り (ます)	iri(masu)	ee-ree(-mah-soo)
要って	itte	eet-teh

When you think about travel necessities, I sure hope toiletries come to mind. Here's how to talk about some common toiletry items in Japanese:

» 歯ブラシ **haburashi** (hah-boo-rah-shee) (*toothbrush*)

» 歯磨き粉 **hamigakiko** (hah-mee-gah-kee-koh) (*toothpaste*)

» 剃刀 **kamisori** (kah-mee-soh-ree) (*razor*)

» 化粧品 **keshōhin** (keh-shohh-heen) (*cosmetics*)

» くし **kushi** (koo-shee) (*comb*)

» 石鹸 **sekken** (sehk-kehn) (*soap*)

» タオル **taoru** (tah-oh-roo) (*towel*)

Other items that may be useful to pack include the following:

>> 地図 **chizu** (chee-zoo) (*map*)

>> 日焼け止め **hiyakedome** (hee-yah-keh-doh-meh) (*sunscreen*)

>> 懐中電灯 **kaichūdentō** (kah-ee-chooo-dehn-tohh) (*flashlight*)

>> カメラ **kamera** (kah-meh-rah) (*camera*)

>> カーナビ **kānabi** (kahh-nah-bee) (*car navigation system*)

>> 傘 **kasa** (kah-sah) (*umbrella*)

Exploring Nature

Every place has its own natural charm. Even when you are working in your office, a tree you can see through the window may give you great comfort! When you travel, you will enjoy varied landscapes and **shizen** (shee–zehn) (*nature*). The following sections help you prepare to explore nature.

Taking in the landscape

When you head outside for a little R and R, you may want to enjoy a few of the following places:

>> ビーチ **bīchi** (beee-chee) (*beach*)

>> 海岸 **kaigan** (kah-ee-gahn) (*shoreline*)

>> 川 **kawa** (kah-wah) (*river*)

>> 火山 **kazan** (kah-zahn) (*volcano*)

>> 湖 **mizuumi** (mee-zoo-oo-mee) (*lake*)

>> 山脈 **sanmyaku** (sahn-myah-koo) (*mountain range*)

>> 滝 **taki** (tah-kee) (*waterfall*)

>> 海 **umi** (oo-mee) (*sea/ocean*)

>> 山 **yama** (yah-mah) (*mountain*)

Beyond admiring the scenery, you may want to do one of the following activities:

» ハイキング **haikingu** (hah-ee-keen-goo) (*hiking*)

» キャンプ **kyanpu** (kyahn-poo) (*camping*)

» サイクリング **saikuringu** (sah-ee-koo-reen-goo) (*cycling*)

Changing with the seasons

When you want to explore nature, the season is the most important factor to take into account. Does your part of the world have **shiki** (shee–kee) (*four seasons*)? The four seasons are

» 春 **haru** (hah-roo) (*spring*)

» 夏 **natsu** (nah-tsoo) (*summer*)

» 秋 **aki** (ah-kee) (*fall*)

» 冬 **fuyu** (foo-yoo) (*winter*)

REMEMBER

If you want to make a suggestion (for example, swimming, singing, diving, and traveling), take the stem form of a verb and add one of these verb suffixes:

» **masen ka** (mah-sehn kah) (*why don't we*), as in **Gorufu o shimasen ka.** (goh-roo-foo oh shee-mah-sehn ka.) (*Why don't we play golf?*)

» **mashō** (mah-shohh) (*let's*), as in **Gorufu o shimashō!** (goh-roo-foo oh shee-mah-shohh!) (*Let's play golf!*)

Examples of these two endings are in the nearby Talkin' the Talk dialogue.

GRAMMAR CHAT

You can ask for permission by using a verb in the **te**–form and adding **mo ii desu ka** to it. If you're giving permission, adding the sentence final particle **yo** (yoh) after **mo ii desu** is nice; it shows your willingness. (Turn to Chapter 3 for more about the particle **yo**.) For example,

泳いでもいいですか。 **Oyoide mo ii desu ka.** (oh-yoh-ee-deh moh eee deh-soo kah.) (*Is it okay to swim?*)

泳いでもいいですよ。 **Oyoide mo ii desu yo.** (oh-yoh-ee-deh moh eee deh-soo yoh.) (*You may swim.*)

ピアノを弾いてもいいですよ。 **Piano o hiite mo ii desu yo.** (pee-ah-noh oh heee-teh moh eee deh-soo yoh.) (*It's okay to play the piano.*)

CULTURAL WISDOM

ENJOYING THE FOUR SEASONS IN JAPAN

Like most of places on Earth, Japan has spring, summer, fall, and winter. The seasons play a significant role in Japanese culture. For example, Japanese aesthetics often involve four seasons in poetry, architecture, tea ceremony, traditional paintings, and other artistic forms. Japanese people admire and respect the transformations of nature. As you can see on the cover of this book, **Fuji-san** (foo-jee-sah-n) (*Mt. Fuji*) and **sakura** (sah-koo-rah) (*cherry blossoms*) are often considered symbols of awe-inspiring natural beauty. When you visit Japan, you can experience the Japanese ways of admiring nature. Here are some examples of seasonal fun activities!

- In spring, don't miss 花見 **hanami** (hah-nah-mee) (*flower viewing*).

- In summer, go to the countryside and experience 盆祭り **Bon matsuri** (bohn mah-tsoo-ree) (*Bon festivals*) and 盆踊り **Bon odori** (bohn oh-doh-ree) (*Bon dancing*), where you can dance with the crowd. (**Bon** is the Buddhist festival of the dead.)

- In fall, drive around in the mountains and enjoy 紅葉 **kōyō** (kohh-yohh) (*the changing of leaves' colors*).

- In winter, go to 雪祭り **yukimatsuri** (yoo-kee-mah-tsoo-ree) (*the snow festival*) in 北海道 **Hokkaidō** (hohk-kah-ee-dohh) (*Hokkaido*) and see the huge, magnificent snow sculptures.

To express prohibition, saying *must not*, add **wa ikemasen** rather than **mo ii desu**, as in the following examples:

泳いではいけません。**Oyoide wa ikemasen.** (oh-yoh-ee-deh wah ee-keh-mah-sehn.) (*You must not swim.*)

レスリングをしてはいけません。**Resuringu o shite wa ikemasen.** (reh-soo-reen-goo oh shee-teh wah ee-keh-mah-sehn.) (*You must not wrestle.*)

Talkin' the Talk

Yoko and Lisa work at a small company in Tokyo. Lisa came to Tokyo only a month ago, so Yoko and Lisa are planning to take a trip to Kyoto together this weekend. It's spring. Cherry blossoms have started blooming.

Yoko: **Risa-san, Kyoto wa sakura ga sakimashita yo.**
Ree-sah-sah-n, kyoh-toh wah sah-koo-rah gah sah-kee-mah-shee-tah yoh.
Lisa, the cherry trees have started to bloom in Kyoto.

Lisa: **Ii taiming desu ne. O-hanami o shimasho!**
Ee-ee tah-ee-mee-n-goo deh-soo neh. Oh-hah-nah-mee oh shee-mah-shohh!
It's good timing. Why don't we go flower viewing?

Yoko: **Ii desu ne! So shimashō. Jā, shinkansen no kippu o kattemo iidesu ka.**
Eee deh-soo neh! Sohh shee mah shohh. Jhahh, sheen-kahn-sehn noh keep-poo o kaht-teh-moh eee-deh-soo kah.
That sounds good! Well then, is it okay (for me) to buy our Shinkansen tickets?

Lisa: **Hai, yoroshiku onegai shimasu.**
Hah-ee, yoh-roh-shee-koo oh-neh-gah-ee shee-mah-soo.
Yes, thank you for taking care of it.

Yoko: **Tochu, shinkansen kara Fuji-san ga mieru to omoimasu yo.**
Toh-choo, sheen-kahn-sehn kah-rah Foo-jee-sahn gah mee-eh-roo toh oh-moh-ee-mah-soo yoh.
On the way, I think we can see Mt. Fuji from the Shinkansen.

Lisa: **Tanoshimi desu!**
Tah-noh-shee-mee deh-soo!
I look forward to it!

• •

WORDS TO KNOW

sakura	sah-koo-rah	cherry (tree)
saku	sah-koo	to bloom
hanami	hah-nah-mee	flower viewing
Shinkansenkippu	sheen-kahn-sehhn-keep-poo	Bullet train ticket
Fuji-san	Foo-jee-sahn	Mt. Fuji
mieru	mee-eh-roo	can be seen

FUN & GAMES

Name the marked items in Japanese. The answers are in Appendix C.

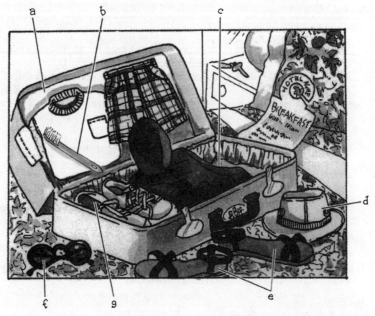

Illustration by Elizabeth Kurtzman

a. _____

b. _____

c. _____

d. _____

e. _____

f. _____

g. _____

IN THIS CHAPTER

» Embarking and disembarking with noru and oriru

» Deciding on the best mode of transportation

» Flying through the airport with the greatest of ease

» Traveling by train and boat

» Trying public transportation and road driving

Chapter **14**

Making Your Way Around: Planes, Trains, Taxis, and More

Kōtsū **kikan** (kohh-tsooo kee-kahn) (*transportation*) is an indispensable part of life. Choose the method that meets your needs. Which costs less, driving a car or taking a train? Which is less hectic, taking a subway or taking a cab? Which makes you feel safer, flying or driving? This chapter provides you with the essential phrases that you need to get around town by using various types of **kōtsū kikan.**

REMEMBER

You can listen to all the Talkin' the Talk dialogues featured in this chapter. Go to www.dummies.com/go/japanesefd and click on the dialogue you want to hear.

Getting On and Off with the Verbs Noru and Oriru

The verb **noru** (noh-roo) is used for all forms of transportation, including bicycles, buses, trains, ships, and airplanes. So its translation can be *to ride, to get on,* or *to get in* any form of transportation, depending on the context. Conjugate this **u**–verb as follows, paying close attention to the **r** syllables as you conjugate it:

Japanese Script	Rōmaji	Pronunciation
乗る	noru	noh-roo
乗らない	noranai	noh-rah-nah-ee
乗り(ます)	nori(masu)	noh-ree(-mah-soo)
乗って	notte	noht-teh

When using **noru** in a sentence, remember to mark the form of transportation that you're taking with the particle **ni** (nee), as in the following examples:

電車に乗る **densha ni noru** (dehn-shah nee noh-roo) (*to get on a train*)

飛行機に乗る **hikōki ni noru** (hee-kohh-kee nee noh-roo) (*to get on an airplane*)

自転車に乗る **jitensha ni noru** (jee-tehn-shah nee noh-roo) (*to ride a bicycle*)

タクシーに乗る **takushī ni noru** (tah-koo-sheee nee noh-roo) (*to get in a taxi*)

If you know the verb **noru,** you have to know the verb **oriru** (oh-ree-roo) (*to get off*), unless you want to live on an airplane. Conjugate this **ru**–verb as follows:

Japanese Script	Rōmaji	Pronunciation
降りる	oriru	oh-ree-roo
降りない	orinai	oh-ree-nah-ee
降り(ます)	ori(masu)	oh-ree(-mah-soo)
降りて	orite	oh-ree-teh

Like **noru,** you can use **oriru** for any form of transportation. Mark the place you're getting off from with the particle **kara** (kah-rah) (*from*) or the direct object particle **o** (oh). Here are a few examples:

飛行機から降りました。 **Hikōki kara orimashita.** (hee-kohh-kee kah-rah oh-ree-mah-shee-tah.) (*I got off the airplane.*)

後ろの出口から降りてください。**Ushiro no deguchi kara orite kudasai.** (oo-shee-roh noh deh-goo-chee kah-rah oh-ree-teh koo-dah-sah-ee.) (*Please get off [the plane] via the rear exit.*)

新宿で電車を降りてバスに乗ります。**Shinjuku de densha o orite basu ni norimasu.** (sheen-joo-koo deh dehn-shah oh oh-ree-teh bah-soo nee noh-ree-mah-soo.) (*I'll get off the train at Shinjuku and get on the bus.*)

GRAMMAR CHAT

In Japanese, saying you're taking some form of transportation isn't the same as saying you're going somewhere by some form of transportation. To specify what form of transportation you're using to go somewhere, use the particle **de** (deh). Place **de** at the end of the word for the mode of transportation, and place both of them somewhere before the verb. For example, **Hikōki de Hokkaidō ni ikimasu.** (hee-kohh-kee deh hohk-kah-ee-dohh nee ee-kee-mah-soo.) means *I'll go to Hokkaido by airplane.*

The general function of **de** is to specify how you perform a given action. Specifying the form of transportation is just one instance in which you use **de**. For other examples, flip to Chapter 3.

Asking about the Best Method of Transportation

Although you can access all kinds of transportation information — from schedules to fares — online nowadays, you still need to be able to ask the right questions when you're wondering about the best transportation method for your purpose.

GRAMMAR CHAT

To ask questions like *Which transportation method is convenient?* or *Which one can we take to get there?*, use the question words **dono** (doh–noh) (*which*) and **dore** (doh–reh) (*which one*). So how do you know which *which* is which? If you're asking about *which* of a particular thing, use **dono** and add the thing you're asking about right after it, as in the following examples:

どのバスに乗れますか。**Dono basu ni noremasu ka.** (doh-noh bah-soo nee noh-reh-mah-soo kah.) (*Which bus can I get on?*)

どの電車で行けますか。**Dono densha de ikemasu ka.** (doh-noh dehn-shah deh ee-keh-mah-soo kah.) (*By which train can I go there?*)

Note that **noremasu** and **ikemasu** in the preceding sentences are the potential forms of **norimasu** and **ikimasu,** respectively. By *potential forms*, I mean the verb forms that bear the meaning of *can* as explained in Chapter 7.

If the name of the thing that you're asking about is understood in the context or is stated separately, you don't have to repeat that word. Just use **dore** rather than **dono.**

> どれに乗れますか。 **Dore ni noremasu ka.** (doh-reh nee noh-reh-mah-soo kah.)
> (*Which one can I get on?*)

> どれで行けますか。 **Dore de ikemasu ka.** (doh-reh deh ee-keh-mah-soo kah.)
> (*By which one can I go there?*)

REMEMBER

Perhaps you're wondering how to ask which transportation method is fastest, most convenient, or most inexpensive. You just have to use the adverb **ichiban** (ee–chee–bahn) (*the most/-est*) for that. (If you recognize the word **ichiban** as the Japanese word for *first*, you're right. It literally means *number one*.) Check out the following examples, and see Chapter 10 for more details on using **ichiban** to express *the most*:

> どのバスが一番はやいですか。 **Dono basu ga ichiban hayai desu ka.** (doh-noh bah-soo gah ee-chee-bahn hah-yah-ee deh-soo kah.) (*Which bus is the fastest?*)

> どの電車が一番便利ですか。 **Dono densha ga ichiban benri desu ka.** (doh-noh dehn-shah gah ee-chee-bahn behn-ree deh-soo kah.) (*Which train is the most convenient?*)

> どれが一番安いですか。 **Dore ga ichiban yasui desu ka.** (doh-reh gah ee-chee-bahn yah-soo-ee deh-soo kah.) (*Which one is the cheapest?*)

If you want to make a comparison and alert listeners that they must choose from the list that you provide, you can list the items at the beginning of a question. Chapter 10 tells you how to do it in detail. For now, here are some examples:

> タクシーと, 電車と, バスでは, どれが一番はやいですか。 **Takushī to, densha to, basu de wa, dore ga ichiban hayai desu ka.** (tah-koo-sheee toh, dehn-shah toh, bah-soo deh wah, doh-reh gah ee-chee-bahn hah-yah-ee deh-soo kah.) (*Which are the fastest: taxis, trains, or buses?*)

> 飛行機と, 車と, 電車と, バスでは, どれが一番安全ですか。 **Hikōki to, kuruma to, densha to, basu de wa, dore ga ichiban anzen desu ka.** (hee-kohh-kee toh, koo-roo-mah toh, dehn-shah toh, bah-soo deh-wah, doh-reh gah ee-chee-bahn ahn-zehn deh-soo kah.) (*Which are the safest: airplanes, cars, trains, or buses?*)

REMEMBER

If you're comparing people, use **dare** (dah-reh) (*who*) rather than **dore**. And if you're comparing locations, substitute **doko** (doh-koh) (*where*) for **dore**. To ask a question that compares just two items, use the question word **dochira** (doh-chee-rah) (*which one out of the two*), regardless of what the two items are. See Chapter 10 for more information about **dochira** and a complete discussion of comparisons.

Navigating the Airport

A **hikōki** (hee-kohh-kee) (*airplane*) is often necessary for speedy vacation travel and business trips, even if you're afraid of heights. And hopping on a commercial plane means jumping all the hurdles that come with going to the **kūkō** (kooo-kohh) (*airport*). Check out the following sections for vocabulary that helps you navigate the boarding process, go through immigration and customs, and exit the airport to explore your destination.

Now boarding: Making it to the plane

Arrive at the airport early to check your luggage and get through security so you can enjoy the time at the airport before boarding instead of making a mad dash for the plane as the door closes. You'll need these words for that:

>> 便 **bin** (been) (*flight*)

>> チケット **chiketto** (chee-keht-toh) (*ticket*)

>> ゲート **gēto** (gehh-toh) (*gate*)

>> 保安検査場 **hoan kensajō** (hoh-ahn kehn-sah-johh) (*security*)

>> 窓 **mado** (mah-doh) (*window*)

>> 窓側の席 **mado gawa no seki** (mah-doh gah-wah noh seh-kee) (*window seat*)

>> 免税店 **menzeiten** (mehn-zehh-tehn) (*duty-free shops*)

>> 席 **seki** (seh-kee) (*seat*)

>> シートベルト **shītoberuto** (sheee-toh-beh-roo-toh) (*seat belt*)

>> 出国手続き **shukkoku tetsuzuki** (shook-koh-koo teh-tsoo-zoo-kee) (*embarkation procedure [filling out paperwork when leaving Japan]*)

>> 搭乗券 **tōjōken** (tohh-johh-kehn) (*boarding pass*)

>> 搭乗手続き **tōjō tetsuzuki** (tohh-johh teh-tsoo-zoo-kee) (*check-in*)

>> 通路側の席 **tsūro gawa no seki** (tsooo-roh gah-wah noh seh-kee) (*aisle seat*)

REMEMBER

Bin is a word that means *flight,* and it also functions as a counter that specifies which flight. If you need to specify a flight with its flight number, add **-bin** right after the number. For example, **18-bin** (jooo-hah-chee-been) means *Flight 18.*

After you get on the plane, just relax. Ask the **kyabin atendanto** (kyah-been ah-tehn-dahn-toh) *(flight attendants)* any questions you may have, such as the following:

どのターミナルに着きますか。**Dono tāminaru ni tsukimasu ka.** (doh-noh tahh-mee-nah-roo nee tsoo-kee-mah-soo kah.) *(Which terminal are we arriving at?)*

毛布がありますか。**Mōfu ga arimasu ka.** (moh-foo-gah ah-ree-ma-soo kah.) *(Do you have a blanket?)*

何番ゲートに着きますか。**Nan-ban gēto ni tsukimasu ka.** (nahn-bahn gehh-toh nee tsoo-kee-mah-soo kah.) *(Which gate are we arriving at?)*

何時に着きますか。**Nan-ji ni tsukimasu ka.** (nahn-jee nee tsoo-kee-mah-soo kah.) *(What time will we arrive?)*

You may wonder how to say *to fly* in Japanese because you say things like *I flew from New York to San Francisco last week* or *He's going to fly to Las Vegas next week* all the time. Well, Japanese usually say *to go* in such contexts and say *to fly* only figuratively because it's the airplane that flies, not the people themselves. But if you want to be figurative, here's how to conjugate the **u-verb tobu** (toh-boo) *(to fly)*.

Japanese Script	Rōmaji	Pronunciation
飛ぶ	tobu	toh-boo
飛ばない	tobanai	toh-bah-nah-ee
飛び(ます)	tobi(masu)	toh-bee(-mah-soo)
飛んで	tonde	tohn-deh

Going through immigration

Before entering a foreign country, you have to meet the very serious folks in the **nyūkoku shinsa** (nyooo-koh-koo sheen-sah) *(immigration)* area. Here, everyone has to stand in line, and the line can be very long if multiple jumbo planes arrive at the same time. Make sure to have your passport in hand and be ready for some of these questions and requests:

>> ビザは。 **Biza wa.** (bee-zah wah.) (*How about your visa?*)

>> どこに泊まりますか。 **Doko ni tomarimasu ka.** (doh-koh nee toh-mah-ree-mah-soo kah.) (*Where are you staying?*)

>> 住所は。 **Jūsho wa.** (jooo-shoh wah.) (*Your address?*)

>> 住所を書いてください。 **Jūsho o kaite kudasai.** (jooo-shoh oh kah-ee-teh koo-dah-sah-ee.) (*Please write your address.*)

>> 観光ですか。 **Kankō desu ka.** (kahn-kohh deh-soo kah.) (*Are you here for sightseeing?*)

>> お名前は。 **O-namae wa.** (oh-nah-mah-eh wah.) (*Your name?*)

>> パスポートを見せてください。 **Pasupōto o misete kudasai.** (pah-soo-pohh-toh oh mee-seh-teh koo-dah-sah-ee.) (*Please show me your passport.*)

>> 仕事ですか。 **Shigoto desu ka.** (shee-goh-toh deh-soo kah.) (*Are you here for business?*)

Chapter 13 gives you more details and Japanese terminology related to passports and visas.

Getting through customs

After you get through immigration, go to the **tenimotsu hikiwatashijō** (teh-nee-moh-tsoo hee-kee-wah-tah-shee-johh) (*baggage claim*) and pick up your suitcases, bags, boxes, or whatever. Head straight to **zeikan** (zehh-kahn) (*customs*) after you have all your belongings. The lines at customs usually aren't as long as the lines at immigration because not many people have items to declare. However, you should be sure to pay the **zeikin** (zehh-keen) (*tax*), if necessary. Certain items are **menzei** (mehn-zehh) (*duty-free*) only if you bring less than a certain amount or quantity of the item with you. Don't forget to fill out 税関申告書 **zeikan shinkokusho** (zehh-kahn sheen-koh-koo-shoh) (*customs declaration*). Be familiar with the following questions and phrases to breeze through customs:

>> あそこで税金を払ってください。 **Asoko de zeikin o haratte kudasai.** (ah-soh-koh deh zehh-keen oh hah-raht-teh koo-dah-sah-ee.) (*Pay the tax over there, please.*)

>> 身の回りのものです。 **Minomawari no mono desu.** (mee-noh-mah-wah-ree noh moh-noh deh-soo.) (*They're my personal belongings.*)

>> 申告するものはありませんか。 **Shinkoku suru mono wa arimasen ka.** (sheen-koh-koo soo-roo moh-noh wah ah-ree-mah-sehn kah.) (*Is there anything you want to declare?*)

You may be asked to **Sūtsukēsu o akete kudasai.** (sooo-tsoo-kehh-soo oh ah-keh-teh koo-dah-sah-ee.) (*Open your suitcase, please.*), so you want to be able to conjugate the **ru**-verb **akeru** (ah-keh-roo) (*to open*):

Japanese Script	Rōmaji	Pronunciation
開ける	akeru	ah-keh-roo
開けない	akenai	ah-keh-nah-ee
開け(ます)	ake(masu)	ah-keh(-mah-soo)
開けて	akete	ah-keh-teh

Leaving the airport

When you're done at customs, grab your bags, pass through the exit, and go to the **tōchaku robī** (tohh-chah-koo roh-beee) (*arrival gate*). You may see hundreds of people looking at you, which can make you feel like you are a movie star! Enjoy your grand entrance to the arrival lobby after a long tiring trip.

If no one is meeting you, you can find ground transportation information at the **chiketto kauntā** (chee-keht-toh kah-oon-tahh) (*ticket counter*) or **annaijo** (ahn-nah-ee-joh) (*information counter*). You can use questions like the following to arrange your transportation from the airport or any other location:

モノレールはどこで乗れますか。 **Monorēru wa doko de noremasu ka.** (moh-noh-rehh-roo wah doh-koh deh noh-reh-mah-soo kah.) (*Where can I catch the monorail?*)

東京まで成田エクスプレスでいくらかかりますか。 **Tōkyō made Narita Ekusupuresu de ikura kakarimasu ka.** (tohh-kyohh mah-deh nah-ree-tah ehk-koo-soo-poo-reh-soo deh ee-koo-rah kah-kah-ree-mah-soo kah.) (*How much does it cost to go to Tokyo by the Narita Express?*)

品川行きのリムジンバスはありますか。 **Shinagawa yuki no rimujin basu wa arimasu ka.** (shee-nah-gah-wah yoo-kee noh ree-moo-jeen bah-soo wah ah-ree-mah-soo kah.) (*Do you have a limousine bus to Shinagawa?*)

次の東京駅行きのリムジンバスは何時ですか。 **Tsugi no Tōkyō eki yuki no rimujin basu wa nan-ji desu ka.** (tsoo-gee noh tohh-kyohh eh-kee yoo-kee noh ree-moo-jeen bah-soo wah nahn-jee deh-soo kah.) (*What time is the next limousine bus bound for Tokyo Station?*)

All Aboard: Hopping on a Train or Boat

Trains and boats are some of the oldest methods of transportation — at least since people quit using chariots — but they're still popular in the modern world. The following sections give you the terminology you need to talk about these rides in Japanese. (Sorry, I ran out of room to add a section on chariots.)

Now entering the station: Riding the train

Traveling by **densha** (dehn–shah) (*train*) is special because you go through many **eki** (eh–kee) (*train stations*), each of which represents the people who live or work in that town. In some **eki,** you see many businesspeople, but in others you see mostly children and their moms.

Check the direction of your train:

» 下り電車 **kudari densha** (koo-dah-ree dehn-shah) (*down train*)

» 上り電車 **nobori densha** (noh-boh-ree dehn-shah) (*up train*)

» 大阪行き **Ōsaka yuki** (ohh-sah-kah yoo-kee) (*bound for Osaka*)

CULTURAL WISDOM

You may be asking yourself, "What in the world are up trains and down trains?" You're in luck; I have the answer. **Nobori densha** (*up train*) refers to any train in Japan traveling toward Tokyo, and **kudari densha** (*down train*) refers to any train traveling away from Tokyo. Tokyo really is the center of Japan, as a glance at a map of Japan shows you. *Note:* These strange terms may give you the impression that Tokyo is the highest point in Japan and that the farthest location from Tokyo must therefore be below sea level. But the allusion to altitude is only figurative, even if somewhat elitist on the part of Tokyo. The point of using these two terms is just to distinguish the directions of each railroad line, not the altitude.

When you take a train, make sure you know what time it leaves and arrives. Conjugate the verb **deru** (deh–roo) (*to leave*) and **tsuku** (tsoo-koo) (*to arrive*). **Deru** is a **ru**–verb, but **tsuku** is an **u**–verb.

Japanese Script	Rōmaji	Pronunciation
出る	deru	deh-roo
出ない	denai	deh-nah-ee
出(ます)	de(masu)	deh(-mah-soo)
出て	dete	deh-teh

Japanese Script	Rōmaji	Pronunciation
着く	tsuku	tsoo-koo
着かない	tsukanai	tsoo-kah-nah-ee
着き(ます)	tsuki(masu)	tsoo-kee(-mah-soo)
着いて	tsuite	tsoo-ee-teh

REMEMBER

Remember to check the **jikokuhyō** (jee–koh–koo–hyohh) (*timetable*) at the station. Be ready for the 24-hour system if you're traveling in Japan. **Jūgo–ji** (jooo–goh–jee) (*15:00 [fifteen o'clock]*) means **gogo 3-ji** (goh–goh sahn–jee) (*3:00 p.m.*). Watch out for two important keywords on the timetable: **hatsu** (hah–tsoo) (*departure*) and **chaku** (chah–koo) (*arrival*). They're short forms of **hassha suru** (hahs–shah soo–roo) (*to depart*) and **tōchaku suru** (tohh–chah–koo soo–roo) (*to arrive*). Take a look at a few examples (for complete coverage on telling time, check out Chapter 4):

> 16時15分発 **16-ji 15-fun hatsu** (jooo–roh–koo–jee jooo–goh–foon hah–tsoo) (*16:15 [4:15 p.m.] departure*)

> 20時57分着 **20-ji 57-fun chaku** (nee–jooo–jee goh–jooo–nah–nah–foon chah–koo) (*20:57 [8:57 p.m.] arrival*)

> 7時5分東京発10時7分大阪着 **7-ji 5-fun Tōkyō hatsu 10-ji 7-fun Ōsaka chaku** (shee–chee–jee goh–foon tohh–kyohh hah–tsoo jooo–jee nah–nah–foon ohh–sah–kah chah–koo) (*7:05 a.m. Tokyo departure, 10:07 a.m. Osaka arrival*)

Depending on how much of a hurry you're in, choose from one of these types of trains, listed in descending order of speed and distance:

> » 新幹線 **shinkansen** (sheen-kahn-sehn) (*bullet train*)

> » 特急 **tokkyū** (tohk-kyooo) (*super-express*)

> » 快速 **kaisoku** (kah-ee-soh-koo) (*rapid*)

> » 急行 **kyūkō** (kyooo-kohh) (*express*)

> » 普通 **futsū** (foo-tsooo) (*regular* or *local*)

CULTURAL WISDOM

Shinkansen got its English name, *bullet train*, from the bullet shape of the lead car in the 0 series, or first generation, of the train. These trains run on special tracks at top speeds of about 300 kilometers per hour (186 miles per hour) and connect all the major cities of **Honshū** (hohn-shooo), the main island of Japan. **Shinkansen** service is also available to a number of cities in Kyushu. Lines connecting parts of Hokkaido are under construction.

For all trains, the **unchin** (oon-cheen) (*fare*) is different for adults and children. Be sure to specify the number of adults and the number of children when buying your tickets. And ask whether discounts and special assistance are available for seniors and people with disabilities.

Use the counter **-mai** to express the number of tickets you want to purchase. (See Chapter 4 for information on counters.) Also specify whether you need a round-trip or one-way ticket. If you're taking the **shinkansen** or another super-express train in Japan, you need to buy two tickets: a super-express ticket plus the regular passenger ticket. Here are some common ticket terms:

>> 乗車券 **jōshaken** (johh-shah-kehn) (*passenger ticket*)

>> 片道 **katamichi** (kah-tah-mee-chee) (*one-way ticket*)

>> 切符 **kippu** (keep-poo) (*tickets*)

>> 往復 **ōfuku** (ohh-foo-koo) (*round-trip ticket*)

>> 特急券 **tokkyūken** (tohk-kyooo-kehn) (*super-express ticket*)

You may make a request like the following as you purchase your ticket:

名古屋まで大人3枚往復お願いします。**Nagoya made otona san-mai ōfuku onegaishimasu.** (nah-goh-yah mah-deh oh-toh-nah sahn-mah-ee ohh-foo-koo oh-neh-gah-ee-shee-mah-soo.) (*To Nagoya, three round-trip tickets for adults, please.*)

大阪まで大人1枚と子ども2枚お願いします。**Ōsaka made otona ichi-mai to kodomo ni-mai onegaishimasu.** (ohh-sah-kah mah-deh oh-toh-nah ee-chee-mah-ee toh koh-doh-moh nee-mah-ee oh-neh-gah-ee-shee-mah-soo.) (*To Osaka, one ticket for an adult and two tickets for children, please.*)

東京まで片道1枚。**Tōkyō made katamichi ichi-mai.** (tohh-kyohh mah-deh kah-tah-mee-chee ee-chee-mah-ee.) (*To Tokyo, one one-way ticket, please.*)

東京までの乗車券と特急券を下さい。**Tōkyō made no jōshaken to tokkyūken o kudasai.** (tohh-kyohh mah-deh noh johh-shah-kehn toh tohk-kyooo-kehn oh koo-dah-sah-ee.) (*A passenger ticket and a super-express ticket to Tokyo, please.*)

Find out which **hōmu** (hohh-moo) (*platform*) you're leaving from, say the number with the counter **-ban** (bahn), and add **hōmu**, as in **ichi-ban hōmu** (ee-chee-bahn hohh-moo) (*platform one*), **ni-ban hōmu** (nee-bahn hohh-moo) (*platform two*), and **san-ban hōmu** (sahn-bahn hohh-moo) (*platform three*).

Setting sail: Cruising around by boat

You may have a lot of chances to go to nearby islands or to towns across a lake, bay, or cove near your home. Some people even commute to work by ferry. What a romantic way to start the workday! Use some of the following terms to travel by water or just to have fun:

>> ボート **bōto** (bohh-toh) (*boat*)

>> フェリー **ferī** (feh-reee) (*ferry*)

>> 船 **fune** (foo-neh) (*ship*)

>> ヨット **yotto** (yoht-toh) (*yacht*)

If you don't know how to swim, find the life jackets right after you board. I'm just kidding. Relax and enjoy the nice breeze. If you spend some time on the water, you'll come ashore feeling refreshed!

Conquering Public Transportation

Sometimes the best way of getting around in larger cities is to take public transportation. Whether you intend to travel by **basu** (bah-soo) (*bus*), **chikatetsu** (chee-kah-teh-tsoo) (*subway*), or **takushī** (tah-koo-sheee) (*taxi*), the next sections have you covered.

TIP

When you make up your mind about which form of public transportation you want to use, say **ni suru** (nee soo-roo) (*to decide on*). The verb **suru** is an irregular verb, and its polite counterpart is **shimasu**. Now you can understand the following decisions:

>> 地下鉄にします。 **Chikatetsu ni shimasu.** (chee-kah-teh-tsoo nee shee-mah-soo.) (*I'll choose the subway.*)

>> タクシーにします。 **Takushī ni shimasu.** (tah-koo-sheee nee shee-mah-soo.) (*I'll take a taxi.*)

Riding a bus

Basu (bah-soo) (*buses*) are inexpensive and convenient, and they can take you across town or across the country. Taking a long-distance bus rather than a plane or train can save you a lot of money.

Go to a bus terminal or a bus stop, and find out which **basu** you should take. The **unchin** (oon-cheen) (*fare*) may be a flat rate, or it may vary depending on how far you go. Either way, put the **unchin** in the designated box. Here's how to conjugate the **ru**-verb **ireru** (ee-reh-roo) (*to put*).

Japanese Script	Rōmaji	Pronunciation
入れる	ireru	ee-reh-roo
入れない	irenai	ee-reh-nah-ee
入れ(ます)	ire(masu)	ee-reh(-mah-soo)
入れて	irete	ee-reh-teh

I also recommend memorizing the following words:

» バスターミナル **basu tāminaru** (bah-soo tahh-mee-nah-roo) (*bus terminal*)

» バス停 **basu-tei** (bah-soo-tehh) (*bus stop*)

» 乗り換え **norikae** (noh-ree-kah-eh) (*transfer*)

TIP

Don't forget to ask the driver for a transfer if you need to change buses.

Taking the subway

The **chikatetsu** (chee-kah-teh-tsoo) (*subway*) is inexpensive, especially compared to taking a taxi. It can also bring you to your destination much more quickly than a bus can. Considering all these factors, the **chikatetsu** may offer you the most convenience for your dollar, especially in big cities.

When you take a subway, be careful not to miss your station. To express which station is yours — **hito-tsu-me** (hee-toh-tsoo-meh) (*the first one*), **futa-tsu-me** (foo-tah-tsoo-meh) (*the second one*), and so on — head to the discussion of ordinal numbers in Chapter 4 and use the ordinal counter **-me**.

Hailing a taxi

Takushī (tah-koo-sheee) (*taxis*) are very convenient — they come to where you are, so you don't need to walk anywhere. Unlike subways, you don't need to figure out which one you should take. And unlike buses, you don't need to wait for them. Just call a taxi to pick you up wherever you are. If you have three or four people in your group, taking a **takushī** may be cheaper than taking a train or a bus!

Here are some phrases you may say or hear in a taxi:

» 美術館までお願いします。**Bijutsukan made onegai shimasu.** (bee-joo-tsoo-kahn mah-deh oh-neh-gah-ee shee-mah-soo.) (*Please go to the art museum.*)

» どちらまで。**Dochira made.** (doh-chee-rah mah-deh.) (*To where?*)

» 空港までいくらぐらいかかりますか。**Kūkō made ikura gurai kakarimasu ka.** (kooo-kohh mah-deh ee-koo-rah goo-rah-ee kah-kah-ree-mah-soo kah.) (*How much does it cost to the airport?*)

» 着きましたよ。**Tsukimashita yo.** (tsoo-kee-mah-shee-tah yoh.) (*We're here.*)

TIP

When the **takushī** driver is about to give you the **otsuri** (oh-tsoo-ree) (*change*), you can refuse it by saying **Otsuri wa kekkō desu.** (oh-tsoo-ree wah kehk-kohh deh-soo.) (*Please keep the change.*) **Kekkō desu** (kehk-kohh deh-soo) means *good* or *fine* in some contexts, but it means *no thank you* in other contexts. It may sound like a contradiction, but in English you sometimes say *I'm fine.* after being asked *Would you like some coffee?* when what you mean is *no thank you*, right? That's the spirit of **kekkō desu** as *no thank you*.

Talkin' the Talk

Kent is trying to hail a taxi. A taxi finally stops in front of him, and the door opens.

Kent: **Akagi Eigo Gakkō made onegaishimasu.**
ah-kah-gee ehh-goh gahk-kohh mah-deh oh-neh-gah-ee-shee-mah-soo.
To Akagi English School, please.

Driver: **Yokohama Eki no mae desu ne.**
yoh-koh-hah-mah eh-kee noh mah-eh deh-soo neh.
That's in front of Yokohama Station, right?

Kent: **Hai.**
hah-ee.
Yes.

Driver: **O-kyaku-san wa eigo no sensei desu ka.**
oh-kyah-koo-sahn wah ehh-goh noh sehn-sehh deh-soo kah.
Are you an English teacher?

Kent: **Hai.**
hah-ee.
Yes.

The taxi arrives in front of Akagi English School.

Driver: **Hai, tsukimashita yo.**
            hah-ee, tsoo-kee-mah-shee-tah yoh.
            Okay, we're here.

Kent: **Ikura desu ka.**
            ee-koo-rah deh-soo kah.
            How much?

Driver: **750-en desu.**
            nah-nah-hyah-koo-goh-jooo-en deh-soo.
            750 yen.

Kent: **Jā, dōzo. Otsuri wa kekkō desu.**
            jahh, dohh-zoh. oh-tsoo-ree wah kehk-kohh deh-soo.
            Here you are. Keep the change.

Driver: **Ā, arigatō gozaimasu.**
            ahh, ah-ree-gah-tohh goh-zah-ee-mah-soo.
            Oh, thank you very much.

WORDS TO KNOW

eigo gakkō	ehh-goh gahk-kohh	English school
made	mah-deh	up to
no mae	noh mah-eh	in front of
Tsukimashita.	tsoo-kee-mah-shee-tah.	(We) arrived.
otsuri	oh-tsoo-ree	change

Driving Around

In smaller communities, driving a **kuruma** (koo–roo–mah) (*car*) may be your only option for getting around. (And even in bigger communities, you may just prefer to drive.) To talk about driving in Japanese, use **unten suru** (oon–tehn soo–roo) (*to drive*). Conjugating this verb is a piece of cake if you know how to conjugate the irregular verb **suru** (soo–roo) (*to do*).

Japanese Script	Rōmaji	Pronunciation
運転する	unten suru	oon-tehn soo-roo
運転しない	unten shinai	oon-tehn shee-nah-ee
運転し(ます)	unten shi(masu)	oon-tehn shee(-mah-soo)
運転して	unten shite	oon-tehn shee-teh

If you're on a trip and you didn't drive to your destination, you'll need to rent a car. And if you're driving in Japan, you'll need a crash course in Japanese road signs. The following sections give you the necessary vocabulary for renting a vehicle and provide an overview of the most important road signs.

CULTURAL WISDOM

Driving a car in Japan is a bit tricky. You have to drive on the left side, and your steering wheel is on the right side. The roads are clean and nice but very narrow. Bicycles and pedestrians always have the right of way on the neighborhood streets. And the highways are in great condition, but the tolls are outrageous.

Renting a car

To rent a **kuruma**, head to a **rentakā shoppu** (rehn-tah-kahh shohp-poo) (*car rental shop*). Be sure to ask about the rental car's features:

>> エアコン **eakon** (eh-ah-kohn) (*air-conditioning*)

>> エコカー **ekokā** (eh-koh-kahh) (*eco-friendly car*)

>> カーナビ **kānabi** (kahh-nah-bee) (*car navigation, GPS*)

>> マニュアル **manyuaru** (mah-nyoo-ah-roo) (*stick shift*)

>> オートマチック **ōtomachikku** (ohh-toh-mah-cheek-koo) (*automatic transmission*)

>> ステレオ **sutereo** (soo-teh-reh-oh) (*stereo*)

Show your **unten menkyoshō** (oon-tehn-mehn-kyoh-shohh) (*driver's license*) to the clerk at the car-rental agency. Note that you need a **kokusai unten menkyoshō** (koh-koo-sah-ee oon-tehn mehn-kyoh-shohh) (*international driving permit*) in addition to your driver's license from your home country when you drive in Japan, unless you have a Japanese license. After that's out of the way, you can get to the details. Following are some common phrases that you may find useful when renting a car:

>> 保険をかけます。 **Hoken o kakemasu.** (hoh-kehn oh kah-keh-mah-soo.) (*I'll take the insurance policy.*)

THE INTERNATIONAL DRIVING PERMIT

国際運転免許証 **Kokusai Unten Menkyoshō** (koh-koo-sah-ee oon-tehn mehn-kyoh-shohh) (*International Driving Permit*) is a document recognized by more than 100 countries, including Japan and the United States. It's supplemental to your official government-issued license and serves translation and identification purposes, so you must also carry your driver's license from your home country when you use it.

Note that **Kokusai Unten Menkyoshō** is only for short-term travelers. If you want to stay in Japan longer term, you need to convert your license from your home country to a Japanese license.

» 小型の車を借りたいんですが。**Kogata no kuruma o karitai-n-desu ga.** (koh-gah-tah noh koo-roo-mah oh kah-ree-tah-een-deh-soo gah.) (*I'd like to rent a small-size car [but do you have one?].*)

» 今日から金曜日まで使いたいんです。**Kyō kara kinyōbi made tsukai-tai-n-desu.** (kyooo kah-rah keen-yohh-bee mah-deh tsoo-kah-ee-tah-een-deh-soo.) (*I want it today through Friday.*)

» 木曜日に返します。**Mokuyōbi ni kaeshimasu.** (moh-koo-yohh-bee nee kah-eh-shee-mah-soo.) (*I'll return it on Thursday.*)

Conjugate the verbs **kariru** (kah-ree-roo) (*to rent*) and **kaesu** (kah-eh-soo) (*to return*) — two essential words for visiting a rental-car agency. **Kariru** is a **ru**-verb, and **kaesu** is an **u**-verb. The conjugation table for **kariru** is in Chapter 9. Here's the one for **kaesu**:

Japanese Script	Rōmaji	Pronunciation
返す	kaesu	kah-eh-soo
返さない	kaesanai	kah-eh-sah-nah-ee
返し(ます)	kaeshi(masu)	kah-eh-shee(-mah-soo)
返して	kaeshite	kah-eh-shee-teh

Deciphering road signs

I bet you can understand most **dōro hyōshiki** (dohh-roh hyohh-shee-kee) (*road signs*) in Japan, but just in case, Table 14-1 shows you the essential ones.

TABLE 14-1 **Japanese Road Signs**

Road Sign	Japanese	Pronunciation	Meaning
止まれ (sign)	止まれ **tomare**	toh-mah-reh	*Stop*
(Do Not Enter sign)	進入禁止 **shinnyū kinshi**	sheen-nyooo keen-shee	*Do Not Enter*
(One Way arrow sign)	一方通行 **ippō tsūkō**	eep-pohh tsooo-kohh	*One Way*
(Parking sign)	駐車可 **chūshaka**	chooo-shah-kah	*Parking Permitted*
(No Parking sign)	駐車禁止 **chūsha kinshi**	chooo-shah keen-shee	*No Parking*

Are you ready to drive in Japan? Here are a couple of final reminders: In Japan, left turns on a red light aren't permitted like right turns on red lights are in the United States. Also, keep in mind that the colors of the traffic lights in Japan are the same, but they call the three colors red, yellow, and blue (rather than red, yellow, and green like in the United States).

FUN & GAMES

Write the Japanese word for the following types of transportation on the corresponding line. The answers are in Appendix C.

1. _____

2. _____

3. _____

4. _____

5. _____

Illustrations by Elizabeth Kurtzman

IN THIS CHAPTER

» **Finding accommodations**

» **Reserving the room**

» **Navigating the check-in process**

» **Knowing how to claim your stuff**

» **Cruising through check-out**

Chapter **15**

Finding a Place to Stay

Selecting the right **shukuhaku shisetsu** (shoo-koo-hah-koo shee-seh-tsoo) (*accommodations*) can make any trip you take more enjoyable. After all, each day of your adventure starts and ends there. This chapter walks you through the process of finding your **shukuhaku shisetsu**: choosing the right place, making a reservation, checking in, and checking out. Enjoy your visit!

REMEMBER

You can listen to all the Talkin' the Talk dialogues featured in this chapter. Go to www.dummies.com/go/japanesefd and click on the dialogue you want to hear.

Picking the Right Accommodations for Your Needs

Select your accommodations according to your needs and budget. For example, if you're planning a family trip to a resort area near the coast, get a nice **hoteru** (hoh-teh-roo) (*hotel*) that features easy access to the beach. Here are the many options available to you:

» ビジネスホテル **bijinesu hoteru** (bee-jee-neh-soo hoh-teh-roo) (*business hotel*)

» ホテル **hoteru** (hoh-teh-roo) (*hotel*)

» 観光ホテル **kankō hoteru** (kahn-kohh hoh-teh-roo) (*tourist's hotel*)

>> カプセルホテル **kapuseru hoteru** (kah-poo-seh-roo hoh-teh-roo) (*capsule hotel*)

>> 民宿 **minshuku** (meen-shoo-koo) (*a private home that offers lodging and meals to tourists*)

>> モーテル **mōteru** (mohh-teh-roo) (*motel*)

>> リゾートホテル **rizōto hoteru** (ree-zoh-toh hoh-teh-roo) (*resort hotel*)

>> 旅館 **ryokan** (ryoh-kahn) (*Japanese-style inn*)

>> ユースホステル **yūsu hosuteru** (yooo-soo hoh-soo-teh-roo) (*youth hostel*)

CULTURAL WISDOM

A **hoteru** is a Western-style hotel. You can speak English in most major **hoteru** in Japan. You can also eat a Western-style breakfast, sleep on a bed rather than a **futon** (foo-tohn) (*thin, quilted mattress*), and use a Western-style bath. (Flip to Chapter 5 for info on the traditional Japanese **futon** sleeping experience.) These amenities may be familiar to you and put you at ease. If you prefer to stay even more inside your comfort zone, you may want to stay at a property owned by a well-known hotel chain.

For more-authentic, Japanese-style accommodations, go to a **ryokan.** At the entrance to the inn, a **nakai-san** (nah-kah-ee-sahn) (*attendant*) in a kimono welcomes you. Enjoy a big bath with other guests if you aren't shy (see the nearby sidebar on Japanese-style bathing). When you get back to your room for the evening, the **futon** is already spread out on the **tatami** (tah-tah-mee) (*straw mat*) floor in your bedroom, and dinner is brought right to the living/dining area of your room. Wear a special kimono-like cotton robe, a **yukata** (yoo-kah-tah), while you enjoy your dinner. In the morning, have a Japanese-style breakfast (turn to Chapter 5 for examples of these dishes).

A **minshuku** is similar to a bed-and-breakfast in Western countries, but it often provides dinner as well as breakfast. All the **minshuku** guests eat their meals together in a big dining room with a **tatami** floor. Each guest has to spread out her own **futon** when she sleeps and fold it up again in the morning. It's like visiting your uncle's or aunt's big house in the countryside.

If you're young and your budget is very tight (or does that go without saying?), you can stay in a **yūsu hosuteru.** You have to share a room and/or a bathroom with other travelers and follow the hostel's strict rules, but you can save your money for another part of your trip.

BATHING JAPANESE-STYLE

A Japanese bath is very different from a Western-style bath. A Japanese bathtub is very deep, and the water is very hot. The bath is only for soaking and relaxing; washing your body, face, or hair in the bath is taboo. You wash yourself outside the tub, in a space with faucets, showers, and mirrors on the wall where you can sit on a low stool as you wash. Entering the bath prior to washing or rinsing your body is considered a major breach of etiquette.

Public baths including **sentō** (sehn-toh) (*communal bath houses*) and **onsen** (ohn-sehn) (*natural hot springs*) are very popular in Japan, although almost every Japanese house has its own bath and shower system. People go to these public baths to relax and enjoy the facilities that often offer food areas or even restaurants. The public baths are usually separated by gender with some exceptions in natural hot springs. In a Japanese public bath, you have to get completely naked. No swimsuits. Stripping down around strangers may be a bit embarrassing, but you don't know any of the other people, so what the heck? Go for it! The tub in a public bath is huge — it's like a giant hot tub (but it's not a heated swimming pool, so don't plan on taking a few laps). And come out of the tub every 15 minutes or so; otherwise, you'll become dizzy from the heat.

If you just need to stay somewhere for your business trip, opt for **bijinesu hoteru**. Their rooms are simple but neat, relatively comfortable, very functional, and convenient for businesspeople. If you need a much cheaper hotel than business hotels in major business cities in Japan, you can stay in a unique, interesting, super-simple hotel called **kapuseru hoteru**. Each room is just as big as a single bed; one person can barely stand up in it. You can think of these hotels as beehives. Each room has a TV and a radio. The hotel has a sauna on some floor of the building that can be shared by guests. The capsule hotels charge very little; they're mostly used by male office workers, who tend to work late and often miss the last train of the day. In fact, many capsule hotels are for men only.

Of course, all these accommodation options will fulfill your most basic need: They'll all provide you with a place to sleep! Here's how to conjugate the **ru-**verb **neru** (neh-roo) (*to sleep*).

Japanese Script	Rōmaji	Pronunciation
寝る	neru	neh-roo
寝ない	nenai	neh-nah-ee
寝 (ます)	ne(masu)	neh(-mah-soo)
寝て	nete	neh-teh

Narrowing Your Choice Further

After you know the type of accommodations you're interested in, you can start looking into specific places. Consider the size of the rooms, the various amenities offered, and the overall cost to help you make your decision. The following sections help you do just that, in addition to helping you figure out how to express possible scenarios with *if*.

Looking into room size and amenities

Ask the folks at the front desk about the types of **heya** (heh-yah) (*rooms*) the hotel has. Suppose you're traveling with your mother, spouse, and two teenage children. Would you prefer to get a big room that everyone can stay in together, or do you want a separate room for your kids and mom? (I know what my answer would be.) Is anyone in your family a heavy snorer? You need a good night's sleep to have some energy for your trip, so you may want to consider multiple smaller rooms (or just bring earplugs). Here's the vocabulary you need to talk about room sizes:

>> ダブル **daburu** (dah-boo-roo) (*double/a room with a big bed for two people*)

>> シングル **shinguru** (sheen-goo-roo) (*single/a room with a twin-size bed for one person*)

>> スイート **suīto** (soo-eee-toh) (*suite*)

>> ツイン **tsuin** (tsoo-een) (*twin/a room with two twin-size beds for two people*)

If you're not sure whether a twin room is bigger than a double room, just ask **Dochira no heya ga hiroi desu ka.** (doh-chee-rah noh heh-yah gah hee-roh-ee deh-soo kah.) (*Which room is bigger?*) Expect to hear this line in response: **Tsuin no heya ga hiroi desu.** (tsoo-een noh heh-yah gah hee-roh-ee deh-soo.) (*A twin room is bigger.*) (For more info on using **dochira** [*which one*] and making other comparisons, see Chapter 10.)

TIP

Ask whether the place you're interested in staying at has the following amenities:

>> 売店 **baiten** (bah-ee-tehn) (*shop*)

>> ビジネスセンター **bijinesu sentā** (bee-jee-neh-soo sehn-tahh) (*business center*)

>> 駐車場 **chūshajō** (choo-shah-johh) (*parking lot*)

» フィットネスクラブ **fittonesu kurabu** (fheet-to-neh-soo koo-rah-boo) (*fitness club*)

» ジム **gimu** (gee-moo) (*gym*)

» インターネット **intānetto** (een-tahh-neht-toh) (*Internet*)

» 自動販売機 **jidōhanbaiki** (jee-dohh-hahn-bah-ee-kee) (*vending machine*)

» 金庫 **kinko** (keen-koh) (*safe*)

» 無線LAN **musen LAN** (moo-sehn rahn) (*wireless LAN [local area network]*)

» プール **pūru** (pooo-roo) (*swimming pool*)

» 冷蔵庫 **reizōko** (rehh-zohh-koh) (*refrigerator*)

» レストラン **resutoran** (reh-soo-toh-rahn) (*restaurant*)

Also ask about any service you may need during your stay. Popular services include

» マッサージ **massāji** (mahs-sahh-jee) (*massage*)

» モーニングコール **mōningu kōru** (mohh-neen-goo kohh-roo) (*wake-up call*)

» ランドリーサービス **randorī sābisu** (rahn-doh-reee sahh-bee-soo) (*laundry service*)

» ルームサービス **rūmu sābisu** (rooo-moo sahh-bee-soo) (*room service*)

If you have a special request, ask for it when you make a reservation. For example:

広い部屋はありますか。 **Hiroi heya wa arimasu ka.** (hee-roh-ee heh-yah wah ah-ree-mah-soo kah.) (*Do you have a spacious room?*)

喫煙ルームですか。 **Kitsuen rūmu desu ka.** (kee-tsoo-ehn rooo-moo deh-soo kah.) (*Is it a smoking room?*)

禁煙の部屋ですか。 **Kin'en no heya desu ka.** (keen-ehn noh heh-yah deh-soo kah.) (*Is it a nonsmoking room?*)

静かな部屋をお願いします。 **Shizuka na heya o onegai shimasu.** (shee-zoo-kah nah heh-yah oh oh-neh-gah-ee shee-mah-soo.) (*A quiet room, please.*)

冷蔵庫のある部屋がいいんですが。 **Reizōko no aru heya ga ii n desu ga.** (rehh-zohh-koh noh ah-roo heh-yah gah een-deh-soo gah.) (*I prefer a room with a refrigerator.*)

スイートをお願いします。 **Suīto o onegai shimasu.** (soo-eee-toh oh oh-neh-gah-ee shee-mah-soo.) (*Suite, please.*)

Comparing costs

Cost is a major criterion when you choose a hotel. Suppose one hotel charges you $150 per day, and another hotel charges you $200 per day. That $50 difference may seem small, but if you're staying for ten days, the difference becomes $500. That's quite a bit of money. (Note that most Japanese hotels charge for each person even if multiple people share one room, so watch out!) Figuring out the total cost isn't always simple, but talking about it in Japanese can be with the info in this section. I show you how to compare prices, how to express concepts like *twice* and *three times as expensive*, and how to express percentages.

Chapter 10 shows you in detail how to use the particle **yori** (yoh-ree) (*than*). You can use that same particle to compare your accommodation options. For example, **Yūsu hosuteru wa yasui desu.** (yooo-soo-hoh-soo-teh-roo wah yah-soo-ee deh-soo.) means *Youth hostels are cheap.* If you want to say *Youth hostels are cheaper than hotels.*, just stick in **hoteru yori** (hoh-teh-roo yoh-ree) (*than hotels*) right before the adjective **yasui desu.** So **Yūsu hosuteru wa hoteru yori yasui desu.** (yooo-soo hoh-soo-teh-roo wah hoh-teh-roo yoh-ree yah-soo-ee deh-soo.) means *Youth hostels are cheaper than hotels.*

TIP

To make a comparison by saying that something is a number of times more (or less) than something else, use the counter **-bai** (bah-ee). For example, to say *Japanese-style inns are three times more expensive than youth hostels.*, say **Ryokan wa yūsu hosuteru yori san-bai takai desu.** (ryoh-kahn wah yooo-soo hoh-soo-teh-roo yoh-ree sahn-bah-ee tah-kah-ee deh-soo.) Following are the possible counters you may want to use when comparing hotel costs:

>> 2倍 **ni-bai** (nee-bah-ee) (*twice*)

>> 3倍 **san-bai** (sahn-bah-ee) (*three times*)

>> 3.5倍 **san-ten-go-bai** (sahn-tehn-goh-bah-ee) (*three and a half times*)

>> 4倍 **yon-bai** (yohn-bah-ee) (*four times*)

>> 5倍 **go-bai** (goh-bah-ee) (*five times*)

And here's one more convenient phrase that you can use when you compare prices. To express percentages, use the counter **-pāsento** (pahh-sehn-toh) (*percent*). For example, to say *Canadian hotels are 25 percent cheaper than American hotels.*, say **Kanada no hoteru wa Amerika no hoteru yori 25-pāsento yasui desu.** (kah-nah-dah noh hoh-teh-roo wah ah-meh-ree-kah noh hoh-teh-roo yoh-ree nee-jooo-goh-pahh-sehn-toh yah-soo-ee deh-soo.) You can also use the same percentage symbol (%) in Japanese as you do in English, as you can see in the following list of percentages you may find handy to use in your comparisons of different accommodation costs.

» 10% **jūp-pāsento** (joop-pahh-sehn-toh) (*10 percent*)

» 15% **jū-go-pāsento** (jooo-goh-pahh-sehn-toh) (*15 percent*)

» 20% **ni-jūp-pāsento** (nee-joop-pahh-sehn-toh) (*20 percent*)

» 100% **hyaku-pāsento** (hyah-koo-pahh-sehn-toh) (*100 percent*)

Considering each possible scenario with nara

You have to think about so many different possibilities when you're planning your trip accommodations, such as "If Bob and Sue come, we'll need to get an extra room." or "We can save $100 if we go in May rather than June." One way to express these hypothetical scenarios in Japanese is to use **nara** (nah–rah) to mean *if*.

GRAMMAR CHAT

You can add **nara** at the end of a verb or an adjective in the plain/informal form, except that the linking **da** (the plain present affirmative form of **desu**) that directly follows a noun or a **na**–type adjective must drop. Check out the following examples.

日本に行くなら旅館に泊まりましょう。**Nihon ni iku nara ryokan ni tomarimashō.** (nee-hohn nee ee-koo nah-rah ryoh-kahn nee toh-mah-ree-mah-shohh.) (*Let's stay at a Japanese-style inn if we're going to Japan.*)

安いなら泊まります。**Yasui nara tomarimasu.** (yah-soo-ee nah-rah toh-mah-ree-mah-soo.) (*If it's cheap, I'll stay there.*)

観光なら京都がいいですよ。**Kankō nara Kyōto ga ii desu yo.** (kahn-kohh nah-rah kyohh-toh gah eee deh-soo yoh.) (*If you're interested in sightseeing, Kyoto is good.* [Literally: *If for sightseeing, Kyoto is good.*])

買い物が好きなら新宿がいいですよ。**Kaimono ga suki nara Shinjuku ga ii desu yo.** (kah-ee-moh-noh gah soo-kee nah-rah sheen-joo-koo gah eee deh-soo yoh.) (*If you like shopping, Shinjuku is a great place for you.*)

朝食が付くならこのホテルにしましょう。**Chōshoku ga tsuku nara kono hoteru ni shimashō.** (chohh-shoh-koo gah tsoo-koo nah-rah koh-noh hoh-teh-roo nee shee-mah-shohh.) (*If breakfast is included, let's stay in this hotel.*)

お金がないならカプセルホテルに泊まった方がいいですよ。**O-kane ga nai nara kapuseru hoteru ni tomatta hō ga ii desu yo.** (oh-kah-neh gah nah-ee nah-rah kah-poo-seh-roo hoh-teh-roo nee toh-maht-tah hohh gah eee deh-soo yoh.) (*If you don't have money, you'd better stay at capsule hotels.*)

TIP

The final example in the preceding list gives advice by using the past tense and the phrase **hō ga ii desu**. Refer to Chapter 16 for more details about **hō ga ii desu**.

Making a Room Reservation

REMEMBER

Japanese doesn't have simple verbs that mean *to plan* or *to make a reservation*. To say *to plan* and *to make a reservation*, you combine the verb **suru** (soo-roo) (*to do*) with a noun — **keikaku** (kehh-kah-koo) (*plan*) and **yoyaku** (yoh-yah-koo) (*reservation*). So **keikaku suru** means *to plan*, and **yoyaku suru** means *to make a reservation*. You simply conjugate the **suru** part of the verb. **Suru** is an irregular verb; I conjugate it for you in Chapter 7.

Before calling a hotel to make a reservation, you need to have a clear idea of how long you're planning to stay. To start, conjugate the **u**–verb **tomaru** (*to stay*).

Japanese Script	Rōmaji	Pronunciation
泊まる	tomaru	toh-mah-roo
泊まらない	tomaranai	toh-mah-rah-nah-ee
泊まり (ます)	tomari(masu)	toh-mah-ree(-mah-soo)
泊まって	tomatte	toh-maht-teh

REMEMBER

Remember to use the particles **kara** (kah-rah) (*from*) and **made** (mah-deh) (*until*) to talk about the duration of your visit. **Kara** and **made** look like English prepositions, but they have to follow, not precede, the relevant phrases. For example, *from the 15th* in English is *the 15th from* in Japanese. And *until the 23rd* in English is *the 23rd until* in Japanese. So you now know **15-nichi kara** (jooo-goh-nee-chee kah-rah) means *from the 15th*, and **23-nichi made** (nee-jooo-sahn-nee-chee mah-deh) means *until the 23rd*. Take a look at a few more examples to really help this tidbit sink in:

来週の月曜日から木曜日までお願いします。 **Raishū no getsuyōbi kara mokuyōbi made onegaishimasu.** (rah-ee-shooo noh geh-tsoo-yohh-bee kah-rah moh-koo-yohh-bee mah-deh oh-neh-gah-ee-shee-mah-soo.) (*From Monday to Thursday of next week, please.*)

このコースは6月から8月までです。 **Kono kōsu wa roku-gatsu kara hachi-gatsu made desu.** (koh-noh kohh-soo wah roh-koo-gah-tsoo kah-rah hah-chee-gah-tsoo mah-deh deh-soo.) (*This course is from June to August.*)

今日からあさってまで泊まります。 **Kyō kara asatte made tomarimasu.** (kyohh kah-rah ah-saht-teh mah-deh toh-mah-ree-mah-soo.) (*I'll stay from today until the day after tomorrow.*)

Use the counter **-haku** (hah-koo) to specify the number of nights that you're staying. **-haku** is the counter for nights that one stays outside of his home. Some numbers use **-paku** (pah-koo), though, so remember to watch out for the **-haku/-paku** alternation. You may not like it, but you just have to memorize it.

- » 一泊 **ip-paku** (eep-pah-koo) (*one night*)

- » 二泊 **ni-haku** (nee-hah-koo) (*two nights*)

- » 三泊 **san-paku** (sahn-pah-koo) (*three nights*)

- » 四泊 **yon-haku** (yohn-hah-koo) (*four nights*)

- » 五泊 **go-haku** (goh-hah-koo) (*five nights*)

- » 六泊 **rop-paku** (rohp-pah-koo) (*six nights*)

Checking In

As soon as you arrive at a hotel, bell staff helps you with your baggage. (If you're in Japan, you don't need to tip the person. Isn't that amazing?) Go to the **furonto** (foo-rohn-toh) (*front desk*).

TIP

If you don't have a **yoyaku** (yoh-yah-koo) (*reservation*), ask whether a **kūshitsu** (koo-shee-tsoo) (*vacant room*) is available.

- » 予約はしませんでしたが, 空室はありますか。**Yoyaku wa shimasen deshita ga, kūshitsu wa arimasu ka.** (yoh-yah-koo wah shee-mah-sehn deh-shee-tah gah, kooo-shee-tsoo wah ah-ree-mah-soo kah.) (*I didn't make a reservation, but do you have any vacancy?*)

- » 今日泊まりたいんですが, 部屋は空いていますか。**Kyō tomaritai-n-desu ga, heya wa aite imasu ka.** (kyohh toh-mah-ree-tah-een-deh-soo gah, heh-yah wah ah-ee-teh ee-mah-soo kah.) (*I'd like to stay here tonight, but do you have a vacancy?*)

You may hear one of the following statements in reply:

- » 申し訳ございません。只今, 空室はございません。**Mōshiwake gozaimasen. Tadaima, kūshitsu wa gozaimasen.** (mohh-shee-wah-keh goh-zah-ee-mah-sehn. tah-dah-ee-mah, kooo-shee-tsoo wah goh-zah-ee-mah-sehn.) (*I'm terribly sorry. We don't have any vacancy now.*)

>> 今日は満室です。**Kyō wa manshitsu desu.** (kyohh wah mahn-shee-tsoo deh-soo.) (*No vacancy tonight.*)

>> シングルの部屋がございます。**Shinguru no heya ga gozaimasu.** (sheen-goo-roo noh heh-yah gah goh-zah-ee-mah-soo.) (*There's a single room.*)

If you have a reservation or the hotel has a vacancy, check in! Hotel clerks are trained to speak very politely. Before they find out your **namae** (nah-mah-eh) (*name*), they address you as **okyaku-sama** (oh-kyah-koo-sah-mah), which literally means something along the lines of *Mr./Ms./Mrs. Customer.* After they learn your name, they address you with your last name followed by **-sama** (sah-mah) (*Mr./Ms./Mrs.*), which is the super-polite, businesslike version of **-san** (sahn). (Note that they never address you as **anata** [ah-nah-tah] [*you*]; for the scoop on **anata,** see Chapter 3.) Next, they ask you for your **jūsho** (jooo-shoh) (*address*) and **denwa-bangō** (dehn-wah-bahn-gohh) (*telephone number*). You know they're asking for *your* information because they add a polite prefix **o-** or **go-** before these words. (See Chapters 6 and 12 for more on the prefixes **o-** and **go-,** respectively.) So they may say something like one of the following:

お客様のお名前は。**O-kyaku-sama no o-namae wa.** (oh-kyah-koo-sah-mah noh oh-nah-mah-eh wah.) (*Your name?*)

ご住所は。**Go-jūsho wa.** (goh-jooo-sho wah.) (*Your address?*)

ご自宅のお電話番号は。**Go-jitaku no o-denwa bangō wa.** (goh-jee-tah-koo noh oh-dehn-wah bahn-gohh wah.) (*Your home telephone number?*)

After that process is complete, get your room number and the **kagi** (kah-gee) (*key*) or **kādo kī** (kahh-doh keee) (*key card*) for your room to complete the check-in. The clerk tells you which floor your room is on by using a numeral plus the counter **-kai** (see Chapters 4 and 10 for full details on the counter **-kai**). So the clerk may say something like the following:

>> 7階の705号室でございます。**Nana-kai no nanahyaku-go-gōshitsu de gozaimasu.** (nah-nah-kah-ee noh nah-nah-hyah-koo-goh-gohh-shee-tsoo deh goh-zah-ee-mah-soo.) (*Your room is Room 705 on the seventh floor.*)

>> こちらがカードキーでございます。**Kochira ga kādo kī de gozaimasu.** (koh-chee-rah gah kahh-doh keee deh goh-zah-ee-mah-soo.) (*This is your key card.*)

TIP

Refer to your room by using a numeral plus the counter **-gōshitsu** (gohh-shee-tsoo). Is it **502-gōshitsu** (goh-hyah-koo-nee-gohh-shee-tsoo) (*Room 502*) or **2502-gōshitsu** (nee-sehn-goh-hyah-koo-nee-gohh-shee-tsoo) (*Room 2502*)?

As you check in, you may want to ask some of the following questions:

» 駐車場はどこですか。**Chūshajō wa doko desu ka.** (chooo-shah-johh wah doh-koh deh-soo kah.) (*Where is the parking garage?*)

» チェックアウトは何時ですか。**Chekku-auto wa nan-ji desu ka.** (chehk-koo-ah-oo-toh wah nahn-jee deh-soo kah.) (*When is the check-out time?*)

» 朝食は何時からですか。**Chōshoku wa nan-ji kara desu ka.** (chohh-shoh-koo wah nahn-jee kah-rah deh-soo kah.) (*What time do you start serving breakfast?*)

» 朝食は何時までですか。**Chōshoku wa nan-ji made desu ka.** (chohh-shoh-koo wah nahn-jee mah-deh deh-soo kah.) (*Until what time do you serve breakfast?*)

Talkin' the Talk

Yoshi Kitayama has just arrived at Hotel Tokyo and is checking in.

Yoshi: **Sumimasen. Kyō kara yon-haku yoyaku shita-n-desu ga.**
soo-mee-mah-sehn. kyohh kah-rah yohn-hah-koo yoh-yah-koo shee-tahn-deh-soo gah.
Excuse me. I made a reservation for a four-night stay starting today.

Clerk: **O-namae wa.**
oh-nah-mah-eh wah.
Your name, sir?

Yoshi: **Kitayama Yoshi desu.**
kee-tah-yah-mah yoh-shee deh-soo.
Yoshi Kitayama.

Clerk: **Kitayama Yoshi-sama de gozaimasu ne.**
kee-tah-yah-mah yoh-shee-sah-mah deh goh-zah-ee-mah-soo neh.
Mr. Yoshi Kitayama, correct?

Yoshi: **Hai.**
hah-ee.
Yes.

The clerk checks the computer.

Clerk: **Kyō kara yon-haku, o-hitori-sama, shinguru no o-heya de gozaimasu ne.**
kyohh kah-rah yohn-hah-koo, oh-hee-toh-ree-sah-mah, sheen-goo-roo noh oh-heh-yah deh goh-zah-ee-mah-soo neh.
Starting today — four nights, one person, a single room, right?

Yoshi: **Hai.**
hah-ee.
Yes.

Clerk: **703-gōshitsu de gozaimasu. Kochira ga kagi de gozaimasu.**
nah-nah-hyah-koo-sahn-gohh-shee-tsoo deh goh-zah-ee-mah-soo. koh-chee-rah gah kah-gee deh goh-zah-ee-mah-soo.
It's Room 703. Here's your key.

Yoshi: **Ā, dōmo.**
ahh, dohh-moh.
Thank you.

. . . .

WORDS TO KNOW

yoyaku	yoh-yah-koo	reservation
kyō kara	kyohh kah-rah	starting today
hitori	hee-toh-ree	one person
shinguru	sheen-goo-roo	single
heya	heh-yah	room
kagi	kah-gee	key

Keeping Track of What's Yours during Your Stay

Lots of mix-ups can happen when you're staying in a big hotel with 300 other guests. Keep track of your **sūtsukēsu** (sooo-tsoo-kehh-soo) (*suitcases*) and **kagi** (kah-gee) (*keys*). The following sections show you a couple of ways to do just that.

Using possessive pronouns

Possessive pronouns allow you to indicate who owns what. To say *yours* and *mine* in Japanese, take the words that mean *you* and *I* and add the particle **no** after them. For example, **anata** (ah-nah-tah) is *you*, and **anata no** (ah-nah-tah noh) is *yours*. How about *mine*? **Watashi** (wah-tah-shee) is *I*, so **watashi no** (wah-tah-shee noh) is *mine*. Piece of cake, right? Now you can say **Watashi no desu!** (wah-tah-shee noh deh-soo!) (*That's mine!*) to someone who is very clearly reaching for your keys. Just don't say **Watashi no desu!** every time a guest touches stuff in your house. You'll sound like a 5-year-old child who doesn't know how to share his toys.

GRAMMAR CHAT

Although **anata no** (*yours*) is perfectly correct grammatically, you should avoid saying it as best you can because the use of **anata** (*you*) sounds snobby or even rude when used for one's superiors such as teachers, elders, bosses, and customers. Here's a helpful breakdown of how you can avoid using **anata**:

» If you know the person's name, use the name followed by **san** rather than あなた **anata,** as in 田中さんのですか。**Tanaka-san no desu ka.** (tah-nah-kah-sahn noh deh-soo kah.) (*Is it yours, Mr. Tanaka?*)

» If you don't know the person's name and she is your customer, you can use お客様 **o-kyaku-sama** (oh-kyah-koo-sah-mah), as in お客様のですか。**O-kyaku-sama no desu ka.** (oh-kyah-koo sah-mah noh deh-soo kah.) (*Is it yours?*)

» If the stranger is someone who was sitting behind you and you just noticed that he left something on the chair, you can say お宅 **otaku,** as in お宅のですか。 **Otaku no desu ka.** (oh-tah-koo-noh deh-soo kah.) (*Is it yours?*) Otaku is a polite "you."

And luckily, if you know *yours* and *mine* in Japanese, you already know *your* and *my* in Japanese. They're exactly the same — almost like a buy-one-get-one-free coupon at the supermarket. If **watashi no** is followed by a noun, such as **kagi,** it means *my*: **Watashi no kagi desu.** (wah-tah-shee noh kah-gee deh-soo.) means *That's my key.*

Take a look at Table 15-1. It contains all the basic personal pronouns and their possessive counterparts.

TABLE 15-1   ## Personal and Possessive Pronouns

Personal Pronouns	Ownership Words
私 **watashi** (wah-tah-shee) (*I/me*)	私の **watashi no** (wah-tah-shee noh) (*my/mine*)
私たち **watashi tachi** (wah-tah-shee tah-chee) (*we/us*)	私たちの **watashi tachi no** (wah-tah-shee tah-chee noh) (*our/ours*)
あなた **anata** (ah-nah-tah) (*you* [singular])	あなたの **anata no** (ah-nah-tah noh) (*your/yours* [singular])
あなたたち **anata tachi** (ah-nah-tah tah-chee) (*you* [plural])	あなたたちの **anata tachi no** (ah-nah-tah tah-chee noh) (*your/yours* [plural])
彼 **kare** (kah-reh) (*he/him*)	彼の **kare no** (kah-reh noh) (*his*)
彼女 **kanojo** (kah-noh-joh) (*she/her*)	彼女の **kanojo no** (kah-noh-joh noh) (*her/hers*)
彼ら **karera** (kah-reh-rah) (*they/them*)	彼らの **karera no** (kah-reh-rah noh) (*their/theirs*)

Using "uchi" possessively

Even though the word **uchi** (oo–chee) means *house, household,* or *inside,* Japanese use **uchi no** (oo–chee noh) to mean *my* or *our.* Here are some examples of **uchi no** in action:

うちの社員はよく働きます。 **Uchi no shain wa yoku hatarakimasu.** (oo-chee noh shah-een wah yoh-koo hah-tah-rah-kee-mah-soo.) (*Our [company's] employees work very hard.*)

うちの大学には図書館が二つあります。 **Uchi no daigaku ni wa toshokan ga futatsu arimasu.** (oo-chee noh dah-ee-gah-koo nee wah toh-shoh-kahn gah foo-tah-tsoo ah-ree-mah-soo.) (*There are two libraries in our university.*)

うちの子供はあまり野菜を食べません。**Uchi no kodomo wa amari yasai o tabemasen.** (oo-chee noh koh-doh-moh wah ah-mah-ree yah-sah-ee oh tah-beh-mah-sehn.) (*Our children don't eat vegetables very much.*)

うちの庭には桜の木があります。**Uchi no niwa ni wa sakura no ki ga arimasu.** (oo-chee noh nee-wah nee wah sah-koo-rah noh kee gah ah-ree-mah-soo.) (*There's a cherry tree in my/our garden.*)

うちの旅行会社は本社が名古屋にあります。**Uchi no ryokō-gaisha wa honsha ga Nagoya ni arimasu.** (oo-chee noh ryoh-kohh-gah-ee-shah wah hohn-shah gah nah-goh-yah nee ah-ree-mah-soo.) (*The headquarters of our travel agency is located in Nagoya.*)

Checking Out

It's **chekku-auto** (chehk-koo-ah-oo-toh) (*check-out*) time! Pack up your stuff and don't forget anything in your room. Go to front desk to **chekku-auto** and pay your bill. You may see some additional charges on your bill, such as the following:

» 電話料 **denwaryō** (dehn-wah-ryohh) (*telephone usage charge*)

» 飲食料 **inshokuryō** (een-shoh-koo-ryohh) (*food and drink charge*)

» インターネット利用料 **intānetto riyōryō** (een-tahh-neht-toh ree-yohh-ryohh) (*Internet usage charge*)

» クリーニング代 **kurīningudai** (koo-reee-neen-goo-dah-ee) (*laundry charge*)

» 税金 **zeikin** (zehh-keen) (*tax*)

If you need further assistance from the hotel staff after checking out, just ask them.

5時まで荷物を預かってください。**Go-ji made nimotsu o azukatte kudasai.** (goh-jee mah-deh nee-moh-tsoo oh ah-zoo-kaht-teh koo-dah-sah-ee.) (*Please keep my baggage here until 5:00.*)

領収書を下さい。**Ryōshūsho o kudasai.** (ryohh-shooo-shoh oh koo-dah-sah-ee.) (*Please give me the receipt.*)

タクシーをよんでくださいませんか。**Takushī o yonde kudasai masen ka.** (tah-koo-sheee oh yohn-deh koo-dah-sah-ee mah-sehn kah.) (*Would you mind calling a taxi?*)

TIP

By adding **masen ka** (mah-sehn kah) at the end of a request, you can make the request sound a bit softer and more polite. That is, **Takushī o yonde kudasai masen ka.** sounds much more polite than **Takushī o yonde kudasai. Masen** is just a polite suffix in the negative form, and **ka** is the question particle. **Masen ka** means something like *Wouldn't you?* or *Would you mind?*

FUN & GAMES

Fill in each blank with the appropriate Japanese word from the following list.

朝食 **chōshoku**

ルームサービス **rūmu sābisu**

チェックアウト **chekku-auto**

無線LAN **musen LAN**

空室 **kūshitsu**

The answers are in Appendix C.

1. _____ は何時ですか。

_____ **wa nan-ji desu ka.**

When is the check-out time?

2. _____ はありますか。

_____ **wa arimasuka.**

Do you have wireless LAN?

3. _____ はありますか。

_____ **wa arimasu ka.**

Do you offer room service?

4. _____ はありますか。

_____ **wa arimasu ka.**

Any vacancies?

5. _____ は付きますか。

_____ **wa tsukimasu ka.**

Is breakfast included?

Chapter **16**

Handling Emergencies

F ocusing on all the good things in life (like eating, shopping, having fun, and making friends) is great, but knowing what to do when an illness, injury, or emergency pops up is important. Handling these situations isn't a big deal when you know the ABCs of emergencies and sickness. This chapter provides you with the confidence and the Japanese to act wisely when faced with an emergency, whether that emergency is medical or legal.

REMEMBER

You can listen to all the Talkin' the Talk dialogues featured in this chapter. Go to www.dummies.com/go/japanesefd and click on the dialogue you want to hear.

Asking (or Shouting!) for Help

The simplest and quickest way to ask for help is to say **Tasukete.** (tah-soo-keh-teh.) (*Help me.*) **Tasukete** is the **te-**form of the verb **tasukeru** (tah-soo-keh-roo) (*to help*). It's in the **te-**form because it's the product of omitting **kudasai** (koo-dah-sah-ee) from the complete request sentence **Tasukete kudasai.** (tah-soo-keh-teh koo-dah-sah-ee.) (*Please help me.*) As I explain in Chapter 10, you express a request by using a verb in the **te-**form plus **kudasai. Kudasai** is a sort of helping verb for expressing a request. In an informal context or in an emergency, you can omit it. See Chapter 10 to find out more about **kudasai.**

Conjugate the **ru**-verb **tasukeru**.

Japanese Script	Rōmaji	Pronunciation
助ける	tasukeru	tah-soo-keh-roo
助けない	tasukenai	tah-soo-keh-nah-ee
助け(ます)	tasuke(masu)	tah-soo-keh(-mah-soo)
助けて	tasukete	tah-soo-keh-teh

When you're really in a panic, what should you shout? Just the vowel **a** (ah)? Its longer counterpart **ā** (aah)? Or maybe its super-long counterpart **āāāāā** (aaaaaaaaaah)? Even a crow can do that. To be more sophisticated than a crow, use the following phrases and scream as loudly as possible:

» だれか! **Dareka!** (dah-reh-kah!) (*Someone help!*)

» 泥棒! **Dorobō!** (doh-roh-bohh!) (*A thief!*)

» 火事! **Kaji!** (kah-jee!) (*Fire!*)

If you see someone who appears to be having a non-life-threatening problem, don't scream. Just ask one of the following questions:

» だいじょうぶですか。 **Daijōbu desu ka.** (dah-ee-johh-boo deh-soo kah.) (*Are you all right?*)

» どうしたんですか。 **Dōshita-n-desu ka.** (dohh-shee-tahn-deh-soo kah.) (*What happened?*)

GRAMMAR CHAT

Be a good person and offer help to those in need. The best way to express your helpful intentions is to ask a question that ends in **-mashō ka** (mah-shohh kah) (*shall I*). **-mashō ka** follows a verb in the stem form. The stem form of **yobu** (yoh-boo) (*to call*) is **yobi** (yoh-bee); therefore, **Keisatsu o yobimashō ka.** (kehh-sah-tsoo oh yoh-bee-mah-shohh kah.) means *Shall I call the police?* Following are some additional examples of **-mashō ka** in action:

ご家族に電話しましょうか。 **Go-kazoku ni denwa shimashō ka.** (goh-kah-zoh-koo nee dehn-wah shee-mah-shohh kah.) (*Shall I telephone your family?*)

救急車を呼びましょうか。 **Kyūkyūsha o yobimashō ka.** (kyooo-kyooo-shah oh yoh-bee-mah-shohh kah.) (*Shall I call an ambulance?*)

荷物を持ちましょうか。 **Nimotsu o mochimashō ka.** (nee-moh-tsoo oh moh-chee-mah-shohh kah.) (*Shall I hold your luggage?*)

運転しましょうか。 **Unten shimashō ka.** (oon-tehn shee-mah-shohh kah.) (*Shall I drive?*)

If you think you can't handle a situation alone, ask the people around you to help out too. To express your request, use a verb in the **te-**form and add **kudasai** (koo-dah-sah-ee), as noted earlier in this section. Here are a few examples:

ちょっと手伝ってください。**Chotto tetsudatte kudasai.** (choht-toh teh-tsoo-daht-teh koo-dah-sah-ee.) (*Please give me a hand.*)

警察に電話してください。**Keisatsu ni denwa shite kudasai.** (kehh-sah-tsoo nee dehn-wah shee-teh koo-dah-sah-ee.) (*Phone the police, please.*)

救急車を呼んでください。**Kyūkyūsha o yonde kudasai.** (kyooo-kyooo-shah oh yohn-deh koo-dah-sah-ee.) (*Call an ambulance, please.*)

消防署に電話してください。**Shōbōsho ni denwa shite kudasai.** (shohh-bohh-shoh nee dehn-wah shee-teh koo-dah-sah-ee.) (*Please phone the fire department.*)

Seeking Medical Attention

If you find yourself in need of medical care while in a predominantly Japanese-speaking area, you're going to wish you had a grasp of some basic doctor-related terminology. Never fear. The following sections walk you through a visit to a doctor's office or a hospital.

Looking for a doctor

If you happen to get sick in Japan, you may want to see an **isha** (ee-shah) (*medical doctor*), or more respectfully, **o-isha-san** (oh-ee-shah-sahn) (*medical doctor*). When you address your doctor, say **sensei** (sehn-sehh). **Sensei** works as a title not only for teachers but also for doctors, lawyers, and politicians.

CULTURAL WISDOM

AN INSIGHT INTO JAPANESE HEALTHCARE

In the United States, people usually see their doctors by appointment, but in Japan, they usually walk in. If you arrive early in the morning, you can get in to see the doctor earlier. If you come a bit late, you may have to wait for a few hours. Not having to make an appointment is nice, but the trade-off is that you have to wait for quite a while in the waiting room.

The Japanese government offers a uniform health insurance policy to all, and the premium and copay are pretty affordable except for special cases. Japan also has a very organized care-management system for elderly and handicapped people.

Depending on your problem, you may have to find a specialist. One way to refer to specialists is to add **i** (ee) after the name of the specialty. **I** (ee) means a *medical doctor,* but you can't use it by itself. It makes sense only if you combine it with another word or a meaning unit. For example, **ganka** (gahn-kah) means *ophthalmology,* and **ganka-i** (gahn-kah-ee) means *ophthalmologist.* Check out the following list:

» 眼科医 **ganka-i** (gahn-kah-ee) (*eye doctor*)

» 皮膚科医 **hifuka-i** (hee-foo-kah-ee) (*dermatologist*)

» 耳鼻咽喉科医 **jibi-inkōka-i** (jee-bee-een-kohh-kah-ee) (*ear/throat/mouth doctor*)

» 内科医 **naika-i** (nah-ee-kah-ee) (*internist*)

» 産婦人科医 **sanfujinka-i** (sahn-foo-jeen-kah-ee) (*obstetrician and gynecologist*)

» 整形外科医 **seikei-geka-i** (sehh-kehh-geh-kah-ee) (*orthopedist*)

» 歯科医 **shika-i** (shee-kah-ee) (*dentist*)

» 小児科医 **shōnika-i** (shohh-nee-kah-ee) (*pediatrician*)

Going to a hospital

Japanese have a couple different kinds of hospitals: **daigaku byōin** (dah-ee-gah-koo byohh-een) (*university hospital*) and **kyūkyū byōin** (kyooo-kyooo byohh-een) (*emergency hospital/emergency room*). If you have a medical emergency, head straight to the nearest **kyūkyū byōin.** Make sure you have your identification and insurance cards with you, though, because you'll have to present them when you arrive. These words will be helpful:

» 健康保険 **kenkō hoken** (kehn-kohh hoh-kehn) (*health insurance*)

» 健康保険証 **kenkō hokenshō** (kehn-kohh hoh-kehn-shohh) (*health insurance card*)

» 身分証明書 **mibun shōmeisho** (mee-boon shohh-mehh-shoh) (*identification*)

Also, you may well hear the following questions, so you'd best get familiar with them:

» 胸は痛くありませんか。 **Mune wa itaku arimasen ka.** (moo-neh wah ee-tah-koo ah-ree-mah-sehn kah.) (*Do you have chest pain?* [Literally: *Don't you have chest pain?*])

» 吐き気はしますか。**Hakike wa shimasu ka.** (hah-kee-keh wah shee-mah-soo kah.) (*Do you feel nauseous?*)

» 呼吸は苦しくありませんか。**Kokyū wa kurushiku arimasen ka.** (koh-kyooo wah koo-roo-shee-koo ah-ree-mah-sehn kah.) (*Do you have any discomfort in breathing? [Literally: Don't you have any discomfort in breathing?]*)

GRAMMAR CHAT

If you want to recommend that your friend do something, like go to the hospital, place **hō ga ii** (hohh gah eee) (*it's better to*) after a verb in the past tense. Yes, strangely, even though such a recommendation refers to the future, you use the past tense of the verb. If you think someone should eat, say **Tabeta hō ga ii.** (tah-beh-tah hohh gah eee.) (If you were to insist on a literal translation, this sentence would translate as *the ate-alternative is good*, and that, my friend, is why you can't always rely on literal translations.) The past tense of the verb **taberu** (tah-beh-roo) (*to eat*) is **tabeta** (tah-beh-tah). It's very easy to form the past tense of a verb if you know the **te-**form. Replace the final **e** in the **te-**form with an **a**, and you instantly get the past tense. And if you want to speak politely, add **desu** to the end of **hō ga ii.** Check out these examples:

病院に行った方がいいですよ。**Byōin ni itta hō ga ii desu yo.** (byohh-een nee eet-tah hohh gah eee deh-soo yoh.) (*You'd better go to the hospital.*)

医者に見てもらった方がいいよ。**Isha ni mite moratta hō ga ii yo.** (ee-shah nee mee-teh moh-raht-tah hohh gah eee yo.) (*It's better to have your doctor check you.*)

休んだ方がいいよ。**Yasunda hō ga ii yo.** (yah-soon-dah hohh gah eee yoh.) (*You'd better rest.*)

薬をのんだ方がいいですよ。**Kusuri o nonda hō ga ii desu yo.** (koo-soo-ree oh nohn-dah hohh gah eee deh-soo yoh.) (*It's better to take medicine.*)

Interestingly, for saying that it's better *not* to do something, you can just use the present negative form in the plain/informal form. No need to get the past tense involved.

お酒は飲まない方がいいですよ。**O-sake wa nomanai hō ga ii desu yo.** (oh-sah-keh wah noh-mah-nah-ee hohh gah eee deh-soo yoh.) (*You'd better not drink alcohol.*)

無理しない方がいいですよ。**Muri shinai hō ga ii desu yo.** (moo-ree shee-nah-ee hohh gah eee deh-soo yoh.) (*You'd better not work/try too hard.*)

Check out Chapter 3 for the present negative form in the plain/informal style.

Navigating a Doctor's Visit

Understanding doctor–talk in your own language can be hard enough, let alone trying to decipher it in a foreign one. How are you supposed to get the doctor's help if you can't tell her what's wrong or comprehend her diagnosis and advice? Luckily, the following sections tell you how to refer to parts of your body, how to describe pains and other symptoms, and how to understand any basic diagnosis and treatment you may receive.

Referring to your body parts

To tell a doctor or nurse where you're experiencing pain or discomfort, you need Japanese words for body parts. Go over the terms in the following bullets, touching your body parts as you say the words for extra reinforcement.

- 頭 **atama** (ah-tah-mah) (*head*)
- 目 **me** (meh) (*eyes*)
- 耳 **mimi** (mee-mee) (*ears*)
- 鼻 **hana** (hah-nah) (*nose*)
- 口 **kuchi** (koo-chee) (*mouth*)
- 歯 **ha** (hah) (*tooth*)
- 首 **kubi** (koo-bee) (*neck*)
- 喉 **nodo** (noh-doh) (*throat*)
- 肩 **kata** (kah-tah) (*shoulder*)
- 胸 **mune** (moo-neh) (*chest/breast*)
- 背中 **senaka** (seh-nah-kah) (*back*)
- おなか **onaka** (oh-nah-kah) (*belly*)
- おしり **oshiri** (oh-shee-ree) (buttocks)
- 腕 **ude** (oo-deh) (*arm*)
- 肘 **hiji** (hee-jee) (*elbow*)
- 手首 **tekubi** (teh-koo-bee) (*wrist*)
- 手 **te** (teh) (*hand/arm*)
- 指 **yubi** (yoo-bee) (*finger*)
- 腰 **koshi** (koh-shee) (*lower back*)

>> 膝 **hiza** (hee-zah) (*knee*)

>> 関節 **kansetsu** (kahn-seh-tsoo) (*joints*)

>> 足首 **ashikubi** (ah-shee-koo-bee) (*ankle*)

>> 足 **ashi** (ah-shee) (*foot/leg*)

>> 足の指 **ashi no yubi** (ah-shee noh yoo-bee) (*toes*)

TIP

If the word **ashi** (ah–shee) means both *foot* and *leg*, and the word **te** (teh) means both *hand* and *arm*, how do you know which is which? Context is everything, as you can see from the following examples:

兄は足が短い。**Ani wa ashi ga mijikai.** (ah-nee wah ah-shee gah mee-jee-kah-ee.) (*My older brother's legs are short.*)

弟が私の足を踏んだ。**Otōto ga watashi no ashi o funda.** (oh-tohh-toh gah wah-tah-shee noh ah-shee oh foon-dah.) (*My little brother stepped on my foot.*)

ピザは手で食べる。**Piza wa te de taberu.** (pee-zah wah teh deh tah-beh-roo.) (*We eat pizza by hand.*)

ゆみは手がながい。**Yumi wa te ga nagai.** (yoo-mee wah teh gah nah-gah-ee.) (*Yumi has long arms.*)

You may also want to know what to call your important internal organs:

>> 腸 **chō** (chohh) (*intestine*)

>> 肺 **hai** (hah-ee) (*lungs*)

>> 胃 **i** (ee) (*stomach*)

>> 腎臓 **jinzō** (jeen-zohh) (*kidney*)

>> 肝臓 **kanzō** (kahn-zohh) (*liver*)

>> 脳 **nō** (nohh) (*brain*)

>> 心臓 **shinzō** (sheen-zohh) (*heart*)

>> 膵臓 **suizō** (soo-ee-zoho) (*pancreas*)

Complaining about your pain

Expect to be asked questions like the following at the doctor's office or in the emergency room:

>> どうしましたか。**Dō shimashita ka.** (dohh shee-mah-shee-tah kah.) (*What happened?*)

» いつからですか。 **Itsu kara desu ka.** (ee-tsoo kah-rah deh-soo kah.) (*For how long?* [Literally: *Since when is it going on?*])

» どこが痛いんですか。 **Doko ga itai-n-desu ka.** (doh-koh gah ee-tah-een-deh-soo kah.) (*Where does it hurt?*)

» 熱はありますか。 **Netsu wa arimasu ka.** (neh-tsoo wah ah-ree-mah-soo kah.) (*Do you have a fever?*)

If some part of your body hurts, say the body part hurts (refer to the preceding section), plus **ga** (gah), plus **itai** (ee-tah-ee) or "X (your body part) **ga itai-n-desu.**" (X gah ee-tah-een deh-soo). By adding **–n-desu,** you sound polite and emphasize/explain your problem at the same time. **Itai** (ee-tah-ee) is an **i**-type adjective meaning *painful*, although in English, you often say "*it hurts*" using the verb "hurt." **Itai** is also what Japanese say for *ouch*. If someone steps on your foot in a crowded train, you would say "**Itai!**" This word can be used in sentences as well. **Atama ga itai** means *head is ouch — I have a headache.* If more than one part hurts, list all the parts, using the particle **to** (toh) which means *and.* Place **to** after each body part, except the last one, as in the following examples.

肩と首がとても痛いんです。 **Kata to kubi ga totemo itai-n-desu.** (kah-tah toh koo-bee gah toh-teh-moh ee-tah-een-deh-soo.) (*My shoulder and neck hurt a lot.*)

肩と腰と首が痛いんです。 **Kata to koshi to kubi ga itai-n-desu.** (kah-tah toh koh-shee toh koo-bee gah ee-tah-een-deh-soo.) (*My shoulder, back, and neck hurt.*)

TIP

To describe how something hurts, you can use funny image-sound words like the ones in the following list. These words are actually a small subset of Japanese sound symbolism that includes onomatopoeia, and they usually consist of a repetition of one or two syllables. You can find more expressions in Chapter 3.

» チクチク **chiku-chiku** (chee-koo-chee-koo): Sharp, needle-like pain, like you may have with stomach complaints

» ガンガン **gan-gan** (gahn-gahn): Hammering or banging pain, as with a pounding headache

» ゴホンゴホン **gohon-gohon** (goh-hohn-goh-hohn): Deep coughing sounds

» ヒリヒリ **hiri-hiri** (hee-ree-hee-ree): Smarting pain, as with a bad sunburn

» ゼーゼー **zē-zē** (zehh-zehh): Wheezing sound in the chest

» ズキズキ **zuki-zuki** (zoo-kee-zoo-kee): Nailing or screwing pain in the head

Here are some examples of how you can weave these expressions into sentences:

頭がズキズキ痛いんです。 **Atama ga zuki-zuki itai-n-desu.** (ah-tah-mah gah zoo-kee-zoo-kee ee-tah-een-deh-soo.) (*I have a screwing pain in the head.*)

火傷したところがヒリヒリします。 **Yakedo shita tokoro ga hiri-hiri shimasu.** (yah-keh-doh shee-tah toh-koh-roh gah hee-ree-hee-ree shee-mah-soo.) (*The part I burned hurts.*)

胃がチクチクするんです。 **I ga chiku-chiku suru-n-desu.** (ee gah chee-koo-chee-koo soo-roon-deh-soo.) (*My stomach hurts with a tingling sensation.*)

Describing your symptoms

Expressing exactly how you're feeling with specific **shōjō** (shohh–johh) (*symptoms*) is crucial for receiving the right diagnosis. A few **shōjō** may occur together. For example, bad stomach viruses cause nausea, which is usually followed by diarrhea. Upper respiratory infections can give you a runny nose, a cough, and a very stuffy and congested night's sleep (or lack of sleep). Think about your **shōjō** and then find them in the following list so you know how to describe what you're experiencing before you go to the doctor:

» 便秘をしている **benpi o shite iru** (behn-pee oh shee-teh ee-roo) (*to have constipation*)

» 下痢をしている **geri o shite iru** (geh-ree oh shee-teh ee-roo) (*to have diarrhea*)

» 吐き気がする **hakike ga suru** (hah-kee-keh gah soo-roo) (*to have nausea*)

» 鼻がつまっている **hana ga tsumatte iru** (hah-nah gah tsoo-maht-teh ee-roo) (*to have a stuffy nose*)

» 鼻水がでる **hanamizu ga deru** (hah-nah-mee-zoo gah deh-roo) (*to have a runny nose*)

» クシャミがでる **kushami ga deru** (koo-shah-mee gah deh-roo) (*to sneeze*)

» 目がかゆい **me ga kayui** (meh gah kah-yoo-ee) (*to have itchy eyes*)

» 目眩がする **memai ga suru** (me-mah-ee gah soo-roo) (*to have dizziness*)

» 耳が痛い **mimi ga itai** (mee-mee gah ee-tah-ee) (*to have an earache*)

» 胸が痛い **mune ga itai** (moo-neh gah ee-tah-ee) (*to have chest pain*)

» 熱がある **netsu ga aru** (neh-tsoo gah ah-roo) (*to have a fever*)

» 喉が痛い **nodo ga itai** (noh-doh gah ee-tah-ee) (*to have a sore throat*)

» 寒気がする **samuke ga suru** (sah-moo-keh gah soo-roo) (*to have the chills*)

» 咳が出る **seki ga deru** (seh-kee gah deh-roo) (*to cough*)

» 頭痛がする **zutsū ga suru** (zoo-tsoo gah soo-roo) (*to have a headache*)

» ゼーゼーする **zē-zē suru** (zehh-zehh soo-roo) (*to wheeze*)

Conjugate the **ru**-verb **deru** (deh-roo) (*to come out*). You need it to describe all the annoying mucus that comes out when you cough, sneeze, and blow your nose when you have a code — sorry, that's stuffy-speak for "cold."

Japanese Script	Rōmaji	Pronunciation
出る	deru	deh-roo
出ない	denai	deh-nah-ee
出(ます)	de(masu)	deh(-mah-soo)
出て	dete	deh-teh

Receiving a diagnosis

A doctor can usually diagnose a minor cold or the flu just by talking with you, but sometimes you have to have tests done. No one wants to have a painful or time-consuming test, but if the doctor tells you that you need it, you'd better take it.

A few tests and procedures that a doctor may recommend are

» CATスキャン **CAT sukyan** (kyaht-toh soo-kyahn) (*CAT scan*)

» 超音波検査 **chōonpa kensa** (chohh-ohn-pah kehn-sah) (*ultrasound/sonogram*)

» CT **CT** (sheee-teee) (*CT scan*)

» 血液検査 **ketsueki kensa** (keh-tsoo-eh-kee kehn-sah) (*blood test*)

» MRI **MRI** (eh-moo-ahh-roo-ah-ee) (*MRI*)

» 尿検査 **nyō kensa** (nyohh kehn-sah) (*urine test*)

» レントゲン **rentogen** (rehn-toh-gehn) (*X-ray*)

After you explain your symptoms to the doctor, have an exam, and undergo any necessary tests, it's judgment time. For your sake, I hope the **shindan** (sheen-dahn) (*diagnosis*) isn't serious. Possible **shindan** include the following:

» アレルギー **arerugī** (ah-reh-roo-geee) (*allergies*)

» 炎症 **enshō** (ehn-shohh) (*inflammation*)

» 肺炎 **haien** (hah-ee-ehn) (*pneumonia*)

» インフルエンザ **infuruenza** (een-foo-roo-ehn-zah) (*influenza/flu*)

» 花粉症 **kafunshō** (kah-foon-shohh) (*hay fever*)

>> 感染 **kansen** (kahn-sehn) (*infection*)

>> 関節炎 **kansetsuen** (kahn-seh-tsoo-ehn) (*arthritis*)

>> 風邪 **kaze** (kah-zeh) (*cold*)

>> 気管支炎 **kikanshien** (kee-kahn-shee-ehn) (*bronchitis*)

>> 骨折 **kossetsu** (kohs-seh-tsoo) (*broken bone*)

>> 盲腸 **mōchō** (mohh-chohh) (*appendicitis*)

>> 捻挫 **nenza** (nehn-zah) (*sprain*)

>> 脳震盪 **nōshintō** (nohh-sheen-tohh) (*concussion*)

>> 食中毒 **shokuchūdoku** (shoh-koo-chooo-doh-koo) (*food poisoning*)

>> ウィルス **wirusu** (wee-roo-soo) (*virus*)

>> 喘息 **zensoku** (zehn-soh-koo) (*asthma*)

Getting treatment

Your doctor may give you some **kusuri** (koo-soo-ree) (*medication*) that makes you a bit more comfortable, such as one of the following:

>> アスピリン **asupirin** (ah-soo-pee-reen) (*aspirin*)

>> 鎮痛剤 **chintsūzai** (cheen-tsooo-zah-ee) (*pain reliever*)

>> 解熱剤 **genetsuzai** (geh-neh-tsoo-zah-ee) (*fever reducer*)

>> 抗生物質 **kōsei busshitsu** (kohh-sehh boos-shee-tsoo) (*antibiotic*)

>> 咳止め **sekidome** (seh-kee-doh-meh) (*cough suppressant*)

There's no cure for a cold, so all you can do is try to treat your symptoms and make your life a little less miserable. Ask your grandma for her natural home remedy. One Japanese traditional cold remedy is **tamago zake** (tah-mah-goh zah-keh) (*egg sake*) — heated sake with beaten egg. What's your secret remedy? Ginger tea? Chicken soup? Honey? Orange juice?

The doctor should ask you **Yakubutsu arerugī wa arimasu ka.** (yah-koo-boo-tsoo ah-reh-roo-gee wah ah-ree-mah-soo kah.) (*Are you allergic to any medication?*) before prescribing any medication, but if for some reason she doesn't and you know you're allergic to some medications, don't forget to mention it. For example, you can say **Penishirin ni arerugī ga arimasu.** (peh-nee-shee-reen nee ah-reh-roo-geee gah ah-ree-mah-soo.) (*I'm allergic to penicillin.*)

If you have an injury, you may come home with one of these:

» ギプス **gipusu** (gee-poo-soo) (*cast*)

» 包帯 **hōtai** (hohh-tah-ee) (*bandage*)

» 松葉杖 **matsubazue** (mah-tsoo-bah-zoo-eh) (*crutches*)

» 湿布 **shippu** (sheep-poo) (*hot or cold compress*)

Contacting the Police

CULTURAL WISDOM

The police emergency number in Japan is 110. Japanese call it **110-ban** (hyah-koo-tohh-bahn). Yes, they usually say **hyakutō-ban** (hyah-koo-tohh-bahn) rather than **hyakujū-ban** (hyah-koo-jooo-bahn) — just one of those things. The number for an accident or a fire is different: **119-ban** (hyah-koo-jooo-kyooo-bahn). Don't confuse these numbers with your own emergency number — 911 in the United States, for example.

When you call emergency numbers in any country, calm down and first tell the dispatcher where you are. Then explain what happened. The following sections explain how to report an accident to the police and report lost or stolen possessions.

Reporting an accident to the police

If you see a **jiko** (jee-koh) (*accident*), report it to the **keisatsu** (kehh-sah-tsoo) (*police*). The verb you need to report a **jiko** is **aru** (ah-roo) (*to exist*); use it in the past tense — *There was an accident.* — and the polite/neutral style (because you're talking to a police officer). So you need to conjugate **aru** into the polite past tense form, **arimashita** (ah-ree-mah-shee-tah), as in the following examples:

事故がありました。**Jiko ga arimashita.** (jee-koh gah ah-ree-mah-shee-tah.) (*There was an accident.*)

高田町で事故がありました。**Takada-chō de jiko ga arimashita.** (tah-kah-dah-chohh deh jee-koh gah ah-ree-mah-shee-tah.) (*There was an accident in Takada Town.*)

I don't want you **au** (ah-oo) (*to be involved in*) an accident, but if you are, make sure to mark **jiko** with the particle **ni** when you use the verb **au**, as in **jiko ni au** (jee-koh nee ah-oo) (*to be involved in an accident*). The polite past tense form of **au** is **aimashita: Hidoi jiko ni aimashita.** (hee-doh-ee jee-koo nee ah-ee-mah-shee-tah.) (*I was involved in a terrible accident.*)

Conjugate the **u**-verb **au.** Watch out for the **w** sound in the negative form.

Japanese Script	Rōmaji	Pronunciation
遭う	au	ah-oo
遭わない	awanai	ah-wah-nah-ee
遭い(ます)	ai(masu)	a-ee(-mah-soo)
あって	atte	aht-teh

Unfortunately, at some point you may be the one to cause the accident. In that case, you need to conjugate the **u**-verb **okosu** (o-koh-soo) (*to cause*). Create **s/ sh**- syllables.

Japanese Script	Rōmaji	Pronunciation
起こす	okosu	oh-koh-soo
起こさない	okosanai	oh-koh-sah-nah-ee
起こし(ます)	okoshi(masu)	oh-koh-shee(-mah-soo)
起こして	okoshite	oh-koh-shee-teh

You often need to specify the nature of an accident so that the people responding know what to expect. The following list gives you an idea of some of the types of **jiko** you may encounter:

>> バイクの事故 **baiku no jiko** (bah-ee-koo noh jee-koh) (*motorcycle accident*)

>> ガス漏れ事故 **gasumore jiko** (gah-soo-moh-reh jee-koh) (*gas leak accident*)

>> 自動車事故 **jidōsha jiko** (jee-dohh-shah jee-koh) (*auto accident*)

>> 火事 **kaji** (kah-jee) (*fire*)

>> 怪我 **kega** (keh-gah) (*injury*)

>> 交通事故 **kōtsū jiko** (kohh-tsoo jee-koh) (*traffic accident*)

Unfortunately, **kōtsū jiko** are everyday events in most cities. If you're involved in an accident and no one gets hurt, consider yourself lucky in an unlucky situation, even if it's your fault.

To avoid future legal complications over responsibilities, call the police, tell them where you are, and wait for the police officer to arrive. To tell the police how to find you, use the location and direction words listed in Chapter 8. And while you're waiting for them to arrive, you may as well conjugate the **u**–verb **matsu** (mah–tsoo) (*to wait*).

Japanese Script	Rōmaji	Pronunciation
待つ	matsu	mah-tsoo
待たない	matanai	mah-tah-nah-ee
待ち(ます)	machi(masu)	mah-chee(-mah-soo)
待って	matte	maht-teh

Talkin' the Talk

Takeshi was just involved in a collision. He calls the police with his cellphone.

Takeshi: **Moshimoshi. Ima kuruma no jiko ni atta-n-desu.**
moh-shee-moh-shee. ee-mah koo-roo-mah noh jee-koh nee aht-tahn-deh-soo.
Hello. I was just in a car accident.

Police: **Dareka kega o shimashita ka.**
dah-reh-kah keh-gah oh shee-mah-shee-tah kah.
Did anyone get injured?

Takeshi: **Īe.**
eee-eh.
No.

Police: **Ima doko desu ka.**
ee-mah doh-koh deh-soo kah.
Where are you now?

Takeshi: **Takada-chō no yūbinkyoku no mae no kōsaten desu.**
tah-kah-dah-chohh noh yooo-been-kyoh-koo noh mah-eh noh kohh-sah-tehn deh-soo.
I'm at the intersection in front of the post office in Takada Town.

Police: **Sugu kēsatsukan ga ikimasu. Go-fun gurai matte kudasai.**
soo-goo kehh-sah-tsoo-kahn gah ee-kee-mah-soo. goh-foon goo-rah-ee maht-teh koo-dah-sah-ee.
An officer will be there soon. Please wait for about five minutes.

WORDS TO KNOW

moshimoshi	moh-shee-moh-shee	hello
kega	keh-gah	injury
yūbinkyoku	yooo-been-kyoh-koo	post office
no mae	noh mah-eh	in front of
kōsaten	kohh-sah-tehn	intersection
sugu	soo-goo	soon
keisatsukan	kehh-sah-tsoo-kahn	police officer

Reporting a crime

Japan is a quite safe country and has a relatively low crime rate. Women can walk around in the city at night feeling pretty safe. The contribution of police boxes called **kōban** (kohh–bahn) is absolutely significant for the high level of safety in Japan. However, if you're attacked, involved in a crime, or witness any criminal act in Japan, report it to the police immediately. You may need to know some of these nouns related to crimes:

>> 暴行 **bōkō** (bohh-kohh) (*assault*)

>> 強盗 **gōtō** (gohh-tohh) (*robbery, robber*)

>> 放火 **hōka** (hohh-kah) (*arson*)

>> 詐欺 **sagi** (sah-gee) (*fraud*)

>> 殺人 **satsujin** (sah-tsoo-jeen) (*murder*)

>> 窃盗 **settō** (seht-tohh) (*theft*)

>> 誘拐 **yūkai** (yoo-kah-ee) (*kidnapping*)

Reporting lost or stolen belongings

If you lose a **handobaggu** (hahn–doh–bahg–goo) (*handbag*), **saifu** (sah-ee-foo) (*wallet*), or **sūtsukēsu** (sooo-tsoo-kehh-soo) (*suitcase*), tell the authorities where you lost it and what it looks like. (Use the words from Chapter 10 to describe the item's color and size.) And think about what was in it so you can list those items on the police report. If your **handobaggu** or **saifu** is stolen, you may also be missing the following:

>> 現金 **genkin** (gehn-keen) (*cash*)

>> 鍵 **kagi** (kah-gee) (*keys*)

>> クレジットカード **kurejitto kādo** (koo-reh-jeeht-toh kahh-doh) (*credit card*)

>> 写真 **shashin** (shah-sheen) (*photos*)

>> 運転免許証 **unten menkyoshō** (oon-tehn mehn-kyoh-shohh) (*driver's license*)

To describe the contents of your bag or wallet, use the phrase **haitte iru** (hah-eet-teh ee-roo) (*to be in it*). **Haitte** is the **te**-form of the verb **hairu** (hah-ee-roo) (*to be placed in somewhere*). Conjugate the **u**-verb **hairu,** which also means *to enter* in some contexts.

Japanese Script	Rōmaji	Pronunciation
入る	hairu	hah-ee-roo
入らない	hairanai	hah-ee-rah-nah-ee
入り(ます)	hairi(masu)	hah-ee-ree(-mah-soo)
入って	haitte	hah-eet-teh

If you add the verb **iru** (ee-roo) (*to exist*) after another verb in the **te**-form, you're talking about a state. For example, **haitte iru** is the state after something entered. This concept — that something would be in the state of having entered somewhere — is hard to understand in English, but it just means "something is in it." That's it.

So **Genkin ga haitte iru.** (gehn-keehn gah hah-eet-teh ee-roo.) means *Some cash is in it.* But in a polite/neutral context, such as when you're talking to the police, say **Genkin ga haitte imasu.** (gehn-keen gah hah-eet-teh ee-mah-soo.) instead. And if you have more than one item in your bag, list everything by using the particle **to** (toh) after each item except the last one. These examples help you explain to the police what your missing item contains:

写真が入っています。**Shashin ga haitte imasu.** (shah-sheen gah hah-eet-teh ee-mah-soo.) (*It has a photo in it.* [Literally: *A photo is in it.*])

財布とパスポートが入っています。**Saifu to pasupōto ga haitte imasu.** (sah-ee-foo toh pah-soo-pohh-toh gah hah-eet-teh ee-mah-soo.) (*My wallet and my passport are in it.*)

現金とクレジットカードと写真が入っています。**Genkin to kurejitto kādo to shashin ga haitte imasu.** (gehn-keen toh koo-reh-jeet-toh kahh-doh toh shah-sheen gah hah-eet-teh ee-mah-soo.) (*Some cash, a credit card, and a photograph are in it.*)

If you want to list the items as examples, implying that there are other items, use the particle **ya** (yah) rather than **to** (toh). For example, if you say **Genkin ya kurejitto kādo ya shashin ga haitte imasu.** (gehn-keen yah koo-reh-jeet-toh kahh-doh yah shah-sheen gah hah-eet-teh ee-mah-soo.) (*Some cash, a credit card, a photograph, and so on are in it.*), it sounds like there are other items in the bag as well.

If you lose something in a store, airport, or train station, listen for an announcement. If you're paged over the public address system, it's a good sign. An announcement states your name and **o-koshi kudasai** (oh-koh-shee koo-dah-sah-ee). This term is a super-polite, businesslike phrase that means *please come* and uses the stem form — **koshi** — of the verb **kosu** (koh-soo) (*to come*). If you're curious about what the **o** and **kudasai** are doing, take a look at Chapter 9.

Getting Legal Help

Japan isn't a very litigious society, and Japanese don't settle disputes through the courts as often as Americans seem to, but if you find that you need legal assistance in Japan, you can always talk to a **bengoshi** (behn-goh-shee) (*lawyer*). Contacting your country's **ryōjikan** (ryohh-jee-kahn) (*consulate*) is also a good idea if you run into trouble.

You may find these sentences helpful if you require legal assistance while traveling in Japan:

>> アメリカ領事館に連絡してください。**Amerika ryōjikan ni renraku shite kudasai.** (ah-meh-ree-kah ryohh-jee-kahn nee rehn-rah-koo shee-teh koo-dah-sah-ee.) (*Please contact the American consulate.*)

>> 弁護士を呼んでください。**Bengoshi o yonde kudasai.** (behn-goh-shee oh yohn-deh koo-dah-sah-ee.) (*Please call a lawyer.*)

>> 私の弁護士に話してください。**Watashi no bengoshi ni hanashite kudasai.** (wah-tah-shee noh behn-goh-shee nee hah-nah-shee-teh koo-dah-sah-ee.) (*Please talk to my lawyer.*)

Foreigners in Japan are subject to the laws of Japan. If you're arrested, know that you have your right to remain silent, to hire a lawyer at your own expense, and to have the embassy or the consulate notified of your arrest.

FUN & GAMES

Write the Japanese words for the following body parts on the corresponding lines. Check the answers in Appendix C.

Illustration by Elizabeth Kurtzman

1. _____
2. _____
3. _____
4. _____
5. _____
6. _____
7. _____
8. _____
9. _____
10. _____
11. _____

The Part of Tens

IN THIS PART . . .

Get practical tips that you can keep in mind as you immerse yourself in the Japanese language.

Discover ten ways to pick up Japanese quickly.

Be aware of ten things you should not say in Japanese.

Find out how to impress Japanese people with a few expressions and phrases.

Chapter **17**

Ten Ways to Pick Up Japanese Quickly

anguage immersion programs work for a reason: They surround you with the language you're trying to learn and force you to speak it in order to communicate with others. You can create an immersion-type environment to help you pick up Japanese quickly by applying the ten methods I list in this chapter. With these ten tricks, you'll be rattling off Japanese phrases and sentences in no time.

Use Digital Technologies

Thanks to smartphones and computers, which provide convenient dictionary and translation tools, a tremendous amount of information is only a finger tap away, anytime and anywhere. You can download Japanese language apps for use when you're on the go. You can use your smartphone or computer's Internet browser to search for Japanese cultural keywords such as **kimono** and **sushi,** Japanese artists' names such as **Utada** and **Arashi,** or Japanese place names such as **Asakusa** and **Akihabara.** You'll be amazed by the tons of useful information these searches return, and you can surely learn some Japanese keywords. Moreover, you can use note-taking apps on your smartphone to take note of new Japanese words as soon as you see or hear them, wherever you are.

Cook or Eat Japanese Foods

Find a Japanese cookbook at your local bookstore or on the Internet — preferably one with photos that show each step of cooking. Pick a dish that really makes your mouth water and whip up a Japanese meal next weekend! As you read over the recipe for your fabulous feast with step-by-step photos, be sure to have your trusty Japanese-English dictionary close by. After you understand the entire recipe, memorize keywords for ingredients and actions. Now, it's time to start cookin', good lookin'. Each time you wash, cut, grate, mix, bake, or grill, say what you're doing aloud in Japanese. And call out the ingredients as you add them.

If you don't want to cook, go to a Japanese restaurant. Talk to a Japanese waiter, waitress, or sushi chef. Make it a goal to master the names of at least five Japanese dishes, ingredients, or whatever's on the table before you leave the restaurant.

Read Japanese Comic Books

Japanese comic books, called **manga** (mahn-gah), are very popular among readers both young and old. With thousands of pictures that show detailed background scenes, actions, and facial expressions of characters plus written speech in balloons, **manga** is a rich source for hundreds of words for sound symbolism, including onomatopoeia. The words for sound symbolism are often written in **katakana**, and just sounding them out is already so much fun. **Manga** usually include **furigana** (foo-ree-gah-nah), **hiragana** specification of the pronunciation of **kanji** characters, so you can always check the meaning of **kanji** characters by using a **kanji** dictionary. (See Chapter 2 to understand what **katakana, hiragana,** and **kanji** mean.)

TIP

You can also purchase a comic book that comes with English translation. Look for them in Japanese bookstores, comic book shops, and larger bookstores in your town or city.

Watch Japanese Anime, Films, and Sports

Your local public library probably has DVDs of Japanese movies and animation with English subtitles. Pick one that looks interesting. Try one of Akira Kurosawa's movies, such as *Seven Samurai* and *Ran*, or other Japanese films that have received good reviews, such as *Departures* and *Shall We Dance?* You may also want to check out Hayao Miyazaki's animated films *My Neighbor Totoro* and *Spirited Away*. When you watch a Japanese film for the first time, just watch the whole thing for enjoyment. Then watch it a second time and try to catch some Japanese words and phrases. Feel free to pause as many times as you need; just try to refrain from turning on the English subtitles. You'll learn the meaning of words, and you'll also figure out what context they're used in.

If you're a sports fan, try watching Japanese-language broadcasts of sports such as sumo and baseball in addition to anime and films. Japanese-language sport broadcasts are easy to follow because you can hear the language in context, just like when you watch anime and films. It's also useful for getting used to the polite/neutral speech style.

Do Karaoke

Get a Japanese karaoke set and sing as you read the lyrics that appear on the screen. If you like the song, memorize it. Imitate the real singer's pronunciation very closely. After you master it perfectly, sing it in front of your friends and family. They'll be impressed by your use of Japanese, even if your singing ability leaves something to be desired! (Check out Chapter 11 for more on karaoke.)

Spend Time with Japanese

Look around you. Okay, now stop looking around and read the rest of this paragraph. Do you know of any Japanese in your school, company, neighborhood, or church? If you find a few Japanese folks, become friends with them. Exchange cellphone numbers or email addresses, message each other on social networks such as Facebook and Twitter, and make plans to get together sometime.

REMEMBER

Understanding Japanese culture and society is indispensable for learning the language. So why not make plans to spend a nice afternoon with your new Japanese friends, discussing Japanese culture, society, and daily life over tea? You may be communicating with them in English, but they'll surely let you know some Japanese words that are important for what you're talking about. Make a mental note of these words.

Exchange Language Lessons

Did you know that helping others helps you a lot? Find a Japanese who wants to learn English and teach him the language. In exchange, ask him her to teach you Japanese. Not only will you learn Japanese for free, but you'll also create a precious friendship.

TIP

Contact local colleges and universities; they may have some Japanese international students who need English help. You can also check with local Japanese associations. Find them in your local phone book. I'm sure you can find at least one Japanese person in your area who needs some help perfecting her English.

Get to Know a Monolingual Japanese

Spend time with someone whose *only* language is Japanese. In order to engage in activities such as shopping, cooking, or crafting with a monolingual Japanese person, you need to speak Japanese just because you won't have the luxury of using your English language. As you speak nothing but Japanese, your tongue and lips will definitely get a workout. This kind of immersion can be a bit painful at the beginning, but it will bring the best result. Feeling that you have to speak Japanese to do something is a great driving force to increase your natural speaking ability.

If you don't know a word in Japanese, use hand gestures or drawings to express it. And listen carefully to what the Japanese person says. If you do this friendly immersion for a few hours each day for a week, by the end of the week, you'll be using fewer and fewer hand gestures and drawings and more and more Japanese words. Think of it as a study abroad program without ever leaving your home.

Travel to Japan

Nothing is more enjoyable than learning Japanese while traveling to Japan. After you're there, look around you! You see Japanese characters all over. Tune in to your surroundings. You hear teenagers chatting with their friends, mothers scolding their kids, and store clerks greeting their customers — all in Japanese. You just have to keep guessing what they're saying. What a fun way of learning the language!

Be Positive, Curious, and Creative

One of the keys of language learning is to remain positive about and engaged in your studies. Don't worry about making mistakes. Relax your mind when you talk. It's not a job interview. It won't be recorded or aired on TV. Be positive and praise yourself when you communicate in Japanese!

Also, don't wait until someone talks to you in Japanese. Initiate conversations yourself. Ask questions in Japanese. Regain the curious and worry-free spirit of your childhood.

Be creative and make opportunities to use Japanese in your daily life. Write down your weekly schedule in Japanese. Say the time and date in Japanese. Memorize your home phone number in Japanese. Address your family in Japanese. Greet your friends in Japanese. Don't wait until someone helps you; help yourself. Be creative, be curious, stay positive, and enjoy talking!

Chapter **18**

Ten Things Never to Say in Japanese

S ocial customs are culturally created rules that differ from country to country because they're often tied to the histories of nations and peoples. Pasts rooted in democracy, feudalism, totalitarianism, pioneer spirit, or liberal or conservative values, to name a few, obviously tend to give rise to different customs. Because U.S. society and Japanese society are built on different customs, what's considered polite for folks from the United States may be rude for Japanese at times. To help you avoid unintentionally offending your Japanese cohorts, this chapter alerts you to ten things that you shouldn't say when you're with Japanese people.

"San" after Your Own Name

When you talk with Japanese people, they'll say your name and then say -**san** (sahn) all the time. But don't copy them by placing -**san** after your own name when you refer to yourself. For example, don't say **Watashi wa Sumisu-san desu.** (wah-tah-shee wah soo-mee-soo-sahn deh-soo.) (*I'm Mr. Smith.*) You'll sound like a kid if you do. Instead, say **Watashi wa Sumisu desu.** (wah-tah-shee wah soo-mee-soo deh-soo.) (*I'm Smith.*)

REMEMBER

The function of **-san** is to show respect to others; therefore, use it after other people's names but not after your own name. You can use **-san** after a family name or a given name, but for adults, it's more common to use a family name than a given name when addressing someone.

Your Boss's or Teacher's First Name

Never call your Japanese bosses or teachers by their first names, no matter how long you've worked or studied with them. Call them by their last names with the appropriate titles that show their professional positions or functions, like **shachō** (shah-chohh) (*company president*) or **sensei** (sehn-sehh) (*professor*): **Tanaka shachō** (tah-nah-kah shah-chohh) (*President Tanaka*) or **Tanaka sensei** (tah-nah-kah sehn-sehh) (*Professor Tanaka*), for example. If their titles are unclear, use the suffix **-san** (sahn) following their last names, as in **Tanaka-san** (tah-nah-kah-sahn) (*Mr./Ms. Tanaka*).

"O-genki Desu Ka" to the Person You Saw Yesterday

In America, you can say *How are you?* to a person regardless of whether you just saw him yesterday. However, that usage is inappropriate for the closest Japanese equivalent, **O-genki desu ka.** (oh-gehn-kee deh-soo kah.), which literally means *Are you well?* Use this phrase only when you see someone you haven't seen for a while.

Note: Young people have started to say the short version, **Genki.** (gehn-kee.) (*Fine?*), as if it's for daily greeting. However, this expression is still quite different from the usage of **O-genki desu ka.**

"Sayōnara" to Your Family

Although many Westerners equate the word **sayōnara** (sah-yohh-nah-rah) with a casual *goodbye,* Japanese really only use it when they part with non-family members. When they leave their family members for school or work in the morning, they say **Ittekimasu.** (eet-teh-kee-mah-soo.), which literally means *I'll leave and come back.* (That translation may sound a little clunky, but this phrase is a customary Japanese goodbye.) In other contexts where Japanese have to part with their families, they usually say **Jā ne.** (jahh neh.) (*Okay? Well, see you?*) or **Jā mata ne.** (jahh mah-tah neh.) (*Okay, see you later.*) (For more information about **sayōnara,** see Chapter 6.)

"Thank You" for a Compliment

In English, if someone says "You look pretty in that dress" or "You're really smart," you usually say "Thanks!" right away, right? Otherwise, the other person may think you're snotty. However, Japanese custom is to deny the compliment by saying **Īe.** (eee-eh.) (*No.*) or **Zenzen.** (zehn-zehn.) (*Not at all.*) Now, I'm not saying you shouldn't give Japanese people compliments. After all, who doesn't love to receive a little positive feedback? Just be aware that Japanese people may deny your compliments verbally even though they're extremely happy when they hear them. It's just part of the Japanese modesty.

So if you're traveling in Japan and someone says **Nihongo ga jōzu desu ne.** (nee-hohn-goh gah johh-zoo deh-soo neh.) (*Your Japanese is good, isn't it?*), you'll impress that person even further if you skip the **Arigatō.** (ah-ree-gah-tohh.) (*Thanks.*) and say **Īe., Zenzen.,** or **Mada mada.** (mah-dah mah-dah.) (*Not yet, not yet.*)

"My Mom Is Pretty" to Outsiders

Another aspect of Japanese modesty (see the preceding section) is that you shouldn't tell outsiders (as in people other than your family) that your mom is pretty. Doing so sounds childish and immodest to Japanese. The same principle applies to other members of your family and other types of characteristics; don't tell outsiders that your little brother or your child is smart even if the kid is a valedictorian. The division between insiders and outsiders greatly limits what you can say.

Interestingly, this insider/outsider distinction can be extended to business contexts: For Japanese, their colleagues are their insiders while their clients are outsiders. So pay close attention when you're about to do business with Japanese.

"Yes" Right after Being Offered Food

When Japanese people are offered food or drink, they often say **Īe, ii desu.** (eeh-eh, eee deh-soo.) or **Īe, kekkō desu.** (ee-ee-eh, kehk-kohh deh-soo.), which both mean *No, thank you.* The host or hostess almost always offers the items again, so the guests eventually accept the offer by saying something like **Jā, itadakimasu. Arigatō gozaimasu.** (jahh, eeh-tah-dah-kee-mah-soo. ah-ree-gah-tohh goh-zah-ee-mah-soo.) (*Oh, then, I'll have some. Thank you.*)

However, when food or drinks are already brought, you can accept the offer right away, saying **jā, itadakimasu,** without trying to decline them once.

"Anata" When Talking to Someone

Although using someone's name and title repeatedly in a conversation may sound strange to you, that's precisely what you should do when speaking to a Japanese person. Your inclination is probably to use the pronoun **anata** (ah-nah-tah) (*you*), but don't; the pronoun **anata** is almost forbidden in Japanese conversations. For some reason, it sounds snobby or arrogant unless you're a wife addressing her husband. A wife can say to her husband, **Kore wa anata no?** (koh-reh wah ah-nah-tah noh.) (*Is this yours?*) In addition, a wife can call her husband by saying **anata,** as if saying *Honey!* That's a strange use of *you*, right?

"Aishite Imasu" to Express Likes

The literal translation of *to love* in Japanese is **aishite imasu** (ah-ee-shee-teh ee-mah-soo). However, people say this phrase in very serious occasions or contexts only, like when they're proposing. In English, you often hear people say they love something, like *I love dogs!*, but if you say **Inu o aishite iru.** (ee-noo oh ah-ee-shee-teh ee-mah-soo.) just to mean you love dogs, people may think you're weird; you'll sound like you want to get married to a dog or to dedicate the rest of your life to dogs. Similarly, if you say **Ano sūgaku no sensei o aishite imasu.** (ah-noh sooo-gah-koo noh senh-sehh oh ah-ee-shee-teh ee-mah-soo.) (*I love the math teacher.*), you'll sound scandalous or unethical.

TIP

To say you like someone or something in a general sense, use **suki desu** (soo-kee deh-soo) (*to like*) or **dai-suki desu** (dah-ee-soo-kee deh-soo) (*to like very much*), and mark the person or item you like with the particle **ga** (gah). For example, **Inu ga suki desu.** (ee-noo gah soo-kee deh-soo.) (*I love dogs.*) See Chapter 6 for more about **suki desu** and **dai-suki desu.**

"Do You Want Coffee?"

Japanese people feel shy about expressing their desire for foods and drinks to nonfamily members, so asking them **Kōhī ga hoshii desu ka.** (kohh-heee gah hoh-shee-ee deh-soo kah.) (*Do you want coffee?*) directly may make them uncomfortable. Instead, say **Kōhī wa ikaga desu ka.** (kohh-heee wah ee-kah-ga deh-soo kah.) (*How about coffee?*) Or if you're talking to your close friend or roommate, you can just say **Kōhī wa dō.** (kohh-heee wah dohh.) (*How about coffee?*) with a rising question intonation. **Dō** and **ikaga** both mean *how*, and **ikaga** is just the polite counterpart of **dō.**

Chapter **19**
Ten Favorite Japanese Expressions

L ife is full of **ki-do-ai-raku** (kee-doh-ah-ee-rah-koo) (*delight-anger-sorrow-fun*), and some phrases slip out of Japanese mouths repeatedly in response to different daily situations. Mastering these common expressions, whether they're simple adverbs or full sentences, is essential. That's why I give you ten popular Japanese expressions in this chapter.

REMEMBER

Although I note in Chapter 3 that Japanese doesn't use question marks, I've included them in some phrases in this chapter when the expression is very short and doesn't contain a question particle that would otherwise tip you off. That way, you can be sure to use these expressions with the proper intonation.

Yatta!

やった! **Yatta!** (yaht-tah!) (*I did it!*)

Say **Yatta!** when you accomplish something big, receive a great opportunity, or feel victorious. Passing a difficult test, getting the job you wanted, or winning the lottery — these all qualify as **Yatta!** material. I hope you get the opportunity to use this expression every day.

Hontō?

本当? **Hontō?** (hohn-tohh?) (*Really?*)

Say **Hontō?** with a rising intonation to confirm what you've just heard. Suppose your colleague tells you that she's getting married to your boss. Respond to the news by saying **Hontō?** What if your friend says that he'll give his car to you for free? Say **Hontō?** before saying thank you. You can say **Hontō?** in a lot of situations because so many unbelievable things happen every day.

Sasuga!

さすが! **Sasuga!** (sah-soo-gah!) (*I'm impressed by you, as usual!*)

The literal meaning of **sasuga** is *as might have been expected,* but the expression is commonly used as a compliment when someone who had a good reputation has done an impressive job as expected. Suppose your friend is a good athlete, and he has just won the gold medal in a skiing competition. You can tell him **Sasuga!**, meaning *I knew that you could win the prize! You were cool, as usual.* If your company president has just created a new day-care center and a recreation facility for the employees, you can say **Sasuga shachō!** (sah-soo-gah shah-chohh!) to her. It means *I admire your usual thoughtfulness, president.*

TIP

The difference between the adjective **sugoi** (soo-goh-ee) (*great*) and the saying **sasuga** is that **sasuga** means not just *great* but *great as always.*

Mochiron!

もちろん! **Mochiron!** (moh-chee-rohn!) (*Of course!*)

Mochiron is the favorite adverb of confident people. Use it when you're 100 percent confident in your opinion. So if your spouse ever asks you, "Would you marry me if you had a chance to do it all over again?" take my advice: Just say **mochiron** because you only live once and will never actually be faced with the decision (or with sleeping on the couch because you gave the wrong answer).

Ā, Yokatta.

ああ、よかった。**Ā, yokatta.** (ahh, yoh-kaht-tah.) (*Oh, good.*)

Say **Ā, yokatta.** every time you feel like saying *What a relief!* or *Oh, good.* If you're Mr. or Ms. Worrier, you may say **Ā, yokatta** ten times a day. For example

> Did I turn off the stove?
>
> Yes, you did.
>
> **Ā, yokatta.**
>
> My daughter was kidnapped!
>
> No, she's right there behind you.
>
> **Ā, yokatta.**

Zenzen.

ぜんぜん。**Zenzen.** (zehn-zehn.) (*Not at all.*)

Zenzen is an adverb used with a negative verb or adjective, but it's often used by itself as the phrase of denial. Suppose that someone asks you, "Am I disturbing you?" when he's not bothering you at all. Say **zenzen** and shake your head. (If he's your boss, though, you may still want to say **zenzen** even if he is disturbing you.)

Nani?

何? **Nani?** (nah-nee?) (*What?*)

Nani is a question word that's handy when you talk with a Japanese person. Say **Nani?** with a rising intonation when you don't hear or understand what the other person said.

TIP

You can also say **Nani?** when you can't believe or don't like what you hear. For example, suppose your significant other suddenly announces, "I'm getting married to Tom." If your name isn't Tom, you can surely say **Nani?** — assuming you have the ability to form words at that point.

Dōshiyō?

どうしよう。 **Dōshiyō?** (dohh-shee-yohh?) (*What shall I do?*)

Say **dōshiyō** when you're in a panic and have no idea what to do. You can repeat it over and over while you try to think of what to do: **Dōshiyō, dōshiyō, dōshiyō.** Now you sound like you're in big trouble. What happened? Oh, you've locked your car door with your keys and your dog inside? Maybe you should check out Chapter 18 for advice on contacting the police.

Yappari.

やっぱり。 **Yappari.** (yahp-pah-ree.) (*I knew it would happen.*)

Sometimes you have a vague suspicion that something will happen, and then it actually happens. At times like that, say **yappari.** Suppose that you haven't received a newspaper for the last month, but the newspaper delivery person says that he has dropped it off in front of your door every day. You suspect your neighbor is the culprit. One day, you wake up earlier than usual and see your neighbor picking up your newspaper. Your suspicion is confirmed, and you can say **yappari.**

Ā, Bikkurishita!

ああ、びっくりした。 **Ā, bikkurishita!** (ahh, beek-koo-ree-shee-tah!) (*What a surprise!*)

Say **Ā, bikkurishita!** when you're very surprised. If your family throws you a surprise party, say **Ā, bikkurishita!** after they shout out *Surprise!*

Chapter **20**

Ten Phrases That Make You Sound Fluent in Japanese

All languages have some obscure or unique expressions that provide an authentic flavor of the culture. The literal translations are often not transparent, and your command of these expressions depends on a deep understanding of the culture and values behind the language. This chapter introduces ten phrases that can make you sound Japanese. Master these expressions and use them in the right context to feel the Japanese mentality and spirit.

Enryo Shinaide.

遠慮しないで。 **Enryo shinai de.** (ehn-ryoh shee-nah-ee deh.) (*Don't be shy.*)

Japanese guests often appear to be very shy. They usually refuse offers of food or drink at least once, no matter what; it's just a part of their politeness. If you're the host, the customary response is to say **Enryo shinaide** right after your guest says

No, thank you. Using this phrase indicates that you're a gracious host and encourages your guest to accept your kind offer the second time.

Mottainai.

もったいない。**Mottainai.** (moht-tah-ee-nah-ee.) (*What a waste./It's too good.*)

Even though Japanese have become spoiled by disposable goods — such as plastic diapers, paper cups, and paper towels — they still hate to waste things. They constantly express their objections to waste by saying **mottainai.** *What? Are you going to throw away that sweater?* **Mottainai.** *Give it to me.*

TIP

This phrase doesn't just express your objection to throwing away things; you can also say **mottainai** if someone lacks a true appreciation for something of value, such as when your children don't appreciate good food. *What? You gave steak to the dog?* **Mottainai.**

You can also use **mottainai** for discussing how somebody is wasting her time with a particular romantic partner. For example, when you hear that Emily — the valedictorian and the most popular girl in school — is going out with Devin — a guy who's far from good-looking and spends all his time eating and sleeping — you may want to say **mottainai!**

O-saki Ni.

おさきに。**O-saki ni.** (oh-sah-kee nee.) (*Pardon me, but I'm leaving now.*)

Although the literal meaning of **o-saki ni** is *earlier*, Japanese use this expression to politely say goodbye in all sorts of contexts and locations — a waiting room, a restaurant, a library, a party, and so on. The **o** at the beginning of the expression **o-saki ni** is the honorific prefix. When you have to leave someplace earlier than a friend who is staying behind, or even a stranger that you've struck up a conversation with, tell those people **O-saki ni.** to display your thoughtfulness for the people who can't leave the place yet. In a business context, like at your workplace, you can add **shitsurei shimasu** (shee-tsoo-rehh shee-mah-soo) after **o-saki ni.** **Shitsurei shimasu** literally means *I'll be rude,* but it's a very polite way of saying goodbye to your superiors and business clients. (Flip to Chapter 6 for more about **shitsurei shimasu.**)

Kanpai!

乾杯! **Kanpai!** (kahn-pah-ee!) (*Toast!/Cheers!*)

When celebrating something, hold a glass of wine or sake and have a toast by saying **Kanpai! Kanpai** is used in almost all formal and informal gatherings in Japan. The one exception may be funeral and memorial services, where **kenpai** (kehn-pah-ee) or **itadakimasu** (ee-tah-dah-kee-mah-soo) is used instead. So the next time you have something to celebrate, don't hesitate to say **Kanpai!**

Ganbatte!

がんばって! **Ganbatte!** (gahn-baht-teh!) (*Try your best, and good luck!*)

Japanese often believe that the effort is more important than the result. Trying one's best is the only way to go. When your friend is going to take an important exam, tell him or her **Ganbatte!** And if you're seriously studying Japanese, I want to tell you **Ganbatte!**

Shikata ga nai.

仕方がない。**Shikata ga nai.** (shee-kah-tah gah nah-ee.) (*There's no choice.*) **Shikata** means *method*, so it literally means *A method does not exist.*

When you're in a difficult situation, look at all the possible solutions. If none of them will work well, choose a solution that you know isn't part of the best-case scenario and say **Shikata ga nai.** to convey your disappointment and acceptance of the given fact.

Suppose that you miss your plane home and no other flights are departing until tomorrow morning. You have to give up the idea of going home today. In such a context, say **Shikata ga nai.** and start looking for a hotel. Suppose that you can't find a hotel and have to give up the idea of sleeping on a bed. Say **Shikata ga nai.** again and sleep on a bench at the airport. The expression somehow smoothes out inevitably bad situations. Life goes on. **Shikata ga nai.**

Okage-sama De.

おかげさまで。**O-kage-sama de.** (oh-kah-geh-sah-mah de.) (*Luckily, thanks to you and other people.*)

If someone asks you **O-genki desu ka** (oh-gehn-kee deh-soo kah) (*How are you?*), answering with **Genki desu** (gehn-kee deh-soo) (*I'm fine*) is perfectly okay. However, you'll sound modest, thankful, and sophisticated if you say **O-kage-sama de.** instead. The original meaning of this very modest expression is that your well-being and health are due to gods, nature, and other people, including the person you're talking to. By the way, how are you?

Tsumaranai Mono Desu Ga.

つまらないものですが。**Tsumaranai mono desu ga.** (tsoo-mah-rah-nah-ee moh-noh deh-soo gah.) (*It's a trivial/boring item, but. . . .*)

Japanese people always bring a gift when invited to other people's houses for a meal. The items are usually quite expensive, but the givers always say **Tsumaranai mono desu ga,** an expression based on Japanese modesty. It's just a sentence fragment that means *It's a trivial or boring item, but [please accept it].* Next time you go to your Japanese friend's house for dinner, give her your gift as you say **Tsumaranai mono desu ga.,** even if you think it's an exceptionally good gift.

Yoroshiku.

宜しく。**Yoroshiku.** (yoh-roh-shee-koo.) (*I'm pleased to meet you./I appreciate your helping me.*)

Using the phrase **Yoroshiku.** shows your polite and modest attitude. The literal meaning of **yoroshiku** is *appropriately*, *favorably*, or *as needed*, but you can say it when you meet someone for the very first time. The concept behind this usage is *Please treat me appropriately.*; you wouldn't want to say such a thing directly, but alluding to it with **Yoroshiku.** speaks to the Japanese modesty. Just don't think about the literal meaning; use **Yoroshiku.** as an equivalent to *Nice to meet you.*

You can also say **yoroshiku** right after asking a favor of someone. The underlying idea is *Thank you for helping me, and I hope you handle it for me appropriately.*, which roughly means *I appreciate your helping me.*

Taihen Desu Ne.

大変ですね。**Taihen desu ne.** (tah-ee-hen deh-soo neh.) (*That's tough.*)

This expression is a phrase of sympathy. Use it when your friends tell you about their hardships related to sickness, financial problems, relationship troubles, or any other kind of difficult situation that requires physical efforts and/or causes mental stress, worries, or financial expense. Suppose that your friend tells you that he has to pay for five kids to go to college. You can tell him **Taihen desu ne.**

5
Appendixes

Use the mini-dictionary to look up words you can expect to use most often in Japanese conversations.

Reference some handy verb tables for when you aren't so sure about how to conjugate verbs.

Use the answer keys to check your work on the Fun & Games sections in each chapter.

Appendix A
Japanese-English Mini-Dictionary

A

agaru (ah-gah-roo) u: to rise

ageru (ah-geh-roo) ru: to give, to raise

aida (ah-ee-dah): between

aisu kurīmu (ah-ee-soo koo-reee-moo): ice cream

aka (ah-kah): red

akeru (ah-keh-roo) ru: to open

aki (ah-kee): autumn, fall

ame (ah-meh): rain, candy

Amerika (ah-meh-ree-kah): America

Amerikajin (ah-meh-ree-kah-jeen): American person

anata (ah-nah-tah): you

ane (ah-neh): older sister (plain)

ani (ah-nee): older brother (plain)

anime (ah-nee-meh): anime

ao (ah-oh): blue

apāto (ah-pahh-toh): apartment

apurikēshon (ah-poo-ree-keh-shohn): application software

are (ah-reh): that one (over there)

arigatō gozaimasu (ah-ree-gah-tohh goh-zah-ee-mah-soo): thank you

aru (ah-roo) irr: to exist

aruku (ah-roo-koo) u: to walk

asa (ah-sah): morning

asagohan (ah-sah-goh-hahn): breakfast

ashi (ah-shee): foot, leg

ashita (ah-shee-tah): tomorrow

asobu (ah-soh-boo) u: to play

asoko (ah-soh-koh): over there

atama (ah-tah-mah): head

atarashii (ah-tah-rah-sheee) i: new

atatakai (ah-tah-tah-kah-ee) i: warm

atsui (ah-tsoo-ee) i: hot (temperature)

B

banana (bah-nah-nah): banana

bangohan (bahn-goh-hahn): dinner

basu (bah-soo): bus

beddo (behd-doh): bed

bengoshi (behn-goh-shee): lawyer

benkyō suru (behn-kyohh soo-roo) irr: to study

bentō (behn-tohh): boxed meals

bijutsukan (bee-joo-tsoo-kahn): art museum

bīru (beee-roo): beer

biza (bee-zah): visa

bōshi (bohh-shee): hat

burausu (boo-rah-oo-soo): blouse

butaniku (boo-tah-nee-koo): pork

byōin (byohh-een): hospital

byōki (byohh-kee): illness

C

chairo (chah-ee-roh): brown

chawan (chah-wahn): teacup, rice bowl

chichi (chee-chee): father (plain)

chikaku (chee-kah-koo): near

chikatetsu (chee-kah-teh-tsoo): subway

chīsai (cheee-sah-ee) i (irr): small

chizu (chee-zoo): map

chīzu (cheee-zoo): cheese

chokorēto (choh-koh-rehh-toh): chocolate

chōshoku (chohh-shoh-koo): breakfast

Chūgoku (chooo-goh-koo): China

chūshajō (chooo-shah-johh): parking lot

chūshoku (chooo-shoh-koo): lunch

D

daidokoro (dah-ee-doh-koh-roh): kitchen

daigaku (dah-ee-gah-koo): university

daigakuin (dah-ee-gah-koo-een): graduate school

daijōbu (dah-ee-johh-boo) na: all right

dainingu (dah-ee-neen-goo): dining room

damasu (dah-mah-soo) u: to deceive

dare (dah-reh): who

dareka (dah-reh-kah): somebody

deguchi (deh-goo-chee): exit

dekiru (deh-kee-roo) ru: to be able to do

demo (deh-moh): but

denki (dehn-kee): electricity

densha (dehn-shah): train

denwa (dehn-wah): telephone

denwa-bangō (dehn-wah-bahn-gohh): telephone number

depāto (deh-pahh-toh): department store

dezāto (deh-zahh-toh): dessert

dō (dohh): how

Doitsu (doh-ee-tsoo): Germany

doko (doh-koh): where

dokoka (doh-koh-kah): somewhere

dōmo (dohh-moh): thanks

dore (doh-reh): which one

dorobō (doh-roh-bohh): thief

doru (doh-roo): dollar

dōryō (dohh-ryohh): co-worker

dōshite (dohh-shee-teh): why

doyōbi (doh-yohh-bee): Saturday

E

e (eh): picture (painting or drawing)

eakon (eh-ah-kohn): air-conditioning

ebi (eh-bee): shrimp

eiga (ehh-gah): movie

eigakan (ehh-gah-kahn): movie theater

Eigo (ehh-goh): English

eki (eh-kee): station (for trains and subways)

enpitsu (ehn-pee-tsoo): pencil

enpitsu kezuri (ehn-pee-tsoo keh-zoo-ree): pencil sharpener

erabu (eh-rah-boo) u: to select, to choose

erebētā (eh-reh-behh-tahh): elevator

F

fakkusu (fahk-koo-soo): fax
fōku (fohh-koo): fork
fude (foo-deh): brush
  (for calligraphy)
fugu (foo-goo): blowfish
fukai (foo-kah-ee) i: deep
fuku (foo-koo): clothes
fuku (foo-koo) u: to wipe
fukuro (foo-koo-roh): sack (bag)
fun (foon): minute
fune (foo-neh): ship
Furansu (foo-rahn-soo): France
furoba (foo-roh-bah): bathing room
furui (foo-roo-ee) i: old
  (for inanimate items)
fūtō (fooo-tohh): envelope
fuyu (foo-yoo): winter

G

gaika (gah-ee-kah): foreign money
gaikoku (gah-ee-koh-koo): foreign
  country
gaikokujin (gah-ee-koh-koo-jeen):
  foreigner
gakkō (gahk-kohh): school
gakusei (gah-koo-sehh): students
gamu (gah-moo): chewing gum
garō (gah-rohh): gallery
gasorin sutando (gah-soh-reen
  soo-tahn-doh): gas station
geijutsu (gehh-joo-tsoo): art
geijutsuka (gehh-joo-tsoo-kah):
  artist
geki (geh-kee): play
gekijō (geh-kee-johh): theater
  (for plays and performances)
gengo (gehn-goh): language

genkan (gehn-kahn): entrance
genki (gehn-kee) na: fine (healthy)
genkin (gehn-keen): cash
geta (geh-tah): clogs
getsuyōbi (geh-tsoo-yohh-bee):
  Monday
gin (geen): silver (metal)
ginkō (geen-kohh): bank
gitā (gee-tahh): guitar
go (goh): five
gogo (goh-goh): p.m., afternoon
go-gatsu (goh-gah-tsoo): May
gohan (goh-hahn): cooked rice
gomi (goh-mee): garbage, trash
gomibako (goh-mee-bah-koh):
  trash can
gorufu (goh-roo-foo): golf
gōtō (gohh-tohh): burglar
gyūniku (gyooo-nee-koo): beef
gyūnyū (gyooo-nyooo): milk

H

ha (hah): leaf, tooth
hachi (hah-chee): eight, bee
hachi-gatsu (hah-chee-gah-tsoo):
  August
hachimitsu (hah-chee-mee-tsoo):
  honey
hae (hah-eh): fly (insect)
haha (hah-hah): mother (plain)
hairu (hah-ee-roo) u: to enter
haisha (hah-ee-shah): dentist
haitatsu (hah-ee-tah-tsoo): delivery
haiyū (hah-ee-yooo): actor
hajimeru (hah-jee-meh-roo)
  ru: to begin (something)
hako (hah-koh): box
hakobu (hah-koh-boo) u: to carry

hakubutsukan (hah-koo-boo-tsoo-kahn): museum

hamigakiko (hah-mee-gah-kee-koh): toothpaste

hana (hah-nah): flower, nose

hanabi (hah-nah-bee): fireworks

hanashi (han-nah-shee): story

hanasu (hah-nah-soo) u: to speak

hanbun (hahn-boon): half

harau (hah-rah-oo) u: to pay

hari (hah-ree): needle

haru (hah-roo): spring

hasami (hah-sah-mee): scissors

hashi (hah-shee): chopsticks, bridge

hashigo (hah-shee-goh): ladder

hashira (hah-shee-rah): pillar

hashiru (hah-shee-roo) u: to run

hata (hah-tah): flag

hataraku (hah-tah-rah-koo) u: to work

hatsuon (hah-tsoo-ohn): pronunciation

hayai (hah-yah-ee) i: early, fast

hayaku (hah-yah-koo): quickly, early

hayashi (hah-yah-shee): woods

hebi (heh-bee): snake

heiwa (hehh-wah): peace

hen (hehn) na: weird, strange

henji (hehn-jee): reply (response)

henshin suru (hehn-sheen soo-roo): to send a reply through email or letters

heya (heh-yah): room

hi (hee): day, fire

hidari (hee-dah-ree): left

hidoi (hee-doh-ee) i: terrible

higashi (hee-gah-shee): east

hikari (hee-kah-ree): light (illumination)

hikidashi (hee-kee-dah-shee): drawer

hikōki (hee-kohh-kee): airplane

hiku (hee-koo) u: to pull

hikui (hee-koo-ee) i: low

hima (hee-mah): free time

himitsu (hee-mee-tsoo): secret

hiroi (hee-roh-ee) i: wide, spacious

hirugohan (hee-roo-goh-han): lunch

hisho (hee-shoh): secretary

hitai (hee-tah-ee): forehead

hito (hee-toh): person

hitsuji (hee-tsoo-jee): sheep

hiza (hee-zah): knee

hō (hohh): cheek

hōki (hohh-kee): broom

hon (hohn): book

honbako (hohn-bah-koh): bookcase

hondana (hohn-dah-nah): bookshelf

hone (hoh-neh): bone

hontō ni (hohn-tohh nee): really (truly)

hon'ya (hohn-yah): bookstore

hon'yaku (hohn-yah-koo): translation

hon'yakusha (hohn-yah-koo-shah): translator

hōrensō (hohh-rehn-sohh): spinach

hōritsu (hohh-ree-tsoo): law

hoshi (hoh-shee): star (in the sky)

hoshii (hoh-sheee) i: to want

hotchikisu (hoht-chee-kee-soo): stapler

hoteru (hoh-teh-roo): hotel

hyaku (hyah-koo): hundred

I

i (ee): stomach

ichi (ee-chee): one

ichi-gatsu (ee-chee-gah-tsoo): January

ichigo (ee-chee-goh): strawberry

ichiman (ee-chee-mahn): ten thousand

ie (ee-eh): house

Igirisu (ee-gee-ree-soo): England

ii (eee) i: good

ijiwaru (ee-jee-wah-roo) na: mean (unkind)

ika (ee-kah): squid

ike (ee-keh): pond

iku (ee-koo) irr: to go

ikura (ee-koo-rah): how much (price); salmon roe

ikutsu (ee-koo-tsoo): how many

ima (ee-mah): now, living room

imin (ee-meen): immigrant

imōto (ee-mohh-toh): younger sister

inaka (ee-nah-kah): countryside

infuruenza (een-foo-roo-ehn-zah): flu

instōru (een-soo-tohh-roo): to install software

inu (ee-noo): dog

iriguchi (ee-ree-goo-chee): entrance

iro (ee-roh): color

iroiro (ee-roh-ee-roh) na: various

iru (ee-roo) ru: to exist

iru (ee-roo) u: to need

isha (ee-shah): physician

ishi (ee-shee): stone

isogashii (ee-soh-gah-sheee) i: busy

isogu (ee-soh-goo) u: to hurry

issho ni (ees-shoh nee): together

isu (ee-soo): chair

itai (ee-tah-ee) i: painful

Itaria (ee-tah-ree-ah): Italy

ito (ee-toh): thread

itoko (ee-toh-koh): cousin

itsu (ee-tsoo): when

itsuka (ee-tsoo-kah): someday

itsumo (ee-tsoo-moh): always

iu (ee-oo or yoo-oo) u: to say

J

jagaimo (jah-gah-ee-moh): potato

jaketto (jah-keht-toh): jacket

ji (jee): o'clock

jigoku (jee-goh-koo): hell

jikan (jee-kahn): hour, time

jiko (jee-koh): accident

jinja (jeen-jah): Japanese shrine

jīnzu (jeeen-zoo): jeans

jisho (jee-shoh): dictionary

jitensha (jee-tehn-shah): bicycle

jiyū (jee-yooo): liberty

jōdan (johh-dahn): joke

joyū (joh-yooo): actress

jū (jooo): ten

jū-gatsu (jooo-gah-tsoo): October

jūgyōin (jooo-gyohh-een): employee

jūichi-gatsu (jooo-ee-chee-gah-tsoo): November

jūni-gatsu (jooo-nee-gah-tsoo): December

jūsho (jooo-shoh): address

jūsu (jooo-soo): juice

K

kaban (kah-bahn): bag

kabe (kah-beh): wall

kabin (kah-been): vase

kaeru (kah-eh-roo): frog

kaeru (kah-eh-roo) ru: to change

kaeru (kah-eh-roo) u: to return

kagaku (kah-gah-koo): science, chemistry

kagami (kah-gah-mee): mirror

kagi (kah-gee): key

kago (kah-goh): basket

kagu (kah-goo): furniture

kai (kah-ee): shellfish

kaisha (kah-ee-shah): company

kaishain (kah-ee-shah-een): company employee

kaji (kah-jee): fire (conflagration)

kaku (kah-koo) u: to write, to draw

kakusu (kah-koo-soo) u: to hide (something)

kame (kah-meh): turtle

kamera (kah-meh-rah): camera

kami (kah-mee): hair, paper, god

kaminari (kah-mee-nah-ree): thunder

Kanada (kah-nah-dah): Canada

kanashii (kah-nah-sheee) i: sad

kanban (kahn-bahn): sign (shop)

kangoshi (kahn-goh-shee): nurse

kani (kah-nee): crab

kanja (kahn-jah): patient (of a doctor)

Kankoku (kahn-koh-koo): South Korea

kanojo (kah-noh-joh): she, girlfriend

kanpai (kahn-pah-ee): toast (ceremonial drink)

kantan (kahn-tahn) na: easy, simple

kao (kah-oh): face

karada (kah-rah-dah): body (of a person or an animal)

karai (kah-rah-ee) i: hot (spicy)

kare (kah-reh): he, boyfriend

karendā (kah-rehn-dahh): calendar

kariru (kah-ree-roo) ru: to borrow

kasa (kah-sah): umbrella

kasu (kah-soo) u: to lend

kata (kah-tah): shoulder

katsu (kah-tsoo) u: to win

kau (kah-oo) u: to buy

kawa (kah-wah): river

kawaii (kah-wah-eee) i: cute

kayōbi (kah-yohh-bee): Tuesday

kazan (kah-zahn): volcano

kaze (kah-zeh): wind, cold (virus)

keisatsu (kehh-sah-tsoo): police

kēki (kehh-kee): cake

ki (kee): tree

kiiro (keee-roh): yellow

kinō (kee-nohh): yesterday

kinyōbi (keen-yohh-bee): Friday

kirei (kee-rehh) na: beautiful, clean

kiru (kee-roo) ru: to wear

kita (kee-tah): north

kitchin (keet-cheen): kitchen

kitte (keet-teh): postage stamp

kodomo (koh-doh-moh): child

kōen (kohh-ehn): park

kōhī (kohh-heee): coffee

koi (koh-ee): carp

kōjō (kohh-johh): factory

kōka (kohh-kah) na: expensive

kōkō (kohh-kohh): high school

koko (koh-koh): here

kokuseki (koh-koo-seh-kee): nationality

kome (koh-meh): uncooked rice

komugiko (koh-moo-gee-koh): flour

konban (kohn-bahn): tonight

kongetsu (kohn-geh-tsoo): this month

konnichiwa (kohn-nee-chee-wah): hello, good afternoon

konshū (kohn-shooo): this week

kore (koh-reh): this one

kōri (kohh-ree): ice

kōsaten (kohh-sah-tehn): intersection

koshi (koh-shee): hip

kōsui (kohh-soo-ee): perfume

kotae (koh-tah-eh): answer

kotoshi (koh-toh-shee): this year

kowai (koh-wah-ee) i: scary

kubi (koo-bee): neck

kuchi (koo-chee): mouth

kudamono (koo-dah-moh-noh): fruit

ku-gatsu (koo-gah-tsoo): September

kūkō (kooo-kohh): airport

kuni (koo-nee): country

kurai (koo-rah-ee) i: dark

kurejitto kādo (koo-reh-jeet-toh kahh-doh): credit card

kureru (koo-reh-roo) ru: to give

kuro (koo-roh): black

kuru (koo-roo) irr: to come

kuruma (koo-roo-mah): car

kūshitsu (koo-shee-tsoo): vacant room

kusuri (koo-soo-ree): medicine

kusuriya (koo-soo-ree-yah): drugstore

kutsu (koo-tsoo): shoe

kyō (kyohh): today

kyōkai (kyohh-kah-ee): church

kyonen (kyoh-nehn): last year

kyū (kyooo): nine

kyūkyūsha (kyooo-kyooo-shah): ambulance

kyūryō (kyoo-ryohh): salary

M

mado (mah-doh): window

mae (mah-eh): front

magaru (mah-gah-roo) u: to (make a) turn

mago (mah-goh): grandchildren

maguro (mah-goo-roh): tuna

majime (mah-jee-meh) na: serious

makura (mah-koo-rah): pillow

mame (mah-meh): beans

manabu (mah-nah-boo) u: to learn

manga (mahn-gah): Japanese comics

massugu (mahs-soo-goo): straight

mata (mah-tah): again

matsu (mah-tsoo) u: to wait

me (meh): eye

megane (meh-gah-neh): eyeglasses

michi (mee-chee): street

midori (mee-doh-ree): green

migi (mee-gee): right

mikan (mee-kahn): orange (fruit)

mimi (mee-mee): ear

minami (mee-nah-mee): south

mise (mee-seh): store

mizu (mee-zoo): water

mizuumi (mee-zoo-oo-mee): lake

mokuyōbi (moh-koo-yohh-bee): Thursday

mono (moh-noh): (tangible) thing

mori (moh-ree): forest

moshimoshi (moh-shee-moh-shee): hello (telephone)

motsu (moh-tsoo) u: to hold (to have in hand)

mukai gawa (moo-kah-ee gah-wah):
opposite side

mune (moo-neh): chest

mura (moo-rah): village

murasaki (moo-rah-sah-kee): purple

mushi (moo-shee): insect

muzukashii (moo-zoo-kah-sheee) i:
difficult

N

nabe (nah-beh): pot

naifu (nah-ee-foo): knife

naka (nah-kah): inside

namae (nah-mah-eh): name

nami (nah-mee): wave

namida (nah-mee-dah): tear

nana (nah-nah): seven

nani (nah-nee): what

nanika (nah-nee-kah): something

naru (nah-roo) u: to become

nashi (nah-shee): pear

natsu (nah-tsoo): summer

naze (nah-zeh): why

nedan (neh-dahn): price

nekkuresu (nehk-koo-reh-soo):
necklace

neko (neh-koh): cat

nekutai (neh-koo-tah-ee): tie

nemui (neh-moo-ee) i: sleepy

neru (neh-roo) ru: to sleep

netsu (neh-tsoo): fever

ni (nee): two

nichiyōbi (nee-chee-yohh-bee):
Sunday

nigai (nee-gah-ee) i: bitter

ni-gatsu (nee-gah-tsoo): February

Nihon (nee-hohn): Japan

Nihongo (nee-hohn-goh): Japanese
language

Nihonjin (nee-hohn-jeen): Japanese
person

niku (nee-koo): meat

nimotsu (nee-moh-tsoo): luggage

ningyō (neen-gyohh): doll

Nippon (neep-pohn): Japan

nishi (nee-shee): west

nodo (noh-doh): throat

nomu (noh-moo) u: to drink

noru (noh-roo) u: to get on
(transportation)

O

oba (oh-bah): aunt (plain)

obasan (oh-bah-sahn): aunt (polite)

obāsan (oh-bahh-sahn): grandmother
(polite)

oboeru (oh-boh-eh-roo) ru: to
memorize

o-cha (oh-chah): green tea

odoru (oh-doh-roo) u: to dance

ohayō (oh-hah-yohh): good morning

oji (oh-jee): uncle (plain)

ojisan (oh-jee-sahn): uncle (polite)

ojīsan (oh-jeee-sahn): grandfather
(polite)

o-kane (oh-kah-neh): money

okāsan (oh-kahh-sahn): mother
(polite)

ōkii (ohh-keee) i (irr): big

oku (oh-koo) u: to put

omoshiroi (oh-moh-shee-roh-ee) i:
interesting

omou (oh-moh-oo) u: to think

onaji (oh-nah-jee): same

onaka (oh-nah-kah): abdomen

onēsan (oh-nehh-sahn): older sister
(polite)

ongaku (ohn-gah-koo): music

onigiri (oh-nee-gee-ree): rice ball

onīsan (oh-neee-sahn): older brother (polite)

onna (ohn-nah): female

onna no hito (ohn-nah noh hee-toh): woman

oriru (oh-ree-roo) ru: to get off (transportation)

osoi (oh-soh-ee) i: late, slow

Ōsutoraria (ohh-soo-toh-rah-ree-ah): Australia

otoko (oh-toh-koh): male

otoko no hito (oh-toh-koh noh hee-toh): man

otōsan (oh-tohh-sahn): father (polite)

otōto (oh-tohh-toh): younger brother

owaru (oh-wah-roo) u: to end

oyasuminasai (oh-yah-soo-mee-nah-sah-ee): good night

oyogu (oh-yoh-goo) u: to swim

P

pan (pahn): bread

pan'ya (pahn-yah): bakery

pasokon (pah-soh-kohn): computer

pasupōto (pah-soo-pohh-toh): passport

pātī (pahh-tee): party (event)

piano (pee-ah-noh): piano

piza (pee-zah): pizza

R

raigetsu (rah-ee-geh-tsoo): next month

rainen (rah-ee-nehn): next year

raishū (rah-ee-shooo): next week

rajio (rah-jee-oh): radio

reizōko (rehh-zohh-koh): refrigerator

remon (reh-mohn): lemon

renshū (rehn-shooo): practice (exercise)

reshīto (reh-sheee-toh): receipt

resutoran (reh-soo-toh-rahn): restaurant

ribingu (ree-been-goo): living room

rimokon (ree-moh-kohn): remote control

ringo (reen-goh): apple

roku (roh-koo): six

roku-gatsu (roh-koo-gah-tsoo): June

ryōjikan (ryohh-jee-kahn): consulate

ryokō (ryoh-kohh): trip

ryōri (ryohh-ree): cooking

ryōshūsho (ryohh-shooo-shoh): receipt

S

saifu (sah-ee-foo): wallet

sakana (sah-kah-nah): fish

sake (sah-keh): rice wine, salmon

sakka (sahk-kah): writer (author)

sakkā (sahk-kahh): soccer

sakura (sah-koo-rah): cherry (tree)

samishii (sah-mee-sheee) i: lonely

samui (sah-moo-ee) i: cold (temperature)

san (sahn): three

sandaru (sahn-dah-roo): sandal

san-gatsu (sahn-gah-tsoo): March

sangurasu (sahn-goo-rah-soo): sunglasses

sara (sah-rah): dish (plate)

sarada (sah-rah-dah): salad

saru (sah-roo): monkey

satō (sah-tohh): sugar

sayōnara (sah-yohh-nah-rah): goodbye

seiseki (seh-ee-seh-kee): grade (rating in school)

seito (sehh-toh): pupil

sekai (seh-kah-ee): world

semai (seh-mah-ee) i: narrow

sengetsu (sehn-geh-tsoo): last month

sensei (sehn-sehh): teacher

senshū (sehn-shooo): last week

sētā (sehh-tahh): sweater

shachō (shah-chohh): company president

shakkuri (shahk-koo-ree): hiccup

shashin (shah-sheen): photograph

shatsu (shah-tsoo): shirt

shi (shee): four

shichi (shee-chee): seven

shichi-gatsu (shee-chee-gah-tsoo): July

shi-gatsu (shee-gah-tsoo): April

shigoto (shee-goh-toh): job

shinbun (sheen-boon): newspaper

shinshitsu (sheen-shee-tsoo): bedroom

shinu (shee-noo) u: to die

shio (shee-oh): salt

shiro (shee-roh): white

shita (shee-tah): under

shitsumon (shee-tsoo-mohn): question

shizen (shee-zehn): nature

shizuka (shee-zoo-kah) na: quiet

shōhizei (shohh-hee-zehh): sales tax

shokugyō (shoh-koo-gyohh): occupation

shokuji (shoh-koo-jee): meal

shomei (shoh-mehh): signature

shū (shooo): week

shuccho suru (shooch-choh soo-roo): go on a business trip

shukkin suru (shook-keen soo-roo): come to work

shukudai (shoo-koo-dah-ee): homework

shumi (shoo-mee): hobby

sobo (soh-boh): grandmother (plain)

sofu (soh-foo): grandfather (plain)

soko (soh-koh): there (near you)

sore (soh-reh): that one (near you)

soto (soh-toh): outside

sugiru (soo-gee-roo) ru: to pass by

suiei (soo-ee-ehh): swimming

suītsu (soo-eee-tsu): sweets

suiyōbi (soo-ee-yohh-bee): Wednesday

sukāto (soo-kahh-toh): skirt

suki (soo-kee) na: to like

sūpā (sooo-pahh): supermarket

supagettī (soo-pah-geht-teee): spaghetti

Supein (soo-peh-een): Spain

suru (soo-roo): to do

sūtsu (sooo-tsoo): suit

sūtsukēsu (sooo-tsoo-kehh-soo): suitcase

suwaru (soo-wah-roo): to sit down

suzushii (soo-zoo-sheee) i: cool (temperature)

T

tabako (tah-bah-koh): tobacco

taberu (tah-beh-roo): to eat

taishikan (tah-ee-shee-kahn): embassy

taiyō (tah-ee-yohh): sun

takai (tah-kah-ee) i: expensive

takushī (tah-koo-sheee): taxi

tamago (tah-mah-goh): egg

te (teh): hand, arm

tegami (teh-gah-mee): letter

tengoku (tehn-goh-koo): heaven

tenisu (teh-nee-soo): tennis

tenpu suru (tehn-poo soo-roo): to attach a document

terebi (teh-reh-bee): TV

tōi (tohh-ee) i: far

tomodachi (toh-moh-dah-chee): friend

tonari (toh-nah-ree): next door

toriniku (toh-ree-nee-koo): chicken (meat)

toru (toh-roo) u: to take

totemo (toh-teh-moh): very

tsukau (tsoo-kah-oo) u: to use

tsuku (tsoo-koo) u: to arrive

tsukuru (tsoo-koo-roo) u: to make

tsumetai (tsoo-meh-tah-ee) i: cold (temperature)

U

ude (oo-deh): arm

ue (oo-eh): above

uma (oo-mah): horse

umi (oo-mee): ocean

unagi (oo-nah-gee): eel

unten suru (oon-tehn soo-roo) irr: to drive

ureshii (oo-reh-sheee) i: glad

uru (oo-roo) u: to sell

urusai (oo-roo-sah-ee) i: noisy

usagi (oo-sah-gee): rabbit

ushiro (oo-shee-roh): behind

uso (oo-soh): lie

uta (oo-tah): song

utau (oo-tah-oo) u: to sing

W

wain (wah-een): wine

wakai (wah-kah-ee) i: young

wakaru (wah-kah-roo) u: to understand

warui (wah-roo-ee) i: bad

wasureru (wah-soo-reh-roo) ru: to forget

wataru (wah-tah-roo) u: to cross over

watashi (wah-tah-shee): I

Y

yakyū (yah-kyooo): baseball

yama (yah-mah): mountain

yasai (yah-sah-ee): vegetable

yasui (yah-soo-ee) i: cheap

yasumi (yah-soo-mee): vacation

yasumu (yah-soo-moo) u: to rest

yomu (yoh-moo) u: to read

yon (yohn): four

yoyaku (yoh-yah-koo): reservation

yubi (yoo-bee): finger

yūbin bangō (yooo-been bahn-gohh): zip code

yūbinkyoku (yooo-been-kyoh-koo): post office

yuki (yoo-kee): snow

yume (yoo-meh): dream

yūshoku (yooo-shoh-koo): dinner

Z

zenzen (zehn-zehn): not at all

zubon (zoo-bohn): pants

English-Japanese Mini-Dictionary

A

abdomen: **onaka** (oh-nah-kah)

above: **ue** (oo-eh)

accident: **jiko** (jee-koh)

actor: **haiyū** (hah-ee-yooo)

actress: **joyū** (joh-yooo)

address: **jūsho** (jooo-shoh)

afternoon: **gogo** (goh-goh)

again: **mata** (mah-tah)

air-conditioning: **eakon** (eh-ah-kohn)

airplane: **hikōki** (hee-kohh-kee)

airport: **kūkō** (kooo-kohh)

all right: **daijōbu** (dah-ee-johh-boo) na

always: **itsumo** (ee-tsoo-moh)

ambulance: **kyūkyūsha** (kyooo-kyooo-shah)

America: **Amerika** (ah-meh-ree-kah)

American person: **Amerikajin** (ah-meh-ree-kah-jeen)

anime: **anime** (ah-nee-meh)

answer: **kotae** (koh-tah-eh)

apartment: **apāto** (ah-pahh-toh)

apple: **ringo** (reen-goh)

application (software): **apurikēshon** (ah-poo-ree-keh-shohn)

April: **shi-gatsu** (shee-gah-tsoo)

arm: **ude** (oo-deh), **te** (teh)

to arrive (v.): **tsuku** (tsoo-koo) u

art: **geijutsu** (gehh-joo-tsoo)

art museum: **bijutsukan** (bee-joo-tsoo-kahn)

artist: **geijutsuka** (gehh-joo-tsoo-kah)

attach (a document): **tenpu suru** (tehn-poo soo-roo)

August: **hachi-gatsu** (hah-chee-gah-tsoo)

aunt: **oba** (oh-bah), **obasan** (oh-bah-sahn)

Australia: **Ōsutoraria** (ohh-soo-toh-rah-ree-ah)

autumn: **aki** (ah-kee)

B

bad: **warui** (wah-roo-ee) i

bag: **kaban** (kah-bahn)

bakery: **pan'ya** (pahn-yah)

banana: **banana** (bah-nah-nah)

bank: **ginkō** (geen-kohh)

baseball: **yakyū** (yah-kyooo)

basket: **kago** (kah-goh)

bathing room: **furoba** (foo-roh-bah)

to be able to do (v.): **dekiru** (deh-kee-roo) ru

beans: **mame** (mah-meh)

beautiful: **kirei** (kee-rehh) na

to become: **naru** (nah-roo) u

bed: **beddo** (behd-doh)

bedroom: **shinshitsu** (sheen-shee-tsoo)

bee: **hachi** (hah-chee)

beef: **gyūniku** (gyooo-nee-koo)

beer: **bīru** (beee-roo)

to begin (something) (v.): **hajimeru** (hah-jee-meh-roo) ru

behind: **ushiro** (oo-shee-roh)

between: **aida** (ah-ee-dah)

bicycle: **jitensha** (jee-tehn-shah)

big: **ōkii** (ohh-keee) i (irr)

bitter: **nigai** (nee-gah-ee) i

black: **kuro** (koo-roh)

blouse: **burausu** (boo-rah-oo-soo)

blowfish: **fugu** (foo-goo)

blue: **ao** (ah-oh)

body (of a person or animal): **karada** (kah-rah-dah)

bone: **hone** (hoh-neh)

book: **hon** (hohn)

bookcase: **honbako** (hohn-bah-koh)

bookshelf: **hondana** (hohn-dah-nah)

bookstore: **hon'ya** (hohn-yah)

to borrow (v.): **kariru** (kah-ree-roo) ru

box: **hako** (hah-koh)

boyfriend: **kare** (kah-reh)

bread: **pan** (pahn)

breakfast: **asagohan** (ah-sah-goh-hahn), **chōshoku** (chohh-shoh-koo)

bridge: **hashi** (hah-shee)

broom: **hōki** (hohh-kee)

brother (older): **ani** (ah-nee), **onīsan** (oh-neee-sahn)

brother (younger): **otōto** (oh-tohh-toh)

brown: **chairo** (chah-ee-roh)

brush (for calligraphy): **fude** (foo-deh)

burglar: **gōtō** (gohh-tohh)

bus: **basu** (bah-soo)

busy: **isogashii** (ee-soh-gah-sheee) i

but: **demo** (deh-moh)

to buy (v.): **kau** (kah-oo) u

C

cake: **kēki** (kehh-kee)

calendar: **karendā** (kah-rehn-dahh)

camera: **kamera** (kah-meh-rah)

Canada: **Kanada** (kah-nah-dah)

candy: **ame** (ah-meh)

car: **kuruma** (koo-roo-mah)

carp: **koi** (koh-ee)

to carry (v.): **hakobu** (hah-koh-boo) u

cash: **genkin** (gehn-keen)

cat: **neko** (neh-koh)

chair: **isu** (ee-soo)

to change (v.): **kaeru** (kah-eh-roo) ru

to chat on an electornic device (v): **chatto suru** (chaht-toh soo-roo)

cheap: **yasui** (yah-soo-ee) i

cheek: **hō** (hohh)

cheese: **chīzu** (cheee-zoo)

chemistry: **kagaku** (kah-gah-koo)

cherry (tree): **sakura** (sah-koo-rah)

chest: **mune** (moo-neh)

chicken (meat): **toriniku** (toh-ree-nee-koo)

child: **kodomo** (koh-doh-moh)

China: **Chūgoku** (chooo-goh-koo)

chocolate: **chokorēto** (cho-koh-rehh-toh)

to choose (v.): **erabu** (eh-rah-boo) u

chopsticks: **hashi** (hah-shee)

church: **kyōkai** (kyohh-kah-ee)

clean: **kirei** (kee-reh-ee) na

clogs (wooden): **geta** (geh-tah)

clothes: **fuku** (foo-koo)

coffee: **kōhī** (kohh-heee)

cold (virus): **kaze** (kah-zeh)

cold (temperature): **samui** (sah-moo-ee) i; **tsumetai** (tsoo-meh-tah-ee) i

color: **iro** (ee-roh)

to come (v.): **kuru** (koo-roo) irr

company: **kaisha** (kah-ee-shah)

comics (Japanese): **manga** (mahn-gah)

company employee: **kaishain** (kah-ee-shah-een)

company president: **shachō** (shah-chohh)

computer: **pasokon** (pah-soh-kohn)

conditioner: **kondhishonā** (kohn-dhee-shoh-nahh)

consulate: **ryōjikan** (ryohh-jee-kahn)

cookie: **kukkiī** (kook-keee)

cooking: **ryōri** (ryohh-ree)

cool (temperature): **suzushii** (soo-zoo-sheee) i

country: **kuni** (koo-nee)

countryside: **inaka** (ee-nah-kah)

cousin: **itoko** (ee-toh-koh)

co-worker: **dōryō** (dohh-ryohh)

crab: **kani** (kah-nee)

credit card: **kurejitto kādo** (koo-reh-jeet-toh kahh-doh)

to cross over (v.): **wataru** (wah-tah-roo) u

custom declaration: **zeikan shinkokusho** (zehh-kahn sheen-koh-koo-shoh)

cute: **kawaii** (kah-wah-eee) i

D

to dance (v.): **odoru** (oh-doh-roo) u

dark: **kurai** (koo-rah-ee) i

day: **hi** (hee)

to deceive (v.): **damasu** (dah-mah-soo) u

December: **jūni-gatsu** (jooo-nee-gah-tsoo)

deep: **fukai** (foo-kah-ee) i

delivery: **haitatsu** (hah-ee-tah-tsoo)

dentist: **haisha** (hah-ee-shah)

department store: **depāto** (deh-pahh-toh)

dessert: **dezāto** (deh-zahh-toh)

dictionary: **jisho** (jee-shoh)

to die (v.): **shinu** (shee-noo) u

difficult: **muzukashii** (moo-zoo-kah-sheee) i

dining room: **dainingu** (dah-ee-neen-goo)

dinner: **bangohan** (bahn-goh-hahn), **yūshoku** (yooo-shoh-koo)

dish (plate): **sara** (sah-rah)

to do (v.): **suru** (soo-roo) irr

dog: **inu** (ee-noo)

doll: **ningyō** (neen-gyohh)

dollar: **doru** (doh-roo)

to download (a file): **daunrōdo** (dah-oon-roh-doh)

to draw (v.): **kaku** (kah-koo) u

drawer: **hikidashi** (hee-kee-dah-shee)

dress: **wanpīsu** (wahn-peee-soo)

to drink (v.): **nomu** (noh-moo) u

to drive (v.): **unten suru** (oon-tehn soo-roo) irr

drugstore: **kusuriya** (koo-soo-ree-yah)

E

ear: **mimi** (mee-mee)

early: **hayai** (hah-yah-ee) i, **hayaku** (hah-yah-koo)

east: **higashi** (hee-gah-shee)

easy: **kantan** (kahn-tahn) na

to eat (v.): **taberu** (tah-beh-roo) ru

eel: **unagi** (oo-nah-gee)

eight: **hachi** (hah-chee)

electricity: **denki** (dehn-kee)

elevator: **erebētā** (eh-reh-behh-tahh)

email address: **mēru adoresu** (mehh-roo ah-doh-reh-soo)

embassy: **taishikan** (tah-ee-shee-kahn)

employee: **jūgyōin** (jooo-gyohh-een)

to end (v.): **owaru** (oh-wah-roo) u

England: **Igirisu** (ee-gee-ree-soo)

English: **eigo** (ehh-goh)

to enter (v.): **hairu** (hah-ee-roo) u

entrance: **genkan** (gehn-kahn), **iriguchi** (ee-ree-goo-chee)

envelope: **fūtō** (fooo-tohh)

to exist (v.): **aru** (ah-roo) u (irr); **iru** (ee-roo) ru

exit: **deguchi** (deh-goo-chee)

expensive: **kōka** (kohh-kah) na, **takai** (tah-kah-ee) i

eye: **me** (meh)

eyeglasses: **megane** (meh-gah-neh)

F

face: **kao** (kah-oh)

factory: **kōjō** (kohh-johh)

fall (autumn): **aki** (ah-kee)

far: **tōi** (tohh-ee) i

fast: **hayai** (hah-yah-ee) i

father: **chichi** (chee-chee), **otōsan** (oh-tohh-sahn)

fax: **fakkusu** (fahk-koo-soo)

February: **ni-gatsu** (nee-gah-tsoo)

female: **onna** (ohn-nah)

fever: **netsu** (neh-tsoo)

fine (healthy): **genki** (gehn-kee) na

finger: **yubi** (yoo-bee)

fire (flame): **hi** (hee)

fire (conflagration): **kaji** (kah-jee)

fireworks: **hanabi** (hah-nah-bee)

fish: **sakana** (sah-kah-nah)

fitness club: **fittonesu kurabu** (feet-toh-neh-soo kuh-rah-boo)

five: **go** (goh)

flag: **hata** (hah-tah)

flour: **komugiko** (koh-moo-gee-koh)

flower: **hana** (hah-nah)

flu: **infuruenza** (een-foo-roo-ehn-zah)

fly (insect): **hae** (hah-eh)

foot: **ashi** (ah-shee)

forehead: **hitai** (hee-tah-ee)

foreign country: **gaikoku** (gah-ee-koh-koo)

foreigner: **gaikokujin** (gah-ee-koh-koo-jeen)

foreign money: **gaika** (gah-ee-kah)

forest: **mori** (moh-ree)

to forget (v.): **wasureru** (wah-soo-reh-roo) ru

fork: **fōku** (fohh-koo)

four: **shi** (shee), **yon** (yohn)

France: **Furansu** (foo-rahn-soo)

free time: **hima** (hee-mah)

Friday: **kinyōbi** (keen-yohh-bee)

friend: **tomodachi** (toh-moh-dah-chee)

frog: **kaeru** (kah-eh-roo)

front: **mae** (mah-eh)

fruit: **kudamono** (koo-dah-moh-noh)

furniture: **kagu** (kah-goo)

G

gallery: **garō** (gah-rohh)

garbage: **gomi** (koh-mee)

gas station: **gasorin sutando**
(gah-soh-reen soo-tahn-doh)

Germany: **Doitsu** (doh-ee-tsoo)

to get off (transportation) (v.):
oriru (oh-ree-roo) ru

to get on (transportation) (v.):
noru (noh-roo) u

girlfriend: **kanojo** (kah-noh-joh)

to give (v.): **ageru** (ah-geh-roo) ru,
kureru (koo-reh-roo) ru

glad: **ureshii** (oo-reh-sheee) i

glasses (eyeglasses): **megane**
(meh-gah-neh)

to go (v.): **iku** (ee-koo)
u (irr)

god: **kami** (kah-mee)

golf: **gorufu** (goh-roo-foo)

good: **ii** (eee) i (irr)

good afternoon: **konnichiwa**
(kohn-nee-chee-wah)

goodbye: **sayōnara**
(sah-yohh-nah-rah)

good morning: **ohayō** (oh-hah-yohh)

good night: **oyasuminasai**
(oh-yah-soo-mee-nah-sah-ee)

grade (rating in school): **seiseki**
(seh-ee-seh-kee)

graduate school: **daigakuin**
(dah-ee-gah-koo-een)

grandchildren: **mago** (mah-goh)

grandfather: **ojisan** (oh-jeee-sahn),
sofu (soh-foo)

grandmother: **obāsan** (oh-bahh-
sahn), **sobo** (soh-boh)

green: **midori** (mee-doh-ree)

guitar: **gitā** (gee-tahh)

H

hair: **kami** (kah-mee)

half: **hanbun** (hahn-boon)

hamburger: **hanbāgā**
(hahn-bahh-gahh)

hand: **te** (teh)

hat: **bōshi** (bohh-shee)

he: **kare** (kah-reh)

head: **atama** (ah-tah-mah)

heaven: **tengoku** (tehn-goh-koo)

hell: **jigoku** (jee-goh-koo)

hello: **konnichiwa**
(kohn-nee-chee-wah)

hello (telephone greeting):
moshimoshi
(moh-shee-moh-shee)

here: **koko** (koh-koh)

hiccup: **shakkuri** (shahk-koo-ree)

to hide (something) (v.): **kakusu**
(kah-koo-soo) u

high school: **kōkō** (kohh-kohh)

hip: **koshi** (koh-shee)

hobby: **shumi** (shoo-mee)

to hold (to have in hand) (v.): **motsu**
(moh-tsoo) u

homepage: **hōmupēji**
(hoh-moo-peh-jee)

homework: **shukudai**
(shoo-koo-dah-ee)

honey: **hachimitsu**
(hah-chee-mee-tsoo)

horse: **uma** (oo-mah)

hospital: **byōin** (byohh-een)

hot (spicy): **karai** (kah-rah-ee) i

hot (temperature): **atsui**
(ah-tsoo-ee) i

hotel: **hoteru** (hoh-teh-roo)

hour: **jikan** (jee-kahn)

house: **ie** (ee-eh)

how: **dō** (dohh)

how many: **ikutsu** (ee-koo-tsoo)

how much (price): **ikura** (ee-koo-rah)

hundred: **hyaku** (hyah-koo)

to hurry (v.): **isogu** (ee-soh-goo) u

I

I: **watashi** (wah-tah-shee)

ice: **kōri** (kohh-ree)

ice cream: **aisu kurīmu** (ah-ee-soo koo-reee-moo)

illness: **byōki** (byohh-kee)

immigrant: **imin** (ee-meen)

insect: **mushi** (moo-shee)

inside: **naka** (nah-kah)

to install software: **instōru** (een-soo-tohh-roo)

interesting: **omoshiroi** (oh-moh-shee-roh-ee) i

Internet: **intānetto** (een-tah-neht-toh)

intersection: **kōsaten** (kohh-sah-tehn)

Italy: **Itaria** (ee-tah-ree-ah)

J

jacket: **jaketto** (jah-keht-toh)

January: **ichi-gatsu** (ee-chee-gah-tsoo)

Japan: **Nihon** (nee-hohn), **Nippon** (neep-pohn)

Japanese language: **Nihongo** (nee-hohn-goh)

Japanese person: **Nihonjin** (nee-hohn-jeen)

jeans: **jīnzu** (jeeen-zoo)

job: **shigoto** (shee-goh-toh)

joke: **jōdan** (johh-dahn)

juice: **jūsu** (jooo-soo)

July: **shichi-gatsu** (shee-chee-gah-tsoo)

June: **roku-gatsu** (roh-koo-gah-tsoo)

K

key: **kagi** (kah-gee)

kitchen: **daidokoro** (dah-ee-doh-koh-roh), **kitchin** (keet-cheen)

knee: **hiza** (hee-zah)

knife: **naifu** (nah-ee-foo)

L

ladder: **hashigo** (hah-shee-goh)

lake: **mizuumi** (mee-zoo-oo-mee)

language: **gengo** (gehn-goh)

last month: **sengetsu** (sehn-geh-tsoo)

last week: **senshū** (sehn-shooo)

last year: **kyonen** (kyoh-nehn)

late: **osoi** (oh-soh-ee) i

law: **hōritsu** (hohh-ree-tsoo)

lawyer: **bengoshi** (behn-goh-shee)

leaf: **ha** (hah)

to learn (v.): **manabu** (mah-nah-boo) u

left: **hidari** (hee-dah-ree)

leg: **ashi** (ah-shee)

lemon: **remon** (reh-mohn)

to lend (v.): **kasu** (kah-soo) u

letter: **tegami** (teh-gah-mee)

liberty: **jiyū** (jee-yooo)

lie: **uso** (oo-soh)

light (illumination): **hikari** (hee-kah-ree)

to like (v.): **suki** (soo-kee) na

living room: **ima** (ee-mah), **ribingu** (ree-been-goo)

log in: **roguin** (roh-goo-een)

log out: **roguauto** (roh-goo-ah-oo-toh)

lonely: **samishii** (sah-mee-sheee) i

low: **hikui** (hee-koo-ee) i

luggage: **nimotsu** (nee-moh-tsoo)

lunch: **chūshoku** (chooo-shoh-koo), **hirugohan** (hee-roo-goh-han)

M

to make (v.): **tsukuru** (tsoo-koo-roo) u

male: **otoko** (oh-toh-koh)

man: **otoko no hito** (oh-toh-koh noh hee-toh)

March: **san-gatsu** (sahn-gah-tsoo)

May: **go-gatsu** (goh-gah-tsoo)

meal: **shokuji** (shoh-koo-jee)

mean (unkind): **ijiwaru** (ee-jee-wah-roo) na

meat: **niku** (nee-koo)

medicine: **kusuri** (koo-soo-ree)

to memorize (v.): **oboeru** (oh-boh-eh-roo) ru

milk: **gyūnyū** (gyooo-nyooo)

minute: **fun** (foon)

mirror: **kagami** (kah-gah-mee)

Monday: **getsuyōbi** (geh-tsoo-yohh-bee)

money: **o-kane** (oh-kah-neh)

monkey: **saru** (sah-roo)

morning: **asa** (ah-sah)

mother: **haha** (hah-hah), **okāsan** (oh-kahh-sahn)

mountain: **yama** (yah-mah)

mouth: **kuchi** (koo-chee)

movie: **eiga** (ehh-gah)

movie theater: **eigakan** (ehh-gah-kahn)

museum: **hakubutsukan** (hah-koo-boo-tsoo-kahn)

music: **ongaku** (ohn-gah-koo)

N

name: **namae** (nah-mah-eh)

narrow: **semai** (seh-mah-ee) i

nationality: **kokuseki** (koh-koo-seh-kee)

nature: **shizen** (shee-zehn)

near: **chikaku** (chee-kah-koo)

neck: **kubi** (koo-bee)

to need: **iru** (ee-roo) u

needle: **hari** (hah-ree)

new: **atarashii** (ah-tah-rah-sheee)

newspaper: **shinbun** (sheen-boon)

next door: **tonari** (toh-nah-ree)

next month: **raigetsu** (rah-ee-geh-tsoo)

next week: **raishū** (rah-ee-shooo)

next year: **rainen** (rah-ee-nehn)

nine: **kyū** (kyooo)

noisy: **urusai** (oo-roo-sah-ee) i

north: **kita** (kee-tah)

nose: **hana** (hah-nah)

not at all: **zenzen** (zehn-zehn)

November: **jūichi-gatsu** (jooo-ee-chee-gah-tsoo)

now: **ima** (ee-mah)

nurse: **kangoshi** (kahn-goh-shee)

O

occupation: **shokugyō** (shoh-koo-gyohh)

ocean: **umi** (oo-mee)

o'clock: **ji** (jee)

October: **jū-gatsu** (jooo-gah-tsoo)

old (inanimate item): **furui** (foo-roo-ee) i

one: **ichi** (ee-chee)

to open (something) (v.): **akeru** (ah-keh-roo) ru

opposite side: **mukai gawa**
(moo-kah-ee gah-wah)

orange (fruit): **mikan** (mee-kahn)

outside: **soto** (soh-toh)

over there: **asoko** (ah-soh-koh)

P

painful: **itai** (ee-tah-ee) i

pancreas: **suizō** (soo-ee-zohh)

pants: **zubon** (zoo-bohn)

paper: **kami** (kah-mee)

park: **kōen** (kohh-ehn)

parking lot: **chūshajō**
(chooo-shah-johh)

party (event): **pātī** (pahh-tee)

to pass by (v.): **sugiru**
(soo-gee-roo) ru

passport: **pasupōto**
(pah-soo-pohh-toh)

password: **pasuwādo**
(pah-soo-wahh-doh)

patient (doctor's): **kanja** (kahn-jah)

to pay (v.): **harau** (hah-rah-oo) u

peace: **heiwa** (hehh-wah)

pear: **nashi** (nah-shee)

pencil: **enpitsu** (ehn-pee-tsoo)

pencil sharpener: **enpitsu kezuri**
(ehn-pee-tsoo keh-zoo-ree)

perfume: **kōsui** (kohh-soo-ee)

person: **hito** (hee-toh)

photograph: **shashin** (shah-sheen)

physician: **isha** (ee-shah)

piano: **piano** (pee-ah-noh)

picture (painting or drawing): **e** (eh)

pillar: **hashira** (hah-shee-rah)

pillow: **makura** (mah-koo-rah)

pizza: **piza** (pee-zah)

play (drama): **geki** (geh-kee)

to play (v.): **asobu** (ah-soh-boo) u

p.m.: **gogo** (goh-goh)

police: **keisatsu** (kehh-sah-tsoo)

pond: **ike** (ee-keh)

pork: **butaniku** (boo-tah-nee-koo)

post office: **yūbinkyoku**
(yooo-been-kyoh-koo)

pot: **nabe** (nah-beh)

potato: **jagaimo** (jah-gah-ee-moh)

practice (exercise): **renshū**
(rehn-shooo)

presentation: **purezentēshon**
(poo-reh-zehn-tehh-shohn)

price: **nedan** (neh-dahn)

pronunciation: **hatsuon**
(hah-tsoo-ohn)

to pull (v.): **hiku** (hee-koo) u

pupil: **seito** (sehh-toh)

purple: **murasaki** (moo-rah-sah-kee)

to put (v.): **oku** (oh-koo) u

Q

question: **shitsumon**
(shee-tsoo-mohn)

quickly: **hayaku** (hah-yah-koo)

quiet: **shizuka** (shee-zoo-kah) na

R

rabbit: **usagi** (oo-sah-gee)

radio: **rajio** (rah-jee-oh)

rain: **ame** (ah-meh)

to raise (v.): **ageru** (ah-geh-roo) ru

to read (v.): **yomu** (yoh-moo) u

really (truly): **hontō ni** (hohn-
tohh nee)

receipt: **reshīto** (reh-sheee-toh)

red: **aka** (ah-kah)

refrigerator: **reizōko** (rehh-zohh-koh)

remote control: **rimokon** (ree-moh-kohn)

reply (response): **henji** (hehn-jee)

reservation: **yoyaku** (yoh-yah-koo)

to rest (v.): **yasumu** (yah-soo-moo) u

restaurant: **resutoran** (reh-soo-toh-rahn)

to return (v.): **kaeru** (kah-eh-roo) u

rice bowl: **chawan** (chah-wahn)

rice (cooked): **gohan** (goh-hahn)

rice (uncooked): **kome** (koh-meh)

rice wine: **sake** (sah-keh)

right: **migi** (mee-gee)

to rise (v.): **agaru** (ah-gah-roo) u

river: **kawa** (kah-wah)

room: **heya** (heh-yah)

to run (v.): **hashiru** (hah-shee-roo) u

S

sack (bag): **fukuro** (foo-koo-roh)

sad: **kanashii** (kah-nah-sheee) i

salad: **sarada** (sah-rah-dah)

salary: **kyūryō** (kyoo-ryohh)

sales tax: **shōhizei** (shohh-hee-zehh)

salmon: **sake** (sah-keh)

salmon roe: **ikura** (ee-koo-rah)

salt: **shio** (shee-oh)

same: **onaji** (oh-nah-jee)

sandal: **sandaru** (sahn-dah-roo)

sandwich: **sandoicchi** (sahn-doh-eech-chee)

Saturday: **doyōbi** (doh-yohh-bee)

to say (v.): **iu** (ee-oo *or* yoo-oo) u

scary: **kowai** (koh-wah-ee) i

school: **gakkō** (gahk-kohh)

science: **kagaku** (kah-gah-koo)

scissors: **hasami** (hah-sah-mee)

secret: **himitsu** (hee-mee-tsoo)

secretary: **hisho** (hee-shoh)

to select (v.): **erabu** (eh-rah-boo) u

to sell (v.): **uru** (oo-roo) u

September: **ku-gatsu** (koo-gah-tsoo)

serious: **majime** (mah-jee-meh) na

seven: **nana** (nah-nah) or **shichi** (shee-chee)

shampoo: **shanpū** (shahn-pooh)

she: **kanojo** (kah-noh-joh)

sheep: **hitsuji** (hee-tsoo-jee)

shellfish: **kai** (kah-ee)

ship: **fune** (foo-neh)

shirt: **shatsu** (shah-tsoo)

shoe: **kutsu** (koo-tsoo)

shoulder: **kata** (kah-tah)

shrimp: **ebi** (eh-bee)

sign (shop): **kanban** (kahn-bahn)

signature: **shomei** (shoh-mehh)

silver (metal): **gin** (geen)

simple: **kantan** (kahn-tahn) na

to sing (v.): **utau** (oo-tah-oo) u

sister (older): **ane** (ah-neh), **onēsan** (oh-nehh-sahn)

sister (younger): **imōto** (ee-mohh-toh)

to sit down (v.): **suwaru** (soo-wah-roo) u

six: **roku** (roh-koo)

skirt: **sukāto** (soo-kahh-toh)

to sleep (v.): **neru** (neh-roo) ru

sleepy: **nemui** (neh-moo-ee) i

slow: **osoi** (oh-soh-ee) i

small: **chīsai** (cheee-sah-ee) i (irr)

smartphone: **sumāto fon** (soo-mahh-toh)

snake: **hebi** (heh-bee)

snow: **yuki** (yoo-kee)

soccer: **sakkā** (sahk-kahh)

somebody: **dareka** (dah-reh-kah)

something: **nanika** (nah-nee-kah)

somewhere: **dokoka** (doh-koh-kah)

song: **uta** (oo-tah)

south: **minami** (mee-nah-mee)

South Korea: **Kankoku** (kahn-koh-koo)

spacious: **hiroi** (hee-roh-ee) i

spaghetti: **supagettī** (soo-pah-geht-teee)

Spain: **Supein** (soo-peh-een)

to speak (v.): **hanasu** (hah-nah-soo) u

spinach: **hōrensō** (hohh-rehn-sohh)

spring: **haru** (hah-roo)

squid: **ika** (ee-kah)

stamp (postage stamp): **kitte** (keet-teh)

stapler: **hotchikisu** (hoht-chee-kee-soo)

star (in the sky): **hoshi** (hoh-shee)

station (for trains and subways): **eki** (eh-kee)

stomach: **i** (ee)

stone: **ishi** (ee-shee)

store: **mise** (mee-seh)

story: **hanashi** (han-nah-shee)

straight: **massugu** (mahs-soo-goo)

strange: **hen** (hehn) na

strawberry: **ichigo** (ee-chee-goh)

streaming: **sutorēmingu** (soo-toh-reee-meen-goo)

street: **michi** (mee-chee)

students: **gakusei** (gah-koo-sehh)

to study (v.): **benkyō suru** (behn-kyohh soo-roo) irr

subway: **chikatetsu** (chee-kah-teh-tsoo)

sugar: **satō** (sah-tohh)

suit: **sūtsu** (sooo-tsoo)

suitcase: **sūtsukēsu** (sooo-tsoo-kehh-soo)

summer: **natsu** (nah-tsoo)

sun: **taiyō** (tah-ee-yohh)

Sunday: **nichiyōbi** (nee-chee-yohh-bee)

sunglasses: **sangurasu** (sahn-goo-rah-soo)

supermarket: **sūpā** (sooo-pahh)

sweater: **sētā** (sehh-tahh)

to swim (v.): **oyogu** (oh-yoh-goo) u

swimming: **suiei** (soo-ee-ehh)

T

tobacco: **tabako** (tah-bah-koh)

to take (v.): **toru** (toh-roo) u

taxi: **takushī** (tah-koo-sheee)

tea (green tea): **o-cha** (oh-chah)

teacher: **sensei** (sehn-sehh)

teacup: **chawan** (chah-wahn)

tear: **namida** (nah-mee-dah)

telephone: **denwa** (dehn-wah)

telephone number: **denwa-bangō** (dehn-wah-bahn-gohh)

ten: **jū** (jooo)

tennis: **tenisu** (teh-nee-soo)

ten thousand: **ichiman** (ee-chee-mahn)

terrible: **hidoi** (hee-doh-ee) i

thank you: **arigatō gozaimasu** (ah-ree-gah-tohh goh-zah-ee-mah-soo), **dōmo** (dohh-moh)

that one (near you): **sore** (soh-reh)

that one (over there): **are** (ah-reh)

theater (for plays and performances): **gekijō** (geh-kee-johh)

there (near you): **soko** (soh-koh)

thief: **dorobō** (doh-roh-bohh)

thing: **mono** (moh-noh)

to think (v.): **omou** (oh-moh-oo) u

this month: **kongetsu** (kohn-geh-tsoo)

this one: **kore** (koh-reh)

this week: **konshū** (kohn-shooo)

this year: **kotoshi** (koh-toh-shee)

thread: **ito** (ee-toh)

three: **san** (sahn)

throat: **nodo** (noh-doh)

thunder: **kaminari** (kah-mee-nah-ree)

Thursday: **mokuyōbi** (moh-koo-yohh-bee)

tie: **nekutai** (neh-koo-tah-ee)

time: **jikan** (jee-kahn)

toast (ceremonial drink): **kanpai** (kahn-pah-ee)

today: **kyō** (kyohh)

together: **issho ni** (ees-shoh nee)

tomorrow: **ashita** (ah-shee-tah)

tonight: **konban** (kohn-bahn)

tooth: **ha** (hah)

toothpaste: **hamigakiko** (hah-mee-gah-kee-koh)

train: **densha** (dehn-shah)

translation: **hon'yaku** (hohn-yah-koo)

translator: **hon'yakusha** (hohn-yah-koo-shah)

trash: **gomi** (goh-mee)

tree: **ki** (kee)

trip: **ryokō** (ryoh-kohh)

Tuesday: **kayōbi** (kah-yohh-bee)

tuna: **maguro** (mah-goo-roh)

to (make a) turn (v.): **magaru** (mah-gah-roo) u

turtle: **kame** (kah-meh)

TV: **terebi** (teh-reh-bee)

two: **ni** (nee)

U

umbrella: **kasa** (kah-sah)

uncle: **oji** (oh-jee), **ojisan** (oh-jee-sahn)

under: **shita** (shee-tah)

to understand (v.): **wakaru** (wah-kah-roo) u

university: **daigaku** (dah-ee-gah-koo)

to upload (a file): **appurōdo** (ahp-poo-roh-doh)

to use (v.): **tsukau** (tsoo-kah-oo) u

user: **yūzā** (yooo-zahh)

V

vacant room: **kūshitsu** (koo-shee-tsoo)

vacation: **yasumi** (yah-soo-mee)

various: **iroiro** (ee-roh-ee-roh) na

vase: **kabin** (kah-been)

vegetable: **yasai** (yah-sah-ee)

very: **totemo** (toh-teh-moh)

village: **mura** (moo-rah)

volcano: **kazan** (kah-zahn)

W

to wait (v.): **matsu** (mah-tsoo) u

to walk (v.): **aruku** (ah-roo-koo) u

wall: **kabe** (kah-beh)

wallet: **saifu** (sah-ee-foo)

to want (v.): **hoshii** (hoh-sheee) i

warm: **atatakai** (ah-tah-tah-kah-ee) i

water: **mizu** (mee-zoo)

wave: **nami** (nah-mee)

to wear (v.): **kiru** (kee-roo) ru

Wednesday: **suiyōbi** (soo-ee-yohh-bee)

week: **shū** (shooo)

weird: **hen** (hehn) na

west: **nishi** (nee-shee)

what: **nani** (nah-nee)

when: **itsu** (ee-tsoo)

where: **doko** (doh-koh)

which one: **dore** (doh-reh)

white: **shiro** (shee-roh)

who: **dare** (dah-reh)

why: **dōshite** (dohh-shee-teh), **naze** (nah-zeh)

wide: **hiroi** (hee-roh-ee) i

to win (v.): **katsu** (kah-tsoo) u

wind: **kaze** (kah-zeh)

window: **mado** (mah-doh)

wine: **wain** (wah-een)

winter: **fuyu** (foo-yoo)

to wipe (v.): **fuku** (foo-koo) u

woman: **onna no hito** (ohn-nah noh hee-toh)

woods: **hayashi** (hah-yah-shee)

to work (v.): **hataraku** (hah-tah-rah-koo) u

world: **sekai** (seh-kah-ee)

to write (v.): **kaku** (kah-koo) u

writer (author): **sakka** (sahk-kah)

Y

yellow: **kiiro** (keee-roh)

yesterday: **kinō** (kee-nohh)

you: **anata** (ah-nah-tah)

young: **wakai** (wah-kah-ee) i

Z

zip code: **yūbin bangō** (yooo-been bahn-gohh)

Appendix B
Verb Tables

Note: The plain/informal affirmative present form and the plain/informal negative present form are also called the dictionary form and the **nai**-form, respectively, in this book.

Regular Japanese Verbs

Regular Ru-verbs Ending with –eru
For example: 食べる taberu (*to eat*)

	Affirmative Present	Affirmative Past	Negative Present	Negative Past
Plain/Informal	食べる taberu	食べた tabeta	食べない tabenai	食べなかった tabenakatta
Polite/Neutral	食べます tabemasu	食べました tabemashita	食べません tabemasen	食べませんでした tabemasen deshita
Te-Form		食べて tabete		食べなくて tabenakute 食べないで tabenai de
Stem Form			食べ tabe	

Regular Ru-verbs Ending with -iru

For example: 着る kiru (*to wear*)

	Affirmative Present	Affirmative Past	Negative Present	Negative Past
Plain/Informal	着る kiru	着た kita	着ない kinai	着なかった kinakatta
Polite/Neutral	着ます kimasu	着ました kimashita	着ません kimasen	着ませんでした kimasen deshita
Te-Form		着て kite		着なくて kinakute 着ないで kinai de
Stem Form			着 ki	

Regular U-verbs Ending with -ku

For example: 書く kaku (*to write*)

	Affirmative Present	Affirmative Past	Negative Present	Negative Past
Plain/Informal	書く kaku	書いた kaita	書かない kakanai	書かなかった kakanakatta
Polite/Neutral	書きます kakimasu	書きました kakimashita	書きません kakimasen	書きませんでした kakimasen deshita
Te-Form		書いて kaite		書かなくて kakanakute 書かないで kakanai de
Stem Form		書き kaki		

Regular U-verbs Ending with -gu

For example: 泳ぐ oyogu (*to swim*)

	Affirmative Present	Affirmative Past	Negative Present	Negative Past
Plain/Informal	泳ぐ oyogu	泳いだ oyoida	泳がない oyoganai	泳がなかった oyoganakatta
Polite/Neutral	泳ぎます oyogimasu	泳ぎました oyogimashita	泳ぎません oyogimasen	泳ぎませんでした oyogimasen deshita
Te-Form		泳いで oyoide		泳がなくて oyoganakute 泳がないで oyoganai de
Stem Form			泳ぎ oyogi	

Regular U-verbs Ending with -su

For example: 貸す kasu (*to lend*)

	Affirmative Present	Affirmative Past	Negative Present	Negative Past
Plain/Informal	貸す kasu	貸した kashita	貸さない kasanai	貸さなかった kasanakatta
Polite/Neutral	貸します kashimasu	貸しました kashimashita	貸しません kashimasen	貸しませんでした kashimasen deshita
Te-Form		貸して kashite		貸さなくて kasanakute 貸さないで kasanai de
Stem Form			貸し kashi	

Regular U-verbs Ending with -mu
For example: 飲む nomu (*to drink*)

	Affirmative Present	Affirmative Past	Negative Present	Negative Past
Plain/Informal	飲む nomu	飲んだ nonda	飲まない nomanai	飲まなかった nomanakatta
Polite/Neutral	飲みます nomimasu	飲みました nomimashita	飲みません nomimasen	飲みませんでした nomimasen deshita
Te-Form		飲んで nonde		飲まなくて nomanakute 飲まないで nomanai de
Stem Form			飲み nomi	

Regular U-verbs Ending with -nu
For example: 死ぬ shinu (*to die*)

	Affirmative Present	Affirmative Past	Negative Present	Negative Past
Plain/Informal	死ぬ shinu	死んだ shinda	死なない shinanai	死ななかった shinanakatta
Polite/Neutral	死にます shinimasu	死にました shinimashita	死にません shinimasen	死にませんでした shinimasen deshita
Te-Form		死んで shinde		死ななくて shinanakute 死なないで shinanai de
Stem Form			死に shini	

Regular U-verbs Ending with -bu

For example: 飛ぶ tobu (*to fly*)

	Affirmative Present	Affirmative Past	Negative Present	Negative Past
Plain/Informal	飛ぶ tobu	飛んだ tonda	飛ばない tobanai	飛ばなかった tobananakatta
Polite/Neutral	飛びます tobimasu	飛びました tobimashita	飛びません tobimasen	飛びませんでした tobimasen deshita
Te-Form		飛んで tonde		飛ばなくて tobanakute 飛ばないで tobanai de
Stem Form			飛び tobi	

Regular U-verbs Ending with a Vowel Directly Followed by -u

For example: 買う kau (*to buy*)

	Affirmative Present	Affirmative Past	Negative Present	Negative Past
Plain/Informal	買う kau	買った katta	買わない kawanai	買わなかった kawanakatta
Polite/Neutral	買います kaimasu	買いました kaimashita	買いません kaimasen	買いませんでした kaimasen deshita
Te-Form		買って katte		買わなくて kawanakute 買わないで kawanai de
Stem Form			買い kai	

Regular U-verbs Ending with –ru
For example: 切る kiru (*to cut*)

	Affirmative Present	Affirmative Past	Negative Present	Negative Past
Plain/Informal	切る kiru	切った kitta	切らない kiranai	切らなかった kiranakatta
Polite/Neutral	切ります kirimasu	切りました kirimashita	切りません kirimasen	切りませんでした kirimasen deshita
Te-Form		切って kitte		切らなくて kiranakute 切らないで kiranai de
Stem Form			切り kiri	

Regular U-verbs Ending with –tsu
For example: 待つ matsu (*to wait*)

	Affirmative Present	Affirmative Past	Negative Present	Negative Past
Plain/Informal	待つ matsu	待った matta	待たない matanai	待たなかった matanakatta
Polite/Neutral	待ちます machimasu	待ちました machimashita	待ちません machimasen	待ちませんでした machimasen deshita
Te-Form		待って matte		待たなくて matanakute 待たないで matanai de
Stem Form			待ち machi	

Irregular Japanese Verbs

		Affirmative Present	Affirmative Past	Negative Present	Negative Past
する **suru**	*Plain/Informal*	する suru	した shita	しない shinai	しなかった shinakatta
to do	*Polite/Neutral*	します shimasu	しました shimashita	しません shimasen	しませんでした shimasen deshita
	Te-Form		して shite		しなくて shinakute しないで shinai de
	Stem Form			し shi	

		Affirmative Present	Affirmative Past	Negative Present	Negative Past
来る **kuru**	*Plain/Informal*	来る kuru	来た kita	来ない konai	来なかった konakatta
to come	*Polite/Neutral*	来ます kimasu	来ました kimashita	来ません kimasen	来ませんでした kimasen deshita
	Te-Form		来て kite		来なくて konakute 来ないで konai de
	Stem Form			き ki	

		Affirmative Present	Affirmative Past	Negative Present	Negative Past
ある **aru**	*Plain/Informal*	ある aru	あった atta	ない nai	なかった nakatta
to exist	*Polite/Neutral*	あります arimasu	ありました arimashita	ありません arimasen	ありませんでした arimasen deshita
	Te-Form		あって atte		なくて nakute
	Stem Form			あり ari	

		Affirmative Present	Affirmative Past	Negative Present	Negative Past
行く **iku**	*Plain/Informal*	行く iku	行った itta	行かない ikanai	行かなかった ikanakatta
to go	*Polite/Neutral*	行きます ikimasu	行きました ikimashita	行きません ikimasen	行きませんでした ikimasen deshita
	Te-Form		行って itte		行かなくて ikanakute 行かないで ikanai de
	Stem Form			行き iki	

		Affirmative Present	Affirmative Past	Negative Present	Negative Past
いらっしゃる **irassharu** *to exist* (honorific)	*Plain/Informal*	いらっしゃる irassharu	いらっしゃった irasshatta	いらっ しゃらない irassharanai	いらっしゃらなかった irassharanakatta
	Polite/Neutral	いらっ しゃいます irass- haimasu	いらっし ゃいました irass- haimashita	いらっし ゃいません irass- haimasen	いらっしゃいま せんでした irasshaimasen deshita
	Te-Form	いらっしゃって irasshatte		いらっしゃらなくて irassharanakute いらっしゃらないで irassharanai de	
	Stem Form	いらっしゃり irasshari			

		Affirmative Present	Affirmative Past	Negative Present	Negative Past
下さる **kudasaru** *to give to* *me/us* (honorific)	*Plain/Informal*	下さる kudasaru	下さった kudasatta	下さらない kudasaranai	下さらなかった kudasaranakatta
	Polite/Neutral	下さいます kuda- saimasu	下さいました kuda- saimashita	下さいません kuda- saimasen	下さいませんでした kudasaimasen deshita
	Te-Form	下さって kudasatte		下さらなくて kudasaranakute 下さらないで kudasaranai de	
	Stem Form	下さり kudasari			

Appendix C

Answer Key

The following are all the answers to the Fun & Games activities.

Chapter 2: Checking out the Japanese Sounds and Scripts

1. おばあさん **obāsan;** 2. おじいさん **ojīsan;** 3. きって **kitte;** 4. かんぱい **kanpai;**
5. 日本人 **Nihonjin**

Chapter 3: Warming up with Japanese Grammar Basics

Activity 1: 1. a; 2. b; 3. a; 4. b; 5. b; 6. b

Activity 2: 何 **nan;** これ **kore;** あれ **are**

Chapter 4: Getting Your Numbers, Times, and Measurements Straight

1. d; 2. c; 3. b; 4. a; 5. e

Chapter 5: Speaking Japanese at Home

1. b; 2. d; 3. c; 4. f; 5. a; 6. e

Chapter 6: Ice Breakers and Conversation Starters

1. c; 2. d; 3. e; 4. b; 5. a

Chapter 7: Getting to Know You

1. d; 2. a; 3. b; 4. c

Chapter 8: Asking for Directions

1. d; 2. g; 3. e; 4. c; 5. h; 6. b; 7. f; 8. a

Chapter 9: Dealing with Money in a Foreign Land

1. 15,000円 **ichi-man go-sen en**; 2. 6,000円 **roku-sen en**; 3. 160円 **hyaku roku-jū en**; 4. 1,500円 **sen go-hyaku en**; 5. 7円 **nana en**

Chapter 10: Shopping Made Easy

1. c; 2. b; 3. a; 4. e; 5. d

Chapter 11: Going Out on the Town

ā	w	u	r	y	z	i	d	f	b	f	ō
g	e	k	i	j	ō	z	p	d	i	h	t
a	b	t	h	ī	e	a	a	k	j	p	r
r	h	o	k	o	s	k	z	k	u	r	h
ō	i	s	ī	ō	t	a	ā	h	t	k	e
ū	o	h	b	w	ā	y	ē	f	s	h	ō
k	ā	o	k	m	t	a	z	ē	u	t	u
h	a	k	u	b	u	t	s	u	k	a	n
ē	y	a	n	j	t	z	ā	u	a	u	ī
n	f	n	e	i	g	a	k	a	n	o	ō

Chapter 12: Taking Care of Business and Telecommunications

1. e; 2. c; 3. k; 4. j; 5. a; 6. b; 7. d; 8. g; 9. h; 10. i; 11. f

Chapter 13: Planning a Trip

a. スーツケース **sūtsukēsu**; b. 歯ブラシ **haburashi**; c. プルオーバーパーカー **puruōbā pākā**; d. 帽子 **bōshi**; e. サンダル **sandaru**; f. サングラス sangurasu; g. スニーカー **sunīkā**

Chapter 14: Making Your Way Around: Planes, Trains, Taxis, and More

1. タクシー **takushī**; 2. 飛行機 **hikōki**; 3. 新幹線 **shinkansen** *or* 電車 **densha**; 4. バス **basu**; 5. 船 **fune** *or* フェリー **ferī**

Chapter 15: Finding a Place to Stay

1. チェックアウト **chekku-auto**; 2. 無線LAN **musen LAN**; 3. ルームサービス **rūmu sābisu**; 4. 空室 **kūshitsu**; 5. 朝食 **chōshoku**

Chapter 16: Handling Emergencies

1. 頭 **atama**; 2. 耳 **mimi**; 3. 目 **me**; 4. 口 **kuchi**; 5. 首 **kubi**; 6. 肩 **kata**; 7. 腕 **ude** *or* 手 **te**; 8. 胸 **mune**; 9. 手 **te**; 10. 膝 **hiza**; 11. 足 **ashi**

Index

boat travel, 278

body language, 22

body parts, 308–309, 310

borrowing office supplies, 234

borrow/rent (verb), 170–171, 283

bosses, addressing, 231, 330

bowing, 22, 118

box lunches, from train stations, 260

breakfast dishes, 97–98

bring (verb), 225

-bu, verbs ending with, 375

building areas, 234–235

buildings, historical, 254

bullet train, 276

bus travel, 278–279

business cards, exchanging, 117

business hotels, 287, 289

business hours, 183

business-related terminology. *See* work

but, 188, 206, 237–238, 243

butcher shops, 177

buy (verb), 195, 375. *See also* shopping

C

calls, telephone. *See* telephone conversations

can form of verbs (potential form), 141–142, 171, 215, 270

capsule hotels, 288, 289

car travel, 281–284

cardinal points, 150–151

cash, 169–171

casual Japanese-style bars, 217–218, 219

categories, comparing, 194–195

cause (verb), 315

celebrating, expression used when, 341

characters

kana, 9–10, 23–27

kanji, 9–10, 27–30, 68–69

Cheat Sheet, 5

check, requesting at restaurant, 215–216

checking in to accommodations, 295–298

checking out of accommodations, 301

Chinese (kanji) characters, 9–10, 27–30, 68–69

cleaning, 101

clerks

bank, 165–167

hotel, 295–298, 301

clients, calling, 238–240

climate, in Japan, 257

close (verb), 202

clothes

packing for trips, 261

shopping for, 184–189

clubs, 216–218

coat sizes, 187

coffee, offering politely, 333

coins used in Japan, 169–170

colors, 185, 188–189

come (verb), 141, 224–225, 319, 377

come out (verb), 312

comic books, Japanese, 324

commands, giving, 139

comparisons, making

of costs, 292–293

with like, 136–137

of room sizes, 290

of transportation methods, 270–271

when shopping, 189–195

compliments, 132, 135, 331, 336

computer terms, 245–246

confirmation, words for, 60

conjugating adjectives, 55–56

conjugating verbs, 2, 46, 48–52. *See also specific verbs*; verbs

conjunction words, 255

consonants, 9, 19–20

content questions, 41–42

contents of stolen item, describing, 318–319

contrasts, using particles for, 206

convenience stores, 179

conversations

about art, 137–138

about doing things, 140–141

about family, 126–129

about games, 139–140

about music, 138–139

about sports, 137

H

habits, talking about, 102–103

hate, expressing, 100, 101

have (verbs), 129–132, 234. *See also* exist

healthcare, Japanese, 305. *See also* medical attention

help
  asking for, 303–304, 305
  offering, 304–305

hiragana characters, 23–27, 28, 38

historical buildings, 254

hobbies, talking about, 137–140

hospitals, 306–307

hostels, 288

hotels, 287–288. *See also* accommodations

hours, 71–73

house
  bathroom terms, 91–92
  bedroom terms, 91
  common activities in, 101–102
  dining room terms, 89–90
  inviting others to, 224–227
  kitchen terms, 88–89
  laundry room terms, 92–93
  living room terms, 90
  naming items in, 11
  rooms and structures, 87–88
  storage room terms, 93–95
  using Japanese in, 9, 87

how, 41, 154

"How are you?," 113, 330

how much, 41

however, 255

hurt (verb), 310

hypothetical scenarios, expressing, 293

I

"I knew it would happen," 338

icebreakers, 114–117

icons, explained, 4

if, 293

illness. *See* medical attention

"I'm sorry," 121

I/me, 44–45

immersion programs, 323

immigration, going through, 272–273

include (verb), 258–259

inflection part, adjectives, 55, 56–57

informal speech style. *See* plain/informal speech style

injuries, treatment for, 314. *See also* medical attention

in-laws, terms for, 129

inns, Japanese-style, 288

insider/outsider distinction, 331

instruments, musical, 138–139

interests, discussing, 137–140

internal organs, 309

International Driving Permit, 283

intonation, 3, 20–21

introductions, 111, 117–119

invitations
  to go out, 221–224
  to house, 224–227

"involved in," 314–315

irregular adjectives, 56–57

irregular verbs
  can form, 141
  conjugating, 48, 50–51
  tables for learning, 377–379

-iru, verbs ending with, 372

i-type adjectives, 54–57, 55

J

Japan rail pass, 254

Japanese climate, 257

Japanese comic books, 324

Japanese healthcare, 305

Japanese language. *See also specific language parts*
  learning quickly, 323–327
  overview, 1–5

Japanese musical instruments, 138

Japanese-style bars, 217–218, 219

Japanese-style baths, 289

Japanese-style inns, 288

jobs. *See* work

"just like," 136–137

K

Kabuki theater, 204

kana characters (phonetic symbols), 9–10, 23–27

kanji (Chinese) characters, 9–10, 27–30, 68–69

karaoke, 218–220, 325

katakana characters, 23–27

kitchen terms, 88–89

-ku, verbs ending with, 372

L

landmarks, referring to, 155

language immersion programs, 323

language lessons, exchanging, 326

language skills, discussing, 135–137

laundry room terms, 92–93

learning Japanese quickly, 323–327

leave (verb), 275

leaving messages, 240–244

legal help, getting, 319

lend (verb), 170–171, 373

length of time, telling, 74

lessons, exchanging language, 326

"let's go," 222

license, driver's, 282, 283

like (verb), 100–101, 332

LINE social media system, 248

literal translations, 3

live (verb), 132–133

living room terms, 90

location

  basic answers regarding, 147–150

  exact, getting, 150–153

  expressing, 130

  question words for, 194

  to travel to, choosing, 253–257

lodging. *See* accommodations

long vowels, 18, 26

look for, 180

lost belongings, reporting to police, 317–319

love (verb), 332

luggage, 261

lunch dishes, 98–99

M

manga, 324

may (verb), 60, 94

me, 44–45

meals, paying for, 215–216. *See also* restaurants, eating at

mealtimes, 95

measurements, 84

meat, purchasing, 177

medical attention

  body parts, referring to, 308–309

  diagnosis, receiving, 312–313

  doctors, types of, 305–306

  hospitals, 306–307

  Japanese healthcare, 305

  overview, 305

  pain, explaining, 309–311

  symptoms, explaining, 311–312

  treatment, getting, 313–314

medication, 313

meeting people, expression used when, 342

meetings, work, 244–245

messages, leaving, 240–244

metric system, 84, 188

mine, 299–301

mini-dictionaries, explained, 3

minutes, 71–73

missing work, explaining to supervisor, 232–233

mobile phone use, 247–248

modesty, expressing, 118, 132, 135, 331, 342

money

  ATM use, 168–169

  cash, 169–171

  credit cards, 171–172

  exchanging, 162–165

  opening bank account, 165–167

  overview, 13, 161–162

  paying for purchases, 195–198

  spending, 169–172

  withdrawing, 167

monolingual Japanese friends, learning with, 326

months, 75–76

most, 192, 270

sounds
  can form of verbs, 141
  consonants, 19–20
  overview, 2, 9, 17
  pitch and intonation, 20–21
  rhythm, 21
  stress, 20
  voiced and voiceless, 25
  vowels, 18–19
souvenirs, shopping for, 180–182
speak (verb), 121–122
speaking on phone. *See* telephone conversations
special requests, at accommodations, 291
specialists, 306
speech styles, 33–34. *See also specific speech styles*
speed, speech, 22
spending money, 169–172
sports
  discussing, 137
  learning Japanese with, 325
state, expressing, 318
stations
  subway, 279
  train, 275–277
stay (verb), 294
stem form, verbs
  conjugation, 49–50
  irregular verbs, 377–379
  overview, 47
  polite suffix, 51–52
  regular verbs, 371–376
stem part, adjectives, 55, 56–57
stolen belongings, reporting, 317–319
storage room terms, 93–95
stores, terms for, 175–176
strangers, addressing, 110–112
streets, versus roads, 155
stressed syllables, 20
-su, verbs ending with, 373
subject-marking particle, 35, 36, 100, 127, 142, 192
subordinates, addressing, 231
subway travel, 279

suffixes. *See also* counters
  can form of verbs, 141–142
  polite, 45–46, 51–52
suggestions, making, 221–222, 263
suit sizes, 187
superiors, addressing, 231, 330
supermarket, shopping at, 176–177
supplies, office, 233–234
surprises, reacting to, 338
swim (verb), 373
syllables, stressed versus unstressed, 20
symbols, phonetic (kana characters), 9–10, 23–27
sympathy, expressing, 343
symptoms, explaining, 311–312

T

table manners, 96–97
take (verb), 168–169
Talkin' the Talk dialogues, explained, 2–3, 5
taxis, 279–281
teachers, addressing, 330
technology
  email, sending, 246–247
  for learning Japanese quickly, 323
  mobile phones and social media, 247–248
  terms related to, 14, 245–246
te-form verbs
  conjugation, 49–51
  giving directions, 156–157
  habits, expressing with, 102
  irregular, 377–379
  overview, 47–48
  past tense, 51
  regular, 371–376
telephone conversations
  asking to speak with someone, 236–238
  calling clients, 238–240
  in emergencies, 314
  leaving messages, 240–244
  mobile phone use, 247–248
  overview, 235
  vocabulary for, 235–236

tellers, bank, 165–167

tests, medical, 312

than, 191–192, 292

thank you, 120–121, 211

that, 43–44, 190–191

theater, 203–204

theft, reporting, 317–319

then, 158, 255

therefore, 255

"there's no choice," 341

these, 43–44

think (verb), 259–260

this, 43–44, 190

those, 43–44

tickets
  for shows and movies, 203
  train, 277

time
  business hours, 183
  dates, 76–78, 79–83
  distance measured by, stating, 151–152
  era names, 80
  hours and minutes, 71–73
  months, 75–76
  overview, 70
  phrases for expressing, 73–74
  reservations, restaurant, 208
  specifying, 79–83
  weekdays, 74–75
  weeks, 79
  years, 79

timetable, at train stations, 276

Tip icon, explained, 4

tips, at restaurants, 216

titles, 110, 111, 231, 330

toasts, 341

toiletries, 261

topic phrases, 39

train stations, box lunches from, 260

train travel, 254, 275–277

transportation
  airports, navigating, 271–274
  asking about, 154, 269–271

boats, 278

driving, 281–284

getting on/off, 268–269

overview, 15, 267

public, 154, 278–281

trains, 254, 275–277

travel. *See also* accommodations; emergencies; transportation; trip planning
  conversations about, 115–116
  instructions for, requesting, 153–154
  to Japan, learning Japanese through, 326
  overview, 15–16

travel agencies, 258–259

treatment, for illness, 313–314

trip planning. *See also* transportation
  exploring nature, 262–265
  location to visit, choosing, 253–257
  overview, 15, 253
  packing, 261–262
  passports and visas, 257
  stating opinions when, 259–260
  with travel agency, 258–259

"try your best, and good luck!," 341

trying clothes on, 185–186, 188–189

-tsu, verbs ending with, 376

Tsukiji Market, 178

24-hour system, 73

U

understood words, dropping, 39–40

unit baths, 92

unstressed syllables, 20

until, 36, 294

up trains, 275

use (verb), 171

u-verbs
  can form, 141
  conjugating, 48–50
  tables for learning, 372–376

V

vacancies, asking about, 295–296

vegetables, shopping for, 178–179

verbs. *See also specific verbs*
  adverbs, 57–58
  auxiliary, 48
  can form, 141–142, 171, 215, 270
  conjugating, 2, 46, 48–52
  dictionary form, 46–47, 49–50, 51, 156–157
  for getting on/off transportation, 268–269
  for giving directions, 156–157
  irregular, 48, 50–51, 141, 377–379
  nai-form, 47, 49–50
  overview, 45–46
  for playing instruments, 138–139
  regular, 48–50, 371–376
  stem form, 47, 49–50, 371–379
  te-form, 47–51, 102, 156–157, 371–379
  word order, 35
visas, for travel, 257
voice mail, leaving message on, 241
voiced sounds, 25
voiceless sounds, 25
vowels, 9, 18–19, 26, 375

W

wait (verb), 316, 376
waiters, talking to, 215
walking distance, asking about, 154
want (verb), 236–238
Warning icon, explained, 4
waste, expressions referring to, 340
waving, 22
wear (verb), 186, 372
weather
  discussing, 116–117
  in Japan, 257
weekdays, 74–75
weeks, 79
what, 41, 194, 337

"what shall I do?," 338
when, 41
where
  asking for directions, 145–146
  asking people where they are from, 133–135
  comparisons, making, 194
  expressing where you live, 132–133
  overview, 41
  talking about travel, 115–116
which, 190–191, 192–193, 269–271
which one, 41, 194, 269–271
who, 41, 194
"why don't we?," 221–222
withdrawing money, 167
word order, in sentences, 35
Words to Know blackboards, explained, 3
work. *See also* telephone conversations
  addressing people at, 231
  benefits, 230–231
  building areas, 234–235
  common activities at, 230
  meetings, 244–245
  missing, explaining to supervisor, 232–233
  office equipment and furniture, 233–234
  overview, 14, 229–230
  small talk about, 126
  technology use at, 245–248
write (verb), 372

Y

years, 79, 80
yen, 162–165, 169–170
yes/no questions, 40
yesterday, 42
you, 45, 112, 299, 332
your/yours, 299–300
youth hostels, 288

About the Author

Hiroko Chiba is a professor of Modern Languages (Japanese) at DePauw University in Greencastle, Indiana. She teaches all levels of Japanese language and Japanese culture and directs the Japanese language program there. Her professional life revolves around various interests related to language teaching and learning. Her research interests include language acquisition, cross-cultural studies of aesthetic perceptions, and Japanese science fiction anime. Her research has been published in both domestic and international venues. She has also served as the president for the Association of Indiana Teachers of Japanese. Hiroko loves teaching and enjoys offering action-packed classes every day. When she has free time, she is a devoted student of yoga and an admirer of **kawaii** (*cute*) products such as Hello Kitty and companion robots like Aibo. Hiroko received a PhD in Educational Psychology from the University of Illinois at Urbana-Champaign.

Dedication

To my former, present, and future students

Author's Acknowledgments

This book is a revision of earlier editions of Japanese For Dummies written by Dr. Eriko Sato. I appreciate her wonderful work and was honored to build on her foundation to produce this third edition. Many thanks to the editors — Lindsay Lefevere, Chrissy Guthrie, Christy Pingleton, and Magesh Elangovan — for patiently having worked with me. I'm much obliged to them. A big thank you to Dr. Charles Andrews, who served as a technical reviewer. His comments were helpful and thoughtful. I would also like to extend my appreciation to Dave Berque, who kindly answered questions I randomly asked. And last, but not least, I would like to thank my family members in Japan who helped me pursue this project in many important ways.

Publisher's Acknowledgments

Executive Editor: Lindsay Sandman Lefevere

Editorial Project Manager and Development Editor: Christina N. Guthrie

Copy Editor: Christine Pingleton

Technical Editor: Charles Andrews, PhD

Production Editor: Magesh Elangovan

Illustrator: Elizabeth Kurtzman

Cover Photos: © Goryu/iStock.com

Leverage the power

Dummies is the global leader in the reference category and one of the most trusted and highly regarded brands in the world. No longer just focused on books, customers now have access to the dummies content they need in the format they want. Together we'll craft a solution that engages your customers, stands out from the competition, and helps you meet your goals.

Advertising & Sponsorships

Connect with an engaged audience on a powerful multimedia site, and position your message alongside expert how-to content. Dummies.com is a one-stop shop for free, online information and know-how curated by a team of experts.

- Targeted ads
- Video
- Email Marketing

- Microsites
- Sweepstakes sponsorship

20 **MILLION** PAGE VIEWS EVERY SINGLE MONTH

15 MILLION **UNIQUE** VISITORS PER MONTH

43% OF ALL VISITORS ACCESS THE SITE VIA THEIR MOBILE DEVICES

700,000 NEWSLETT SUBSCRIPTIO TO THE INBOXES OF *300,000* UNIQUE INDIVIDUALS EVERY WEEK

# of dummies

Custom Publishing

Reach a global audience in any language by creating a solution that will differentiate you from competitors, amplify your message, and encourage customers to make a buying decision.

- Apps
- Books
- eBooks
- Video
- Audio
- Webinars

Brand Licensing & Content

Leverage the strength of the world's most popular reference brand to reach new audiences and channels of distribution.

For more information, visit dummies.com/biz

PERSONAL ENRICHMENT

Staying Sharp	Facebook	Guitar	Investing	Beekeeping	Digital Photography
9781119187790	9781119179030	9781119293354	9781119293347	9781119310068	9781119235606
USA $26.00	USA $21.99	USA $24.99	USA $22.99	USA $22.99	USA $24.99
CAN $31.99	CAN $25.99	CAN $29.99	CAN $27.99	CAN $27.99	CAN $29.99
UK £19.99	UK £16.99	UK £17.99	UK £16.99	UK £16.99	UK £17.99

Meditation	Pregnancy	Samsung Galaxy S7	iPhone	Crocheting	Nutrition
9781119251163	9781119235491	9781119279952	9781119283133	9781119287117	9781119130246
USA $24.99	USA $26.99	USA $24.99	USA $24.99	USA $24.99	USA $22.99
CAN $29.99	CAN $31.99	CAN $29.99	CAN $29.99	CAN $29.99	CAN $27.99
UK £17.99	UK £19.99	UK £17.99	UK £17.99	UK £16.99	UK £16.99

PROFESSIONAL DEVELOPMENT

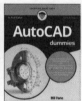

Windows 10	AutoCAD	Excel 2016	QuickBooks 2017	macOS Sierra	LinkedIn	Windows 10
9781119311041	9781119255796	9781119293439	9781119281467	9781119280651	9781119251132	9781119310563
USA $24.99	USA $39.99	USA $26.99	USA $26.99	USA $29.99	USA $24.99	USA $34.00
CAN $29.99	CAN $47.99	CAN $31.99	CAN $31.99	CAN $35.99	CAN $29.99	CAN $41.99
UK £17.99	UK £27.99	UK £19.99	UK £19.99	UK £21.99	UK £17.99	UK £24.99

SharePoint 2016	Fundamental Analysis	Networking	Office 2016	Office 365	Salesforce.com	Coding
9781119181705	9781119263593	9781119257769	9781119293477	9781119265313	9781119239314	9781119293323
USA $29.99	USA $26.99	USA $29.99	USA $26.99	USA $24.99	USA $29.99	USA $29.99
CAN $35.99	CAN $31.99	CAN $35.99	CAN $31.99	CAN $29.99	CAN $35.99	CAN $35.99
UK £21.99	UK £19.99	UK £21.99	UK £19.99	UK £17.99	UK £21.99	UK £21.99

dummies.com

dummies®
A Wiley Brand